TEACHING FOR SUCCESS

Strengthening
Child-Centered
Classrooms

CONTENTS:

FOR DISCUSSION

READINESS / KINDERGARTEN

LEARNING STYLES/NEEDS

MULTIAGE EDUCATION

INTEGRATED CURRICULUM

ASSESSMENT

TEACHING ALL CHILDREN

RESOURCES / BIBLIOGRAPHY

This book is printed on recycled paper.

SDE Sourcebook. © Copyright 1995 by The Society For Developmental Education.
All rights reserved. Printed in the United States of America.
Published by The Society For Developmental Education, Ten Sharon Road, PO Box 577, Peterborough, New Hampshire 03458.
Phone 1-800-924-9621
FAX 603-924-6688

EIGHTH EDITION

President: Jay LaRoche
Executive Director: Jim Grant
Program Director: Irv Richardson
Editor: Aldene Fredenburg
Creative Director, Cover Design: Susan Dunholter
Production Coordinators: Deborah Fredericks, Christine Landry
Type Compositor: Laura Taylor

ISBN 1-884548-02-4 (paperback)

Bringing true reform to schools

Class size

Giving students a chance to succeed

This is the second in a series of articles focusing on issues covered in the proposed Education Reform Act. S-3125.

Some teachers feel like the old woman in the shoe—they have so many children, they don't know what to do.

Class size: Teachers say it affects everything they do with children; parents petition boards of education to reduce it; opinion polls show the public considers it of major importance to pupil achievement. Yet in 1988 newspaper headlines quoted the U.S. Secretary of Education as saying smaller classes would not appreciably increase student achievement.

How can something we *know* to be true be subject to such attack?

Why is it that some contend that research does not substantiate the value of small class size?

In 1986 the Educational Research Service, an independent nonprofit corporation based in Arlington, Va., published an analysis of class size research. In its review of seemingly contradictory research, ERS found that many studies were flawed. However, the analysis, which still stands as the most definitive work on the subject, does conclude that research verifies some benefits of small class size.

Most effective: 15 pupils or less

And one significant fact, cited even in the negative report by the U.S. Department of Education, stands out: Class size has its most significant effect when the number of pupils is 15 or less.

NJEA has promoted a maximum class size of 15 since 1984.

Some NJEA affiliates have pursued this issue in their local school districts. Working with parents, local associations have lobbied local boards of education to deal with overcrowded classes. What one administrator calls the "mad mom phenomenon" sometimes works.

NJEA's members have decided that this issue needs to be addressed statewide. The proposed Education Reform Act (S-3125) calls for class sizes of no more than 15 "except for those classes which by the nature of the activity conducted therein, require participation of more than 15 pupils."

Move to reduce primary grades first

Current regulations governing special education classes would remain. In prekindergarten classes the limit would be 10 students. The bill calls for a phasing-in of these limitations beginning with primary grades.

Why primary grades? For one thing, gradual implementation would enable districts to plan for the change over a period of years.

For another, the ERS survey identifies the primary grades as most clearly benefitting from smaller class size. Moreover, as the Head Start program has demonstrated, children who get off to a good start do better all the way through school.

Affects skills, behavior

In smaller primary classes, ERS says, students' attitudes and behavior, as well as learning, improve. A positive attitude, appropriate behavior, and a good base in learning give children the opportunity to succeed.

The research also indicates that children master mathematics skills and reading skills more quickly in small classes. Obviously students who master the basics early on have a greater chance for educational success.

But primary grades aren't the only ones that benefit from fewer children per class. Class size is especially critical for economically disadvantaged students, the ERS survey found.

Key element in reaching the needy

Children from homes where concern about basic survival comes first and where resources are limited need even more individual attention from school and from the school staff. That's possible only in small classes.

Students of lesser academic ability also prove to benefit from smaller classes. The opportunity to receive individual attention and the more relaxed atmosphere of small classes apparently allow these students more opportunity to succeed.

In small classes, teaching practices and approaches such as individualization, creativity, small-group activity, and interpersonal regard flourish, ERS says while also contending that more research needs to be done to validate the "presumed superiority" of these activities.

Teachers need to adapt techniques

On the other hand, the report also says that class size does not make a significant difference in student achievement if teachers don't adapt their techniques to small groups. The report calls for "providing teachers with the support and training needed to optimize learning conditions."

Education is more than learning what's going to be on a test. It's learning how to get along with others, feeling a sense of self-worth, finding out what we can contribute to our world. Smaller classes offer better opportunity for these aspects of "affective learning."

Staff members also benefit, says the research. Teachers have more positive attitudes toward their work and better perceptions of their own effectiveness in small classes. That's good for the profession and for children.

A better way to measure class size

One of the frustrations of dealing with the class size issue is quantifying the data.

In New Jersey, for example, the student-teacher ratio for 1987 reported by the state was 14-to-one. Impossible, you say?

No, it's just that the way this figure is calculated is misleading. It's done by dividing the number of students in a district by the number of certificated staff. And when guidance counselors, school nurses, child study team members, librarians, special teachers, resource room teachers, compensatory education teachers, part-time staff, and others are added in, the result is a distorted view of class size.

At the same time, the number of students those members serve shouldn't be ignored either and may warrant other studies.

NEA has published a booklet entitled "At Last—A Better Way To Measure Class Size." It provides a formula for coming up with a more accurate figure for class size in a school district and tips for organizing the study.

Dividing students by teachers to determine class size fails to convey important facts about the condition of education in our schools. Instead of counting numbers of students, we should be counting sizes of groups in which students are instructed. Individual students may be members of more than one group.

NEA suggests finding the "median student" in your school.

Finding the elementary school median

A simple method for elementary schools is:
1. Arrange the classes in your school in order of size from the largest to the smallest. For example: 37, 31, 29, 21, 19, 12, 11.
2. Find the total number of students in all the classes by totaling the numbers in each class.

   For example: 37 + 31 + 29 + 21 + 19 + 12 + 11 = 160

3. Add 1 to the total number of students and divide by 2 to find the number of the "median student."

   Using the example: $\dfrac{160 + 1}{2} = 80.5$

4. Count down from the largest class until you come to the median student.

In the example above, there are 68 students in the two largest classes. The 80.5th student would be in the next largest class, which contains 29 students. Consequently, the average class has 29 students.

Measuring at the secondary level

Counting numbers of students and teachers in secondary school classes has been difficult because of the huge variety of special arrangements possible, and the fact that all-day intact classes are rare.

Often the issues of class size and teacher workload—which is also an important topic—become confused. But to measure average class size at the secondary level we ignore the number of teachers.

Instead, we list the number of students who meet for each "period" and these are tallied in a frequency distribution similar to that for elementary schools.

Again, you would find the median student, then count down to find the size of that individual's class.

Include regular classes only

In a survey, ask school staff to report the number of students in each class they teach. Ask them to exclude from that report all classes which don't represent regular classroom instruction, such as individual counseling, therapy, small recital or recitation meetings, small group remediation, etc.

For a copy of "At last—A better way to measure class size," contact NEA Communications, 1201 16th St. NW, Washington, D.C. 20036, (202) 822-7200.

Reprinted with permission from the *NJEA Review*, official publication of the New Jersey Education Association, Vol. 62 No. 7, March 1989, pp. 14-19.

Where We Stand

By Albert Shanker, President
American Federation of Teachers

Inclusion and Ideology

The movement in American education that is taking hold the fastest and is likely to have the profoundest — and most destructive — effect is not what you might think. It's the rush towards full inclusion of disabled children in regular classrooms.

Advocates demand that all disabled children be put into regular classrooms, regardless of their ability to function or benefit and regardless of the effect on other children in the class. And they are being successful. Full inclusion is happening quickly, all over the country, without substantial debate n state legislatures and school boards, through court orders and federal directives.

As a result, we are seeing medically fragile children and children with severe behavioral disorders placed in regular classrooms where teachers who have had little if any special training — and get little if any extra help — struggle to deal with the youngsters' special needs. This could mean suctioning mucus from a child's lungs or giving him a medicated enema. Or it could mean trying to figure out how to handle a child who bites and kicks others with no apparent provocation and shouts or cries and exposes himself throughout the school day. And all this while the teacher is attempting to give other students the grounding they need in math and reading and science.

Full inclusionists argue that all the supports that disabled children have in special education settings must follow them into regular classrooms. This is no more likely to happen for disabled children than it did for mentally ill people who were de-institutionalized years ago. Their supports were also supposed to follow them when institutions were closed, but the supports never materialized; and now, as we know, many of these people are out on the streets. That's one reason why many parents of disabled children oppose full inclusion. They fear their children will lose the range of services now available and end up, like those who were de-institutionalized, with nothing.

We usually think of schools as performing three functions: imparting knowledge and skills; preparing students for the working world; and helping them become good citizens and develop socially. But those demanding full inclusion are interested in only one thing — socialization. Teaching disabled and nondisabled kids to get along together is worthwhile (as many schools that don't practice full inclusion would agree), but it is only one value. And it's certainly not the only reason taxpayers support the schools.

Full inclusion is an ideological position that disabled and nondisabled children must always *be fully integrated, regardless of the circumstances or consequences.*

Full inclusion is often justified by an analogy with the racial segregation practiced during a good portion of our history. Just as "separate but equal" always meant "inferior," inclusionists feel the same is true of any separate classes for any disabled children.

But the analogy is faulty. African-American children have the same range of abilities and needs as white children. They were excluded only because of the color of their skin, which was irrelevant to their ability to function in a regular classroom and benefit from being there. This is quite different from putting a blind youngster into a special class so he can learn Braille or excluding a youngster who is emotionally disturbed because he will disrupt the education of other kids — while deriving little benefit himself.

Recently, I received a letter from Edward Martin, who was the first director of the U.S. Bureau of Education for the Handicapped and now heads on advocacy group for the disabled. He, too, opposes full inclusion, and he is especially troubled by the idea of making sweeping changes without any data or research to support these changes. Where are our figures on how well disabled students in regular classrooms do in comparison with those in special education settings? How many drop out? How many go on to college or vocational programs? Without this kind of information, we have no way of knowing what is working for these youngsters and what is not. "Special education programs," Martin says, "must be judged on t heir success, not on our wishes for a more inclusive society."

Many disabled children can be, and are now, included in regular classrooms and, with adequate supports, many more could be. These decisions should be made on an individual basis — depending on the nature and severity of the disability — and remade if a placement turns out to have been wrong. And they should be based on what is good for all the children involved — the children with disabilities and the others. But full inclusion makes no room for individual judgments. It is an ideological position that disabled and nondisabled children must *always* be fully integrated, regardless of the circumstances or consequences.

Some full inclusionists talk as though they are in a battle pitting the forces of morality against the forces of immorality. In reality, the battle pits ideologues who, without any evidence, would force destructive changes on our schools against people who believe that children's interests come first.

This article first appeared in The New York Times, February 6, 1994. Reprinted with permission of Albert Shanker.

MY TURN

My Turn," is a commentary series of short columns solicited on a rotating basis from noted authors and professionals in the field of LD. Opinions not necessarily those of *The Exchange* or The Network.

By Harley A. Tomey, III

There are students who. . . will require intense systematic instruction that may not be available or is not common in the general education classroom

INCLUSION:
Why the controversy?

The controversy over inclusion comes in part from disagreement among professionals, parents, and others about the meaning of inclusion. Instead of debating this issue, the focus should be on the full implementation of the least restrictive environment. The goal of education should be to provide students, including those with learning disabilities, with the opportunity and necessary supports that will allow them to become independent, productive, and socially involved citizens who are committed to life-long learning. With this goal, the full implementation of the least restrictive environment for many students with learning disabilities will be within the general education classroom, with appropriate supplementary aids and services.

For others, however, the least restrictive environment may mean part-time or full-time education in special classes or special schools. We need to remember that there are students who, due to the nature and severity of their disability, will require intense systematic instruction that may not be available or is not common in the general education classroom. Meeting the unique educational needs of these students may require the use of part-time or full-time special classes and must remain the goal on any discussion of inclusion. With this in mind, there are several issues that must be addressed to make the general education classroom an environment that will enable these students to achieve their goals.

First, a shared vision as articulated by a school's philosophy and mission statement is essential. The development of these statements must involve the entire school community which includes teachers, support personnel, administrators, parents, students, and the community-at-large. However, one must remember that change, regardless of how large or small, is a process, not an event, and takes time.

Second, the school's staff must determine the role and responsibilities of individual teachers, support personnel, and administrators. All those involved with the education of students, including those with learning disabilities, need to develop a common set of expectations about each other.

The third critical issue is staff development. Staff development must be ongoing and well planned and must address the needs of the school community. It should include not only skills in effective communications, team decision making, team interaction, and cooperative learning, but also study skills instruction, social skills instruction, systematic multisensory instruction, direct instruction, understanding learning differences, and the use of collaboration and cooperation. This training should lead to supportive networks for both students and staff. For the student this may include cooperative learning buddy systems, and peer tutoring, while for the school staff it may include collaboration, team teaching, co-teaching, child study committees, and other cooperative arrangements.

Besides staff development, parents must be informed and involved, since they are key stakeholders in the process. They must be considered equal partners and involved in the planning process

While inclusive education in the general education classroom is the ultimate goal. . . it must be accomplished in a reasonable manner.

from the beginning. Remember, parents have concerns that must be addressed. These include:

- Will my child learn as much and as effectively?
- What level of involvement will I have in a decision regarding my child's educational needs and placement?
- Will school staff be provided with training in order to be able to address the educational needs of my child?
- Will flexibility for my child be assured?
- Can I be assured that support systems, including related services, will be available to meet my child's specific needs?

The last issue to be addressed is flexibility in the learning environment. While inclusion is a goal for all students with learning disabilities, placement decisions must be based upon the specific needs of the student as identified in the student's individual education program. Thus, a continuum of alternative placement options must be available to each student. This flexibility allows parents, school staff, and the student to make decisions based upon the educational needs of the student. It is reckless to believe that one environment, either the general or the special education classroom, will adequately meet the educational needs of all students with

learning disabilities at all times. If a placement does not work as well as anticipated, changes should be made quickly. The student should not be made to endure an inappropriate placement.

In conclusion, while inclusive education in the general education classroom is the ultimate goal for all students with learning disabilities, it must be accomplished in a reasonable manner. Forcing inclusion upon an educational community will only create barriers. However, when the educational community has shared goals and makes decisions, when staff roles and responsibilities are defined, when staff is well trained, when parents are informed, and when the educational environment is flexible, inclusion can be successful. It is imperative that the individual education program for the student with a learning disability focus on meeting the student's unique needs. ■

Harley A. Tomey, III, M.A. is a learning disabilities specialist in the Virginia State Department of Education and a Vice President of The Orton Dyslexia Society

REFERENCES

Baker, J., Zigmond, N. 1990. Are regular education classes equipped to accommodate students with learning disabilities? *Exceptional Children* 54:515-526.

Cernosia, A. 1994, July. Full implementation of LRE an overview of the law: From exclusion to full inclusion. Paper presented to the special education staff of the Virginia Department of Education, Richmond, VA.

Fuchs, D., Deshler, D., & Zigmond, N. 1994, March. How expendable is general education? Paper presented at the 31st annual international conference of the Learning Disabilities Association of America, Washington, D.C.

Fuchs, D., & Fuchs, L.S. 1994. Inclusive schools movement and the radicalization of special education reform. *Exceptional Children* 60:294-309.

Mather, N., & Roberts, R. 1994. Learning disabilities: A field in danger of extinction? *Learning Disabilities: Research and Practice* 9:45-58.

Mercer, C.D., Lane, H. 1994. Principles of responsible inclusion. *LDA Newsbriefs* 49(4), 1.

National Center for Learning Disabilities, 1994. An NCLD statement on inclusion. *Their World* 101-104.

National Joint Committee on Learning Disabilities, 1994. Collective perspectives on issues affecting learning disabilities. Position papers and statement. Austin, TX: Pro-Ed.

The Orton Dyslexia Society 1994, May. Position statement on inclusion.

Virginia Department of Education, 1993. Accept, learning together: Integrating students with disabilities. Richmond, VA.

Reprinted with permission of *The Network Exchange*, Spring/Summer, 1995, Vol. 13, No. 1.
The Exchange is published by The Learning Disabilities Network, 72 Sharp St., Hingham, MA 02043.

7

Readiness / Kindergarten

The All Day Kindergarten: Assessing the Need

Nearly 50 percent of all 5-year-olds in this country attend some type of extended or all-day program. Current trends for instruction in an all-day kindergarten urge longer periods of more diverse academic instruction, thus putting today's kindergarteners under pressures that may be too great for their developmental levels. Yet the need for all-day care for children of working parents makes these programs attractive. Experts are proposing a careful look at the all-day kindergarten and some are suggesting a compromise consisting of a half day of a quality kindergarten program followed by a half day of good in-school day care.

In assessing current all-day kindergarten programs, we must ask the following questions and look carefully at the research that provides answers to them.

QUESTION:

Who benefits most from all-day-kindergarten?

RESEARCH FINDINGS:

While a large body of research based on European models of full-day preschool programs is used to support all-day kindergarten, the results are often overstated. The overall effectiveness of pre-school programs is marked especially in children of lower socioeconomic status. There is little or no effect shown on children from the middle class (Adler, 1982; Caruso & Detterman, 1981; Clarke, 1984; Darlington, Royce, Snipper, Murray, & Lazar, 1980).

These positive gains made by some children required support of parents and follow-through programs. The large success of programs such as Head Start was also due to a focus on the whole child — academics, play, and noneducational needs such as health and nutrition.

QUESTION:

Are children today more advanced than those of a decade ago?

RESEARCH FINDINGS:

Those who support all-day kindergarten maintain that various forces influencing today's children — television, pre-school experience, single parent families — make them different from those of a decade ago and therefore in need of a more instructionally challenging curriculum (Helmich, 1985; Herman, 1984; Naron, 1981).

However, there appears to be no empirical data to support the claim that today's children are different from those of 10 years ago. Socioeconomic factors are different, more children have had pre-school experience, and most seem to adapt to the new conditions of early childhood, but there is no proof that their development has been altered or hastened in any significant way (Olsen and Zigler, 1989).

QUESTION:

Does increased time mean increased individualization of instruction?

RESEARCH FINDINGS:

Proponents of all-day kindergarten note that it provides a greater amount of time in which teachers can individualize instruction. In reality, most teachers in all-day programs tend to teach children in groups and not individually (Jarvis & Molnar, 1986, Office of Educational Assessment,

N.Y.C.). All-day kindergarten requires special retraining for many teachers that will prove too costly for the majority of small school districts.

QUESTION:

Is more attention paid to nutrition and parent involvement than in half-day kindergarten?

RESEARCH FINDINGS:

Success of the Head Start program clearly points out that good, nutritious snacks and lunch are important to the child's day. Several studies, however, show that there are problems in many programs with establishing a lunch program for all-day kindergarten (Jarvis & Molnar, 1986).

While parent involvement is cited as a crucial factor in the success of all-day kindergarten, in actuality, it is minimal (Alper & Wright, 1979; Winter & Klein, 1970; Bronfenbrenner, 1974; Deutsch et al., 1983; Radin, 1969; Slater, 1971; Sparrow, Blachman, & Chauncey, 1983; Valentine & Stark, 1979; Waksman, 1980). Given the same socioeconomic factors that are cited as cause for the intellectual advancement of children of the 1980s — working parents, etc. — this type of involvement is very difficult to manage.

QUESTION:

Does a longer school day mean increased standardized test scores?

RESEARCH FINDINGS:

There are sufficient research findings to indicate that the longer school day, which allows more time for concentration on math, reading and language, does increase standardized test scores (Olsen and Ziegler, 1989). In considering these results, however, we must consider whether the increased test scores are consistent across all social class groups and whether these gains are maintained over time.

Several studies show that those who show the greatest increase in test scores are those of low socio-economic status and children who are bilingual and least ready (Jarvis & Molnar, 1985; Lysiak & Evans, 1976; Winter & Klein, 1970). One study involving only white, middle-class children found no positive effect of an all-day program (Evans & Marken, 1984).

QUESTION:

What are the long-term academic effects of all-day kindergarten?

RESEARCH FINDINGS:

Findings on the long-term effects of all-day kindergarten are ambiguous. One study of a group of Title I kindergarteners (followed through eighth grade) found that the gains were maintained throughout grade school (Neiman and Gastright, 1981). Another study showed higher reading test scores, grades, and fewer retentions in upper grades (Humphrey, 1983). Yet another study found no differences between all-day and half-day students on the California Achievement Tests in later grades (Evans & Marken, 1983). Other studies have produced similar statistics.

It appears that achievement gains best maintained long-term are those of lower socioeconomic status children (Neiman & Gastright, 1981; Mueller, 1977).

QUESTION:

What effect does all-day kindergarten have on a child's self-concept, social development and motivation?

RESEARCH FINDINGS:

The philosophy of Frederick Froebel of the whole child approach to education was common in kindergarten programs until about a decade ago. We have seen the shift in concern from the whole child's development to the child's academic achievement. As with findings on the long-term academic effects of all-day kindergarten, findings on self-concept, social development and motivation are also mixed.

Out of eight studies on development of noncognitive skills, three showed no difference between the two groups (Olsen and Ziegler, 1989). Those studies that showed increases in skills of full-day students seem to indicate that the differences were due to teachers' greater familiarity with their students (Gullo and Clements, 1984).

There is evidence that students who attended full-day kindergarten had better self-concept and attitudes toward science and social studies (Humphrey, 1983). Another study shows teachers' ratings of better social skills in all day kindergarteners, but no difference in those students' attitudes toward school in general (Levinson and Lalor, 1986).

One important study by Evans and Marken (1984) suggests that children in half-day kindergarten showed a better attitude toward reading in later grades.

QUESTION:

Is there an alternative to all-day kindergarten that will meet the needs of children and parents?

RESEARCH FINDINGS:

Although the total picture through careful research on the all-day kindergarten issue is not complete, several things are obvious. There is a strong trend toward equating general educational advancement with performance in basic skills, especially standardized test scores. The whole child is being ignored if not forgotten. And there is a trend toward placing on young children the responsibilities that have previously belonged to older children (Elkind, 1981; Cohen, 1975). Common sense tells us that the quality of life, intellectual development and school achievement will not improve simply by being in school for more hours.

What, then, is the alternative given the fact that half of the kindergarteners in America have two working parents?

Experts are proposing the educare alternative — a half day of school combined with quality in-school day care following. This arrangement would meet the needs of children and parents while maintaining developmentally appropriate programs for the kindergarten. Such a program would allow flexibility for parents and children. Working parents would know their children had quality care between the end of school and the end of work, while children of non-working parents could go home at the end of the half-day.

Educare would be "taught" by certified child development aides who are paid less than teachers. Costs can be reduced, and teachers won't have to take on the additional role of care-taking.

Educare would make use of school resources and space, provide appropriate time for play and unstructured activity vital to the development of young children, and provide a safe, affordable alternative to additional after-school care.

Summary of research compiled by Deborah Olsen and Edward Zigler, (1989). "An Assessment of the All-Day Kindergarten Movement." Early Childhood Research Quarterly (Vol. 4, #2, pp. 167-186). Norwood, NJ: Ablex Publishing.

Note: To request resource list of research articles, contact: The Society For Developmental Education, Ten Sharon Road, PO Box 577, Peterborough, NH 03458, (603) 924-9621.

Printed with permission of Deborah Olsen.

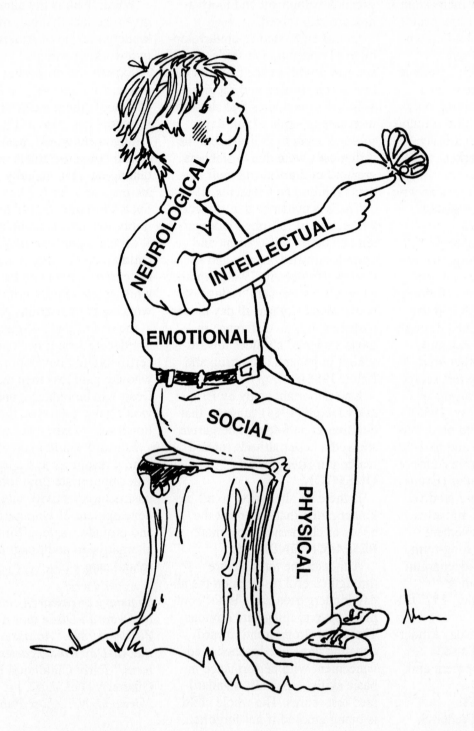

Jim Grant / Bob Johnson

Factors That Influence Developmental Diversity

by James K. Uphoff, Ed.D.
College of Education and Human Services Wright State University
Dayton, OH 45435 • (513) 873-3231

The school bells ring in late summer and thousands of children march through the school house doors without anyone having given any thought as to whether or not these children are ready — physically, socially, emotionally, academically — for the curriculum awaiting them. This document aims to provide you, the parent, with a number of major elements which should be considered as you make this vital decision. These same considerations are also relevant when parents are thinking about giving their child the *gift of time,* another year in the current grade in order to grow and mature, or a year in a readiness, K or a transition K-1 program. Too often parents and school officials alike confuse verbal brightness with readiness for school. *Being bright and being ready for school are not the same thing!* An inappropriate start in school too often "tarnishes" that brightness.

Today's K-3 curriculum has been pushed down by our American "faster is better" culture to the point that what is often found in today's kindergarten was found in late first or early second grade just three decades ago! Many schools are trying to change from the "sit-still, paper-pencil" approach of the present to a more active, involved, manipulative curriculum which enables young children to learn best. However, until this latter learning environment is available for your child, you must consider whether or not the child is ready. The material which follows is presented to help you make this very tough decision!

Each of the following factors indicates a potential for problems. The more of these factors which apply to an individual child, the more likely he/she is to encounter difficulty — academically, socially, emotionally, and/or physically — and each of these areas is crucial to a well-rounded human being. No one factor should be the only basis for making a decision. Look at all of the factors, then decide.

Readiness Factors

Chronological Age at School Entrance: My own research and that of many others indicates that children who are less than five and one-half years of age at the time of school entrance into kindergarten are much more likely to encounter problems. This would put the date at about March 25th for many schools. The younger the child is, the more likely the current academic paper/pencil kindergarten curriculum is inappropriate.

Problems at Birth: When labor lasts a long time or is less than four hours; or when labor is unusually difficult, the child is more likely to experience problems. Long labor too often results in reduced oxygen and/or nourishment for the child just before birth. Some studies have found birth trauma to be associated with later emotional problems including, in the extreme, suicidal tendencies.

Early General Health & Nutrition: Poor nutrition in the pre-school years puts the child at greater risk in terms of school success. The child who experiences many serious ear infections during these years has been found to have more difficulty in learning to read. Allergies, asthma, and other similar problems can also inhibit such learning. Any type of illness or problem which results in a passive child — in bed or just "being very quiet" day after day — is more likely to result in a physically delayed development. Lack of body and muscle control can be a major problem for learners.

Family Status: Any act which lessens the stability of the child's family security is a problem and the closer such acts/events occur to the start of school, the more likely that start is to be a negative one. Such destabilizers as the following should be considered.

1. **Death** of anyone close to the child. This includes family, friends, neighbors, pets, etc.
2. **Moves** from one house/apartment to another even though the adults may see it as a positive relocation—more space, own bedroom for child, etc. The child may miss friends, neighbors, the dog next door, etc.
3. **Separation** from parents or close family members whether by jobs, military duty, divorce, prison, remarriage, moves, etc., can create problems for child in early school experiences.
4. **Birth of a Sibling** or the addition of new step-family members can be very upsetting.

Birth Order: If the gap between child #1 and #2 is less than three years, then #2 is more likely to have problems in school. When there are more than 3 children in a family, the baby of the family (last born) often experiences less independence and initiative. There are exceptions to these factors as with the others, but they remain as predictors, never-the-less.

Low Birth Weight: A premature child with low weight often experiences significant delays in many aspects of his/her development.

Sex: Boys are about one month behind girls in physiological development at birth; about 6 months behind at age 5; and about 24 months behind girls at age 11-12. (Some contend that we males never catch up!) Boys need extra time more than girls, but research shows that girls actually benefit from it more. Their eyes, motor skills, etc., etc., are ahead by nature, and when given time become even "aheader"! Boys fail far more often than do girls and have many more school problems than do girls.

Vision: Being able to see clearly does *not* mean that a child's vision is ready for school work. It is not until age 8 that 90% of children have sufficient eye-muscle development to do *with ease* what reading demands of the eyes. The younger the child is, the more likely he/she does *not* have all of the vision development required. For example, many children have problems with focusing. Their eyes work like a zoom lens on a projector zooming in and out until a sharp focus is obtained. Much time can be spent in this process and much is missed while focusing is taking place. Other eye problems include the muscle ability to maintain focus and smooth movement from left to right, lazy eye, and midline problems.

Memory Level: If a child has difficulty remembering such common items as prayers, commercials, home address/telephone number, etc., then the child may well experience problems with the typical primary grade curriculum. Many times memory success is associated with one's ability to concentrate—attention span, thus this factor is related to the next one.

Attention Span: Research has clearly shown a strong connection between the amount of time a child spends working on skill content (three Rs) and the achievement level reached. The child who is easily distracted and finds it difficult to focus attention for 10-15 minutes at a time on a single activity is also a child who is probably

going to experience much frustration in school. Discipline problems are likely, as are academic ones. Sitting still is very difficult for the typical 5½- to 6½-year-old child and this normal physiological condition is at great odds with the typical sit still/paper-pencil curriculum imposed after Sputnik went up over 30 years ago!

Social Skills: The child with delayed social development is often reluctant to leave the security of a known situation (home/sitter/preschool/etc.). This child is very hesitant about mixing with other children, is passive, and slow to become involved. Noninvolvement is often associated with lower learning levels. Tears, urinary "accidents," morning tummy aches, a return to thumb sucking, etc., are all signals of such a delay. Some research has found correlations between short labor deliveries and problems such as these.

Speaking Skills: The ability of a child to communicate clearly is closely related to maturation. In order to pronounce sounds distinctly and correctly, muscle control is essential. Hearing must also be of good quality and this has often been reduced by early ear infections, allergies, etc. Inappropriate speech patterns (baby talk) and/or incorrect articulation (an "r" sounds like a "w") are major concern signals.

Reading Interest: If a child does not like to be read to, has little desire to watch a TV story all the way through, or rarely picks up a book to read to him/herself, then the odds are high that this child is not ready for the curriculum of the typical kindergarten. Few of us do well those things in which we are not yet interested and our children are no different!

Small Motor Skills: The ability to cut, draw, paste, and manipulate pencils, colors, etc., are very important in today's pushed-down kindergarten. The child who has some difficulty with these, uses an awkward grip on the pencil (ice-pick, one or no fingertips on the pencil, etc.), and/or has trouble holding small cards in the hand during a game is a candidate for frus-

trations. Eye/hand coordination is vital for a high degree of success.

Large Motor Skills: It is typical for a 5- to 6-year-old child to "trip over a piece of string," yet the typical curriculum assumes major control over one's body movements. Ability to skip, jump on one foot at a time, walk a balance beam, hop, jump from a standing position, etc., is an ability which research has found to be related to overall success with some particular skills tested just before starting school predicting reading success levels in 5th and 8th grades!

Summary

"Is my child ready for school?" is a major question for parents to answer. This small document merely highlights some of the key factors one should consider when making such a decision. I urge all schools to adopt a thorough assessment procedure which checks all of these factors so as to provide parents with more information upon which to base their decisions.

A child's self-concept needs to be positive. He/she should see school as a good place to be, a place where he/she finds success and support. Giving the child the best start in school demands that the parent and school work together to be sure that the curriculum available will enable this child to find success and positive experiences. Parents can also provide support for the school in its efforts to reduce the amount of paper work in the early grades. Working together, the home and the school can help each child establish a firm foundation for a lifetime of learning.

For more information on transition and readiness programs, see Dr. Uphoff's book Real Facts from Real Schools, *published by Programs for Education, 1994.*

The book provides a historical perspective on the development of readiness and transition programs, presents an in-depth look at the major issues raised by attacks on such programs, and summarizes more than three dozen research studies.

Jim Grant / Bob Johnson

12

Students Enter Kindergarten on a Broken Front

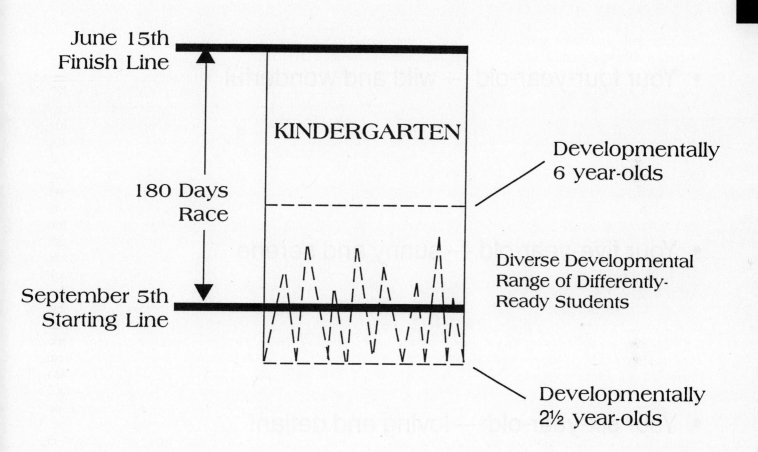

June 15th
Finish Line

KINDERGARTEN

Developmentally
6 year-olds

180 Days
Race

Diverse Developmental
Range of Differently-
Ready Students

September 5th
Starting Line

Developmentally
2½ year-olds

Notes:

Jim Grant / Bob Johnson

Knowing Children: Ages and Stages

**"One cannot possibly serve children
without knowing them first."**
Jim Grant

- Your four-year-old — wild and wonderful

- Your five-year-old — sunny and serene

- Your six-year-old — loving and defiant

- Your seven-year-old — life in a minor key

How to Make a Child Learning Disabled

1. Escalated curriculum

2. Large class size

3. Board copying

4. No recess

5. Textbooks

6. Ditto worksheets

7. Time on task

8. Irrelevant curriculum

9. Departmentalized elementary program

Jim Grant / Bob Johnson

10. Too much curriculum

11. Dysfunctioning home life

12. Tracking

13. Unfair competition

14. Group standardized testing

15. Fixed point curriculum . . . in a fixed time frame

16. Narrow instructional approach

17. Narrow critical period to learn to read

Jim Grant / Bob Johnson

Learners Who May Be Considered At Risk for Remaining in the Same Grade or Program a Second Year

1. A low IQ child

2. An unmotivated student

3. A slow learner

4. An emotionally disturbed child

5. A child with a behavior disorder

6. An economically deprived child

7. A linguistically different child

8. A child who has high absenteeism

9. A child whose parents are opposed to extra time through retention

10. A child who is already a year older than his/her peers

11. A child who is too "street wise" for his age

12. A child who has a multitude of complex problems (high impact child)

13. A child with very low self-esteem

Jim Grant / Bob Johnson

Potential Learners Who May
Possibly Benefit from Grade Expansion

1. A child whose ability is average or above average

2. A developmentally young child who has been assigned to the wrong grade or program

3. A child whose parents want their child to remain in the same grade or program another year

4. A child who wants to remain in the same grade or program another year

5. A child who has never had an extra year of time and is <u>not</u> already a year older

6. A child who doesn't appear to have problems other than being too young developmentally for the assigned grade or program

Jim Grant / Bob Johnson

Grade Expansion Words of Wisdom

1. Never pressure a parent to retain a child.

2. Never cause a child to be more than one year older than the peer group.

3. Always make high stakes decisions with an ad hoc child study team.

4. Never substitute grade retention in place of special education services.

5. If a child needs more time in grade, do it in the early years.

6. Only retain an older student if you have his or her unconditional support.

7. Never make the decision to retain a student based on one factor (i.e. standardized test score) but on a variety of considerations.

Jim Grant / Bob Johnson

The answer is more than intelligence goes to school.

The whole child goes to school—brains, nervous system, muscles, emotions, teeth, hands, feet, arms, legs and much, much more.

Children grow and develop in four major areas: physical, emotional, social, and intellectual. All must be recognized and nurtured. Children have:

1. Physical needs—for food, exercise, sleep, growing;

2. Social needs—for playtime, family, friends, community;

3. Emotional needs—for security, comfort, love, stability;

4. Intellectual needs—for stimulation, creative expression, academics.

All of these individual parts together go to school, all wrapped up in one small, neat package--your child.

It is a myth to think that intelligence alone is the cornerstone for success in school or life. Intelligence alone can't control the pencil in the child's hand unless the muscles have developed. Intelligence alone can't see the print on a page if the eyes are not able to focus. Intelligence alone can't make friends if the child's emotions are fear, frustration, and anxiety. The reality is that even the most intelligent children may fail in school. If their other needs are not met, eventually the struggle of keeping up will create an imbalance.

The child's personality, temperament, motivation, emotional make-up, home environment, learning style— all of these play a role in achievement at school. In fact, many early childhood experts agree that maturity level, the child's developmental age, is the leading factor in determining a child's overall success in school.

How can you tell if your child is ready for school?

1. First, recognize that you, the parent, know your child as no one else can, and you are the best judge of your child's development. Read all you can on the subject. Attend talks on the subject at your child's school.

2. Second, speak with your child's teacher, who has training in childhood development, and experience in working with children. Ask how your child's development compares with others of the same chronological age. Remember, teachers want what is best for children--they are good development barometers.

3. Third, observe what your child can and cannot do, not what you want or wish your child to do. It is difficult to make this distinction. Wanting the best for your child and doing what is actually best for him/her is not always the same.

4. Fourth, if you feel your child may not be ready for a grade, have your child's readiness level evaluated through testing. Evaluations have been developed specifically to assess a child's maturity level and readiness for a particular grade.

If you think your child seems "younger" than others of the same age, if you suspect he or she needs extra growing time, speak to the teachers and principal. Research clearly indicates that the children who are developmentally too young for their assigned grades are the children who most often fail at school.

Jim Grant
More Than Intelligence Goes To School
Copyright © 1988 Jim Grant

Published by Programs for Education, Inc.
Rosemont, NJ 08556

Recommended Reading:

Ames, Louise Bates. **Is Your Child In The Wrong Grade?** Rosemont, NJ: Modern Learning Press, 1978.

Ames, Louise Bates; Gillespie, Clyde; and Streff, John W. **Stop School Failure** Rosemont, NJ: Programs for Education, 1972.

Grant, Jim. **Jim Grant Live.** (Audio tape) Rosemont, NJ: Programs for Education, 1985.

Dialogues on Development. (A collection of articles and research data.) Rosemont, NJ: Programs for Education, 1986.

Perceived Advantages of a Kindergarten/First Grade Blend

- Mixed-age eavesdropping opportunities

- There is a higher ceiling on the curriculum

- There are peer modeling opportunities

- There are over a dozen multiyear placement benefits

- There can be an additional year of learning time without the stigma of "staying back"

- Grade one is afforded more play opportunities

- There is additional time available for "kid watching"

- In some schools kindergartners go home at noon reducing the class size for first grade in the PM

- There are real benefits to proximal development

- There are tutoring opportunities for both groups

- There are 50% fewer new first graders to teach to read

Jim Grant / Bob Johnson

Perceived Disadvantages of a Kindergarten/First Grade Blend

- Kindergartners may be denied play opportunities

- Many of today's kindergartners have very high needs

- Class is too diverse developmentally

- First graders may be shortchanged academically

- Some schools have four-year-olds in kindergarten due to a late entrance date

- The needs of five-year-olds are very different from six-year-olds

- Kindergartners may be overwhelmed by more experienced first graders

- There may not be enough quality kid watching time

- Kindergarten is time intensive to teach

- Some entire kindergarten classes are too disjointed to keep together as a group for multiple years

- Kindergartners who are learning handicapped, yet un-identified, may not qualify for special needs intervention

- If there is an AM and PM kindergarten (2 groups) there may be too much lost time transitioning

Jim Grant / Bob Johnson

Q. Will children who are developmentally young catch up in a multiage classroom?

A. No. Children will not automatically catch up in a multiage classroom. This seems to be wishful thinking on the part of some school officials seeking a "quick fix," no-cost solution to the issue of developmental differences. Students who are developmentally younger than their peers when they enter a multiage classroom will exit the same way — developmentally young.

Some educators claim that the multiage classroom is an education equalizer. It is not. Varying amounts of learning time — the often unacknowledged factor that can make a difference in student performance — is the equalizer. Children who are developing more slowly may need the extra learning time afforded by the multiage continuous progress classroom.

In a first/second grade multiage blended classroom, some learners may take up to three years to complete the program.

Q.

Is a pre-first/first multiage blend a viable alternative to a self-contained pre-first program?

A. Yes! The birth of the pre-first concept in 1966 in New Hampshire was a valiant attempt to break the stranglehold on the inflexible lockstep graded structure. This additional grade level was designed to build in a year of extra learning time for those children who are chronologically six but are developmentally too young and simply need three years to complete the traditional kindergarten and first year program. Thousands of extra-year programs were created as an alternative to school failure. These programs enjoyed great popularity with parents and teachers for the most part; they did what they were intended to do. These programs incorporated developmentally appropriate practices, reduced teacher, parent, and child stress, promoted a child's self-esteem, negated retention, and enhanced performance for many students.

Most school systems that have eliminated the extra year of learning time did so not because it didn't work, but because of the cost of financing the extra year. The program was replaced with the age-old concept called social promotion.

Social promotion is the practice of moving students up through the grades without giving consideration to the students' developmental needs or skills attainment. Social promotion creates a host of other school ills, such as an increase in school-induced learning disabilities and attention deficit disorder, low academic performance, and an increase in discipline problems. Some classroom educators reacted to the loss of this extra learning time option by creating a very real substitute — a pre-first/first grade multiage classroom.

Students are carefully selected based on their developmental needs. Only children whose parents agree to this placement are put in this setting. These students have the option of staying with the class for one or two years based on teacher observation and parental support. This arrangement allows some students additional learning time in a continuous progress configuration without being in a separate extra-year classroom.

Schools should not eliminate the self-contained pre-first program until the pre-first/first multiage classroom is well under way.

Excerpt from *Multiage Q&A: 101 Practical Answers to Your Most Pressing Questions*, by Jim Grant, Bob Johnson and Irv Richardson. Reprinted by permission of Crystal Springs Books, Ten Sharon Road, Peterborough, NH 03458. 1-800-321-0401.

— Introduction —
Signs and Signals of School Stress

With their bodies, their gestures, and the expressions on their faces — not just their words — children communicate their needs. For example, any parent knows what it means when a child's bottom lip begins to quiver. There are many ways children indicate how they feel and what they think, and these signs and signals are important indicators for adults concerned about a child's well-being.

Some signs and signals are unique to a particular age level — they are not likely to appear before a child reaches a certain stage of development, and they are likely to disappear as the child continues to develop and behave in more advanced ways. Other signs and signals span several age levels — they may even continue to appear throughout someone's life if the underlying causes are not identified and resolved.

The signs and signals in this checklist can help you approximate the level of "school stress" that a child is experiencing. School stress occurs when the curriculum in a particular grade or program does not match the developmental needs of a child. This is primarily a matter of **what** the teacher is required to teach, rather than **how** the teacher teaches. It may be possible in some cases to modify both what and how the teacher teaches, but in many cases a variety of regulations and budget limitations prevent the teacher from changing the content and style of instruction.

No grade or program can match the developmental needs of all children all the time, so some school stress is inevitable and will not do any harm. And, most children do not experience severe school stress.

However, when a mismatch between a child's needs and the curriculum is too significant and sustained, the amount of school stress can become overwhelming. This can make school a difficult and unpleasant experience and have long-term effects, such as the development of poor self-esteem and negative attitudes about school.

To avoid this sort of result, you can use this checklist as a "school stress detector." By noting how frequently a child exhibits certain signs at home and in general, and combining this information with the teacher's notes on your child's behavior at school, you are gathering the information you need to make informed decisions. And, you'll find that the checklist includes space for you to list other signs and signals you have noticed which do not appear in the checklist.

Once you have completed the checklist, be sure to read the information that follows it, which explains how to interpret and use the checklist results. You'll also want to discuss this information with your child's teacher. Working effectively and positively with your chid and the child's teacher is the best way to turn school stress into school success.

Jim Grant / Bob Johnson

6-Year-Olds

Signs and Signals of School Stress

Child's Name _____ Birthdate _____

At Home - **How often does this 6-year-old child:**

		Never	Rarely	Often
1.	complain of before-school stomach aches			
2.	revert to bed-wetting			
3.	behave in a manner that seems out of character to the parent			
4.	ask to stay at home			

At School - **How often does this 6-year-old child:**

		Never	Rarely	Often
1.	want to play with 5-year-olds			
2.	want to play with toys during class time			
3.	choose recess, gym and music as favorite subjects			
4.	feel overwhelmed by the size and activity level in the lunchroom			
5.	have a high rate of absenteeism			
6.	try to take frequent "in-house field trips" to the pencil sharpener, bathroom, school nurse, custodian, etc.			
7.	mark papers randomly			
8.	"act out" on the playground			
9.	reverse, invert, substitute, or omit letters and numbers when reading and/or writing (this is also not unusual for properly placed students, either)			
10.	complain about being bored with school work, when in reality he or she cannot do the work			
11.	have a short attention span — unable to stay focused on a twenty-minute reading lesson			
12.	have difficulty understanding the teacher's instructions			

In General - **How often does this 6-year-old child:**

		Never	Rarely	Often
1.	cry easily and frequently			
2.	tire quickly			
3.	need constant reassurance and praise			
4.	become withdrawn and shy			
5.	develop a nervous tic — a twitching eye, a nervous cough, frequent clearing of the throat or twirling of hair			
6.	return to thumbsucking			
7.	lie or "adjust the truth" about school			
8.	revert to soiling his or her pants			
9.	make restless body movements, such as rocking in a chair, jiggling legs, etc.			
10.	dawdle			
11.	seem depressed			
12.	feel harried / hurried			

Parent Notes:

Teacher Notes:

Jim Grant / Bob Johnson

5-Year-Olds

Signs and Signals of School Stress

Child's Name _____ Birthdate _____

At Home - How often does this 5-year-old child:

		Never	Rarely	Often
1.	not want to leave Mom/Dad			
2.	not want to go to school			
3.	suffer from stomach aches or headaches, particularly in the morning before school			
4.	dislike school or complain that school is "dumb"			
5.	complain that the teacher does not allow enough time to finish his or her school work			
6.	need to rest, but resist taking a nap			
7.	revert to bedwetting			

At School - How often does this 5-year-old child:

1.	show little interest in kindergarten "academics"			
2.	ask if it's time to go home			
3.	seem unable to hold scissors as directed by the teacher			
4.	worry that Mom/Dad will forget to pick him or her up after school			
5.	have a difficult time following the daily routine			
6.	talk incessantly			
7.	complain that school work is "too hard" ("I can't do it,") or "too easy" ("It's so easy I'm not going to do it,") or "too boring"			
8.	interrupt the teacher constantly			
9.	seem unable to shift easily from one task to the next			
10.	seem overly restless during class and frequently in motion when supposed to be working at a task			

In General - How often does this 5-year-old child:

1.	become withdrawn			
2.	revert to thumbsucking or infantile speech			
3.	compare herself negatively to other children ("They can do it, but I can't")			
4.	complain that she has no friends			
5.	cry easily and frequently			
6.	make up stories			
7.	bite his or her nails			
8.	seem depressed			

Parent Notes:

Teacher Notes:

Jim Grant / Bob Johnson

How to Interpret & Utilize Checklist Results

All children display some stress signs at times. Severe stress is indicated when a child displays several stress signs frequently and over an extended period of time.

If the checklist indicates severe stress, or if you strongly feel the child is under such stress, further investigation is warranted. You should discuss the situation with your child's teacher and other personnel at the school. Further assessment by a learning specialist or pediatrician who can identify the causes of the stress may be in order.

In particular, a developmental assessment of your child can help to determine whether your child's current stage of development matches the curriculum in your child's grade or program. Children's rates of development vary widely, and a child who is "developmentally young" needs material and instructional strategies appropriate for that child. Also, the children in a grade or program who are younger in terms of their chronological age may experience stress and difficulties in learning, simply because they need more time to grow in order to reach the same developmental level that older children have already reached.

Other factors may also be influencing children's development, learning, and related stress. For example, girls tend to mature faster than boys — and to have an advantage in "fine motor" skills. This means that a boy is more likely to have trouble paying attention and learning, especially if he is also chronologically and/or developmentally young. And, any child who frequently comes to school hungry, tired or sick will have a more difficult time learning because of these problems. Emotional problems stemming from such things as a separation or divorce, the death of someone important to the child, or the relocation to a new community can have a similar impact on a child's school success and level of stress.

These days, many children under stress may be suspected of having a Learning Disability or Attention Deficit Disorder. It is important to remember that this sort of diagnosis can only be made by a trained professional. And, developmentally and/or chronologically young have many of the same symptoms, which may be reduced or relieved when the child is placed in a developmentally appropriate grade or program.

Options for Relieving School Stress

Just as school stress can have a variety of causes, there are many ways in which it can be relieved. If the level of stress is not too severe and related directly to one or two specific areas, additional help may solve the problem. If a specialist believes that a child has a Learning Disability or Attention Deficit Disorder, the specialist should develop a detailed plan for helping the child in cooperation with the child's teacher and parents.

In many cases, however, a child's difficulties in school are not specifically related to just one or two areas, and the child does not actually have a Learning Disability or Attention Deficit Disorder. Instead, the child is experiencing school stress and widespread problems because the child has not yet reached the developmental stage at which he or she can succeed in a particular grade or program. The solution for this sort of child is to provide more time to grow and learn, and a number of educational options which provide this extra time have been found to work successfully in schools across America. Following is a brief summary of some of these options you may want to consider now or in the future:

An extra year of preschool: Allowing developmentally young children to spend an extra year in preschool can be a very positive alternative to sending them off to kindergarten and waiting to find out if they "sink or swim." An extra year to grow and learn in a supportive preschool greatly decreases the odds that such children will flounder and need rescuing in the primary grades.

Readiness classes: Readiness classes provide a year before kindergarten in which children can grow, learn, and make the transition to school in a developmentally appropriate setting. This can help make kindergarten a much more successful educational experience for developmentally young children.

Transition or pre-first grades: These full-day programs provide students with an extra year in which to make the difficult transition from the play-oriented learning of kindergarten to more formal academic tasks, which become increasingly important in first grade. Children who have had this experience are then better prepared to enter first grade with confidence and a reasonable expectation of success.

Multi-age classes: Many schools now offer multi-age, continuous-progress classrooms, in which children of different ages work and learn together with the same teacher for more than one year. These classes are particularly appropriate for children who need extra time to develop, because they already contain a wide range of age levels and a flexible timetable that allows children to "remain" for another year.

Another year in the same grade: Many children feel a great sense of relief when told they will be spending more time in a grade, because they know they won't have to keep trying to do the impossible. An extra year in the same grade gives children time to master the curriculum, and gain the skills and confidence they will need to succeed in upper grades.

Based on information in *I Hate School!* by Jim Grant. Rosemont, NJ: Modern Learning Press, 1994. Reprinted by permission of Jim Grant and Modern Learning Press. All rights reserved. Checklists for 4, 5, 6 year-olds available in packets of 25 from Crystal Springs Books, Ten Sharon Road, PO Box 500, Peterborough, NH 03458. 1-800-321-0401.

Jim Grant / Bob Johnson

READING: READINESS LEVEL

Vocabulary:
Reads by sight:
Own name in print
A personal sight vocabulary (high interest)
20 words from the basic sight vocabulary

Word Meaning:
Understands **beginning** and **end** in relation to:
print
speech
When listening, predicts:
outcome
vocabulary, word, rhyme

Comprehension:
Knows that:
reading makes sense
print represents the sounds of the language
Has a reading attitude.
Listens well to stories.
Has a desire to read:
Looks at books on his/her own
Is interested in words and symbols.

Auditory:
Identifies:
beginning sounds
ending sounds
rhymes
Discriminates the major consonant sounds.

Visual:
Has correct directional habits:
looks at books from front to back
looks at books from left page to right page
begins left top
proceeds left to right
proceeds top to bottom
Identifies:
word
letter

Auditory/Visual
Matches spoken and printed words when someone
reads
Knows most letter names:
upper case
lower case

Oral Reading
Attacks words using context and initial letter checked
by sense

WRITING: READINESS LEVEL

Fluency:
Writes independently
Has confidence as a writer

Composition:
Expresses thoughts in writing
Writes telling sentences
Talks about what he/she has written
Revises one or more words during conferences

Mechanics:
Capitalizes:
First name and initial of last name
I

Handwriting:
Tries to make recognizable letters

Spelling:
Own first name
Uses major consonants: b, d, j, k, l, m, n, p, s, t, z
for beginnings of words

SPEAKING

Expresses his/her needs
Asks questions
Responds appropriately to questions
Maintains the subject line in conversation
Shares experiences in a group
Uses complete sentences
Uses specific vocabulary for objects (book, puzzle,
scissors)

Literacy Learning

"Learning to read and to write ought to be one of the most joyful and successful of human undertakings."

"Children learn to listen and to speak in an unbreakable unity of function." [1] Reading and writing are two sides of an integrated learning process. We approach these skills together — and term them literacy learning. Reading is a developmental process starting early in childhood and continuing throughout life.

The essence of reading is to gain meaning from text, and children learn to read by reading. Therefore we teach reading strategies through quality children's literature, rich in human meaning. The joy of reading a novel is superior to using a commercial series for language learning.

The essence of writing is to communicate ideas in written form. Techniques of grammar and spelling are taught after children experience the thrill of expressing themselves in writing. We believe phonics skills need to be taught in order for children to spell correctly and we incorporate these skills as the child is ready.

"Children taught in this way take pride in their work, take pride in themselves, and take joy in communicating from their own writing and reading." [2]

1. Don Holdaway, *The Foundations of Literacy* (Sydney, Australia: Ashton Scholastic, 1979).

2. Marlene J. McCracken and Robert A. McCracken, *Reading, Writing, and Language, A Practical Guide for Primary Teachers* (Winnipeg, Canada: Peguis Publishers Limited, 1979) Foreward, viii.

Jay Buros

3 Cue Systems

Meaning
(semantic)

Structure
(grammar / syntax)

Visual
(shapes • sounds • graphophonic)

9:00-9:40 Miss Minor	ART Ms. Robinson	GYM Miss Taylor	MEETING Moe	GYM Miss Taylor
9:40-10:15	OPENING	SHARING	CALENDAR	
10:15-10:30		SNACK		
10:30-10:45	NOISY OR SILENT READING	RECESS- IN AUTUMN REST OF YEAR		
10:45-11:45		WRITING		
11:45-12:10		LUNCH		
12:15-12:40		RECESS		✱ DUTY
12:40-2:05	INTEGRATED DAY WHOLE LANGUAGE wed ½ group library (1:30) seniors start writing.			
2:05-2:40	PLAY childs choice			
2:40- EARLY BUS! 3:00- EVERYONE LEAVES	Share outcome of "Play". To go home.		Readiness Schedule J.Buros	
MONDAY—	TUESDAY	WEDNESDAY	THURSDAY	FRIDAY

Jay Buros

Whole Language

1. WARM-UP
   Songs
   Poems
   Nursery Rhymes
   Jingles
   Cheers

2. OLD STORY
   Have a child choose the story

3. NEW STORY
   a. Big Book
   b. Good literature on opaque projector or overhead
   c. Student made Big Book
   d. Teacher published Big Book
   e. Song/Poem, chant on chart paper

4. OUTPUT/DEMONSTRATIONS — Student participation in relationship to new story
   1. Wall chart
   2. Student made, published Big Book
   3. Student made small books (copy of large book)
   4. Murals
   5. Puppets
        hand (made out of socks)
        popsicle stick
   6. Flannel board characters and magnetic board characters
   7. Play of story
   8. Innovation of new story (Creating a new story together — probably after it has been read 8-10 times)
   9. Mobile of all the characters in the story
   10. Personal writing about the story — mine and the children's
   11. Field trips to make story come alive
   12. Invite people — to make story come alive (example: teddy bear collector to talk with children)
   13. Share book with a larger audience

Jay Buros

Whole Language Block

	Monday	Tuesday	Wednesday	Thursday	Friday
			Warm-up		
			Children choose "old" story		
			New story — song — poem — rhyme Teacher's choice from observation of children		
			Demonstration by teacher — Output by children		

Jay Buros

TEACHER:_____ Grade:_____

ARE YOU READY FOR PUBLICATION?

Today's Date:_____

Your first and last name:_____

The title of your book:_____

Dedicated to:_____

Circle the size type you want. _____

Large Type   Small Type

Do you want pictures in your book? _____

    If you do circle where you want the pictures to be.

        Left page (The writing will be on the right page.)

        Top half of the page.

        Bottom half of the page.

        Only one or two pictures . . . Where do you want them?

        All pictures will be drawn on special paper. Get it from your teacher.

What color cover do you want? _____

NOW: 1. Attach **About The Author** to your writing.
          2. Clip your writing and this form together.
          3. Put it on the **manuscript** desk.

CONGRATULATIONS!

_____**Observation**

_____**Date**

I looked at:_____

A picture of what I saw:

[   ]

Here are things I noticed:_____

_____

_____

_____

1 _____
(The Dream)

If you achieved it how would you know?

②

A.

B.

C.

D.

E.

F.

Benchmarks (back plan — include span of time)

④

Where are you today? (in each area listed under ②)

③

A.

B.

C.

D.

E.

F.

Methods you will try. "Be flexible."

⑤

Jay Buros

Why Whole Language
by Jay Buros

What do you want children to accomplish by the end of the year?

FAVORITE SONGS, POEMS, AND RHYMES

HEY THERE NEIGHBOR!

Hey there, neighbor!
What do you say?
It's going to be a wonderful day!
Clap your hands and boogie on down.
Give 'em a bump and pass it around!
                    (or sit on down)

HI! MY NAME IS JOE!

Hi! My name is Joe and I work in the button
    (doughnut) factory.
I have a wife, a dog, and a family!
One day my boss came to me and said,
"Hey Joe, are you busy?"
I said, "No."
He said, "Well then work with your right hand."
    • Repeat each time adding one more body part:
       left hand, right foot, head
       Last line, last time:
I said, "Yes!!!"

TONY CHESTNUT

Toe knee chestnut
Nose eye love you.
Toe knee nose.
Toe knee nose.
Toe knee chestnut nose I love you . . .
That's what toe knee nose.

HI DEE HAY! HI DEE HO!

Leader: *Hi dee hay! Hi dee ho!*
Group: **Hi dee hay! Hi dee ho!**
Leader: *Igglee wigglee wogglee wo!*
Group: **Igglee wigglee wogglee wo!**
Leader: *Raise your voices to the sky.*
Group: **Raise your voices to the sky.**
Leader: *Mrs._____'s class is walking by.*
Group: **Mrs._____ 's class is walking by.**
Leader: *Count off!*
Group: **1, 2, 3, 4, 5**
Leader: *Break it on down now!*
Group: **6, 7, 8, 9, 10 . . .**
Leader: *Let's do it all once again!*

COPY CAT

Let's play copy cat just for fun
Let's copy_____, she's the one.
Whatever she does we'll do the same,
'cause that's how you play the Copy Cat Game

RISE RUBY RISE!

Down in the valley two by two.
Down in the valley two by two.
Down in the valley two by two.
Rise Ruby Rise!

2nd verse:
We can do it your way two by two.
We can do it your way two by two.
We can do it your way two by two.
Rise Ruby Rise!

3rd verse:
We can do it my way two by two.
We can do it my way two by two.
We can do it my way two by two.
Rise Ruby Rise!

OH! MY AUNT CAME BACK

Oh! my aunt came back
Oh! my aunt came back
from_____.

And she brought me back
And she brought me back
_____.

Old Japan	old hand fan
Old Algier	a pair of shears
Belgium too	some gum to chew
London Fair	a rocking chair
Holland too	some wooden shoes
Timbuktu	a nut like you

"Whatever you can do or dream you can begin it.
Boldness has genius, power, and magic in it."
                                    Goethe

Music Resources

Greg and Steve
1-800-444-4287
Vol. II, We All Live Together
Playing Favorites
Holidays and Special Times

Charlotte Diamond
Hug Bug Records
c/o Box 58174
Station L
Vancouver, BC
Canada VSP 6CS

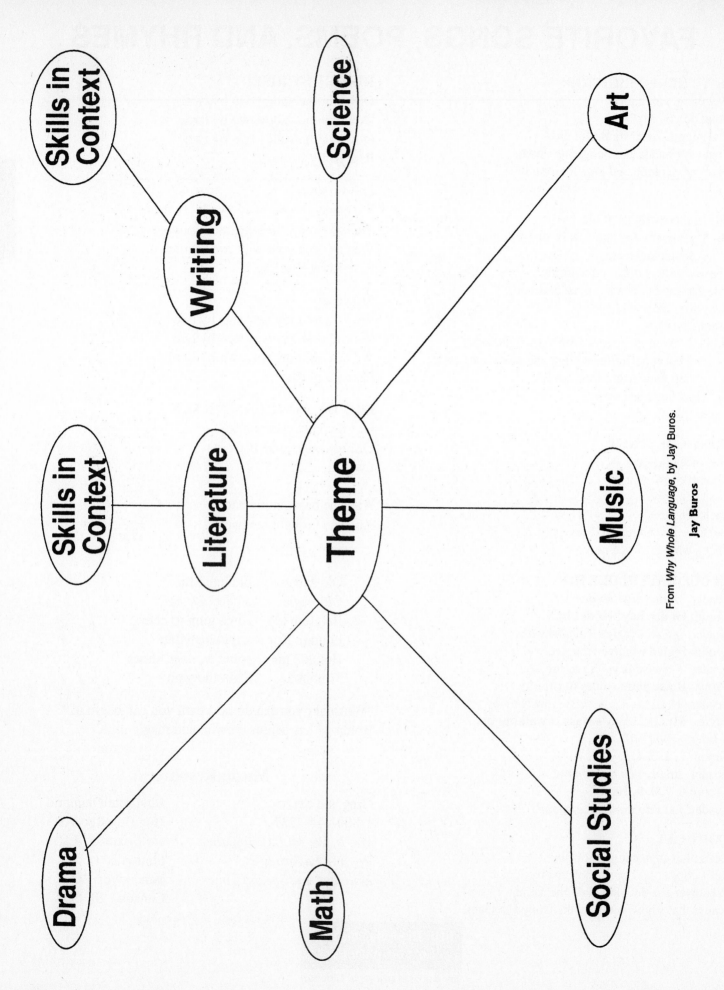

From *Why Whole Language*, by Jay Buros.

Jay Buros

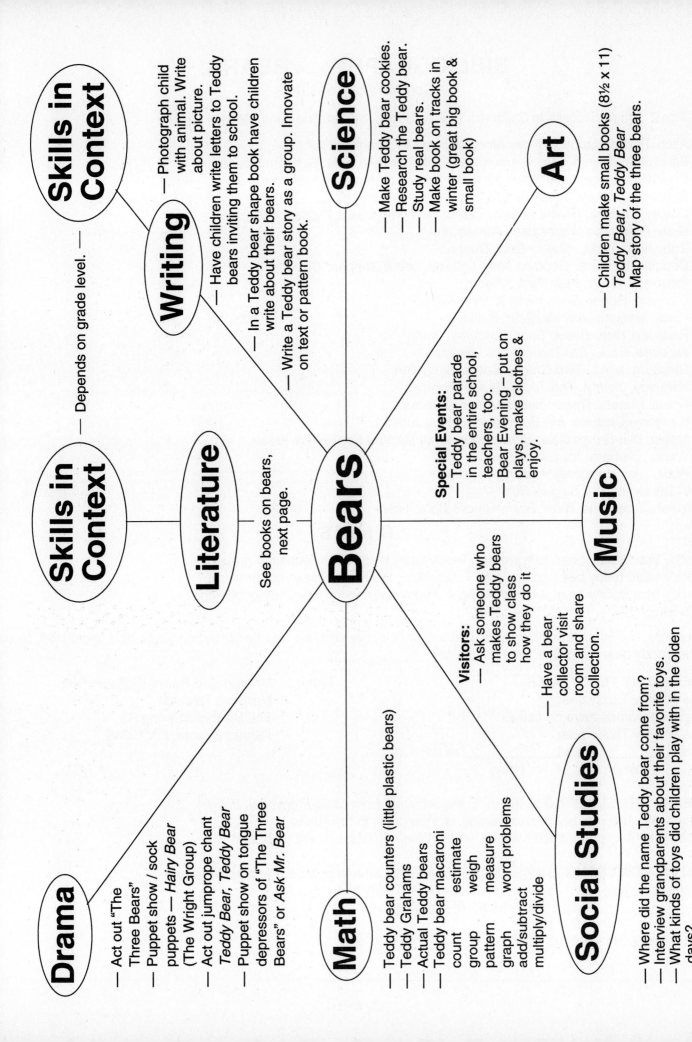

Skills in Context

— Depends on grade level. —

Writing

— Photograph child with animal. Write about picture.
— Have children write letters to Teddy bears inviting them to school.
— In a Teddy bear shape book have children write about their bears.
— Write a Teddy bear story as a group. Innovate on text or pattern book.

Science

— Make Teddy bear cookies.
— Research the Teddy bear.
— Study real bears.
— Make book on tracks in winter (great big book & small book)

Art

— Children make small books (8½ x 11) *Teddy Bear, Teddy Bear*
— Map story of the three bears.

Skills in Context

Literature

See books on bears, next page.

Bears

Special Events:
— Teddy bear parade in the entire school, teachers, too.
— Bear Evening – put on plays, make clothes & enjoy.

Visitors:
— Ask someone who makes Teddy bears to show class how they do it
— Have a bear collector visit room and share collection.

Music

Jay Buros

Drama

— Act out "The Three Bears"
— Puppet show / sock puppets — *Hairy Bear* (The Wright Group)
— Act out jumprope chant *Teddy Bear, Teddy Bear*
— Puppet show on tongue depressors of "The Three Bears" or *Ask Mr. Bear*

Math

— Teddy bear counters (little plastic bears)
— Teddy Grahams
— Actual Teddy bears
— Teddy bear macaroni
  count   estimate
  group   weigh
  pattern measure
  graph   word problems
  add/subtract
  multiply/divide

Social Studies

— Where did the name Teddy bear come from?
— Interview grandparents about their favorite toys.
— What kinds of toys did children play with in the olden days?

41

BIBLIOGRAPHY . . . BEARS!
Compiled by Jay Buros

** A to Z Subject Access to Children's Picture Books. by Caroline Lima, Bowker Co.

* Asch, Frank. *Happy Birthday Moon, Mooncake*. Prentice Hall.
* Berenstein, Stan & Jan. *Bears in the Night, The Bike Ride*. Random House.
  Brustlein, Janice. *Little Bears Pancake Party*. Lothrop, Lee & Shepard.
  Carlstrom, Nancy. *Jesse Bear, What Will You Wear?*
  Cauley, Lorinda. *Bryan, Goldilocks and the Three Bears*. Putnam's Sons.
  Craft, Ruth. *The Winter Bear*. Atheneum.
* Dabcovich, Lydia. *Sleepy Bear*. Dutton.
  Douglas, Barbara. *Good As New*. Lothrop, Lee & Shepard Co., NY.
  DuBois, William. *Bear Party*. Viking.
* Duvoisin, Roger. *Snowy and Woody*. Knopf.
* Flack, Marjorie. *Ask Mr. Bear*. Puffin.
* Freeman, Don. *Beady Bear, Corduroy*. Puffin.
  Galdone, Paul. *The Three Bears*. Seabury.
  Ginsburg, Mirra. *Two Greedy Bears*. Macmillan.
* Kennedy, Jimmy. *The Teddy Bears' Picnic*.
* Kraus, Robert. *Three Friends*. Windmill Books.
  Kuratomi, Chizuko. *Mr. Bear Goes to Sea*. Judson.
* Martin, Bill. *Brown Bear, Brown Bear, What Do You See?* HRW Press.
* Waber, Bernard. *Ira Sleeps Over*.
* Wahl, Jan. *Humphrey's Bear*.
* Ward, Lynn. *The Biggest Bear*.
  Yolen, Jane. *The Three Bears Rhyme Book*. HBJ.

CHARTS

Teddy bear, teddy bear, turn around. Teddy bear, teddy bear, touch the ground.
Teddy bear, teddy bear, go upstairs. Teddy bear, teddy bear, say your prayers.
Teddy bear, teddy bear, turn out the light. Teddy bear, teddy bear, say goodnight,
"Goodnight!"

One little, two little, three little Teddy bears, four little, five little, six little Teddy bears, seven little, eight little, nine little Teddy bears, ten little Teddy bears and _____.

ME AND MY TEDDY BEAR
Me and my Teddy bear
Have no worries have no cares.
Me and my Teddy bear
Just _____ and _____ all day.
    (play)   (play)

Music: **Unbearable Bears** by Kevin Roth
Marlboro Records
845 Marlboro Spring Rd.
Kennet Square, PA 19348

BEARS ARE SLEEPING (Sung to "Frere Jacques" from *More Piggyback Songs*)
Bears are sleeping, bears are sleeping. In their dens, in their dens.
Soon it will be spring, soon it will be spring. Wake up bears, wake up bears!

TEDDY BEAR SONG (Sung to: Mary Had A Little Lamb from *More Piggyback Songs*)
 (child's name) has a Teddy bear, Teddy bear, Teddy bear.
_____ has a Teddy bear. It's (brown) and (furry) all over.

I'M GOING ON A BEAR HUNT

Jay Buros

Trees – Ecology

Skills in Context — Depends on grade level. —

Writing
— Brainstorm names of trees.
— Web a story
— Map stories
— Design a poster that you would carry in a protest march.
— List names of trees that give fruit.

Science
— Talk about a recycle program.
— Observe a leaf / pine cone.
— Compare / observe apples.
— How long does it take garbage to break down?

Art
— Design a poster to encourage recycling programs.
— Illustrate one way you can recycle today.
— Illustrate things in the world that are made out of wood. (Make into a tree mural.)

Skills in Context

Literature
Read:
— *The Man Who Planted Trees* – guided reading
— *My Earth Book*

Game:
— About Ecology

Music
— *Evergreen / Everblue*
Raffi (See drama.)

Drama
— Rap song —
*Recycle Mania /
Billy B. Sings
about Trees*

Math
— Survey the grocery store and count how many shopping bags are used in one hour.
— Homework survey — ½ hour; go to a grocery store and count how many paper bags are used by customers.
— Recycle aluminum cans — count by hundreds — count by hundreds — thousands.
— How many cans do you need to make a pound?
— How much money could the class make per pound?
— How many trees make 1 Sunday edition of the New York Times? Your local paper?

Social Studies
— Game — How much of the world is water? Land?
— Chart on a graph.
— Identify where trees grow / what kinds.
— Name markers on a map, example: land, river, ocean.
— Play a game throwing a globe.

Jay Buros

Ecology Resources

Books:

* Applehof, Mary. *Worms Eat My Garbage.* Michigan Flower Press, 1982.
* Bare, Edith. *This Is the Way We Go To School.*
  Bonnet, Robert L. *Earth Science — 49 Science Fair Projects.* Tab Books, 1990.
* Brandenberg, Aliki. *The Story of Johnny Appleseed.* NY: Simon and Schuster.
  Byars, Betsy. *The Summer of the Swans.* NY: Puffin Press, 1970.
  Caduto, Michael and Bruchac, Joseph. *Keepers of the Earth.* Fulcrum Inc., 1988.
* Cherry, Lynn. *A River Ran Wild.* NY: Harcourt, Brace Jovanovich, 1992.
  _____. *The Great Kapok Tree.* NY: Harcourt, Brace Jovanovich, 1990.
* Child, Lydia Maria. *Over the River and Through the Wood.* NY: Scholastic, 1974.
* Cook, Janet. *How Things Are Made.* Belgium: Usborne Pub. Ltd., 1989.
* Cooney, Barbara. *Island Boy.*
* Dabcovich, Linda. *Busy Beavers.* NY: Scholastic, 1988.
* dePaola, Tomie. *The Legend of Bluebonnet.* NY: G.P. Putnam's Sons, 1983.
* Donahue, Mike. *The Grandpa Tree.*
  Elkington, Hailes Hill. *Going Green.* NY: Puffin Books, 1990.
  Fiarotta, Phyllis. *Ships, Snails, Walnut Whales: Nature Crafts for Children.* NY: Workman Pub. Co.
* Giono, Jean. *The Man Who Planted Trees.* Chelsea Green Pub., 1985.
* Glaser, Linda. *Wonderful Worms.* The Millbrook Press, 1992.
  Goble, Paul. *I Sing for the Animals.* NY: Bradbury Press, 1991.
* Hallinan, P.K. *I'm Thankful Each Day!* Ideals Pub.
  Herman, Marina. *Teaching Kids to Love the Earth.* Pfeifer-Hamilton, 1991.
* Holling, Holling, C. *Paddle to the Sea.*
  Javna, John. *50 Simple Things Kids Can Do to Save the Earth.* NY: Universal Press.
* Jeffers, Susan. *Stopping by Woods on a Snowy Evening.* NY: Dutton, 1978.
* _____. *Brother Eagle, Sister Sky.* NY: Dial Books, 1991.
  Jeunesse, Gallimard. *The Earth and Sky.* NY: Scholastic, 1992.
* Kindersley, Dorling. *My First Green Book.* NY: Alfred Knopf, 1991.
  Lankford, Marg. *Hopscotch Around the World.*
* Lionni, Leo. *Tico and the Golden Wings.* NY: Alfred Knopf, 1964.
* Lobel, Arnold. *Ming Lo Moves the Mountain.*
* Locker, Thomas. *The Land of the Gray Wolf.* NY: Dial Books, 1991.
* MacDonald, G. *Little Island.*
* Maeno, Itoko. *Mother Nature Nursery Rhymes,* Santa Barbara, CA: Advocacy Press, 1990.
* McLerran, Alice. *The Mountain that Loved the Bird.* Picture Book Studio, 1985.
* Orbach, Ruth. *Apple Pigs.* NY: Philomel Books, 1976.
  Paulsen, Gary. *The Night the White Deer Died.* NY: Delacorte Press, 1978.
* Pearce, Fred. *The Big Green Book.* NY: Grosset and Dunlap, 1991.
  Pinnington, Andrea. *Nature.* NY: Random House, 1991.
* Ray, Deborah Kogan. *Little Tree.* NY: Crown Pub., 1987.
* Ryland, Cynthia. *When I Was Young in the Mountains.*
  Schwartz, Linda. *My Earth Book.* Santa Barbara, CA: The Learning Works, 1991.
* Siebert, Diane. *Hartland.*
* Silverstein, Shel. *The Giving Tree.* NY: Harper and Row, 1964.
* Soutter, Perroti, Andrienne. *Earthworm.* Creative Editions, 1993.
* Speare, Elizabeth George. *The Sign of the Beaver.* NY: Dell Pub. Co., 1983.
* Starr, Susan Bryer. *I Was Good to the Earth Today.* Starhouse Pub., 1992.
  Swartz, Linda. *Earth Book for Kids.* Santa Barbara, CA: The Learning Works Inc., 1990.
* Taylor, Barbara. *Green Thumbs Up!* (Experiments and Activities) NY: Random House, 1954.
* _____. *Hear! Hear!* (Experiments) NY: Random House, 1990.
* _____. *Over the Rainbow.* (Experiments) NY: Random House, 1992.
* _____. *Up, Up and Away!* (Experiments) NY: Random House, 1991.
* Udry, Janice May. *A Tree Is Nice.* NY: Harper and Row Pub., 1986.
* Van Allsburg, Chris. *Just a Dream.* Boston: Houghton Mifflin Co., 1990.

Jay Buros

Walker, Colin. *The Great Garbage Mountain.*

_____. *Oceans of Fish.*

_____. *We Need Energy.*

_____. *Our Storehouse Earth.*

_____. *Our Changing Atmosphere.*

_____. *Forests Forever.*

_____. *Food Farming.*

_____. *Ecology — Plants and Animals.*

_____. *The Environmental Teacher Guide,* Bothell, WA: The Wright Group, 1992.

White Deer of Autumn. *Ceremony in the Circle of Life.* Beyond Word Pub. Co., 1983.

* Wildsmith, Brian. *Squirrels.* Toronto: Oxford University Press, 1974.

* _____. *The Trunk.*

* Winter, Jeanette. *Follow the Drinking Gourd.*

Wolfman, Ira. *My World and Globe.* NY: Workman Pub., 1991.

Wood, Douglas. *Old Turtle.*

* Yolen, Jane. *Encounter.*

* _____. *Owl Moon.* NY: Philomel Books, 1987.

* Young, Ed. *Birches.* NY: Holt and Co., 1988.

GAME:

About Ecology
Earthwood, Inc.
Keyport, NJ 07735

MUSIC:

Recycle Mania / Billy B. Sings About Trees
P.O. Box 5423
Takoma Park, MD 19912
301-445-3845

PUZZLES, PROJECTS, FACTS AND FUN:

The Learning Works

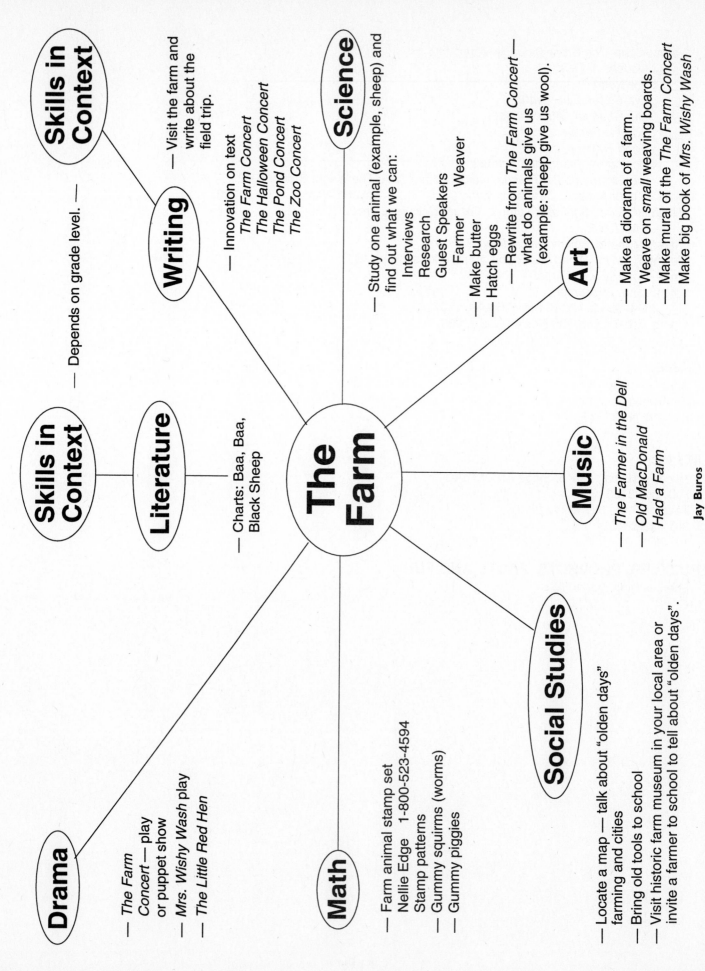

The Farm

Skills in Context

Writing
— Visit the farm and write about the field trip.
— Innovation on text
 The Farm Concert
 The Halloween Concert
 The Pond Concert
 The Zoo Concert

— Depends on grade level. —

Skills in Context

Literature
— Charts: Baa, Baa, Black Sheep

Drama
— *The Farm Concert* — play or puppet show
— *Mrs. Wishy Wash* play
— *The Little Red Hen*

Math
— Farm animal stamp set
 Nellie Edge 1-800-523-4594
 Stamp patterns
— Gummy squirms (worms)
— Gummy piggies

Social Studies
— Locate a map — talk about "olden days" farming and cities
— Bring old tools to school
— Visit historic farm museum in your local area or invite a farmer to school to tell about "olden days".

Science
— Study one animal (example, sheep) and find out what we can:
 Interviews
 Research
 Guest Speakers
  Farmer Weaver
— Make butter
— Hatch eggs
— Rewrite from *The Farm Concert* — what do animals give us (example: sheep give us wool).

Art
— Make a diorama of a farm.
— Weave on *small* weaving boards.
— Make mural of the *The Farm Concert*
— Make big book of *Mrs. Wishy Wash*

Music
— *The Farmer in the Dell*
— *Old MacDonald Had a Farm*

Jay Buros

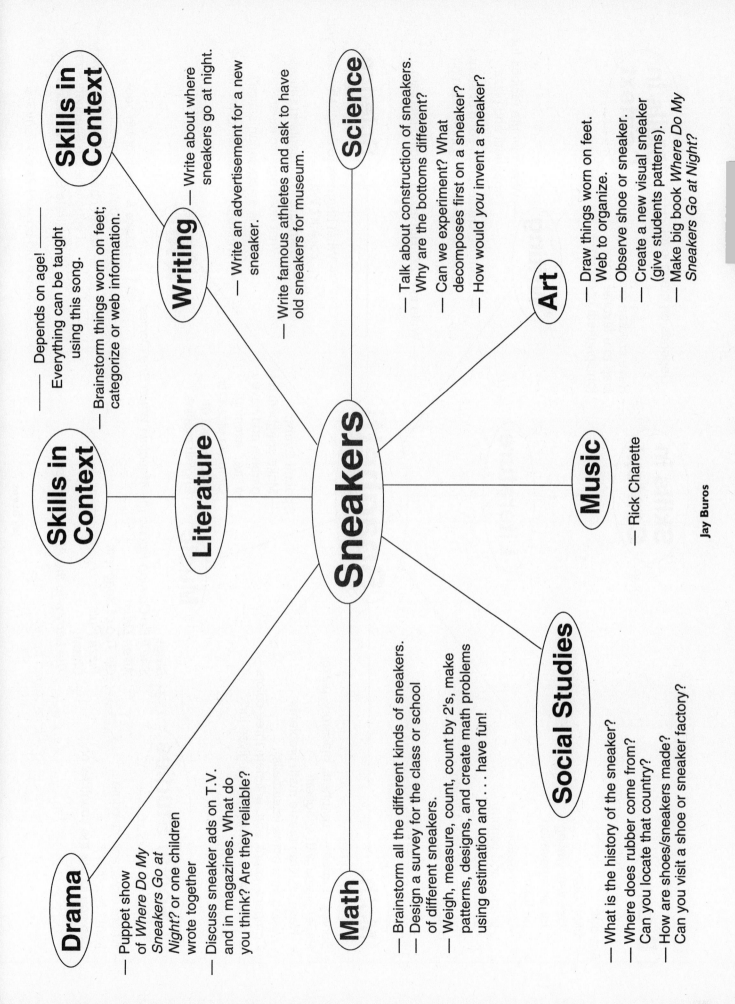

Sneakers

Skills in Context

— Depends on age!
Everything can be taught
using this song.

— Brainstorm things worn on feet;
categorize or web information.

Writing

— Write about where
sneakers go at night.

— Write an advertisement for a new
sneaker.

— Write famous athletes and ask to have
old sneakers for museum.

Science

— Talk about construction of sneakers.
Why are the bottoms different?

— Can we experiment? What
decomposes first on a sneaker?

— How would *you* invent a sneaker?

Skills in Context

Literature

Drama

— Puppet show
of *Where Do My
Sneakers Go at
Night?* or one children
wrote together

— Discuss sneaker ads on T.V.
and in magazines. What do
you think? Are they reliable?

Math

— Brainstorm all the different kinds of sneakers.

— Design a survey for the class or school
of different sneakers.

— Weigh, measure, count, count by 2's, make
patterns, designs, and create math problems
using estimation and . . . have fun!

Social Studies

— What is the history of the sneaker?

— Where does rubber come from?
Can you locate that country?

— How are shoes/sneakers made?

— Can you visit a shoe or sneaker factory?

Art

— Draw things worn on feet.
Web to organize.

— Observe shoe or sneaker.

— Create a new visual sneaker
(give students patterns).

— Make big book *Where Do My
Sneakers Go at Night?*

Music

— Rick Charette

Jay Buros

47

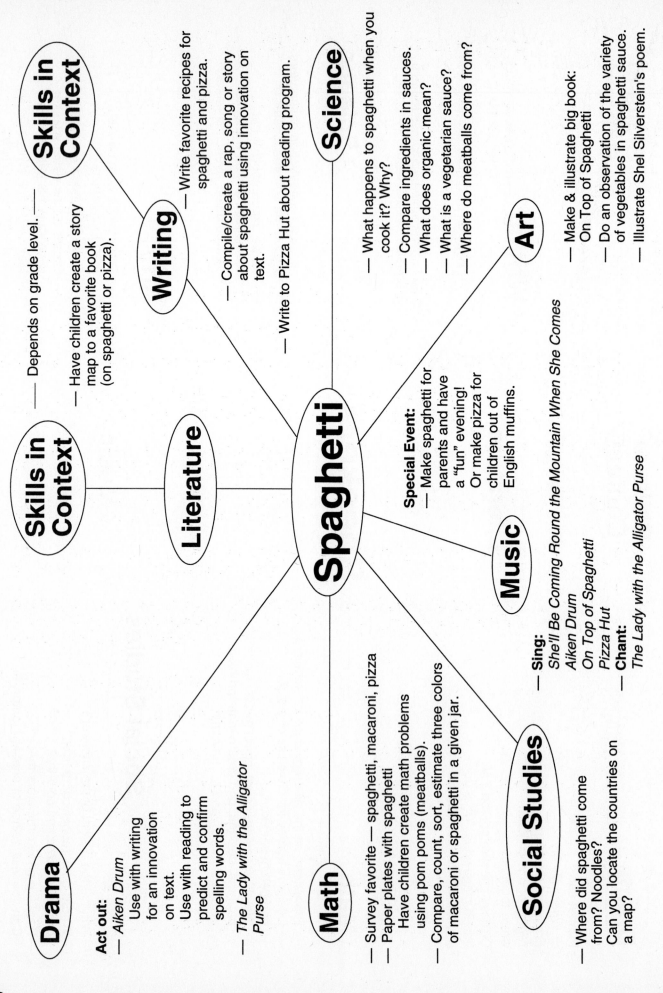

Skills in Context

— Depends on grade level.
— Have children create a story map to a favorite book (on spaghetti or pizza).

Writing

— Write favorite recipes for spaghetti and pizza.
— Compile/create a rap, song or story about spaghetti using innovation on text.
— Write to Pizza Hut about reading program.

Science

— What happens to spaghetti when you cook it? Why?
— Compare ingredients in sauces.
— What does organic mean?
— What is a vegetarian sauce?
— Where do meatballs come from?

Art

— Make & illustrate big book: On Top of Spaghetti
— Do an observation of the variety of vegetables in spaghetti sauce.
— Illustrate Shel Silverstein's poem.

Skills in Context

Literature

Spaghetti

Special Event:
— Make spaghetti for parents and have a "fun" evening! Or make pizza for children out of English muffins.

Music

Sing:
She'll Be Coming Round the Mountain When She Comes
Aiken Drum
On Top of Spaghetti
Pizza Hut
Chant:
The Lady with the Alligator Purse

Drama

Act out:
— *Aiken Drum*
   Use with writing for an innovation on text.
   Use with reading to predict and confirm spelling words.
— *The Lady with the Alligator Purse*

Math

— Survey favorite — spaghetti, macaroni, pizza
— Paper plates with spaghetti
  Have children create math problems using pom poms (meatballs).
— Compare, count, sort, estimate three colors of macaroni or spaghetti in a given jar.

Social Studies

— Where did spaghetti come from? Noodles? Can you locate the countries on a map?

Jay Buros

48

Learning Styles / Multiple Intelligences

Different Kinds of Smart

By Susan Black

*Not everyone is smart in the same way,
says Harvard's Howard Gardner, whose theory of
multiple intelligences could change your schools*

HOWARD GARDNER HAS TWO DREAMS: THE first is for schools to do away with testing and assess children in more natural ways; the second is for society to recognize a full range of intelligences.

Gardner, a researcher in cognitive development at Harvard University, has become a source of inspiration, guidance, and knowledge for many educators who are tussling with tough questions about the nature of intelligence and how it can be measured. Already, many schools are replacing standardized tests with "authentic assessments," using portfolios—collections of students' real work—to determine achievement and progress. (See the February 1993 Research Report, "Portfolio Assessment.")

But getting schools to recognize "a full range of intelligences"—and then change educational practice to promote children's multiple intelligences—appears to be a much more complex and formidable endeavor.

Gardner's theory of multiple intelligences posits that individuals (with the exception of those who are brain-damaged or otherwise severely impaired) are intelligent to some degree in each of the following areas: linguistic, musical, logical-mathematical, spatial, bodily-kinesthetic, interpersonal, and intrapersonal (see the box on page 25). What's more, Gardner claims, with good teaching, individuals can develop, can actually get smarter, in each of these seven intelligences.

Susan Black is an education consultant who lives in Hammondsport, N.Y.

Some schools are taking this theory to heart, but it isn't easy going. "The question is whether we should level our school and start from scratch," says a principal who intends to lead his K-6 elementary building toward a multiple-intelligence approach, "or whether we should take the slow route—one stepping stone at a time."

The limits of IQ

Whether you undertake radical reform or move cautiously in piecemeal fashion toward promoting a spectrum of intelligences, you must deal with some inescapable issues. One is the solid grip of standardized tests—especially when they're used to determine students' IQ.

So pervasive are the tests that supposedly measure and quantify students' intelligence that many schools would be lost without them. Without test data for evidence, how would schools know, for instance, where to place kindergartners? How would schools assign students to programs for the gifted? Who would be routed to special education classes? Which students would be counseled to go on to college, and which students would be told they should settle for vocational training?

In Gardner's ideal school, students wouldn't be categorized or labeled according to machine-scored, paper-and-pencil tests. Such tests, according to Gardner and his research colleagues at Harvard, are useful for one purpose and one purpose only: They predict children's success *in school*. Administering standardized tests to sixth-graders will, for instance, provide a fairly accurate picture of how they'll achieve in junior high. But, according to Gardner and other researchers, schools misuse tests when they use scores to slot kids into ability groups. It's especially unconscionable, they say, to use test scores to place a ceiling on some students' dreams for the future.

Why are IQ tests so limited? For one thing, the test items restrict students to using only what Gardner terms their logical-mathematical and linguistic skills. In fact, Gardner and other critics argue, IQ tests virtually ignore other traits in which many students excel—such as creativity in art or music, dexterity in mechanical or athletic areas, and sensitivity and caring toward others.

For another thing, standardized tests don't take into account such factors as motivation and effort (what some researchers call "task commitment"), which often drive brilliant achievement.

And, Gardner contends, schools doubly fail students by refusing to acknowledge talents and propensities that aren't considered "academic." The first blow is denying students a chance to develop all of their intelligences while they're in school; the second is preventing many from discovering and mastering talents, such as negotiating, which could benefit society.

Putting the theory to work

Schools that take Gardner's theories of multiple intelligences to heart are mapping out new strategies for teaching and learning. In the Key School in Indianapolis—an elementary school begun some seven years ago by a group of enterprising teachers—the staff works at promoting each student's range of abilities. In line with Gardner's theory, teachers provide opportunities for students to explore their seven intelligences. Teachers encourage students to use their strongest domains but help them develop their less dominant abilities.

Perhaps the commitment to helping students discover and develop untapped intelligences is most apparent in the school's Flow Room, a center every student attends at least three times a week. There, guided by clear rules and regulations, and supervised by a skillful teacher, students choose "flow activities" such

---

THE SEVEN INTELLIGENCES

Intelligence	End States	Core Components
1. Logical-mathematical	Scientist, mathematician	Sensitivity to, and capacity to discern, logical or numerical patterns; ability to handle long chains of reasoning.
2. Linguistic	Poet, journalist	Sensitivity to the sounds, rhythms, and meanings of words; sensitivity to different functions of language.
3. Musical	Composer, violinist	Ability to produce and appreciate rhythm, pitch, and timbre; appreciation of the forms of musical expressiveness.
4. Spatial	Navigator, sculptor	Capacity to perceive the visual-spatial world accurately and to perform transformations on one's initial perceptions.
5. Bodily-kinesthetic	Dancer, athlete	Ability to control one's body movements and to handle objects skillfully.
6. Interpersonal	Therapist, salesperson	Capacity to discern and respond appropriately to the moods, temperaments, motivations, and desires of other people.
7. Intrapersonal	Person with detailed, accurate self-knowledge	Access to one's own feelings and the ability to discriminate among them and to draw upon them to guide behavior; knowledge of one's own strengths, weaknesses, desires, and intelligences.

Source: Gardner, Howard, and Hatch, Thomas. "Multiple Intelligences Go to School: Educational Implications of the Theory of Multiple Intelligences." New York: Center for Technology in Education, 1990. ERIC Document No. ED 324366.

as board games, puzzles, books, and toys for free-play time. (Some students might also bring in hobbies—such as kits for building model airplanes—from home.)

But playtime in the Flow Room isn't just a recess period for letting off steam or burning up energy. Here play is serious business—so much so that teachers record students' choices and behavior on observation charts. Data on the students' activities help teachers interpret the children's talents and skills; the records also become part of students' academic profiles and portfolios and are used to plan and design classroom learning activities.

Other pilot programs are under close supervision and direction from Howard Gardner and his colleagues. Project Spectrum, for example, is studying cognitive strengths and capabilities of preschoolers in and around Boston. Spectrum researchers are assembling profiles of students' talents and skills as they observe carefully constructed opportunities—both in free-play activities and in classroom instruction—for students to experiment with each of the seven multiple intelligences.

Another pilot program is Arts PROPEL, a collaborative project with Educational Testing Service and the Pittsburgh Public Schools. This program follows middle and high school students through three forms of artistic expression—imaginative writing, music, and visual arts—to determine how students learn and how their achievement can be assessed. Rather than concentrating on students' finished products as evidence of learning, researchers are looking at "process-folios," which document students' work on artistic productions over time. In line with developing students' multiple intelligences, teachers encourage students not only to create art but to critique, reflect, and judge artistic expression.

The Practical Intelligence for School (PIFS) project, undertaken jointly by Howard Gardner and Robert Sternberg of Yale, targets middle school students in urban Massachusetts schools and rural Connecticut schools. To help students integrate academic knowledge and practical knowledge about themselves and how they learn, teachers introduce lessons designed to help students analyze, reflect, and understand the ways they learn in their math, social studies, science, and English classrooms. Students are asked to identify and then use their intellectual strengths and abilities to tackle assignments such as writing essays or conducting experiments.

Aside from such closely supervised and heavily documented projects as these, teachers here and there are experimenting with Gardner's theories in their own classrooms. In Richmond, Ky., for example, Debbie Brown incorporates multiple-intelligence theories in her nongraded primary class by giving young students lots of flexibility in how they approach solving problems. One student, Brown notes, had considerable difficulty writing out answers to assignments, but that same student did beautifully when he drew pictures to illustrate his answers.

Now Brown has students work at a variety of centers

she's designed to let students explore their different intelligences. The centers, spread throughout her classroom, encourage students to learn about curriculum themes—one such theme is on trees—in creative and unusual ways. Students at one center might map out locations where certain tree species are found, while students at another center design an art portfolio for the class leaf collection.

Schooling children's minds

Gardner describes intelligence as the capacity to solve problems or to fashion products that are valued in one or more cultural settings. It's a definition that challenges schools to rethink and reconceptualize students' abilities and talents. Once students leave school, how far will mathematical and linguistic skills take them? How many careers or other endeavors (such as serious hobbies or avocations) depend on the knowledge a person gains from spending 12 years in school?

To Gardner, much of what passes for serious academic learning in school is simply a barrier that keeps many individuals from putting their inherent intelligences to good use. After years of memorizing facts—imports and exports of countries, names of inventors, dates of world events—students have little more than a repertoire of trivia. Simply having at hand a body of facts—no matter how impressive—is no assurance a person will ever apply that information to solve problems or fashion products that are useful. In other words, most schooling doesn't empower students to act on their intelligences. Sadly, many students leave school thinking it was a waste of time. And for many, it was just that.

Still, some students who cruise along through school without getting much notice for special gifts or talents excel once they're out in the "real world"—just as some brilliant students seem to vanish after high school. What schools need to reckon with, maintains Gardner, is that all students possess each of the seven identified intelligences to some extent, but the combinations and degrees of their intelligences are all different. Schools must figure out which students are "at promise" and which students are "at risk" in each intelligence and then plan education programs accordingly.

But developing every child's array of intelligences isn't the only agenda Gardner presents to schools. He wants schools to come to grips with the misinformation most students carry around in their heads—misinformation that often lasts a lifetime and gets in the way of real learning and understanding. His studies in cognitive development show how ineffective schools are at transforming children's earliest mind-sets—kids' intuitive thinking—about how the world seems to work.

Gardner says schools fail to appreciate that in nearly every student there is the "mind of a 5-year-old struggling to get out." But despite schools' efforts to give students facts that contradict their intuitive (and erroneous) thinking, the intuitive views still stick in students' minds. In fact, Gardner's research shows, schools fail miserably at changing children's understandings. Even college students, he points out, persist at incorrectly interpreting the change of seasons or the laws of motion; despite years of explanations in science courses, they cling to the explanations they developed in early childhood.

To school children's minds, Gardner encourages teachers to help students move from being intuitive learners (preschoolers to about first-graders), to being traditional learners (generally, second-graders to high school graduates), to becoming disciplinary experts who demonstrate mastery in specific areas and who can apply knowledge to new situations. To that end, Gardner recommends that schools set up cognitive apprenticeships so students can study and learn from practicing professionals and experts. Along the way, he says, schools need to help students set aside their original naive understandings—their 5-year-old minds—and move on to more sophisticated knowledge.

Gardner also believes schools should nurture children's interests and abilities, giving students plenty of enrichment and learning opportunities so that they might discover their passion. As an example, Gardner cites Yehudi Menuhin, who was so enchanted with the sound of the violin at a concert that, at age 3, he insisted on getting his own violin; from then on, Menuhin's musical genius was stimulated for a lifetime.

To increase the likelihood that students will encounter such "crystallizing experiences"—events that forcefully shape their futures—schools need to provide opportunities to work with different materials, equipment, and people. Consider how studying cells under a microscope might capture the imagination and the mind of a future microbiologist, or how studying architectural styles might trigger a student to become a leader in historical preservation. Such connections aren't far-fetched, as Gardner's research shows and as many talented and productive adults testify.

Schools also need to provide systematic learning in the symbols (Gardner calls them "notational systems") used in various disciplines. To be successful in math, for instance, students need to master the notations used to represent functions; in music, they must learn how to interpret key signatures and all the other symbols used to translate written music to sound. The same is true throughout the curriculum—students need to learn how to unlock meaning from knowledge coded in notations and symbols.

Finally, Gardner urges schools to counsel students seriously about career possibilities. The purpose of school, Gardner says, "should be to develop intelligences and to help people reach vocational and avocational goals that are appropriate to their particular spectrum of intelligences." It's important, he argues, that schools help people feel more "engaged and competent, and therefore more inclined to serve society in a constructive way." And that, he says, might be the last best thing schools can do for students. 🔢

SELECTED REFERENCES

Armstrong, Thomas. "Learning Differences—Not Disabilities." *Principal*, September 1988, 68, 34-36.

Armstrong, Thomas. 7 *Kinds of Smart: Identifying and Developing Your Many Intelligences*. New York: Plume Books, 1993.

Blythe, Tina, and Gardner, Howard. "A School for all Intelligences." *Educational Leadership*, April 1990, 47, 33-37.

Brandt, Ron. "On Teaching for Understanding: A Conversation with Howard Gardner." *Educational Leadership*, April 1993, 4-7.

Fernie, David E. "Profile: Howard Gardner." *Language Arts*, March 1992, 69, 200-227.

Fowler, Charles. "Recognizing the Role of Artistic Intelligences." *Music Educators Journal*, September 1990, 77, 24-27.

Gardner, Howard. *Art, Mind, and Brain*. New York: Basic Books, 1982.

Gardner, Howard. "Beyond the I.Q.: Education and Human Development." *Harvard Educational Review*, May 1987, 187-193.

Gardner, Howard. *Frames of Mind: The Theory of Multiple Intelligences*. New York: Basic Books, 1983.

Gardner, Howard. *Multiple Intelligences: The Theory in Practice*. New York: Basic Books, 1993.

Gardner, Howard. *The Unschooled Mind: How Children Think and How Schools Should Teach*. New York: Basic Books, 1991.

Gardner, Howard, and Hatch, Thomas. "Multiple Intelligences Go to School: Educational Implications of the Theory of Multiple Intelligences." Technical Report No. 4. New York: Center for Technology in Education, 1990. ERIC Document No. ED 324366.

"Project Zero: An Interdisciplinary Research Group." Technical Report. Cambridge, Mass.: Harvard Graduate School of Education, 1988.

Scherer, Marge. "How Many Ways Is a Child Intelligent?" *Instructor*, January 1985, 94, 32-35.

Walters, Joseph M., and Gardner, Howard. "The Crystallizing Experience: Discovering an Intellectual Gift." Cambridge, Mass.: Harvard Project Zero, 1984.

Walters, Joseph M., and Gardner, Howard. "The Development and Education of Intelligences." Report, 1984, 1-33. ERIC Document No. ED 254545.

Whalen, Samuel P., and Csikszentmihalyi, Mihaly. "Putting Flow Theory into Educational Practice: The Key School's Flow Activities Room." Benton Center for Curriculum and Instruction, May 1991, 1-62. ERIC Document No. ED 338381.

Using the 4MAT System to Bring Learning Styles to Schools

by Bernice McCarthy

In 1972, I developed the 4MAT System to help teachers organize their teaching based on differences in the way people learn. 4MAT is an eight-step cycle of instruction that capitalizes on individual learning styles and brain dominance processing preferences. Designed to raise teacher awareness as to why some things work with some learners while others do not, 4MAT is based on research from the fields of education, psychology, neurology, and management. The theories of David Kolb (1981, 1984, 1985), Carl Jung (1923), Jean Piaget (1970), John Dewey (1958), Joseph Bogen (1969, 1975), Gabriele Rico (1983), Betty Edwards (1979), and John Bradshaw and Norman Nettleton (1983) have contributed to 4MAT's conception.

Research we have conducted in 17 school districts[1] that have committed to long-range implementation of 4MAT has given us interesting insights into the change process. Here, we report on what we are trying to teach them about the 4MAT System and its uses in instruction and staff development planning.[2]

The 4MAT System: An Overview

Inherent to the 4MAT System are two major premises: (1) people have major learning styles and hemispheric (right-mode/left-mode) processing preferences; and (2) designing and using multiple instructional strategies in a systematic framework to teach to these preferences can improve teaching and learning.

All of us feel, reflect, think, and do, but we linger at different places along the way. And these lingerings form our learning style preferences, complex patterns of individuality, developed over time, that bias what we see and how we see it. Differences in our learning styles depend on many things: who we are, where we are, how we see ourselves, what we pay attention to, and what people ask and expect of us.

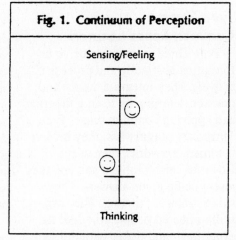

Fig. 1. Continuum of Perception

Sensing/Feeling

Thinking

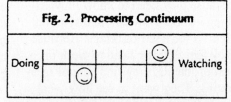

Fig. 2. Processing Continuum

Doing — Watching

Perceiving and Processing

David Kolb (1976, 1984, 1985), whose work forms the theoretical base for 4MAT, described two major differences in how people learn: how they perceive and how they process. People perceive reality differently. Some people, in new situations, respond primarily by sensing and feeling their way, while others think things through. No one uses one response to the total exclusion of the other.

However, in their reactions, people hover near different places on a continuum, and that hovering place is their most comfortable place (fig. 1).

Those who perceive in a sensing/feeling way project themselves into the reality of the now. They attend to the actual experience itself. They immerse themselves directly, they perceive through their senses. They intuit. On the other hand, those who think through experiences attend more to the abstract dimensions of reality. They analyze what is happening. Their intellect makes the first appraisal, they reason experience, they approach experiences logically.

These two kinds of perception are quite different; they complement rather than exclude each other. Both are equally valuable, and both have strengths and weaknesses. Most important of all, every learner needs both for the fullest possible understanding of experience.

Perception alone, however, does not equal learning. The second major difference in how people learn is how they process experience and information, how they make new things part of themselves (fig. 2). Some people are watchers first, others are doers first. The watchers reflect on new things; they filter them through their own experience to create meaning in a slow, deliberate choosing of perspectives. The doers act on new information immediately. They reflect only after they have tried it out. They need to do it, to extend themselves into the world, in order to make it theirs. Both ways of processing information and experience are equally valuable, and each has its own strengths and weaknesses.

The processing dimension is a

continuum that ranges from the need to internalize to the need to act. Watchers need to refine their reflective gifts while developing the courage to experiment and try. And doers need to refine their experimenting gifts while developing the patience to watch reflectively.

The Four Major Learning Styles

When these two dimensions of perceiving and processing are juxtaposed, a four-quadrant model is formed. The resulting structure delineates the qualities of four major learning styles (fig. 3).

Type One: Imaginative Learners

Imaginative learners perceive information concretely and process it reflectively. They integrate experience with the self. Listening and sharing ideas to learn, they are imaginative thinkers who believe in their own experiences. They work for harmony and need to be personally involved. They seek commitment and are interested in people and culture. Sometimes because they see all sides, they have difficulty making decisions. They seek meaning and clarity. They find school too fragmented and disconnected from the personal issues that they find most interesting. They struggle to connect the content of schooling with their need to grow and understand their world.

Type Two: Analytic Learners

Type Two learners perceive information abstractly and process it reflectively. They devise theories by integrating their observations into what they know. They learn by thinking through ideas. They need to know what the experts think. They value sequential thinking. They need details, and are thorough and industrious. They enjoy traditional classrooms and find ideas fascinating. Sometimes they enjoy ideas more than people — they can be cool and

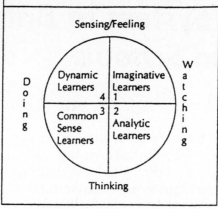

Fig. 3. The Four Major Learning Styles

Sensing/Feeling

Doing

Dynamic Learners 4 | Imaginative Learners 1

Common Sense Learners 3 | 2 Analytic Learners

Watching

Thinking

aloof. Seeking intellectual competence and personal effectiveness, they are highly skilled verbally and, generally, avid readers. They find school well suited to their needs.

Type Three: Common Sense Learners

Type Three learners perceive information abstractly and process it actively. They integrate theory and practice, learning by testing theories and applying common sense. Type Threes are pragmatists: they believe if something works, then use it. Down-to-earth problem solvers, they resent being given answers. They value strategic thinking. They are skills-oriented people who like to experiment and tinker with things because they need to know how things work. They edit reality to cut right to the heart of things. Because they feel a strong need to work on real problems, they find school frustrating. They want to see how what they are learning is of immediate use to them.

Type Four: Dynamic Learners

Dynamic learners perceive information concretely and process it actively. They integrate experience and application, learning by trial and error. Enthusiastic about new things, they are adaptable people who relish change. They excel when flexibility is needed. Type Fours often reach accurate conclusions in the absence of logical justification. They are

risk-takers who are at ease with people, and sometimes they are seen as manipulative and pushy. They seek to influence. For them, school is often tedious and overly sequential. Because they seek to pursue their interests in diverse ways, they too are frustrated with the structure of our schools.

Using 4MAT to Engage the Whole Brain

Other illuminating views of preferences can be derived from research on the different functions of the two hemispheres of the brain. Current brain research has found that (1) the two halves of the brain process information differently; (2) both hemispheres are equally important in terms of whole-brain functioning; and (3) individuals rely more on one information processing mode than the other, especially when they approach new learning (Bogen 1969, 1975).

Research typically describes the left mode as serial, analytic, rational, and verbal. Left-mode processing is systematic. Analysis and planning are key strategies. Problems are solved by looking at the parts, and sequence is critical.

The right mode is global, visual, and holistic, able to see patterns and connections. Right-mode processing seeks patterns and solves problems by looking at the whole picture. Intuition, beliefs, and opinions are key processing strategies.

To illustrate the importance of whole-brain functioning, Jeremy Campbell (1989) remarks on how the human mind forms its notions by mixing up its own nature with the nature of things. When scientists engage in explicit theory development, he observes, they use logical reasoning. But in the discovery phase that must precede the definitive process of creating a new theory, they often use illogical reasoning, reasoning that reflects their own subtle biases.

The reality is that we approach learning with our whole minds, with our intuition, our beliefs, our subjectivity intact. Accordingly, schools should engage the subjective mind more openly and with honor. It is the whole brain that flexes and flows. If the left mode engages in analyses — breaks down, specializes, names things, and agrees on the existence of these things — and if the right mode seizes upon the character of the whole — understands from experience and grasps directly — then it is clear we need to honor both modes of processing in our schools: we must engage the whole brain.

Each of the four learning styles quadrants contains right-mode, left-mode and whole-brained learners, although there are strong tendencies toward left-mode dominance in Quadrants Two and Three and toward right-mode processing in Quadrants One and Four. But because there are right-, left-, and whole-brained learners in each of the quadrants, I made a commonsense decision to alternate right- and left-mode techniques through the four learning styles cycle. If all four learning styles are taught to all learners in a cycle that alternates from right- to left-mode information processing, and if in doing this, all styles are equally valued, this integration will allow learners to be comfortable some of the time and stretched and challenged at other times. And because it is clear that all learners need all segments of the cycle, the entire cycle then becomes more valuable than any one segment.

Thus, teachers can use the 4MAT System to improve their instructional designs by employing diverse strategies in a cycle of learning (fig. 4). This cycle appeals to each learner's most comfortable style in turn, while stretching her or him to function in less comfortable modes. The movement around this circle is a natural learning progression. Humans sense and feel, they experience, then they watch, they reflect, then they think, they develop theories, then they try out theories, they experiment. Finally, they evaluate

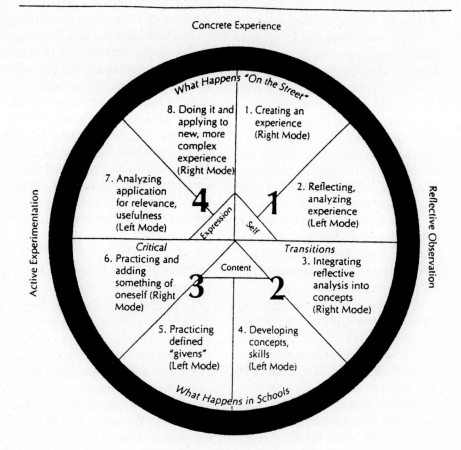

Fig. 4. The 4MAT System

and synthesize what they have learned in order to apply it to their next similar experience. They get smarter. They apply experience to experiences.

The 4MAT Cycle as a Change System

As a learner-focused model for adapting curriculum and instruction to the diverse needs of students, 4MAT benefits teachers by giving them a framework to design learning activities in a systematic cycle. But 4MAT has other applications: administrators can use the 4MAT quadrants to sketch out the desired outcomes of staff development (fig. 5).

By examining the primary characteristics in each quadrant of the cycle, the role shifts of teachers and learners become apparent. Each quadrant has a different emphasis.

Quadrant One's emphasis is on meaning, or how the material to be learned is connected to learners' immediate lives. Quadrant Two's emphasis is on content and curriculum and the importance of delivering instruction through an integrated approach. Quadrant Three addresses the usefulness of learning in the lives of the learners both in and out of school — it emphasizes the transferability of learning. Quadrant Four encompasses creativity, how the learner adds to the original learning in new and unique ways.

When these quadrants are put together, they make up a complete developmental learning cycle, moving from subjective knowing to objective knowing to integrated knowing (Kegan 1982). This cycle can be a valuable framework to those designing staff development strategies.

Quadrant One: Attitude Shifts in Meaning

When we use the 4MAT cycle in staff development, we begin by affirming what teachers already know about good practice. We begin with the teachers themselves: where they live, who they are, and how they learn (by having them find out their own best learning style). As we connect 4MAT principles to the immediate lives and concerns of the teachers, we see changes in three major areas: in teachers' attitudes toward diverse kinds of intelligence, in their attitudes about the act of teaching, and in their sense of responsibility for their students' motivation.

When teachers take the *Learning Style Inventory* (Kolb 1976, 1985) and the *Hemispheric Mode Indicator for Left and Right Information Processing Preferences* (McCarthy, 1986), they begin to address the issue of differences in learners through the eyes of their own preferences. Then their attitudes about the act of teaching begin to change: teaching becomes more dialogue, less monologue — more of an interactive exchange of different realities rather than the mere giving of information. They begin to see student diversity as a positive outcome, one that can enhance learning. Teachers also feel a deeper sense of responsibility for motivating students: they report a new urgency to create curiosity and interest in their students. They develop Quadrant One "hooks" to get their students involved with the content. In addition, teachers' attitudes toward their fellow teachers become more positive. As a new sense of collegiality emerges, their professionalism rises.

Teachers begin talking about instruction: the best ways to introduce new concepts, their reactions to student responses to right-mode techniques, thoughts about students becoming involved in the problem-solving aspects of the cycle, and concerns about the difficulty of zeroing in on the best concepts (best in the sense of structurally important to the content itself and significant in its potentiality for making connections).

Teachers need practice when undertaking innovations, and they need immediate feedback from that practice. The implementation strategy called Learning Partners[3] helps fill that need. This strategy, a form of peer coaching, is a powerful tool in helping teachers master 4MAT. Teachers form new relationships as they come together during feedback sessions to discuss and critique lesson units for improvement and refinement.

Quadrant Two: Changes in Content Approaches

As teachers examine their approaches to content during long-range 4MAT projects, they often find themselves increasingly frustrated with the fragmentation of the curriculum. The writing of a 4MAT lesson necessitates spotlighting the concepts or key issues that underlie the content. In searching for these issues, teachers turn to concepts that connect several ideas together, and they find this difficult. Many dual fields of knowledge, such as bioengineering and neurophysiology, have emerged in our time, yet our curriculums show few programs that merge content successfully. Once teachers rediscover this fragmentation, they encounter the content coverage dilemma. If we are to make the conceptual choices necessary to teach to depth rather than merely to cover material, we must strengthen our ability to understand the structure of content fields.

Teachers often need help in understanding content areas in this higher-order way, since textbooks for the most part have not been written conceptually and, of course, our tests also lack a conceptual approach. For example, a social studies teacher might choose the theme "Exploration," and then integrate the perspectives of geography and history (how particular places influence and become part of historical events), the economic exigencies, the political struggles, and the anthropological cast of humans living out their need to continuously seek and know. Such an integration of content encourages students to construct their own meaning and connections.

Staff developers, perhaps department chairs and supervisory personnel, need to build in this integrated approach to content as they move to conceptual approaches. In 4MAT intermediate training, we give teachers the time and assistance to conceptualize their content areas, and they are most successful when they undertake this task together.

Quadrant Three: Changes in Strategies for Mastery

Quadrant Three calls for tinkering, checking out the validity of the content they are being asked to master. We want our students to question, to ask: *Is this valid? Does it work? What happens when this is applied to life outside school?* The 4MAT cycle requires students to transfer what they are learning into their own lives, and this questioning, validating phase is a crucial step in the process of putting learning to use. Without practical application, there is no real learning. Teachers themselves need to be "tinkerers," to model the act of pondering ambiguities, of facing uncertainties, of highlighting subtleties, in order to help students question, try, struggle with complexities, and then personalize.

Teachers in the 4MAT projects learn to find activities that call for

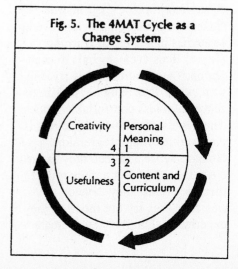

Fig. 5. The 4MAT Cycle as a Change System

experimenting, for doing, for acting. Because these requirements go far beyond workbook pages and chapter questions, teachers report a new sense of extension, of moving students beyond set content objectives. As they tinker with new applications for their learning and begin to take over the responsibility for the learning process, teachable moments proliferate. Staff developers should include strategies for helping teachers to fulfill their new roles as coach and resource. Teachers need help in creating the risk-free environments that invite open-ended learner participation, particularly those whose own learning styles make participation difficult.

Quadrant Four: Changes in Evaluation Techniques

When 4MAT long-range projects move into their second year, teachers begin to feel the inadequacy of traditional evaluation methods, typically Type Two. The need to assist learners in accepting greater responsibility for self-evaluation becomes clear.

If they are going to require their students to function in all four quad-

> **Some people are watchers first, others are doers first.**

rants, teachers must devise and implement techniques for evaluating the 4MAT quadrants, as well as right- and left-mode activities. Most evaluation techniques used by teachers apply mainly to objective test items, with some content areas using essay tests, which they may or may not know how to grade effectively. The nature of objective testing has kept educators from dealing with evaluation process issues such as the clarity of conclusions, the insights brought to bear on a situation, and the elegance of a solution to a complex problem. Our present measurement methods are inadequate to the

task of multiple ways of knowing. Teachers must accept the task of engaging in dialogue with colleagues to create standards of excellence — standards based on subjective judgments about what constitutes excellence. Evaluation methods must be expanded to include Quadrants One, Three, and Four and right-mode processing activities if we are to assess learning in all its forms.

Finally, student self-evaluation must become central to all evaluation. I am not speaking of loose, uneven standards; rather, we must help our teachers teach their students high standards for original and creative work and hold them to this requirement. In Quadrant Four, students are led to self-discovery. The chief responsibility for learning shifts from the teacher (Quadrants One and Two) to the students (Quadrants Three and Four). In Quadrants Three and Four, students practice and personalize, until they finally create and integrate. The essence of Quadrant Four, the last piece in the cycle, occurs when students find original and creative ways to integrate what they have learned into their lives and their communities.

The 4MAT Process as a Systems Approach

None of these changes can happen unless administrators and staff developers take a systems approach to learning styles implementation. To do this, each quadrant of the 4MAT cycle can be divided into principal, teacher, and student perspectives (see fig. 6).

When the 4MAT Wheel is used to plan a systems approach, Quadrant One becomes devoted to the question *Why?*, Quadrant Two becomes *What?*, Quadrant Three, *How does this work?*, and Quadrant Four, *If?* Each question is then addressed to the principal, teacher, and student, whose roles change according to the demands of each question.

In Quadrant One, the principal's

> **Learning style issues lead directly to instructional issues, which lead directly to curriculum issues and their attendant ambiguities about the nature of evaluation.**

role is to articulate the meaning of the school through his or her vision, the teacher's role involves connecting meaning to content, and the student's role is to construct meaning in dialogue with each other and their teachers, dialogue about content that connects to their lives.

In Quadrant Two, the principal is the instructional coordinator, aligning the curriculum with the mission statement. The teachers assume the roles of instructional leaders (it is they, after all, who specialize in content), and the students are the comprehenders of that content.

In Quadrant Three, the student assumes the role of user of content and skills. The teacher becomes the coach, and the principal becomes the facilitator of resources, honoring multiple methods of instruction and arranging time, money, and materials.

And finally, in Quadrant Four, the student becomes the innovator. The teacher becomes the facilitator of creative options and the principal becomes the refocuser, setting up collaboration possibilities, coordinating evaluations, enlarging diffusion networks, and re-articulating meaning and mission.

Through our staff development efforts over the last few years, I have experienced the need to couch our instructional designs and project plans in a systems approach. The complexity of schooling makes it necessary to understand how the parts and the whole fit together and

Fig. 6, The 4MAT Process as System

Quadrant 4

PRINCIPAL
The Refocuser

4

- Rearticulating meaning
- Setting up collaboration possibilities
- Helping people learn from failure
- Championing good tries
- Coordinating evaluation
- Enlarging diffusion networks
- Labeling the successes which will become harbingers of strategic new directions

PRINCIPAL

TEACHER
The Facilitator of Creative Options

- Overseeing student self-discovery
- Arranging student sharing
- Encouraging diverse use of learning
- Elaborating
- Critiquing
- Honoring student originality

TEACHER

STUDENT
The Innovator

- Applying learning in new ways

STUDENT

QUADRANT FOUR: "IF?"
- Maximizing uniqueness   • Encouraging distinct competence
- Discovering together as a school community
- "If?" demands synergy

Quadrant 1

- The WHY of the school
- The spirit communicated with enthusiasm, passion, and hope
- Accomplished by honoring teacher diversity as strength, by aligning and bonding people
- The courage to create a mission statement and to articulate its meaning

PRINCIPAL
The Meaning Articulator

1

PRINCIPAL

- Helping to forge connections between the content and the students' lives
- Honoring student diversity as an aid to learning
- Honoring teacher diversity as resources to each other

TEACHER
The Meaning Connector

TEACHER

- Connecting personal life and the content

STUDENT
The Meaning Maker

STUDENT

QUADRANT ONE: "WHY?"
- Vision is critical   • We have the most compelling need for ideas

Quadrant 3

QUADRANT THREE: "HOW DOES THIS WORK?"
- Ideas do not become mine because I read them. I must act on them.
- Actions inform thought   • Ability must be exercised

STUDENT
The User of Content and Skills

- Practicing and personalizing

STUDENT

TEACHER
The Sponsor and Practice Coach

3

- Guiding and facilitating basic skill development
- Leading students to the identification and articulation of the material learned
- Leading students to the use and integration of the material learned

TEACHER

PRINCIPAL
The Facilitator of Resources

- Honoring multiple methods of instruction
- Arranging time, money, and materials
- Setting up environments open to testing and experimenting
- Generating opportunities
- Guiding the diffusion process

PRINCIPAL

Quadrant 2

QUADRANT TWO: "WHAT?"
- The content must be significant and presented with whole-brained techniques   • Learning must be understood in its multiple forms

- Understanding at the conceptual level

STUDENT
The Comprehender

STUDENT

- Managing and delivering knowledge units with conceptualized themes patterned into meaningful connections
- Relating the parts back to the whole

TEACHER
The Instructional Leader

TEACHER

2

- Aligning curriculum with the mission statement
- Overseer of the entire curriculum conceptualization, systemization, and connection
- Consistently holding the idea of "process" and "product" as parallel goals
- Planner of systematized staff development

PRINCIPAL
The Instructional Coordinator

PRINCIPAL

to plan accordingly. To focus only on instruction (as I believed I would at first) will not work. Learning style issues lead directly to instructional issues, which lead directly to curriculum issues and their attendant ambiguities about the nature of evaluation. The necessity to integrate curriculum leads to questions about teacher time, time away from students for teachers to work together, to construct integrated approaches to content, and to be learning partners to one another. And all of it hinges on outcomes. What are our goals? Do we want our students skilled in multiple forms of conceptualization, or are the present narrow forms of evaluation sufficient for life in contemporary society, where meaning is experienced as multiple and interactive?

I continue to ponder these questions and to experience the complexity of the schooling enterprise as I go. It has become apparent to me that a systems approach is vital. And I become more and more perplexed by — and leery of — people who have easy answers.

[1] Arlington Heights, Ill., District 25; Carleton Board of Education, Nepean, Ontario, Canada; Fairfax County, Va., Area III; Hamilton-Wenham, Mass.; Honolulu Central District, Hawaii; Kamehameha Schools, Honolulu, Hawaii; Kenmore-Tonawanda, N.Y.; Littleton, Colo.; Maine Township High Schools, Park Ridge Ill.; Marion Community Schools, Ind.; Monroe County, Ind.; The State of Nebraska, ESU Units; North York, Ontario, Canada; Salem, N.H.; Scarborough, Ontario, Canada; Upper Moreland School District, Willow Grove, Pa.; Upper Perkiomen School District, East Greenville, Pa.

[2] See also B. McCarthy, (1981, 1987), *The 4MAT System: Teaching to Learning Styles with Right/Left Mode Techniques* (Barrington, Ill.: Excel, Inc.).

[3] Coined by Area III, Fairfax County, Va., teachers as preferable to the term *peer coaches*.

References

Bogen, J. E. (July 1969). "The Other Side of the Brain: An Appositional Mind." *Bulletin of the Los Angeles Neurological Societies* 34, 2: 49-61.

Bogen, J. (1975). "Some Educational Ramifications of the Hemispheric Specialization." *UCLA Educator* 17: 24-32.

Bradshaw, J., and N. Nettleton. (1983). *Human Cerebral Assymmetry.* Englewood Cliffs, N.J.: Prentice-Hall, Inc.

Campbell, J. (1989). *The Improbable Machine.* New York: Simon and Schuster.

Dewey, J. (1958) *Experience and Nature.* New York: Simon and Schuster.

Edwards, B. (1979). *Drawing on the Right Side of the Brain.* Los Angeles: J.P. Tarcher, Inc.

Jung, C. (1923). *Psychological Types.* New York: Harcourt Brace.

Kegan, R. (1982). *The Evolving Self: Problem and Process in Human Development.* Cambridge, Mass.: Harvard University Press.

Kolb, D. A. (1976, 1985). *The Learning Style Inventory.* Boston, Mass.: McBer and Co.

Kolb, D. R. (1984). *Experiential Learning: Experience as the Source of Learning and Development.* Englewood Cliffs, N.J. Prentice-Hall, Inc.

McCarthy, B. (1986). *The Hemispheric Mode Indicator.* Barrington, Ill.: Excel, Inc.

Piaget, J. (1970). *Genetic Epistemology.* New York: Columbia University Press.

Rico, G. (1983). *Writing the Natural Way.* Los Angeles: J. P. Tarcher, Inc.

Bernice McCarthy is President of Excel, Inc.

*D*ream a lot.

Dream what the children in your classroom can become . . .

Then live the dream.

From *Never, EVER Serve Sugary Snacks on Rainy Days,* by Shirley Raines. Beltsville, MD: Gryphon House, 1995.

The Culture/Learning Style Connection

Pat Guild

Cultures do have distinctive learning style patterns, but the great variation among individuals within groups means that educators must use diverse teaching strategies with all students.

Our ability to give every child a chance to succeed in school depends upon a full understanding of culture and learning styles. After all, effective educational decisions and practices must emanate from an understanding of the ways that individuals learn. Consequently, knowing each student, especially his or her culture, is essential preparation for facilitating,

© Arthur Tilley/FPG International

structuring, and validating successful learning for all students.

This imperative leads to three critical questions. Do students of the same culture have common learning style patterns and characteristics? If they do, how would we know it? And most important, what are the implications for educators?

These questions are both important and controversial. They are important because we need all the information we can get to help every learner succeed in school and because our understanding of the learning process is the basis for decisions about curriculum and instruction. They are important because success for the diverse populations that schools serve calls for continual reexamination of educators' assumptions, expectations, and biases. And they are important because, ultimately, every educational decision is evaluated according to its impact on individual students' learning.

One reason that the linkage between culture and learning styles is controversial is that generalizations about a *group* of people have often led to naive inferences about *individuals* within that group. Although people connected by culture do exhibit a characteristic pattern of style preferences, it is a serious error to conclude that all members of the group have the same style traits as the group taken as a whole.

A second source of controversy is the understandable sensitivity surrounding attempts to explain the persistent achievement differences between minority and nonminority students—it is all too easy to confuse descriptions of differences with explanations for deficits. Finally, the relationship between culture and learning styles is controversial because it brings us face to face with philosophical issues that involve deeply held beliefs. Debaters in the uniformity versus diversity dispute, for instance, differ over whether instructional equality is synonymous with educational equity. Another debate concerns the ultimate purpose of schooling.

Is it "cultural pluralism" or the "melting pot"?

A highly public example of how sensitive these issues are occurred in 1987 when the state of New York published a booklet to help decrease the student dropout rate. A small section of the booklet described the learning styles typical of minority students and identified certain patterns associated with African-American students.

These descriptions became the subject of intense scrutiny and animated debate. Eventually, the descriptions were deleted from the booklet. Nonetheless, in the *New York State Regent's Report,* a review panel reiterated that:

> learning style and behavioral tendency do exist, and students from particular socialization and cultural experiences often possess approaches to knowledge that are highly functional in the indigenous home environment and can be capitalized upon to facilitate performance in academic settings (Claxton 1990).

© Arthur Tilley/FPG International

Generalizations about a *group* of people often lead to naive inferences about *individual* members of that group.

How We Know That Culture and Ways of Learning Are Linked

There is very little disagreement that a relationship does exist between the culture in which children live (or from which they are descended) and their preferred ways of learning. This relationship, further, is directly related to academic, social, and emotional success in school.

These conclusions are not as simple or definite as they seem, however. Though many syntheses and surveys have discussed the interdynamics of different cultures and ways of learning, each comes from a very distinctive approach, focusing either on a specific learning style model or a particular cultural group. No work, to my knowledge, claims to be comprehensive on the topic of culture and learning styles.

In general, researchers have reported three kinds of information about culture and learning styles.

The first is the set of *observation-based descriptions of cultural groups*

of learners. For the most part, people who are familiar with each group have written these descriptions to sensitize people outside the culture to the experiences of children inside the culture. They have often contrasted minority students' learning patterns with European-American students' ways of learning and the school practices designed for such students.

Researchers have identified typical learning patterns among African Americans (Hale-Benson 1986, Shade 1989, Hilliard 1989), Mexican Americans (Ramirez 1989, Vasquez 1991, Berry 1979, Cox and Ramirez 1981), and Native Americans (Bert and Bert 1992, More 1990, Shade 1989).

The reports conclude that Mexican Americans regard family and personal relationships as important and are comfortable with cognitive generalities and patterns (Cox and Ramirez 1981, Vasquez 1991). Such traits explain why Mexican-American students often seek a personal relationship with a teacher and are more

comfortable with broad concepts than component facts and specifics.

Research about the African-American culture shows that students often value oral experiences, physical activity, and loyalty in interpersonal relationships (Shade 1989, Hilliard 1989). These traits call for classroom activities that include approaches like discussion, active projects, and collaborative work.

Descriptions indicate that Native-American people generally value and develop acute visual discrimination and skills in the use of imagery, perceive globally, have reflective thinking patterns, and generally value and develop acute visual discrimination and skills in the use of imagery (Shade 1989, More 1990, Bert and Bert 1992). Thus, schooling should establish a context for new information, provide quiet times for thinking, and emphasize visual stimuli.

In contrast, the observers describe mainstream white Americans as valuing independence, analytic thinking, objectivity, and accuracy. These values translate into learning experiences that focus on competition.

information, tests and grades, and linear logic. These patterns are prevalent in most American schools.

A second way that we know about the links between culture and learning styles is *data-based descriptions of specific groups.* In this class of inquiry, researchers administer learning style/cognitive style instruments to produce a profile of a cultural group, compare this group with another previously studied one (usually white Americans), or validate a particular instrument for cross-cultural use.

The various formal assessment instruments that purport to measure learning styles detect differences in two general ways. In the category of instruments that looks for style *preferences,* respondents usually self-report their favored approaches to learning. The best known instrument of this kind is probably the Myers-Briggs Type Indicator. It infers learning style patterns from basic perceptual and judging traits.

Another type of assessment instrument tests style *strengths,* that is, the ability to do tasks with a certain approach. The Swassing-Barbe Modality Index, for example, asks test takers to repeat patterns given auditorily, visually, and tactilely. Another example is the well-known series of assessments that distinguishes between field-dependence and independence. In this series, the test taker tries to find a simple figure embedded in a more complex one. The results show differences in cognitive strengths, such as global, holistic learning in contrast to analytic, part-to-whole approaches.

Formal assessment data should be interpreted (though often, it is not) in the light of the kind of assessment used. An important fact about self-report instruments, for instance, is that

they are language- and culture-specific. In other words, when test takers respond to specific words, they interpret the words through their cultural experiences.

Further, different assessments may yield conflicting results. For instance, someone might self-report a preference for learning something in a certain way and yet test out in a different way on a task involving strengths. It is equally possible for descriptions based on observations to conflict with self-reported preferences.

These inconsistencies do not invalidate the usefulness of each of the ways of assessing learning styles. They do point out, however, that understanding learning patterns is a complex task and that the scope of the diagnostic tool used imposes limits on generalizations that can be drawn on the basis of it. Further, the characteristics of the assessment instruments used often account for the seemingly contradictory information reported about groups of learners.

The third way we know about the relationship of learning and culture is through *direct discussion.* Shade (1989), for instance, comments that:

> perceptual development differs within various ethnocultural groups. It is

[therefore] an erroneous assumption in the teaching-learning process to assume children "see" the same event, idea, or object in the same way.

Cognitive styles research, Ramirez (1989) believes, could help accommodate children who see things differently. The research findings, he notes, provide "a framework to look at and be responsive to diversity within and between cultures."

Bennett (1986) warns that ignoring the effects of culture and learning styles would depress learning among nonmainstream students:

> If classroom expectations are limited by our own cultural orientations, we impede successful learners guided by another cultural orientation. If we only teach according to the ways we ourselves learn best, we are also likely to thwart successful learners who may share our cultural background but whose learning styles deviate from our own.

Accepted Conclusions About Culture and Learning Styles

Those who study culture and those who study learning styles generally agree on at least five points.

1. Educators concur that *students of any particular age will differ in their ways of learning.* (Guild and Garger 1985). Both empirical research and

© Jeffrey Myers/FPG International

When people are asked to respond to specific words, they will interpret the words through their cultural experiences.

experiences validate these learning style differences, which in their cognitive, affective, and behavioral dimensions, help us to understand and talk about individual learning processes.

2. Most researchers believe that *learning styles are a function of both nature and nurture.* Myers (1990) asserts that:

> Type development starts at a very early age. The hypothesis is that *type* is inborn, an innate predisposition like right- or left-handedness, but the *successful development* of type can be greatly helped or hindered by environment.

Some researchers downplay the innate aspects of learning style, preferring to focus on the impact of environment. Many place great importance on the early socialization that occurs within the family, immediate culture, and wider culture.

3. Most researchers also believe that *learning styles are neutral* (Guild and Garger 1985). Every learning style approach can be used successfully, but can also become a stumbling block if applied inappropriately or overused.

This concept in the learning styles literature says a great deal about the effects of different learning approaches with different school tasks. Without

question, for example, an active, kinesthetic learner has a more difficult time in school because of the limited opportunities to use that approach, especially for the development of basic skills. Nonetheless, the kinesthetic approach is a successful way to learn, and many adults, including teachers and administrators, use this approach quite effectively. Howard Gardner's (1983, 1991) identification of various intelligences has helped people appreciate the strengths of various approaches to learning.

4. In both observational and databased research on cultures, one consistent finding is that, *within a group, the variations among individuals are as great as their commonalities.* Therefore, no one should automatically attribute a particular learning style to all individuals within a group (Griggs and Dunn 1989).

This subtle point is often verbally acknowledged, but ignored in practice. Cox and Ramirez (1981) explain the result:

> Recognition and identification of ... average differences have had both positive and negative effects in education. The positive effect has been the development of an awareness of the types of learning that our public schools tend to foster.... The negative effect ... is [that] the great diversity within a culture is ignored and a construct that should be used as a tool for individualization becomes yet another label for categorizing and evaluating.

5. Finally, many *authors acknowledge the cultural conflict between some students and the typical learning experiences in schools.* When a child is socialized in ways that are inconsistent with school expectations and patterns, the child needs to make a

difficult daily adjustment to the culture of the school and his or her teachers. Hale-Benson (1986) points out the added burden this adjustment places on black youngsters:

> Black children have to be prepared to imitate the "hip," "cool" behavior of the culture in which they live and at the same time take on those behaviors that are necessary to be upwardly mobile.

Debates About Applying Theory on Culture and Learning Styles

The published literature recommends caution in applying knowledge about culture and learning styles to the classroom. This prudence seems advisable because, despite the accepted ideas, at least five differences of opinion persist.

1. People differ, for instance, on *whether educators should acquire more explicit knowledge about particular cultural values and expectations.* Proponents say that such knowledge would enable educators to be more sensitive and effective with students of particular cultures. Certain states even mandate such information as part of their goals for multiculturalism.

Other authors argue, however, that describing cultures has resulted in more stereotyping and may well lead to a differentiated, segregated approach to curriculum. For example, Cox and Ramirez (1981) note that "the concept of cognitive or learning styles of minority and other students is one easily oversimplified, misunderstood, or misinterpreted." The authors go on to say that misuse of the concept has led to stereotyping and labeling rather than the identification of educationally meaningful differences among individuals.

2. Authors also debate the *proper response to the fact that the culture-learning styles relationship affects*

student achieve-ment. Evidence suggests that students with partic-ular learning style traits (field-depen-dent, sensing, extraversion) are underachievers in school, irrespective of their cultural group. Students with such dominant learning style patterns have limited opportunities to use their style strengths in the classroom.

Even more disheartening is the practice of remediating problems so that the learner conforms to school expectations, rather than structuring school tasks in ways that respond to students' strengths. With the current emphasis on the inclusion of all learners in classrooms, it seems essential to change that practice.

Another achievement problem is the serious inequity that results when certain cultures value behaviors that are undervalued in school. Will increased attention to culture and learning styles eradicate this problem? Hilliard (1989) thinks not:

> I remain unconvinced that the explana-tion for the low performance of cultur-ally different "minority group" students will be found by pursuing questions of behavioral style.... Children, no matter what their style, are failing primarily because of systemic inequities in the delivery of whatever pedagogical approach the teachers claim to master—not because students cannot learn from teachers whose styles do not match their own.

Bennett (1986) agrees that accom-modating learning styles won't solve all problems:

> We must be careful ... not to view learning styles as the panacea that will eliminate failure in the schools. To

address learning styles is often a neces-sary, but never sufficient, condition of teaching.

3. Another unresolved issue is *how teachers working from their own cultures and teaching styles can successfully reach diverse popula-tions.* Bennett (1986) sums up the problem this way:

> To the extent that teachers teach as they have been taught to learn, and to the extent that culture shapes learning style, students who share a teacher's ethnic background will be favored in class.

Some argue, though, that teachers properly play a special role in repre-senting their own culture. Hale-Benson (1986), for example, says:

> It is incumbent upon black profes-sionals to identify the intelligences found especially in black children and to support the pursuit of their strengths.

Yes, that seems sensible. But we have all learned successfully from teachers who were neither like us in learning style or in culture. Often, these were masterful, caring teachers. Sometimes our own motivation helped us learn in spite of a teacher. Clearly, neither culture nor style is destiny. Just as clearly, though, teachers of all cultures and styles will have to work conscientiously to provide equitable opportunities for all students.

4. *How cultural identity and self-esteem are related* remains an open question, too. Many large city school systems are wrestling with the appro-priateness of ethnically identified schools, such as an African-American academy. Bilingual programs continue to debate the value of instruction in the students' first language.

I would add to this discussion a remark of Carl Jung's: "If a plant is to unfold its specific nature to the full, it must first be able to grow in the soil in which it is planted" (Barger and Kirby 1993). This comment has led me to argue against the approach to learning so prevalent in our schools (especially in special education programs), which emphasizes the identification and remediation of deficiencies.

An acceptance of learning styles demands an approach that develops skills through strengths. Should the same not be said of cultural identity?

5. Perhaps the most weighty of the application issues has to do with *ways to counteract our tendency toward instructional pendulum swings.* This oscillation has become so predictable in schooling in our country. Today it's phonics. Tomorrow whole language. The day after that, phonics again. We are always seeking one right way to teach, and when we accumulate evidence that a strategy is effective with some students, we try to apply it

> When a child is socialized in ways that are inconsistent with school expectations and patterns, the child needs to make a difficult daily adjustment.

to every student in every school.

A deep understanding of culture and learning styles makes this behavior seem naive. If instructional decisions were based on an understanding of each individual's culture and ways of learning, we would never assume that uniform practices would be effective for all. We would recognize that the only way to meet diverse learning needs would be to intentionally apply diverse strategies. As Bennett (1986) says, equitable opportunities for success demand "unequal teaching methods that respond to relevant differences among students."

Ideas about culture and learning styles can be of great help to teachers as they pursue such intentional instructional diversity. A teacher who truly understands culture and learning styles and who believes that all students can learn, one way or another, can offer opportunities for success to all students.

Not Easy, but Crucial

While the culture/learning styles relationship is deceptively simple and the issues surrounding it are complex, it is a crucially important idea to contemplate. We should not be reluctant to do so for fear of repeating past mistakes. With a better understanding of these missteps, we can avoid them in the future. As Hilliard (1989) assures us:

Educators need not avoid addressing the question of style for fear they may be guilty of stereotyping students. Empirical observations are not the same as stereotyping, but the observations must be empirical and must be interpreted properly for each student.

As we try to accommodate students' cultural and learning differences, it is most important to deeply value each person's individuality. If we believe that people do learn—and have the right to learn—in a variety of ways, then we will see learning styles as a comprehensive approach guiding all educational decisions and practices. The ideas will not become ends in themselves, which would merely support the uniformity found in most schools.

Using information about culture and learning styles in sensitive and positive ways will help educators value and promote diversity in all aspects of the school. This task will not be easy, but then teaching is not a profession for the faint of heart. It requires courage and a willingness to grapple with real questions about people and their learning. Many students stand to benefit from that effort. ∎

References
Barger, N. J., and L. K. Kirby. (Fall 1993). "The Interaction of Cultural Values and Type Development: INTP Women Across Cultures." *Bulletin of Psychological Type* 16: 14-16.

Bennett, C. (1986). *Comprehensive Multicultural Education, Theory and Practice.* Boston: Allyn and Bacon.

Berry, J. W. (1979). "Culture and Cognitive Style." In *Perspectives on Cross-Cultural Psychology,* edited by A. Marsella, R. Tharp, and T. Ciborowski. San Francisco: Academic Press.

Bert, C. R. G., and M. Bert. (1992). The Native American: An Exceptionality in Education and Counseling. (ERIC Document Reproduction Service No. ED 351 168).

Claxton, C. S. (Fall 1990) "Learning Styles, Minority Students, and Effective Education." *Journal of Developmental Education* 14: 6-8, 35.

Cox, B., and M. Ramirez III. (1981). "Cognitive Styles: Implications for Multiethnic Education." In *Education in the '80s,* edited by J. Banks. Washington, D. C.: National Education Association.

Gardner, H. (1983) *Frames of Mind.* New York: Basic Books.

Gardner, H. (1991) *The Unschooled Mind: How Children Think and How Schools Should Teach.* New York: Basic Books.

Griggs, S. A., and R. Dunn. (1989). "The Learning Styles of Multicultural Groups and Counseling Implications." *Journal of Multicultural Counseling and Development* 17: 146-155.

Guild, P., and S. Garger. (1985). *Marching to Different Drummers.* Alexandria, Va.: Association for Supervision and Curriculum Development.

Hale-Benson, J. E. (1986). *Black Children: Their Roots, Culture, and Learning Styles.* Rev. ed. Baltimore: Johns Hopkins University Press.

Hilliard, A. G., III. (January 1989). "Teachers and Cultural Styles in a Pluralistic Society." *NEA Today*: 65-69.

More, A. J. (1990). "Learning Styles of Native Americans and Asians." Paper presented at the Annual Meeting of the American Psychological Association, Boston. (ERIC Document Reproduction Service No. ED 330 535)

Myers, I. B. (1990). *Gifts Differing.* 2nd ed. Palo Alto, Calif.: Consulting Psychologists Press.

Ramirez, M., III. (1989). "Pluralistic Education: A Bicognitive-Multicultural Model." *The Clearinghouse Bulletin* 3: 4-5.

Shade, B. J. (October 1989) "The Influence of Perceptual Development on Cognitive Style: Cross Ethnic Comparisons." *Early Child Development and Care* 51: 137-155.

Vasquez, J. A. (1991). Cognitive Style and Academic Achievement. In *Cultural Diversity and the Schools: Consensus and Controversy,* edited by J. Lynch, C. Modgil, and S. Modgil. London: Falconer Press.

Pat Guild is owner of Pat Guild Associates, P. O. Box 99131, Seattle, WA 98199.

Multiage Education

The Return of the Nongraded Classroom

Major changes in school structure have created a promising new climate for an old approach to education.

Robert H. Anderson

as the time for nongradedness in elementary schools finally come? My answer is *yes*! There are powerful forces for educational change in this country that are calling for structural as well as instructional improvements that are wholly consistent with nongraded concepts and approaches. The educational environment has rarely been as favorable as it is today.

Nearly every other dimension of restructuring, including teacher empowerment, teamwork, site-based decision making, and providing more flexible alternatives for students, changes the dynamics of school practice in ways that make a nongraded approach not only more meaningful, but also more attainable.

In virtually every argument for restructuring American schools, there are either explicit references to the rigidity and inappropriateness of the conventional graded structure, or implicit recommendations for continuous progress and changes in present promotion/retention practices. Never before in its checkered history has the graded school, with its lockstep curriculum and competitive-comparative pupil evaluation system, come under such attack not only by thoughtful educators, but also by politicians and business people. No less a figure than W. Edwards Deming, the guru of total quality management, has become a vocal critic of school retention,

Robert H. Anderson is president of Pedamorphosis, Inc., in Tampa, Florida, and coauthor of *The Nongraded Elementary School* and *Nongradedness: Helping It to Happen*.

66
JANUARY 1993

grouping, and competitive grading practices.

The Trouble with Graded Schools

It is strange that the graded school, with its overloaded, textbook-dominated curriculum, and its relatively primitive assumptions about human development and learning, has held its ground this long. To my knowledge there has never been a respectable body of research or scholarly reflection on the academic and social legitimacy of segregating students by age and providing them with a standard curriculum.

The graded school concept, born of administrative practicality and puritanical traditions, was first introduced by Horace Mann to Massachusetts from Prussia in the mid-nineteenth century. It is unfortunate that these justifications for graded schools persist in the 1990s.

Equally persistent is the historic isolation of predominantly female teachers from each other, often combined with supervisory practices that could be labeled as sexist in today's society, as well as punishment practices that could be labeled as child abuse. Add to this the tendency of many educators and business leaders to continue viewing the tax-supported public school system largely as a funnel for producing unskilled workers at a time when there are no longer an abundance of jobs available to them.

Regrettably, John Dewey's visionary concepts of "educating the whole child" and of appealing to children's multidimensional interests and talents failed to gain much momentum until well after World War II. And even today, the use of terms such as "critical thinking," "humane educational practices," or "child-centered classrooms" produce sharply negative reaction in some communities.

Déjà Vu All Over Again?

It is difficult to write an accurate history of nongradedness, partly because there have been so many instances over the years of varied efforts, each with its own label and ground rules, and partly because the extent or success of such efforts were rarely recorded. In the post-Sputnik climate of educational reform, labels such as "nongraded education," "open education," "team teaching," and "individu-

(Photo courtesy of Teaching/K-8, John Flavell (photographer) and Pikeville Elementary School, Pikeville, Kentucky.)

alized instruction" were often used more as expressions of intent than as titles of accomplishment.

However, in many schools and districts across the country, there emerged the forerunners of what is now being defined as nongraded education. The movement began after World War II, when an expanding pupil population produced a corresponding surge of interest in how better to fit schooling practices to emerging understanding of child growth and development. In a climate favorable for "modernizing" schools, a "first wave" of nongradedness began in the 1950s and continued through the early 1970s. In retrospect, however, those early efforts touched only a small fraction of American schoolchildren, and only a few of them led to the establishment of authentic nongraded models.

Therefore, it is inaccurate for any educator to shout "déjà vu!" and to say that nongradedness has already been tried and found wanting. Some fairly good nongraded programs did emerge and thrive over time, notably within the team-taught, multi-aged grouping framework of Individually Guided Education, as developed by the Kettering Foundation and the University of Wisconsin. We are not starting from scratch in the 1990s.

Barbara Pavan, who first surveyed the research literature on nongradedness about 20 years ago, recently completed an update of that research with 64 added studies (Anderson and Pavan 1993). Her findings showed that, in terms of academic achievement and mental health, results favoring graded groups are very rare. Most of the studies show neutral or inconclusive outcomes when graded and nongraded groups are compared, but results favoring the nongraded approach are growing in both quantity and quality.

In a climate favorable for "modernizing" schools, a "first wave" of nongradedness began in the 1950s and continued through the early 1970s.

"There is now," Pavan reports, "definitive research evidence to confirm the theories underlying nongradedness." It appears a nongraded environment especially benefits boys, blacks, underachievers, and students from lower socioeconomic groups, with the benefits increasing the longer that children remain in that environment. Pavan's work also confirms the conclusion that nongradedness is most likely to thrive when teachers work in teams with multi-aged aggregations of children.

What's Holding Us Back?

As seems to be true for all efforts at educational reform, the obstacles to nongradedness are mostly matters of habit and attitude. Some of the more constraining *habits* of teachers include:

• Over-reliance on graded instructional materials and tests;
• Voluntary seclusion in self-contained classrooms;
• Reluctance to take risks or rock the boat;
• Familiarity with graded classes from their own childhoods; and
• Disinclination to pursue new skills through staff development.

Some of the most constraining *attitudes*, closely linked with the foregoing habits, are:

• Resentment (often justified) of administrators' tendencies to embrace every innovation that comes along;
• Skepticism about theoretical, as opposed to practical, ideas;
• Limited acceptance of the slogan, proclaimed by Jerome Bruner, Benjamin Bloom, and others, that "all children can learn"; and
• Conviction that some children can only be motivated extrinsically (*e.g.*, by graded report cards and fear of retention).

On the positive side, the great majority of teachers now in service are better educated, particularly with respect to how children develop and learn, than were their predecessors a generation ago. They are more accepting of individual differences and more aware of the vast array of pedagogical options available to them, including whole language, cooperative learning, and heterogeneous grouping.

Similarly, today's principals are better prepared to assume the role of facilitator, and more willing to share decision-making power with their staffs. Both teachers and principals also understand the great need we have in our schools for professional communication and collaboration.

One of the reasons that nongradedness seems more achievable in the 1990s is that there are now good models available for pupil-peer tutoring and cooperative learning programs, as well as a wider variety of technological aids and instructional materials. Authentic nongraded programs can make good use of these models and materials.

Most advocates of nongradedness believe it is essential for students to belong to a basic aggregation of children that embraces at least two (preferably three) age

Today's principals are better prepared to assume the role of facilitator, and more willing to share decision-making power with their staffs. Both teachers and principals also understand the great need we have in our schools for professional communication and collaboration.

Voices

The first element of superiority in a Prussian school . . . consists in the proper classification of the scholars. In all places where the numbers are significantly large to allow it, the children are divided according to ages and attainments, and a single teacher has the charge only of a single class . . . There is no obstacle whatever . . . to the introduction at once of this mode of dividing and classifying scholars in all our large towns.

— Horace Mann

groups. Thus, a nongraded primary group might include five-, six-, and seven-year-olds, or six-, seven-, and eight-year-olds. We now know that the most natural learning environment for children calls for heterogeneous multi-age groupings, within which all sorts of homogeneous *and* heterogeneous subgroupings can be created as needed.

I believe that an ideal nongraded grouping should number from 70 to 120 children, in the charge of a team of three to six teachers. It has been demonstrated that a truly nongraded environment is much

What Is Authentic Nongradedness?

Authentic nongraded schools should meet, or come close to meeting, the following criteria:

• Replacement of labels associated with gradedness, like first grade and fifth grade, with group titles like "primary unit" that are more appropriate to the concept of continuous progress;

• Replacement of competitive-comparative evaluation systems (and the report cards associated with them) with assessment and reporting mechanisms that respect continuous individual progress and avoid competitive comparisons;

• All groupings to include at least two heterogeneous age cohorts;

• Groups assembled for instructional purposes to be non-permanent, being dissolved and reconstituted as needed;

• Organization of the teaching staff into teams, with teachers having maximum opportunities to interact and collaborate;

• Development of a flexible, interdisciplinary, whole-child-oriented curriculum, with grade-normed books and tests used only as resources (if used at all);

• Adoption of official policies consistent with nongradedness in the school and at the school board level, even where waivers of policy may be required (*e.g.*, reporting enrollments by grades).

"Simply launching a nongraded program is at least a two-year process... To develop a mature and smooth-running operation... may require an additional five years."

easier to produce when the philosophy and practices of nongradedness are combined with multi-age approaches and some form of team teaching. In fact, it is almost impossible to find examples of authentic nongradedness within single-age groups of children taught by lone teachers in self-contained classrooms.

Where do you find authentic nongradedness? This is a tough question to answer, for two reasons. First, schools offering programs that can be considered "authentic" (*see box*) are not abundant; and second, there are few accurate listings of these schools should you wish to visit one. The Canadian province of British Columbia probably has the most such schools at the moment, although states like Kentucky and Oregon may soon provide good models. At present, several organizations are cooperating on a project to establish an international registry of such schools, which would serve as models for nongraded education.

How Do You Go Nongraded?

In our 1993 book, Pavan and I propose that one of the first steps should be to take an inventory of your staff's basic beliefs and intuitions. If too many teachers are uncomfortable with the philosophy and prac-

tices associated with nongradedness, there is little point in taking the plunge. Conversely, if many on your staff are true believers, mountains can be moved!

The next step is for your teachers to immerse themselves in the literature in order to acquire a sound knowledge base about authentic nongradedness. Such immersion should include the resolution of questions about such matters as pupil grouping, teacher teaming, evaluating pupil progress, dealing with the public, and adopting necessary policies.

You should be forewarned that simply *launching* a nongraded program is at least a two-year process. It takes a lot of time to work out policies and procedures, to make curriculum changes, to prepare the community, and to provide appropriate staff development and training. To develop a mature and smooth-running operation, with an integrated, interdisciplinary, and multi-dimensional curriculum may require an additional five years.

But when it comes to developing an exciting and successful nongraded program, it is well to remember that trite but useful motto: "Rome wasn't built in a day!"□

REFERENCES

American Association of School Administrators. *The Nongraded Primary: Making Schools Fit Children.* Arlington, Va.: The Association, 1992.

Anderson, Robert H., and Pavan, Barbara N. *Nongradedness: Helping It to Happen.* Lancaster, Pa.: Technomic Publishing, 1993.

Bloom, Benjamin S. *Human Characteristics and School Learning.* New York: McGraw-Hill, 1976.

Bruner, Jerome S. *The Process of Education.* Cambridge, Mass.: Harvard University Press, 1960.

Gardner, Howard. *Frames of Mind: The Theory of Multiple Intelligences.* New York: Basic Books, 1983.

Gayfer, Margaret. *The Multi-Grade Classroom: Myth and Reality.* Toronto: Canadian Education Association, 1991.

Gaustad, Joan. "Nongraded Education: Mixed-Age, Integrated, and Developmentally Appropriate Education for Primary Children." *OSSC Bulletin* (Oregon School Study Council), March 1992.

Gaustad, Joan. "Making the Transition from Graded to Nongraded Primary Education." *OSSC Bulletin* (Oregon School Study Council), April 1992.

Goodlad, John I., and Anderson, Robert H. *The Nongraded Elementary School*, 3rd edition. New York: Teachers College Press, 1987.

Nongraded Primary Education

by Joan Gaustad

In the mid-1800s, the revolutionary idea of mass public education created the need for an efficient, economical system capable of handling large numbers of students. Graded education — the practice of classifying and dividing students by age — spread rapidly throughout the United States and has remained the standard until the present (Goodlad and Anderson 1987).

In the 1990s, educators and citizens are reevaluating their schools and proposing reforms to meet the needs of diverse social and economic groups. Nongraded primary education is a key component of many reform proposals, including the Kentucky Educational Reform Act and the Oregon Educational Act for the 21st Century.

Many experimental nongraded programs tried in the sixties and early seventies failed due to inadequate understanding, lack of administrative and community support, and poorly planned implementation. Today's nongraded model is supported by additional decades of research and refined by the study of successful programs.

What Is Nongraded Education?

Nongraded education is the practice of teaching children of different ages and ability levels together, without dividing them (or the curriculum) into steps labeled by grade designations. Children move from easier to more difficult material at their own pace, making *continuous progress* rather than being promoted once per year. Curriculum and teaching practices are *developmentally appropriate*. *Integrated* curriculum fosters children's physical, social, emotional, and intellectual growth (Gaustad 1992a).

Various names have been used to describe this approach, including mixed-age grouping, heterogeneous grouping, and open education. In some cases, as with Kentucky's Primary Program, alternative terminology is deliberately used to avoid negative associations with the earlier unsuccessful programs (Robinson-Armstrong 1992). Nongrading can be used with all ages but is particularly appropriate during the primary years.

A nongraded classroom differs physically from a graded one. Rows of desks do not permanently face one direction; instead, tables and chairs are frequently regrouped. "Learning Centers" are scattered around the room: tables holding math, science, and art materials; a sand table with plastic toys for pretend play; a library corner with bean-bag chairs and book-filled shelves.

Materials are geared toward hands-on learning. For example, instead of learning arithmetic solely from workbooks, children discover basic mathematical relationships by sorting, counting, and measuring real objects.

Flexible grouping is a key element of nongraded education. Students are grouped *homogeneously* by achievement for some subjects, such as math and reading. For other subjects children learn in *heterogeneous groups*. At different times students work independently, in pairs, and in large and small groups (Gaustad 1992a).

Children contribute to group projects according to their skill level. For example, in making books to display what they learned about a topic, younger children can create illustrations while older children write the text (Katz and others 1990).

Those unfamiliar with the term *nongraded* often assume it refers to the practice of not giving letter grades. Many nongraded programs do use alternative types of evaluation, such as collections of student work and descriptive reports. However, this is only a small element of the approach.

How Does Research Support Nongraded Primary Education?

Graded education assumes that students who are the same age are at basically the same level of cognitive development, can be taught in the same way, and will progress at the same rate. Intellectual development is assumed to be the goal, and the division of curriculum into discrete skills and subjects to be the most effective organization. Research has discredited all these assumptions.

Young children actually vary in their rates of intellectual development just as they do in physical development. They often progress at different rates in different areas of achievement and may alternately spurt ahead and hit plateaus rather than moving at a steady pace. Goodlad and Anderson (1987) state, "Children entering the first grade differ in mental age by approximately four full years." Even greater variation may be found in subsequent grades.

Swiss psychologist Jean Piaget established that young children are cognitively not ready to think abstractly. They learn best through active, hands-on activities with concrete materials. Research on learning has shown that, whatever the learner's age, information taught in a *meaningful context* is more easily learned than unconnected facts (Gaustad 1992a), and that individuals with different learning styles rely to different degrees on auditory, visual, and kinesthetic cues.

In its influential position statement, the National Association for the Education of Young Children (Bredekamp 1987) summarized this

accumulated knowledge of child development and described appropriate teaching practices for primary-age children. Its list of *developmentally appropriate* practices closely matches the components of nongraded education. The *inappropriate* practices it lists are typical of traditional graded education.

After reviewing studies comparing graded and nongraded programs, Miller (1989) concluded that multiage or multigraded classes are as effective as single-grade classes in terms of academic achievement, and superior in terms of student attitudes toward school and self. Katz and others found that participating in mixed-age groups has social and cognitive benefits for both older and younger children. Cooperative, prosocial behaviors increased and discipline problems were reduced.

What Are Its Disadvantages?

Experts agree that teaching multiage classes requires more preparation time. Teacher burnout due to insufficient planning time was one reason for the failure of earlier nongraded experiments.

Abbie Robinson-Armstrong, director of the Kentucky Department of Education's Division of Early Childhood, points out that it also requires "more knowledge about child development, integrated curriculum, and instructional strategies." Most teachers will require substantial training. Districts that previously relied heavily on single sets of textbooks and manuals will need to acquire hands-on materials and a variety of supplementary books. These changes may be costly.

It may be easier to "pick up a teacher's manual and read verbatim from it" (Robinson-Armstrong) than to use a variety of instructional strategies with groups of varying sizes. It may be more efficient to correct multiple-choice tests than to evaluate collections of student work and write descriptive comments. But as Goodlad and Anderson comment, "Efficiency takes on proper meaning only in relation to the job that should be done. To recognize that something is easy does not justify our doing it."

What Facilitates the Implementation of Nongrading?

Goodlad and Anderson found that understanding and support by teachers and parents were the factors most crucial to the success of nongraded programs. Thus educating and informing teachers and parents is the first priority. Both groups are more likely to support nongrading when they are involved in planning and decision-making (Gaustad 1992b).

Miller calls practical training in multiage teaching "critically important for success." This should include opportunities to observe effective models such as through visits to schools with pilot programs.

Hord and others (1987) found that innovations often fail because policymakers drastically underestimate how long change will take and the amount of training and support teachers will require. Realistically, full implementation of innovations require several years.

Changing to nongraded education involves multiple innovations. It affects basic educational philosophy and often clashes with deeply held expectations. However, a number of its elements can be used in graded settings, and many graded schools already use them to some extent. Adding new elements one at a time is easier than attempting to change everything at once.

How Can Administrators and School Boards Promote Nongrading?

Some districts have adopted policies endorsing nongraded education and encouraged their schools to move in that direction. In other districts, interest in nongrading has originated with teachers. Educators interviewed by Gaustad (1992b) agree that board support is extremely helpful in either case. However, most feel boards should not dictate specific actions.

Boards can help by removing impediments such as requirements for grade-level textbooks and accountability evaluation based on standardized testing. Waiving these grade-oriented regulations lessens pressure on teachers and frees them to focus on mastering nongraded teaching techniques (Gaustad 1992b).

John Thompson, director of policy services for the Kentucky School Boards Association, says boards must do the following to ensure that Kentucky's new primary program succeeds: (1) make sure their teachers receive sufficient training, (2) inform their communities, (3) find funding for transition expenses not covered by the state, and (4) monitor their schools' progress and assist in evaluating and improving the implementation process (Gaustad 1992b).

If a district decides to promote nongraded education, policymakers should acknowledge the magnitude of the change and be realistic about the time and resources it will require. Nonetheless, nongraded primary education is well worth exploring.

RESOURCES

Bredekamp, Sue, Editor. *Developmentally Appropriate Practice in Early Childhood Programs Serving Children from Birth through Age 8.* Washington, D.C.: National Association for the Education of Young Children, 1987.

Gaustad, Joan. *Nongraded Education: Mixed-age, Integrated, and Developmentally Appropriate Education for Primary Children.* OSSC Bulletin. Eugene, Oregon: Oregon School Study Council, March 1992a. 38 pages.

_____. *Making the Transition to Nongraded Primary Education.* OSSC Bulletin. Eugene, Oregon: Oregon School Study Council, April 1992b. 41 pages.

Goodlad, John I., and Robert H. Anderson. *The Nongraded Elementary School,* Revised Edition. New York: Teachers College Press, Columbia University, 1987. 248 pages.

Hord, Shirley M., and others. *Taking Charge of Change.* Alexandria, Virginia: Association for Supervision and Curriculum Development, 1987. 98 pages.

Katz, Lilian G., and others. *The Case for Mixed-age Grouping in Early Education.* Washington, D.C.: National Association for the Education of Young Children, 1990. 59 pages.

Kentucky Department of Education. *Kentucky's Primary School: The Wonder Years, Program Description I.* Frankfort, Kentucky: Author, undated. 115 pages.

Miller, Bruce A. *The Multigrade Classroom: A Resource Handbook for Small, Rural Schools.* Portland, Oregon: Northwest Regional Educational Laboratory, 1989. 279 pages. ED 320 719.

Robinson-Armstrong, Abbie. Unpublished memorandum, March 27, 1992.

A Product of the ERIC Clearinghouse on Educational Management • College of Education, University of Oregon • Eugene, Oregon 97403

This publication was prepared with funding from the Office of Educational Research and Improvement, U.S. Department of Education, under contract No. OERI RI88062004. The ideas and opinions expressed in this Digest do not necessarily reflect the positions or policies of OERI, ED, or the Clearinghouse. This Digest is in the public domain and may be freely reproduced. EA 024 078

Sandra J. Stone

Sandra J. Stone is Assistant Professor, Early Childhood/Literacy Education, Center for Excellence in Education, Northern Arizona University, Flagstaff.

Strategies for Teaching Children in Multiage Classrooms

The multiage classroom is becoming an increasingly popular way to restructure schools. Kentucky, for example, has mandated multiage classrooms in all primary grades (K-3). Mississippi and Oregon have similar mandates. Alaska, California, Florida, Georgia, New York, Pennsylvania, Tennessee and Texas are also considering implementation of multiage classrooms (Gaustad, 1992; Kentucky Department of Education, 1992; Lodish, 1992).

In a multiage classroom a group of mixed-age children stay with the same teacher for several years. Typical primary grade age groups are 5-6-7, 6-7-8 or 7-8-9. The children spend three years with the same teacher (Connell, 1987). While the current multiage movement generally focuses on the primary years, multiage classrooms are also being implemented in upper elementary classes with age groups of 8-9-10 and 9-10-11.

Multiage teachers are frequently asked, "How does one teach students with such a wide range of abilities?" The question implies that teaching several grades of children is impractical and too difficult. On the surface, teaching mixed ages does appear to be overwhelming.

Successful multiage classrooms require teachers to shift attention from teaching *curriculum* to teaching *children*. A multiage class requires teachers to consider children as individuals, each with his or her own continuum of learning. Teachers who try to teach grade-specific curriculum to multiple-grade classrooms may become frustrated and often return to same-age classrooms. Teachers who have instituted appropriate instructional strategies, however, find multiage classes to be exhilarating and professionally rewarding. What are some teaching strategies that will help make multiage classroom teaching successful?

Process Approach to Learning

A key factor in multiage classrooms' success is the use of a process approach to education. This approach emphasizes teaching children, rather than curriculum. Each child is treated as a whole person with a distinct continuum of learning and developmental rate and style. The teacher focuses on developing children's social skills and on teaching broad academic subjects such as reading, writing and problem-solving. Each goal reflects a developmental process, not the learning of discrete skills in a prescribed curriculum.

To facilitate the writing process, for example, the teacher provides daily opportunities to write. First, she models writing and includes broad-based writing conventions. The children's writing is based on their individual developmental continuum. The younger child may write one sentence, using only beginning sounds, while the older child may write paragraphs.

The teacher also provides daily opportunities for children to read. Children read independently and in large and small groups. In large groups, the teacher presents a shared reading experience and focuses on broad-based skills, such as recognizing initial consonants, predicting outcomes and finding compound words. In small groups, the teacher chooses teaching points to fit the children's individual needs, nurturing effective reading strategies and increased comprehension.

Opportunities for children to use math are also available. Children studying dinosaurs, for example, may choose to set up a dinosaur store. Younger children learn to distinguish between nickels and dimes or to compute how many dimes are needed to buy a 30-cent dinosaur. Older children may try more complex calculations, such as adding a series of numbers.

A teacher using the process approach provides opportunities, open-ended activities, experiences or projects in which all the children can participate on their own developmental levels. The strategy is to provide the context where the learning process occurs. Children learn to read by reading, and to write by writing, in meaningful and relevant contexts. The process approach helps children to see themselves as progressive, successful learners.

Facilitator of Learning

The teacher must become a facilitator of learning in order to successfully implement a multiage classroom. A teacher must guide, nurture and support the learning process. Rather than acting simply as the "giver of knowledge," she must facilitate each child's growth in all areas according to individual developmental needs and interests. Therefore, teachers must *know the children*. A teacher can guide a younger child to use beginning sounds in writing only if she *knows* where the child is in the writing process. By facilitating learning, the teacher focuses on teaching children, not curriculum.

An Integrated Curriculum

Teachers choose an integrated curriculum in multiage classrooms that not only applies a holistic approach to learning, but also provides an excellent context for the process of learning. Teachers and/or children select a yearly, quarterly, monthly or even weekly theme. Children's reading, writing, problem-solving, graphing, measuring, painting and playing are based upon that thematic choice. As Connell (1987) notes, "integrating a curriculum around a theme allows children of different ages and stages to work together in a group as well as to practice skills at different levels" (p. 24).

Appropriate Learning Environment

The learning environment should permit all children to engage in the processes of learning. Such an environment includes active, hands-on learning experiences that are based on children's interests and choices. The center and/or the project approach is very effective in multiage classrooms. Centers may include library, writing, listening, art, play, science, social science, social studies, math, drama and computers.

Using bears as a theme, children at the writing center might create stories based on a group reading of "Goldilocks and the Three Bears." At the listening center, children may choose from a selection of fictional and nonfictional stories about bears or related themes. Younger children at the science center could clas-

> **R**ather than acting simply as the "giver of knowledge," she must facilitate each child's growth . . .

Where do we start if we are to improve life in the classroom? By examining how we respond to children. How a teacher communicates is of decisive importance. It affects a child's life for good or for bad. Usually we are not overly concerned about whether our response conveys acceptance or rejection. Yet to a child this difference is fateful, if not fatal.

Teachers who want to improve relations with children need to unlearn their habitual language of rejection and acquire a new language of acceptance. To reach a child's mind a teacher must capture his heart. Only if a child feels right can he think right.

From *Teacher and Child: A Book For Parents and Teachers*, by Dr. Haim Ginott. New York: Collier Books, 1972.

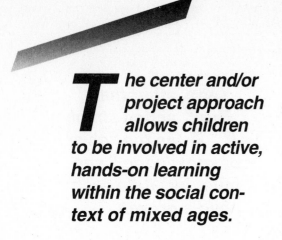

The center and/or project approach allows children to be involved in active, hands-on learning within the social context of mixed ages.

sify bears by type, while older children write descriptive paragraphs for each bear. At the play center, children of mixed ages can dramatize "Goldilocks and the Three Bears." Mixed-age groups could also design and build bear habitats or create a poster campaign to inform the public about endangered bear species.

Children choose their own open-ended activities and monitor their own time. The teacher is free to work with the children in small groups or individually as they become autonomous learners in charge of their own learning. The center and/or project approach allows children to be involved in active, hands-on learning within the social context of mixed ages.

Cross-age Learning

An effective multiage classroom encourages opportunities for cross-age learning. Social interaction in mixed-age groupings positively affects all areas of a child's development. Vygotsky (1978) suggests that children's learning can be enhanced by adults or more capable peers. In a multiage classroom where cooperation replaces competition, older children become mentors to younger children. A multiage classroom is not effective if the children are predominantly isolated in same-age groups or even same-ability groups.

Cooperative learning groups and peer tutoring are effective strategies. Collaboration through social interaction positively affects the children's learning.

Flexible Groupings

The predominant instructional strategy in multiage classrooms relies on small, flexible groupings. Children spend most of their class time in small groups, pairs or on their own.

While children participate in independent, cooperative groupings at centers or projects, the teacher works with small groups characterized by student needs or interests. For example, a teacher may conduct a literature study with a mixed-ability grouping, gather beginning readers together for support on using reading strategies and engage another group that showed interest in solving a particular problem. She may work individually with a child needing help in letter recognition. The breakdown of small groupings and independent study is not based on a predetermined, prescribed curriculum, but rather on the needs and interests of the children.

There is very little large-group instruction in the multiage classroom. Large group instruction times do provide a forum for broad-based skills. These instructional times allow for a wider curriculum presentation. Multiage teachers are amazed at how opening up the curriculum engages children to whom they ordinarily would not have presented certain concepts or skills.

Portfolio Assessment

Because the multiage classroom approach frees teachers to see children as individuals and relies on process learning, a new type of assessment is necessary. Portfolio assessment is an ideal strategy for

documenting the progress of each child. Children are assessed according to their own achievement and potential and not in comparison with other children (Goodlad & Anderson, 1987). The teacher holds different expectations for different children, does not grade portfolios and relies on using report cards that are narrative, rather than traditional.

Portfolios also help the teacher support and guide instruction. The authentic assessments in the portfolio enable teachers to know their students' strengths as well as areas that need further development. Portfolio assessment is an excellent tool for communicating with children and parents. It allows children to see themselves as successful learners and parents to better understand the learning process.

Conclusion

Strategies such as the process approach to learning, teacher as facilitator, appropriate learning environments, cross-age learning, flexible groupings and portfolio assessment all help teachers focus on teaching *children*. These strategies support the implementation of a successful and effective multiage program.

References and Other Resources

American Association of School Administrators. (1992). *The nongraded primary: Making schools fit children.* Arlington, VA: Author.

Anderson, R. H., & Pavan, B. N. (1993). *Nongradedness: Helping it to happen.* Lancaster, PA: Technomic Press.

Barbour, N. H., & Seefeldt, C. (1993). *Developmental continuity across preschool and primary grades: Implications for teachers.* Wheaton, MD: Association for Childhood Education International.

Bredecamp, S. (Ed.). (1987). *Developmentally appropriate practice in early childhood programs serving children from birth through age 8* (expanded edition). Washington, DC: National Association for the

Education of Young Children.

Connell, D. R. (1987). The first 30 years were the fairest: Notes from the kindergarten and ungraded primary (K-1-2). *Young Children, 42*(5), 30-39.

Cushman, K. (1990). The whys and hows of the multi-age classroom. *American Educator, 14*, 28-32, 39.

Elkind, D. (1989). Developmentally appropriate practice: Philosophical and practical implications. *Phi Delta Kappan, 17*(2), 113-117.

Gaustad, J. (1992). Nongraded primary education: Mixed-age, integrated and developmentally appropriate education for primary children. *Oregon School Study Council Bulletin, 35*(7).

Goodlad, J. I., & Anderson, R. H. (1987). *The non-graded elementary school* (rev. ed.). New York: Teachers College Press.

Kasten, W. C., & Clarke, B. K. (1993). *The multiage classroom.* Katonah, NY: Richard C. Owen.

Katz, L. G., & Chard, S. C. (1989). *Engaging children's minds: The project approach.* Norwood, NJ: Ablex.

Katz, L. G., Evangelou, D., & Hartman, J. A. (1990). *The case for mixed-age grouping in early education.* Washington, DC: National Association for the Education of Young Children.

Kentucky Department of Education. (1992). *Kentucky's primary school: The wonder years.* Frankfort, KY: Author.

Lodish, R. (1992). The pros and cons of mixed-age grouping. *Principal, 71*(6), 20-22.

Oberlander, T. M. (1989). A nongraded, multiage program that works. *Principal, 68*(5), 29-30.

Vygotsky, L. S. (1978). *Mind in society: The development of psychological processes.* Cambridge, MA: Harvard University Press.

The Multiage Education Bill of Rights

by Jim Grant

1. Every student has the right to learn in a continuous progress program.

2. Every student should have the option to continue with a teacher for more than one year.

3. Every student has the right to experience continuous success in the academic, social, physical, and emotional areas.

4. Every student has the right to take the time she or he needs to learn in a multiage classroom without the stigma of school failure.

5. Every student has the right to be free from the harmful effects of long-term ability grouping.

6. Every student has the right to learn in a program appropriate for his or her level of development.

7. Every student has the right to learn in a mixed-age classroom with a variety of learners.

8. Every student has the right to learn in a classroom where literacy is taught in an integrated manner.

9. Every student has the right to learn in a classroom where cooperation and conflict resolution are fostered.

10. Every student has the right to be evaluated in a manner that is consistent with how he or she was taught and measures knowledge, skills and attitudes which are meaningful.

Stone, Sandra J. Strategies for teaching children in multiage classrooms. *Childhood Education, 71*, 102-105.
Reprinted by permission of Sandra J. Stone and the Association for Childhood Education International,
11501 Georgia Avenue, Suite 315, Wheaton, MD. Coypright © 1995 by the Association.

Managing Your Multi-Age Classroom

What's it like to be faced with multiple grade level objectives and a wide range of abilities? Here's what one teacher has to say

BY BONNIE WALL

" *Teaching a multi-age class does take more planning initially, but it's not really as hard as it may seem.* **"**

When classes begin this fall at Barnwell Elementary School, 120 students will be sharing the experience with classmates who are significantly younger or older than themselves.

Over one-tenth of our 1,100 students are in multi-age classes – or, as we call them, MAC classes. There are three "primary" MAC classes, each with eight first graders, eight second graders and eight third graders; and two "intermediate" MAC classes, each with 12 fourth graders and 12 fifth graders.

The rapid growth of the MAC program over the past five years is a good indication of its acceptance at Barnwell.

Hellish classroom. In 1989, when other Barnwell teachers heard that I had agreed to teach the pilot MAC class, they kidded me about teaching "The Classroom from Hell."

Why? Well, they reasoned, it was challenging enough to meet objectives for a single grade level in a given day or a given year. How could I maintain my sanity with *multiple* grade level objectives?

Even worse. If I was the kind of teacher whose teaching style relied heavily on assigning the next page in the textbook (I'm not), a multi-age class would be a nightmare.

Actually, I wasn't at all nervous about teaching a multi-age class. I'd been a Montessori teacher and was used to multi-age groupings. If anything, I think I'd have been more nervous about teaching a single grade level class.

If you step back and look at the curriculum, you'll find that it's not really that different for first, second and third graders, nor for fourth and fifth graders. Math, language arts, social studies and science objectives often overlap grade levels. Some new material is added at each grade level, of course, but there's a good deal of repetition.

The key point here is that even in a single grade level class, students have a range of abilities. There's a continuum. A multi-age class simply adds students of different ages to that continuum.

There are certain benefits that come with

Simple science experiments *are easily done by multi-age teams. Here, team members find that adding salt to water will make an egg float.*

Continued

a multi-age environment. For example, because students remain in the same class – two years in an intermediate MAC, three years in a primary MAC – teachers already know half or two-thirds of their students at the beginning of each school year. In my primary MAC class, there are only eight new first graders and 16 eager "experts" to help me with them in every way.

Also, I know what was covered during the previous year, which saves a lot of evaluation and repetition of instruction.

Even more important are the benefits for the children. For example:

• Because there's a wide range of abilities, the multi-age class lends itself to a cooperative spirit. Students are more accepting of the uniqueness of themselves and others

• There are more opportunities for students to work at their own level. An advanced first grader simply works at a higher level; a slow third grader works at a lower level

• Younger students learn from older students; older students, because they're "teaching," reinforce their own learning

• Older students get to be models and leaders, which enhances their self-esteem

• Traditions and memories are built. Kids love this kind of ritual

MAC from a hat. Barnwell offers the MAC program as an alternative to regular classrooms. Teachers teach MAC classes because they choose to and students are in the classes because their parents want them there.

And a great many parents *do* want them there. There are always more requests than vacancies. So to be fair to everyone, we select students' names randomly – from a hat – with the provision that the numbers are balanced by grade and sex.

This method of selection emphasizes that MAC classes are not necessarily better than single grade classes. They're just different.

What does it take to be a MAC teacher? Well, for one thing, you need to be organized, yet flexible and open to trying new things. Also, it helps if you're familiar with curriculum objectives for multiple grade levels.

I've found three techniques to be effec-

tive in teaching a MAC group:

• *Integrate.* I integrate as much as possible, using a unit or theme approach. Units vary from one to six weeks and provide learning activities for all areas of the curriculum.

• *Balance.* I try to balance what we do in the classroom – whole-class with small group activities, cooperative teamwork with individual work.

• *Cooperative teams.* Although I emphasize balance, cooperative teams are the core units of my class. There are six teams, each with four members. Each team includes at least one first, second and third grader. Teams spend some time every day working on a project or activity. I change teams about six times a year.

A typical day. If you were to spend a day in my classroom, here are some of the things you might see.

We begin our reading and writing time each day with journal writing, after which the students share what they've written. Students are exposed to many levels of writing through sharing.

Journal writing is followed by silent reading. Students have their own reading material and write a summary and a supported opinion on a response sheet. The same assignment is given to all students, who are encouraged to respond at their highest level. They are also encouraged to go to members of their cooperative team for help on assignments.

Several times each day, I read poetry, stories or articles (often about our social studies or science theme). This is followed by a whole class discussion.

In addition to independent reading, students meet with me in small groups to work on specific reading and writing skills These "skill groups" are made up of children, regardless of their grade level, who need or are ready to learn a particular skill.

Twice each month, the children present book reports. They use a variety of reporting media, including overhead transparencies, puppets, dioramas, posters, cubes, cans, time lines and so on.

If you were to visit my MAC class, you'd

also see students working on science and social studies units. I use a three-year cycle of unit study to make sure all of the objectives are met without repeating themes and activities each year.

Last year, for example, we studied wetlands. This year, we'll be studying oceans, and next year we'll study the desert. We use trade books, films, activities and computer programs to present material to the entire class.

Sometimes assignments include different activities for different skill levels, but frequently students are all doing the same thing or working with their cooperative teams. For example, during our study of oceans, several experiments were done by teams. Research papers on sea creatures were required of the older students, while the younger ones helped create a mural showing what organisms live at various ocean depths.

In planning math lessons, I look for strands such as problem-solving, operations, geometry, measurement, statistics and probability. All students work on the same strand at the same time, although at different levels.

Whole class lessons or discussions of a math concept may serve as an introduction for young students and a review for older students. Work in skill groups usually follows. Sometimes an older child will direct an activity for a younger skill group.

We use computer-generated math tests on eight levels, ranging from simple addition facts to division facts. The students have three years to complete all eight levels. In addition, the whole class takes a five-minute test each week, with students working at their skill level. They are recognized for improving their scores and passing a level. In a very real sense, they compete against the test, not against each other.

Troublesome texts. You may have noticed that up to this point, we've made no mention of textbooks. That's because we don't use them very much. Textbooks almost inevitably mean assignments and keeping track of pages and in a multi-age environment, that's more trouble than it's worth.

This isn't to say that we never use text-

Bonnie Wall teaches a multi-age class (grades 1-3) at Barnwell Elementary School, Alpharetta, GA.

The entire class enjoyed observing the emergence of their very own luna moth.

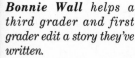
A multi-age team of artists collaborate on a team project for social studies: creating a community

Author study can be a lot of fun especially when it means you can listen to an Eric Carle story.

Bonnie Wall helps a third grader and first grader edit a story they've written.

books. If a chapter in a textbook fits in with our unit of study, the children might "buddy-read" it, with the more advanced readers helping the beginners.

Similar principles. Teaching a multi-age class does take more planning initially, but it's not really as hard as it may seem. It becomes even easier if you can work with other teachers who are doing the same thing, and if you're willing to create an environment where everyone works together. ❧

The Change Process

Change Strategy 1: Let Go of What's Not Working.

The first step in making changes is to stop doing what's not working. Repeating unsuccessful interventions, besides wasting our time and energy, keeps us stuck and makes us feel hopeless.

Change Strategy 2: Shift Gears Realistically.

Whenever we try to implement something new in our lives, we tend to feel unnatural, uncomfortable, and even a little phony. If we expect and accept these feelings, we can proceed to make helpful changes. We'll make some mistakes in the beginning, but if we persevere, we'll achieve the results we want. Be kind to yourself by setting realistic expectations, and be patient with yourself when progress falters.

Change Strategy 3: Give Yourself Encouragement.

We all have voices in our heads that give us both positive and negative self-talk. We need our voices to encourage us by telling us "you can do it," "this is going to work." By feeding yourself this kind of encouragement, you can give yourself the optimism and confidence to implement major changes.

Change Strategy 4: Dramatize Difficult Situations.

Dramatization is particularly valuable because it gives us an opportunity to receive helpful feedback from others. Friends and colleagues can play the roles of students, so we have actual persons to react to.

Change Strategy 5: Form a Support Group.

Advise and encouragement of friends and colleagues will not only fire our enthusiasm, but may keep us from giving up when the going gets rough. Support groups can vary in size from one other interested teacher to an entire school staff. What's important is keeping the atmosphere positive and optimistic, not allowing negative comments or attitudes to overtake us.

Change Strategy 6: Persist, Persist, Persist.

How successful we are at applying new strategies depends not upon how fast we try to implement everything, but rather on how persevering we are in our efforts.

Stephanie Noland

What is Multiage Grouping?

"Age grouping based on physical time denies the fact that children are organisms and that they operate on variable biological and psychological time, not uniform physical time."
— David Elkind

Multiage grouping is . . .

- developmentally appropriate practice in all decisions for primary-age children in accordance with NAEYC research and recommendations.

- a community of learners with a wide range of gifts and abilities.

- supportive of flexible and heterogeneous grouping

- process oriented in the curricular areas — supportive and compatible with whole language.

- active participation on the part of the student — hands-on activities, learning centers, class discussion, cooperative projects, and self-selection of materials, topics and learning.

- the teacher taking the role as facilitator of learning experiences — monitoring, guiding, participating and observing in instructional opportunities.

- instruction organized in integrated thematic units across content areas giving the children meaningful context for concepts learned.

- free of traditional school structures such as ability grouping and grade levels which are unnatural in the "real world" and often unnecessary.

- assessed and evaluated by ongoing, performance-based, meaningful sources including portfolios, anecdotal records, student/teacher conferences, and teacher observation as well as by more formal evaluation methods.

Multiage grouping is not . . .

- grouping two or more ages together due to economic factors alone.

- teaching two distinct grade level curriculums — dividing children by age to do so.

- isolated subjects with little or no opportunity to see how things work together as a whole.

- based on rigid ability groupings.

- learning that has little or no regard for the child's interests, strengths, or motivation to explore.

- the teacher directing every lesson while the students sit quietly at desks.

- based on convergent thinking where students seek to find the one right answer.

Stephanie Noland

Classroom Practices That Facilitate Mulitage Grouping

While there is strong research for multiage grouping as a practice in the elementary grades, there is little "hard and fast" information regarding staff development and training in multiage practices. The strand that continues to emerge from available research indicates that there are many appropriate models for establishing a multiage program — not just one "right" way. And while there is no "one right" staff development, research repeats several teaching strategies and classroom practices that, if teachers are trained in them, will facilitate and aid in establishing a successful multiage program.

- Developmentally appropriate practices — the teacher understands how young children learn and grow at different rates.

- Reading is a daily practice. The teacher as well as students read as part of daily routine. Material provided is on a wide span of levels and interests. Children are encouraged to read self-selected materials. The teacher reads a variety of genres to the children.

- Flexible grouping is used. Children are grouped for specific needs and for short periods of time. Groups are fluid and changing based on the topic or content addressed.

- Manipulative-based mathematics instruction emphasizes problem solving and worksheets are used minimally or not at all.

- Science instruction is organized in a hands-on, discovery, experimentation approach where materials are available for children to manage their own learning.

- Process writing is stressed where children select their own topics and invented spelling is accepted as a part of process.

- Cooperative learning is a regular part of instruction so that children can learn to work together in teams. Student seating is arranged to promote cooperation.

- Integrated thematic instruction is implemented in a way so that content concepts are introduced and extended in meaningful ways.

- Learning centers are used not for when "work" is finished, but as a part of the instruction process for reinforcing and extending instruction.

- Materials necesary for completing both teacher-assigned and student-initiated tasks are accessible to both teacher and students.

The multiage model is not "throwing the baby out with the bathwater," but instead is using the strengths already in place in education to provide developmentally appropriate instruction for all children.

Stephanie Noland

Three Grouping Strategies

Whole Class

Group conferences
Appropriate group lessons
Introductions
Reading to class
Instructional games
Etc.

Small Group Instruction

Group

Skills development
Interest
Work habits
Social
Random
Task/Activity

Other students

Contracts
Centers
Stations
Peer tutoring
Parent volunteers
Choices

Individual Instruction

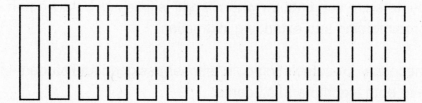

Contracts, centers, stations, peer tutoring, choices, volunteers, projects

Stephanie Noland

The Developmentally Appropriate Classroom:
What Does It Look Like?

When establishing a work environment that is appropriate for young children - especially those of mixed ages, there are many things to consider. Take a look at your own classroom and ask yourself the following questions.

Questions to Consider:

• Are there large spaces for the whole group to meet comfortably?

• Are there medium spaces for small group instruction? If team teaching, are these far enough apart to reduce interference noise?

• Are there small spaces for 2-3 kids to work in together?

• Are there quiet spaces for individual tasks?

• Does table space and arrangement promote cooperation?

• Are there spaces for hands-on science and manipulative-based math? If not, does your routine allow for designating floor or table space for these materials?

• Is safety considered in available supplies?

• Are writing materials, art supplies, and books openly and readily available?

• Are kid spaces and materials well identified?
(labels - Kids can make these!)

• Are there soft spaces with rugs, pillows, etc...

• Are kid messages at kid-eye level?

• Is the environment print-rich?

• Is the work/print displayed meaningful to the children?

• Is the print current?

• Do the children participate in organizing the space?

Remember:
Give the children TIME to adjust to any new arrangements!

Stephanie Noland

Parent/Community Survey

In response to many requests for parent/community assessment of our multi-age program, the attached survey was developed. The following choices are not reflected in the actual piece, but should be carefully considered when implementing a similar assessment tool within your community.

GOAL: to assess attitudes in the community with regard to the site based decision/newly implemented program of multi-age grouping and to take parent concerns into consideration when modifying and refining the program.

ORGANIZATION AND STRUCTURE OF INSTRUMENT: Although implementation was phased in over three years, beginning with K-2 and adding 3-4 and 5-6, all families are surveyed to gain perceptions from both in and out of the program. Different colors were used to designate those two groups and then, after full implementation, to designate which component of the program the family was familiar with - primary, intermediate, or 5-6. This allowed anonymity for all families. Families with siblings were requested to complete a survey in consideration of the effects for each child individually.

Questions and desired information were brainstormed by involved faculty and the multi-age steering committee. Statements to be addressed were phrased in the most positive language possible. Statements were organized to (hopefully) help parents to see the benefits of the program for their child/children before making global statements on the entire picture. It was discussed that some parents may have negative feelings overall about the change and fail to recognize the benefits for their child if, for example, statement #10 was early in the list.

One statement was added to help us get more accurate information. Along the bottom of the survey, the statement "My child has been a part of the multi-age program for _____ years."

All returned surveys are reviewed initially by the site-based steering committee. Any mentioned names are deleted and the survey photocopied. "Attacks" on specific teachers are also deleted. All surveys are currently filed and available in the school office for involved parties to view upon request. The file, however, may not be removed from school grounds or photocopied by parents/community members.

PERMISSION: Permission is granted to use this survey as a model for a similar form to be used in your school. It is not copyrighted information, but credit would be appreciated.

Stephanie Mullins Noland, 1995

Stephanie Noland

Parent/Community Survey – 1992

As you know, our entire school family has worked hard to initiate and implement an instructional program that best meets the needs of our students. The purpose of this opinion survey is to gather input from you about how you think we are doing in that endeavor.

Listed below are statements. Please read each statement and then circle the number which best represent your reaction to the statement. Circling a "5" means that you strongly agree with the statement. Circling a "1" means that you strongly disagree with the statement. The numbers "2", "3", and "4" represent different levels of agreement between the "strong" levels.

	Strongly Disagree — Slightly Disagree — Neutral — Slightly Agree — Strongly Agree
1. The mixed-age grouping program helps my child learn as much as possible .	1 ------ 2 ------ 3 ------ 4 ------ 5
2. The mixed-age grouping program helps my child learn to work well in a student group setting.	1 ------ 2 ------ 3 ------ 4 ------ 5
3. The mixed-age grouping program helps my child gain an appreciation for the unique contribution that each person can make.	1 ------ 2 ------ 3 ------ 4 ------ 5
4. The mixed-age grouping program helps my child develop a strong positive self-image.	1 ------ 2 ------ 3 ------ 4 ------ 5
5. My child receives adequate individual attention in the mixed-age instructional setting.	1 ------ 2 ------ 3 ------ 4 ------ 5
6. There is strong district support for the mixed-age grouping program.	1 ------ 2 ------ 3 ------ 4 ------ 5
7. I feel that adequate communication exists to keep me informed about my child's academic progress.	1 ------ 2 ------ 3 ------ 4 ------ 5
8. The atmosphere or learning climate at Northlake is positive.	1 ------ 2 ------ 3 ------ 4 ------ 5
9. Our school is helping students learn to cope with a rapidly changing society.	1 ------ 2 ------ 3 ------ 4 ------ 5
10. I support the mixed-age grouping program as the organizational structure of the instructional program at Northlake.	1 ------ 2 ------ 3 ------ 4 ------ 5
11. Discipline is not a serious problem in our program.	1 ------ 2 ------ 3 ------ 4 ------ 5
12. Our school has a positive image in the community.	1 ------ 2 ------ 3 ------ 4 ------ 5
13. The morale of students is high.	1 ------ 2 ------ 3 ------ 4 ------ 5

The one thing that has really helped make the mixed-age grouping program successful is:

_____

_____

The one thing that would really help the mixed-age grouping program be more successful is:

_____

_____

_____

If there are any other comments you would like to make about Northlake or the mixed-age grouping program, please feel free to write your comments on the back of this page.

Stephanie Noland

Learning Centers

What is a learning center?

Individual children or small groups working and playing cooperatively or alone on projects they have selected themselves or are guided to by the teacher. Materials and activities are concrete, real, and relevant to children's lives. (NAEYC, 1987)

Component parts of learning centers

Each center needs:

1. **a title and clear instructions** - The learning center should be identified or titled. The instructions should be presented to the entire class or be simple enough so that all students can figure out the instructions independently. The students should be shown how to use the center appropriately.

2. **all necessary equipment and materials necessary to complete the center** - The center should be created so that materials are readily available to the students. Students should know how the materials should be stored so that other students may use the center.

3. **a variety of activities** - The activities in the center should be related to a topic being studied, provide the opportunity to explore an area of interest, or provide practice of a skill. The center should be able to accommodate a variety of ability levels. Open-ended activities do a good job at achieving this goal.

4. **assessment** - The students should know how their work will be evaluated and where to put their completed work. Students may also be given a standard of work and then judge the quality of their own work or the work of their peers.

5. **to be visually attractive** - This seems insignificant, but students will want to work in a center that is attractive.

6. **to have a purpose** - Centers should be more than a replacement for "busy work" or "seatwork". Students should be able to apply what they have learned both in the centers and as a result of working with the centers.

REMEMBER: Many behavior issues are really management issues. If students know what is appropriate -- they're on task and behaving.

adapted from Learning Centers handout developed by Irv Richardson

Stephanie Noland

Center Time is....... LEARNING TIME!!!

Through blocks, a child:
• has opportunity for using large muscles
• chooses sizes and shapes
• learns to use his own ideas
• may enjoy conversation
• learns to put materials away

Through Dramatic Play, a child:
• plays out home experiences
• develops muscular coordination in imitating home actions
• has opportunity to play alone
• has opportunity to "help"
• role plays life like situations
• may begin to cooperate with others
• reveals thoughts and attitudes through conversation
• develops his imagination
• may develop thinking and reasoning skills

Through table games, a child:
• enjoys a sense of achievement
• learns to solve problems
• learns to work independently
• has opportunity for choices
• may enjoy conversation
• develops coordination and fine motor control
• learns to manipulate materials
• forms mathematical concepts

Through Art Materials, a child:
• enjoys sensory experiences
• has opportunity to plan and think for himself
• enjoys manipulation by squeezing, pounding, brushing, and cutting
• experiences creative ways of using materials
• has opportunity for releasing emotional tensions and frustrations
• experiments with color and texture
• learns responsibility for cleaning up

Through Library Materials, a child:
• may enjoy handling and looking at books
• learns to listen to stories
• increases attention/interest span
• develops new concepts and adds to previous experiences
• learns to visually attend to activities
• begins to take responsibility for orderliness

Through Science, a child:
• learns to appreciate beauty
• enjoys sensory experiences
• becomes more aware of his surroundings
• learns to help care for plants and animals
• develops interest in experimentation
• learns to draw conclusions
• accepts change

Through Woodworking, a child:
• has opportunity to plan and carry out ideas
• uses large muscles
• learns to share materials
• has opportunity for releasing emotional tension and aggression
• experiences creativity
• contributes to problem solving activities
• learns measurement principles

Through cooking, a child:
• has opportunity to contribute to the well being of others
• learns concepts of measurement, time, and space
• may enjoy sharing and taking turns
• associates experiences with tangible rewards
• enjoys sensory experiences
• shares cultural background
• develops language

S. Noland, 1995.

Stephanie Noland

Homework Cards
Self-selected, self-directed, meaningful homework experiences for primary children

Tonight at home I will:

- tell someone what I did in school/math/reading/journal writing/etc... today.
- draw/write something to share at school.
- ask someone to read with me.
- look in my kitchen and find ___ things that begin with ___
- find 10 things that will fit in a cup.
- write about/draw 3 things I found in (a room in my house)
- listen to the weather report and be ready to talk about it.
- find 3 labels that I can read.
- count the number of windows/doors/ etc... in my house
- survey my family about ___. (Perhaps something to do with a recently read book?)
- sort my socks(or whatever) by an attribute (color?)
- tell someone what I did in centers today.
- tell/read a bedtime story to someone in my family.
- say "Please" and "Thank you" tonight.
- help set the table and count plates, spoons, forks, etc...
- sing my favorite song from school.
- find a pattern at home, draw a picture of it, and bring it to school.
- watch the news.
- find math in the newspaper.
- conduct an interview with my parent.
- help someone cook.
- find something at home that's my favorite color. Describe it at school.
- plan to share a favorite thing from home.
- count the number of knives, forks, spoons, in your silverware drawer. Graph your findings.

TIPS AND SUGGESTIONS

1. Make homework cards real generic and open-ended. That way, you're providing maximum learning opportunities with a minimum of work for yourself.
2. Color code homework cards to designate activities or content areas. Even emergent readers can "read" the colors and know what the assignment is.
3. Keep generic homework cards available at all times while rotating more specific assignments in and out as themes and instruction dictate.
4. Help parents understand the value of these experiences. For example, tell families that you'll be using collected data for math graphs and comparison.
5. Have each child keep and circulate homework in a pocket folder. Make the child responsible for choice and management. Choices must be made other than at the end of the day.

Stephanie Mullins Noland, 1995.

Stephanie Noland

STRATEGIES TO ELEVATE STUDENT THINKING

- Utilize "Think-Pair-Share"
  Allow individual thinking time, discussion with a partner, and then sharing with the class

- Ask "Follow-ups"
  Why? Do you agree? Can you elaborate? Tell me more.

- Ask for summary to promote active listening
  Please share with the class what your group found.

- Survey the class
  How many people agree . . . (thumbs up/down)

- Ask students to "unpack their thinking"
  Describe how you arrived at your answer.

- Remain aware of your language
  Involve the class with your language — "Can someone share with the class . . . ?" rather than "Can you tell me . . . ?"

- Play Devil's Advocate
  Require students to defend their own reasoning against different points of view.

- Cue student responses
  Let them know that there is not a single correct answer. They should consider alternatives.

- Don't forget wait time
  Provide at least three seconds of thinking time after a question AND after a response.

- Withhold judgement
  Respond to answers in a nonevaluative fashion.

- Allow for student calling
  "Mary, will you please call on someone else to respond?"

- Call on students randomly
  Avoid the pattern of always calling on only those students with raised hands.

- Encourage student questioning
  Let students develop their own questions.

Stephanie Noland

GROUP PROCESSING

How did we do?

1. We took <u>turns</u>.

2. We <u>checked</u> with each other.

    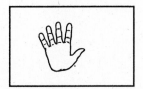

3. We <u>helped</u> each other.

4. We <u>shared</u> materials.

5. We <u>encouraged</u> each other.

    Good job!
    You can do it!
    Cool idea!

On the back of this page list:

* All group members' names
* What we could have done better
* "Bragging rights"

Shared Book Experiences

Story:

Date:

Class:

1. Makes predictions											
2. Listens attentively											
3. Participates in discussions											
4. Answers questions											
5. Can retell story											
6. Skill Focus:											
Follow-up activity:											

Comments:

_____

_____

_____

_____

_____

Often	+
Sometimes	S
Seldom	—
Not Observed	N

Sample   Writing Checklist

Key:

+ introduced
+ reinforced
* mastery

NAMES OF STUDENTS	Capitalize I	Capitalize beginning of sentence	Capitalize proper nouns	End punctuation . ? !	Quotation Marks	Commas in a series	Apostrophes - possessive	Contractions		
1.										
2.										
3.										
4.										
5.										
6.										
7.										
8.										
9.										
10.										
11.										
12.										
13.										
14.										
15.										
16.										
17.										
18.										
19.										
20.										
21.										
22.										
23.										
24.										

Stephanie Noland

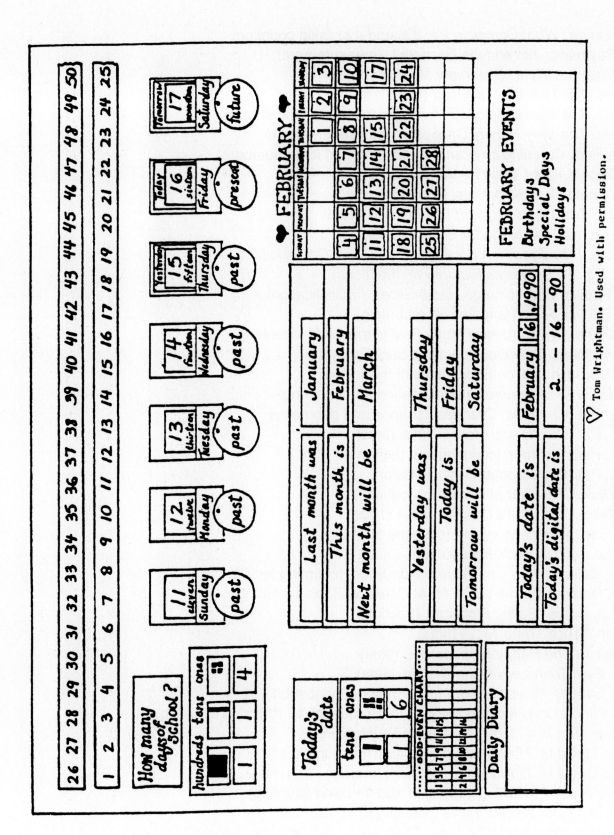

Stephanie Noland

93

Books You Can <u>Count</u> On

Compiled by Stephanie Mullins Noland

Aker, Suzanne. *What Comes in 2's, 3's, and 4's?* (skip counting)

Briggs, Raymond. *Jim and the Beanstalk.* (measurement)

Brown, Margaret Wise. *Goodnight Moon.* (time)

Carle, Eric. *The Grouchy Ladybug.* (time)

Carle, Eric. *The Secret Birthday Message.* (geometry and shapes)

Carle, Eric. *The Very Hungry Caterpillar.* (days of the week)

Clement, Rod. *Counting on Frank.* (estimation and large numbers)

Crews, Donald. *Light.* (look for the clocks!)

Crews, Donald. *Ten Black Dots.* (counting)

Dee, Ruby. *Two Ways to Count to Ten.* (skip counting)

DePaola, Tomie. *Pancakes for Breakfast.* (time)

Ehlert, Lois. *Fish Eyes — A Book You Can Count On.* (addition)

Emberly, Ed. *Ed Emberly's Picture Pie.* (fractions)

Giganti, Paul Jr. *Each Orange Had 8 Slices.* (multiplication)

Giganti, Paul Jr. *How Many Snails?* (counting)

Hamm, Diane Johnston. *How Many Feet in the Bed?* (counting)

Harshman, Marc. *Only One.* (counting backwards)

Hooper, Meredith. *Seven Eggs.* (days of the week)

Hulme, Joy N. *Sea Squares.* (multiplication and squaring)

Hutchins, Pat. *Changes, Changes.* (shapes and geometry)

Hutchins, Pat. *Clocks and More Clocks.* (time)

Hutchins, Pat. *1 Hunter.* (counting and patterns)

Hutchins, Pat. *The Doorbell Rang.* (division)

Inkpen, Mick. *One Bear at Bedtime.* (counting)

Kasza, Keiko. *The Wolf's Chicken Stew.* (100s)

Kitchen, Bert. *Animal Numbers.* (counting to 100)

Lionni, Leo. *Inch by Inch.* (measuring)

Lottridge, Celia Barker. *One Watermelon Seed.* (counting to 100)

McGrath, Barbara Barbieri. *The M&M Counting Book.* (counting)

Macmillian, Bruce. *Eating Fractions.* (fractions)

Macmillian, Bruce. *Time To . . .* (time)

Martin, Bill Jr. *The Happy Hippopotami.* (time)

Merriam, Eve. *Train Leaves the Station.* (time)

Merriam, Eve. *12 Ways to Count to 11.* (number concepts)

Pinczes, Elinor. *One Hundred Hungry Ants.* (counting to 100, skip counting)

Rees, Mary. *Ten In A Bed.* (counting and subtraction)

Schwartz, David M. *How Much is a Million?* (counting)

Schwartz, David M. *If You Made a Million.* (money)

Sloat, Teri. *From 1 to 100.* (counting to 100 and skip counting)

Thornhill, Jan. *The Wildlife 1-2-3.* (counting to 1000)

Viorst, Judith. *Alexander Who Used To Be Rich Last Saturday.* (money)

Wiesner, David. *Tuesday.* (time)

Science in Early Childhood Classrooms

"Imagination is more important than knowledge." - Albert Einstein

Dr. Einstein said that young children engage in thinking and investigation that is truly scientific and that their strong curiosity is similar to that of great scientists.

Children are natural scientists. They have a sense of wonder and curiosity that is the beginning of a scientific attitude. The teacher must provide an environment where children are encouraged to develop the scientific attitude.

Any child can be taught facts if he can memorize. The idea of teaching science is to introduce concepts and allow the learner to <u>experience</u> the facts. Facts only make sense if they are clearly related to a concept. We all know that $E = mc^2$ but, few of us understand the concept behind the math. Concepts are enriched and broadened by facts.

Elementary science education should place more stress on the attitudes and aptitudes it develops than on content. The development of attitudes involves continued participation. If children are to develop a scientific attitude, they must have personal science experiences which are enjoyable (Herbert Zim).

"In teaching children to read, we must begin with the experiences of the child."   *- Marie Clay*

By giving our children hands - on opportunities to explore science materials, not only are we encouraging a scientific attitude, we are also enabling the child to begin to read and understand scientific material. When the child experiences, his mental setting enlarges -- then those experiences support the child in dealing with a print setting.

SCIENCE PROCESSES TAUGHT IN EARLY CHILDHOOD

- Observation - gathering of information
- Comparison - noticing similarities and differences
- Classifying - sorting and grouping according to common attribute
- Measuring - use of standard and non-standard units
- Communication - telling about an event
- Inferring - using observations to venture a guess
- Predicting - using information to anticipate future events
- Hypothesizing - If... then...

Stephanie Noland

LITERATURE FOR THE SCIENCE CURRICULUM

Listed below are several titles for commonly explored scientific topics as well as one terrific way to include parents and home reading in the content connections.

Birds
Ehlert, Lois. Feathers for Lunch.
Heller, Ruth. Chickens Aren't The Only Ones.
Hutchins, Pat. Good Night Owl.
Oppenheim, Joanne. Have You Seen Birds?
Pallotta, Jerry. The Bird Alphabet Book.
Yolen, Jane. Owl Moon.

Ecology
Brown, Ruth. The World That Jack Built.
Cherry, Lynne. The Great Kapok Tree.
Cowcher, Helen. Rain Forest.
Dorros, Arthur. Rain Forest Secrets.
Gibbons, Gail. Recycle!
Greene, Carol. The Old Lady Who Liked Cats.
Jeffers, Susan. Brother Eagle, Sister Sky.
Kellogg, Steven. Island of the Skog.
Kraus, Robert. How Spider Stopped the Litterbugs.
Livingston, Myra Cohn. Earth Songs.
Peet, Bill. The Wump World.
Rand, Ted and Gloria. Prince William.
Yolen, Jane. Welcome to the Greenhouse.

Insects and Spiders
Brown, Ruth. If At First You Do Not See.
Carle Eric. The Grouchy Ladybug.
—— The Very Busy Spider.
—— The Very Hungry Caterpillar.
—— The Very Quiet Cricket.
Dorros, Arthur. Ant Cities.
Pallotta, Jerry. The Icky Bug Alphabet Book.
Parker, Nancy Winslow. Bugs.

Oceans and Ocean Life
Cole, Joanna. The Magic School Bus on the Ocean Floor.
Gibbons, Gail. Whales.
Kalan, Robert. Blue Sea.
Pallotta, Jerry. The Ocean Alphabet Book.
——The Underwater Alphabet Book.
Sheldon, Dyan. The Whale's Song.

Plants
Bash, Barbara. Desert Giant.
Behn, Harry. Trees.
Carle, Eric. The Tiny Seed.
Ehlert, Lois. Planting A Rainbow.
—— Growing Vegetable Soup.
Guilberson, Brenda. Cactus Hotel.
Heller, Ruth. Plants That Never Ever Bloom.
—— The Reason For a Flower.
Lobel, Anita. Alison's Zinnia.
Merrill, Claire. A Seed is A Promise.
Pallotta, Jerry. The Flower Alphabet Book.
—— The Victory Garden Alphabet Book.

Space
Asch, Frank. Happy Birthday Moon.
—— Moondance.
—— Mooncake.
Barton, Byron. I Want To Be An Astronaut.
Brown, Margaret Wise. Goodnight Moon.
Carle, Eric. Papa, Please Get the Moon For Me.
Cole, Joanna. The Magic School Bus: Lost in the Solar System.
Moche, Dinah. What's up There?
Simon, Seymour. Jupiter.
—— The Moon.
—— Saturn.
—— Stars.
—— The Sun.

The Science Backpack - Its purpose is to allow students to independently explore scientific concepts and draw conclusions. Topics could range from those listed to weather, inventions, rocks, and the list goes on and on. Included with the books in the backpack are related activities and necessary materials for the student to work on at home with the parent.

Stephanie Noland

Evaluating a Learner's Development:

- displayed confidence and independence
- increased knowledge of ideas and concepts
- participated in activities
- applied inquiry skills and processes
- broadened means of presentation
- made comparisons; saw alternatives
- collaborated and cooperated
- reflected on and assessed own progess; revised earlier generalizations

1. Make assessment integral part of teaching; ongoing.
2. Use variety of techniques.
3. Assess what students know.
4. Use data collected to guide instruction.

"The curriculum is no longer a prepackaged plan."

LOOPING

Twice the Learning and Twice the Love

A teacher discovers the joys and sorrows of holding on and letting go as she moves with her students from first grade to second grade

After two years *of friendship and learning, Deborah's students have aged emotionally and physically. With a little natural trepidation, they prepare to move to a new teacher and new experiences.*

BY DEBORAH JACOBY

❝ *By the second year, I was able to offer more constructive criticism on the students' academic work without damaging our relationship.* **❞**

In September 1990, with freshly scrubbed faces, brand new clothes, bulging backpacks full of newly purchased school supplies and 20 children tentatively crossed the portal of my first grade classroom. Some were holding an older sibling's hand or hiding behind the protective folds of their mother's skirt. One parent had a videocamera to record the momentous occasion.

Before saying goodbye, their mothers helped them find their names on their cubbies and hung up their jackets. After a quick kiss, a giant bear hug, or a smile and a wave that seemed to say, "I'll be okay, Mom," the new students quietly made their way to the tables

to color or do puzzles and we began our year.

Gradually, we got to know and trust each other. We had a full year – hatching chicks, loose teeth, birthday treats and other significant first grade milestones. One by one, the first graders became more fluent readers and writers as typically happens at this age.

In the spring, my principal approached me about taking them on to second grade. I was hesitant about mastering new curriculum, wondering if I'd be able to continue to challenge and interest the same children in second grade. But knowing how much I enjoyed these children and excited about the prospect of doing something different, I agreed.

Deborah Jacoby teaches first and second graders in Chicago, IL. This is her first article for *Teaching K-8*.

Back in the saddle. In September 1991, amidst a sea of moms, tears and all the trepidation of the first day of school, there were 20 confident second graders who rushed into my classroom and quickly began unpacking their supplies, chatting about summer vacations.

Last spring, the children made their own name labels for their desks and cubbies. There were no first day jitters. Instead, there were feelings of familiarity.

The startup that fall was different for me than in any other year. We jumped right into projects without any of the usual transition time. Behavioral expectations had been set the year before. I tried to make sure certain things about the routine were different, but found that the children preferred the comfort of the same routines.

The continuing curriculum. All year, curriculum was partially defined by my previous experiences with the children. I needed to do very little assessment of skills. I knew where we had left off in the spring. In fact, several children had unfinished stories from the end of first grade that they completed in second.

When we discussed books and authors, we would often compare or contrast a book to one we had read the previous year. I was able to build on known foundations and utilize the children's strengths and talents more than I was ever able to before.

This was perhaps most true in reading and writing. I had watched my students' skills emerge and solidify. I was able to reinforce those skills in a style that was consistent over two years. For example, knowing the process we had used in researching chameleons in the fall of first grade and polar bears in the winter, I was able to build on those steps to plan for researching planets in the winter of second grade. Each project built on the last one.

By the second year, I was able to offer more constructive criticism on the students' academic work without damaging our relationship. They already knew that I believed in them and in their cognitive abilities and they trusted my instincts.

Strengthening the bond. The students' relationships with me and with each other deepened over time. We knew each other's strengths and weaknesses. And as a family, we shared triumphs and tears.

The whole class cheered when Tom finished a 500-piece puzzle. We were all saddened when Andrew's dog died and when Lindsay moved to California. Each time someone celebrated a birthday, the children dictated sentences for the birthday card that described why the birthday child was special. I was impressed by the precise insights the children offered about each other. The sense of the classroom being an interdependent community of learners was so very strong.

The two year sequence benefited the shy, quiet children tremendously as well. There always seem to be one or two children who rarely talk in class, although their parents say that they are never quiet at home. Those children grew increasingly comfortable in the classroom, and by the middle of the second year, came fully out of their shells; as our time together increased, school simulated the comfort and intimacy of home and family.

A time to share. I was also able to develop trusting relationships with parents and families. Together, we charted their children's ups and downs over two years. The parents, children and I were able to reflect on growth and change over a greater time period. When Claire wrote an exceptional story that had rabbits as the theme, I was able to refer back to when she wrote a story about rabbits in first grade and point to specific elements in the second story that had improved from the previous year.

Every child has grown in every way – socially, cognitively and emotionally – even physically. The little desks and chairs are no longer adequate for some whose knees are rubbing against the undersides of their desks.

I had worried that we might grow tired of each other, but as the second year progressed, I found them even more fascinating. Their enthusiasm in their new curriculum never waned. As each unit of study was introduced, the children never failed to bring in relevent books and artifacts.

When Jessica told me that she felt nervous about third grade, I asked her what she felt most nervous about. Without a moment's hesitation she said, "Having a new teacher."

Each year, it's difficult to say goodbye to my class. This year will be the most difficult. As I put away the second grade materials and prepare to return to first grade, I find myself reflecting on how lucky I was to be able to hold on to my class for two years. Now, I'm able to say goodbye and let them go knowing that I have had some of my most rewarding teaching and learning experiences with these children. ⬇

"As I put away the second grade materials and prepare to return to first grade, I find myself reflecting on how lucky I was to be able to hold on to my class for two years."

Looping, the Two-Grade Cycle: A Good Starting Place

by Jim Grant and Bob Johnson

"In this novel approach to teaching, primary graders move ahead by staying right where they are . . . . A two-year span provides a child with greater continuity in experience, both socially and academically . . . . We've had numerous students come out of their shell in the second year because they feel confident about themselves and secure within the group." — Diana Mazzuchi and Nancy Brooks, "The Gift of Time," *Teaching K-8* (February 1992)

What Looping Is

Looping is sometimes called multiyear teaching or multiyear placement. It is a two-year placement for the teacher as well as the children. The children have the same teacher for two successive years. Looping involves a partnership of at least two teachers, who teach two different grade levels, but in alternate years.

For example, in the initial year, Teacher A teaches kindergarten and Teacher B teaches first grade. At the end of the year both Teacher A and the kindergarten children are "promoted" to first grade. Teacher A and her children are together for the second year, but this time as a first grade.

At the end of the second year, Teacher A's children move on to second grade, and the following fall, Teacher A will begin the cycle again with a new crop of kindergarteners.

Meanwhile, at the end of the first year, Teacher B's first graders move on to second grade, and at the beginning of the second year she welcomes a new class of kindergarteners. At the end of the second year Teacher B is "promoted" with her class to first grade and continues as their teacher for the next year.

In schools where kindergarten is half-day, only half of the kindergarteners will continue with the same teacher. The other half will have another first grade teacher. The half that stay in the loop could be either the morning group or the afternoon group. Or, they can be chosen by lot from among those whose parents indicated they would like them to stay with the same teacher.

Although our example is of kindergarten and first grade, looping will work with any two contiguous grades: first and second grade, second and third, third and fourth. It can be started with any two grades where two teachers are willing to get together and give it a try.

What Looping Is Not

Looping is not a multiage configuration. It does, however, open up an appealing window of opportunity for creating a continuous progress program. Over the two-year span, the teacher can see and take advantage of a child's development in a less fragmented, more natural way. In moving toward implementing a full multiage continuous progress program,

> *Over the two-year span, the teacher can see and take advantage of a child's development in a less fragmented, more natural way.*

looping offers teachers, parents, and administrators the chance to see, experience, and appreciate what can happen when a teacher and a child work together for more than one year.

What Looping Makes Possible

"My teacher" is an important person in a young child's life. For a lot of children today, their teacher is often the most stable, predictable adult in their lives. If "my teacher" waves goodbye at the end of 180 days, come September a whole new relationship with a brand new teacher has to be slowly established. Moving into a new grade can be a scary transition for children.

When "my teacher" is the same person for two years, there is stability that the child can build on. By the middle of the first year, the child knows what the teacher expects of him or her, knows what the rules are, knows what pleases *and* what annoys the teacher. Teacher and child have established a working relationship that the child can count on. As the child becomes comfortable in the relationship and begins to count on its stability, s/he can release the tension and energy that have gone into trying to understand the teacher.

It is a jump start from the teacher's point of view as well. It takes time to find out the interests, abilities, and learning styles of each student in the classroom. All aspects of classroom planning are affected by this knowledge. At the beginning of the second year the teacher already has in-depth information and can build on it. S/he knows who is shy, who is aggressive, who is an emergent reader, and who finds reading easy. A few reminders, some review, and both teacher and children are ready to pick up where they left off at the end of the last grade and move ahead.

Looping is effective and efficient. Teachers like being able to spread certain themes over a longer period of time. They report that, in the second year, children frequently mention activities and experiences from the previous year that relate to present activities. Teachers can help children carry over information and build on these connections. The two-year curriculum becomes woven together.

Looping's Effect on High-Stake Decisions

In the spring every teacher has to make high-stake decisions based on evaluation of what each child has accomplished during the year. Some children in the class are clearly ready for the next grade. One or two may have learning disabilities and been referred for special evaluation. But what of the others? Are they "late bloomers"? Do they just need a little more time — "cheddar cheese kids" who simply need to

age to be at their best? What about the borderline children? What should happen with a very verbal girl, for instance, who has mastered words but seems quite young developmentally in other ways? Looping reduces the stakes in decisions made at the end of the first year. There is the chance to keep watching and evaluating these children.

Looping allows teachers and administrators to move into a change that produces a minimum of fear, anxiety, and frustration, not only for children, but for parents and themselves.

At the end of the two-year loop, a child who is developmentally young and needs an extra year of time may be accommodated by moving laterally. S/he could remain in the same grade but with a different teacher in a different classroom.

Where there is the goal of including differently-abled children in the classroom, the stability and continuity of looping is very helpful. A two-year program can be somewhat more flexible than a rigid single grade where the curriculum tends to be very unforgiving to children who are differently-abled.

"Something Easy That Works Well"

Looping allows teachers and administrators to move into a change that produces a minimum of fear, anxiety, and frustration, not only for children, but for parents and themselves. It begins

with the concept of the teacher simply moving with the children up one grade. It involves a philosophical change but not a major school restructuring. It requires no new building or alterations in physical space. Most teachers don't need a great deal of retraining to begin looping.

Many teachers find this a very manageable change. It is a challenge, but it can be done. We have had several teachers tell us that it was particularly satisfying. Typical of these comments are:

"It was refreshing, re-energizing to be able to be doing something innovative that works so well."

"It made me reflect on my teaching and move in a new direction."

"Did I want the same children for two years? Could I create a seamless curriculum? I found out I both liked it and did it well."

"I wasn't so sure when I agreed to do this, because I never thought of myself as a very versatile person. But to my surprise, this brought out a side of me I didn't think I had."

Making a change that works tends to boost teachers' confidence and open them up to the possibilities that a multiage continuous progress classroom has to offer. Having experience teaching a two-cycle looping program, they know they can bond with a family of children and enjoy having them over a longer period of time. They have had experience in creating a semiseamless, integrated curriculum over two grade levels. They have proven to themselves that they can comfortably handle a multiyear program.

What Is Required to Make Looping Work

The first requirement is two teachers who want to try looping. Our advice to principals is to start with good teachers and give them the support they need. In practical terms, this translates into enough materials and enough time to plan and organize a two-year curriculum cycle, time to share day-to-day planning and, later on, their experience and problems. The looping partnership is one opportunity for teachers to collaborate. Though each teacher is in his or her own room, looping encourages ongoing collaboration and mutual support between teachers.

Communicating with parents can be particularly rewarding in a multiyear program. It takes some parents most of the year to become comfortable with a teacher. Multiyear teachers often find that parents who may have been standoffish in the first year will begin to participate in events the second year, volunteer in the classroom, or help in other ways.

Some Hazards of Looping

Every teacher we have ever worked with recalls times when a whole class was in trouble. We remember one class that we called "the year of the summer-born boys." The class was top-heavy with males, almost every one of whom was chronologically young. It was an exceptionally difficult, disjointed year. The individual children would not have been problems in themselves but having so many in the same class threw it out of balance.

If, by October or November, there are clear signs that a class is out of balance and is a difficult, disjointed group of children, plan to divide up the class in the second year. It does not help any children in such a class to keep them together for two years.

When possible, teachers should not feel required to keep a difficult child more than one year. However, a difficult child is often one who is particularly in need of the stability and continuity that a two-year looping program offers. There is no one right answer to this dilemma. This is one of those tough decisions!

There is also the occasional problem of the difficult parent who may be endured for one year but should not have to be endured for two.

In looping, the teacher may spot some borderline children who might or might not need referral for special services. There is some advantage in having more time to make these decisions. The down side of that is the risk of delaying referral for special services. A two-year delay could be disastrous for a child who really needs special services. Kindergarten teachers, particularly, need to bear this in mind.

From *A Common Sense Guide to Multiage Practices* by Jim Grant and Bob Johnson, published by Teachers' Publishing Group, Columbus, Ohio. Reprinted with permission.

Voices

"*H*old childhood in reverence, and do not be in any hurry to judge it for good or ill . . . . Give nature time to work before you take over her task, lest you interfere with her method . . . . A child ill taught is further from virtue than a child who has learned nothing.*"

— Jean Jacques Rousseau

Integrated Curriculum

Introduction

All teachers want children to become confident, competent learners. A competent learner understands the processes of learning: how to define a problem, find information needed to solve the problem, put ideas together in an organized way, and apply knowledge to new situations. The early childhood and elementary school years are when the foundation for life-long learning is established. Therefore, *how* teachers guide children's learning is as important as *what* children are learning.

The teacher's role as a guide in the learning process involves understanding how children learn and knowing what is age-appropriate and individually appropriate for each child. Classroom activities can then be planned so that children construct their own knowledge by actively investigating real problems, representing their growing understandings in a variety of ways, and reflecting on what they have learned.

Principles that Guide Teachers in Planning

Teachers constantly make decisions as they plan curriculum. Some decisions are made in advance and involve scheduling work times for various subjects or long-range planning for studies; other decisions are made on-the-spot as a "teachable moment" arises in the classroom. Whether the decisions are about teaching a specific skill, a new concept, or introducing a long-term study, you can most effectively guide children's learning if you apply the following four principles in your planning: (1) learning should be purposeful and relevant to children's lives; (2) meaningful learning is integrated; (3) communication is central to learning; and (4) learning takes time.

Learning Should Be Purposeful

Think of a time when someone was trying to teach you how to do something in which you had very little interest. Despite an energetic manner, what the person said probably went in one ear and out the other. In contrast, recall a time when you either wanted or had to know something and you eagerly sought the answer yourself. Perhaps you looked in a book, or struggled with the ideas until finally they made sense. Having a reason and desire to find something out increases our willingness to learn.

Children are more motivated to learn when they are challenged to solve real, interesting problems. When children pursue answers to questions of interest to them and apply their learning to something they care about, they are more likely to remember what they have learned than if they are taught skills out of context. As you think about the new skills and content you want to introduce, look for ways to build on children's interests and help them to see the relevance of what they are learning to everyday life.

Responding to Children's Interests

Children's personal observations and interpretations of an experience can be a marvelous stimulus for introducing new information. A teacher who takes advantage of a child's interests by encouraging further investigation helps that child clearly understand the purpose of the task.

After a ferry trip to a nearby island, Sherri, a second grader, asserts the theory that islands float in the water. Some of her classmates agree while others argue that this isn't so. Ms. Kallen asks them how they could find out and the children offer many suggestions. They form groups to test out their ideas. Sherri's group suggests using plasticine and a tub of water to test the theory that islands float. Repeated experiments lead to many sinking balls of plasticine. When finally the ball is big enough to stick out over the top of the water, Jeremiah points to the top and exclaims, "Is this part the island?" Following this, Ms. Kallen sets up other activities for the children to continue their explorations of land forms.

The teacher could have responded to Sherri's statement by giving her the information that islands do not float. Instead, Ms. Kallen builds on Sherri's curiosity about islands. She encourages exploration that can lead to answering Sherri's question and simultaneously captures the interests of other children. She allowed the children to construct their own understanding by encouraging them to generate and test their theories. It didn't take much encouragement because the children were investigating a topic of genuine interest to them. Because they made their own discoveries and came to their own conclusions, they are likely to retain what they learned.

Teaching Skills in Context

Most children are practical: when they learn something new, they want to use it. When children use newly learned skills in practical ways, they are more likely to remember them.

Committed to capturing the excitement he is feeling about a camping trip with his family, eight-year-old Brian makes several revisions to the rough draft of his story before deciding he is ready to "publish" it. In the final editing stages of his writing, Ms. Asche observes that his story contains lots of dialogue. She shows him how to use quotation marks and why they are important. Brian readily uses them because he wants to make his story perfect for publication.

Skills taught in isolation usually have little meaning for children. Skills taught in context—where children can immediately use what they learn—make sense to learners. When Ms. Asche told Brian that quotation marks help the reader know who is talking, she made the purpose of Brian's learning explicit. Giving a reason to learn a new skill that made sense to Brian motivated him to learn it.

Teachers can use moments such as the one with Brian to present new information to everyone in the class. Brian might share his writing with the class during story sharing (discussed in detail in the chapter on Language and Literacy), at which time Ms. Asche can point out to the class how Brian incorporated quotation marks into his story to make it clear to the reader who was talking. At first, she may use the term, "talking marks," until she is sure the children understand what a quote is. Using chart paper, she might write a part of Brian's story large enough for the entire class to see. In this way other children can learn from Brian's experience.

Meaningful Learning Is Integrated

Integrated curriculum means planning activities that enable children to gain knowledge and apply skills across many disciplines. Teachers have long recognized that children are more likely to learn and remember new skills and concepts when they use them in a meaningful context. Because children in any classroom are at different stages in the learning process, integrated learning experiences offer a wide range of possibilities so that all children may participate successfully.

An Integrated Approach Reflects Real Life Experiences

In our everyday lives we do not have experiences that are "math experiences" or "literacy experiences" or "social studies" experiences. We utilize a broad range of knowledge and skills from many disciplines. Shopping in the supermarket is an example of this process: we may select items to buy based on our knowledge of nutrition and good health; determine quantities to buy based on knowledge of weights, measures, and costs; move throughout the store guided by our understanding of categories of organization; and speak with store clerks using our language skills. Shopping is an "integrated experience;" we use skills and knowledge from many different disciplines to accomplish our goals.

Curriculum is naturally integrated. For example, language and literacy includes speaking, listening, reading, and writing. We teach these skills in an integrated way all the time. Children listen and speak as they discuss stories they have read and math problems they solved. In exploring who works in the community, or investigating the life cycle of a butterfly, children use speaking, listening, reading, and writing skills. Mathematical skills are used to answer science and social studies questions: "How many of the eggs in our incubator will hatch?" or, "What are the different jobs in our school and how many people do each job?"

Integrated learning experiences already take place in most classrooms. For example, after reading a story, a teacher may have children draw pictures or make puppets of the characters, create maps of the setting, write about a character, or create a sequel. In each of these choices, children use a range of skills. When curriculum is integrated, children can see connections between the skills they are learning and how to use them.

- To follow a recipe, children realize they have to measure and therefore need a measuring cup and a teaspoon.
- To send a letter to the senior citizen center arranging a visit, children appreciate the importance of writing neatly and using a business letter style.
- To build a model of the city, children measure, consider scale, draw a plan, and research what to include.

Organizing curriculum around real topics and problems enables children to make connections which are a critical part of learning.

Integrated Curriculum Facilitates Planning

Teachers often feel pressured because there is so much to teach and not enough time. Finding ways to integrate curriculum effectively addresses a range of curriculum objectives at once. In thinking about the possibilities for integrating your curriculum, ask yourself the following:

- Do children use math skills as they work on science or social studies projects? Could they?
- During math and science lessons, do children read, write, and discuss? Could they?
- Are children using dramatics and art to represent their interpretations of literature or what they are discussing in social studies? Could they?

Long-term studies are an effective way to integrate curriculum because a teacher can use them to teach skills, process, and content.

Communication Is Central to Learning

Communication—the exchange of knowledge, ideas, and opinions with others—reinforces children's understanding. As children investigate problems or topics of interest, teachers encourage them to talk about what they are learning. In doing so, children learn to value their own thinking as well as to respect the ideas and opinions of others. Effective communication is an important feature of a learning community.

Talking Clarifies Thinking

When children try to put their ideas into words to explain them to others, they must describe, explain, evaluate, and clarify their own thinking. Informal talking around learning tasks takes place in classrooms all the time.

> *Mei and Ben, two first graders, work together on a math problem. Mei, having just learned to count by tens, makes a suggestion: "Let's make stacks of ten, like this (pointing and counting) so we can count by tens." Because Mei attaches words to her thinking, Ben learns a new strategy for counting.*

A more formal way for children to talk with others takes place in meetings. Participating in group discussions promotes the development of critical thinking skills as children express their own thoughts and evaluate the thinking of others. For example, before a work time, several children talk about the model they are going to make. They discuss what size the people will be and therefore how tall the buildings should be, how many to include, the size of doors, and so on. In the process of describing it and making their building decisions, they organize and clarify their thinking and learn to make decisions as a group. Another example of how teachers encourage children to talk about their work is to call a meeting after a writing time so children can share their stories and ask for the questions and comments of their peers.

Just as children bring their individual learning styles to investigating and representing information, they also bring varied comfort levels and styles of speech. Some children readily speak in discussions while others prefer to listen. Some have learned how to engage in discussions at home while other children may have been taught not to express their opinions or ideas in a public setting. By offering options—working in pairs, small groups, one-on-one conferences, or group meetings—teachers demonstrate respect for children's individual preferences and learn more about what each child knows. Based on their observations, teachers can ask questions and offer information to extend children's thinking.

Open-Ended Questions Extend Thinking

Teachers use questions to find out what children know and to encourage children to reflect on their ideas. Depending on their goal, teachers ask one of two types of questions: closed and open-ended.

Closed questions have only one right answer. They simply tell us whether or not a child knows a fact: "How many sides does a triangle have?" or "What is the main idea of the story?" In closed questions, the teacher knows the answer and the child's response is either right or wrong.

Open-ended questions enable children to respond with many possible answers. Rather than asking how many sides the triangle has (a closed question), a teacher might ask, "What do you notice about this shape?" This way, the teacher will find out whether or not children know the number of sides of a triangle as well as their other thoughts and observations.

You can use open-ended questions and comments to help children:

- *label and organize their thinking:* "Tell me about how you estimated the number of jellybeans in the jar," or, "What would you like to happen to the character in your story?"

- *describe what they already know:* "What do you already know about the public library in our town?" or, "What do you know about caterpillars?"

- *anticipate and wonder about what they will see or do or what might happen:* "Let's think about what we might see when we visit the telephone company," or, "Based on the picture on the cover of this book, what do you predict this story will be about?" or "What will happen to each of these fruits if we slice them and leave them on the windowsill for the week-end?"

- *reflect on an experience:* "What did you see on our visit to the court house?" or, "Tell us about the part of the story that you remember," or, "Tell us more about how the machines worked at the bread factory."

- *think about possible ideas or solutions to problems:* "What jobs will we need in our classroom in order for it to remain clean and orderly?" or, "Let's make a list of the ways we can represent a favorite part of the story we just read," or, "Tell us how you solved the problem. That's a good approach. Can anyone think of another way?"

Listening to children's responses to open-ended questions and comments gives teachers vital assessment information and helps them plan appropriate next steps. For example, after asking children what they expect to see when they visit the harbor the next day, a teacher realizes from their responses that several children have not visited a harbor before and have no idea what to expect. She decides to read *Harbor* by Donald Crews, to prepare children for the upcoming trip.

As discussed in the first chapter on Knowing the Children You Teach, it is important to keep in mind that children react differently to different kinds of questions, depending on the experiences with questions they have had previously. Many teachers find that children not familiar with open-ended questions may be hesitant to respond because they wonder what answer the teacher really wants. With experience, these children will become more comfortable as they realize there are no "wrong answers" and the teacher is genuinely interested in their ideas. With open-ended questions, children have room to interpret the question their own way.

Learning Takes Time

Meaningful learning can't be rushed. It doesn't always fit into fifteen or thirty minute time slots. Frequently, the necessity of scheduling the day into brief time periods arises from pressures to "cover the curriculum" and manage the schedules of specialists and resource teachers. Many teachers complain about not having enough time and feeling pressured by scheduling demands. Scrambling from one activity to the next increases the level of stress in the classroom for everyone and is not conducive to learning.

Three ways teachers can allocate time for learning are: (1) scheduling extended work times each day so children can become involved in tasks; (2) recognizing the importance of giving children time to revisit concepts that have been taught; and (3) giving children time to think about and play with ideas.

Schedule Extended Work Times

Each day, try to schedule work times of at least 45 minutes to an hour so children get involved in an activity. Once or twice a week, it's beneficial to plan even longer periods for projects such as model making, murals, or working on skits. Combining subjects means you don't lose time making the transition from one work time to another.

This may sound impossible at first, but it can work if you adjust your schedule by rethinking time allocations. For example, if a work time will involve children in exploring more than one subject (e.g., math and science, or language and math), try allotting an hour for one activity rather than 30 minutes for two separate ones. (See the chapter on Structure for suggestions on planning the daily schedule.)

Children, like all of us, become frustrated when they are busy at work and we expect them to stop and quickly make a transition to the next activity. When you have no choice but to end a work time when the children are engrossed in what they are doing, it helps if you say something like, "I know it's really hard to stop what you are doing when you're so close to finishing. We just don't have a choice today. You can put your things on this tray and get back to work first thing tomorrow morning."

Encourage Children to Revisit Ideas and Concepts

Simply because you have presented a concept or skill to children does not mean that everyone will now understand and be able to use what you have taught. Some children may already know what you introduced; others will have varied levels of understanding. Like adults, children often need time to come back to an idea, to revisit it in other contexts, and to construct their own understanding.

> *During a discussion about birthdays, Ms. Wong talks with the children about their birthdays. Jenny says, "Tomorrow is my half-birthday." Several children ask her what she means. Ms. Wong asks the class if they know why Jenny says it is her "half-birthday." One of the children volunteers that there are 12 months in a year and 6 months in half a year. The children use the calendar to figure out when their half-birthdays occur. The following week in the midst of a math activity related to money, Ann-Marie says to Ms. Wong, "I just figured out that my quarter birthday is next week. I'm going to ask my parents to give me a quarter for my quarter birthday." Ms. Wong realizes that Ann-Marie has continued to mull over the discussion from the previous week. She applied what she learned to solve a problem of interest to her that relates to money, time, and fractions.*

This example provides insight into the importance of allowing children to stay with topics over time and to revisit them.

Give Children Time to Think

Group discussions highlight children's individual differences. In response to a question or statement, some children will immediately raise their hand, bursting to share their thoughts; other children will ponder the question or the concept presented, trying to assemble their thoughts before raising their hands. The eagerness of their classmates often interferes with their ability to think. As a result, they may lose their own train of thought and therefore the opportunity to contribute to the discussion.

Allowing children time to "think about their thinking" is a teaching technique that addresses children's individual learning styles and makes it possible for all children to participate equally. Here are some ways teachers can provide children with thinking time:

- After posing a question during a discussion, say "Take a minute to think of an idea. Don't say anything yet. Close your eyes and just think."

- Before inviting children to share their ideas in the group, invite them to share with a neighbor. "Turn to the person next to you and talk about what you are thinking."

- Model for children your own ways of taking time to think before talking. "That's an interesting question. Give me a minute to think about it. I have lots of ideas and I need to sort them out."

- Prior to sending children off to work after a meeting, check to see if anyone needs more time or help. If so, encourage those children to stay for a minute or two, to talk with each other or with you, until they feel sure and ready to get to work.

When you model the importance of slowing down to think, you reinforce the value of careful thought as part of the learning process.

In this section we have discussed the importance of making learning purposeful, integrating the curriculum, fostering communication, and providing ample time for learning. These four principles can be applied to planning learning experiences that enable children to construct their own knowledge.

Voices

Education has no higher purpose than preparing people to lead personally fulfilling and responsible lives. For its part, science education — meaning education in science, mathematics, and technology — should help students to develop the understandings and habits of mind they need to become compassionate human beings able to think for themselves and to face life head on. It should equip them also to participate thoughtfully with fellow citizens in building and protecting a society that is open, decent, and vital. America's future — its ability to create a truly just society, to sustain its economic vitality, and to remain secure in a world torn by hostilities — depends more than ever on the character and quality of the education that the nation provides for all of its children.

— From *Science for All Americans*, by F. James Rutherford and Andrew Ahlgren. New York, Oxford: Oxford University Press, 1990.

This article has been excerpted from *Constructing Curriculum for the Primary Grades* by Diane Trister Dodge, Judy R. Jablon, and Toni S. Bickart. © Teaching Strategies, Inc. Washington, D.C. 1994, pp. 139, 149-156. The book is available from Teaching Strategies by calling 1-800-637-3652.

Keith J. Topping

Cued spelling: A powerful technique for parent and peer tutoring

In this article Topping presents a new approach to spelling instruction that gives children greater control over their own learning.

Spelling is a curriculum area that is both neglected and controversial. Few teachers enjoy teaching spelling, and fewer children enjoy learning it. The range of strategies, materials, and methods available to teachers is probably smaller and less varied than in any other basic skills area. Yet government and employers continue to assert the importance of spelling.

There is less than full agreement about how specific spelling instruction should be integrated within whole language. From a visual orientation, work on word patterns and word clusters is often popular, but the strategies may not be retained and generalised to free writing. For other teachers, phonic strategies are the method of choice, yet less than half of the words in English are phonically regular. Moreover, the complexity of English means that a vast number of spelling rules and exceptions need to be remembered and applied.

Just as with learning to read, there are many different pathways to becoming a competent speller. Turner and Quinn (1986) found that younger children tend to rely on auditory information irrespective of the nature of the word, while for older children visual information produced better results. They concluded, "The learner must draw on several strategies...no single strategy can be used to overcome all irregularities in written English" (p. 239).

As with reading, overteaching in any specific, narrow instructional channel can do more harm than good, particularly when the type of instruction does not correspond to the child's strongest sensory modality and/or learning style. However, most teachers have no time to analyse the individual spelling profile of every child in the class and prescribe and manage a wide range of individual spelling programmes.

One possible solution is to help children manage their own learning. Teachers can adopt methods that free children to follow their own favoured pathways, yet provide a strongly supportive general framework. This can be done in an interactive way which involves children in evaluating the success of their own strategies. This is what cued spelling is all about. Cued spelling is a technique different from, but complementary to, regular teacher-directed classroom instruction in spelling.

Research background

Teaching styles that encourage children to work out effective learning strategies for themselves are increasingly favored (Pressley, 1990; Scheid, 1993). Scruggs and Laufenberg (1986) carried out a series of experiments on mnemonic strategies, which showed the importance of enhancing recall by representations that are meaningful to the individual. Such strategies were more effective in immediate and delayed recall of spellings than a direct instruction spelling programme (Veit, Scruggs, & Mastropieri, 1986). In a similar vein, Wong (1986) developed a successful self-monitoring strategy for children, while emphasising that they also needed to be taught specific information about words. Coupled with these trends is the growth in organising teaching and learning in cooperative, interactive ways (Slavin, 1990; Topping, 1988).

Intensive rote learning of high frequency commonly misspelt words is now out of favour. Prominence is currently given to relating instruction to developmental stages in children's spelling (Cummings, 1988; Gentry, 1982; Henderson, 1990; Henderson & Beers, 1980; Read, 1975; Templeton & Bear, 1992). Various spelling error analysis methods have been devised to help teachers determine students' levels of development (Gable, Hendrickson, & Meeks, 1988; Hepburn, 1991; Schlagel, 1989). Developmental spelling offers a valuable general framework, but the idiosyncratic needs, motivations, and style of the individual student must still be taken into account.

Approaches to spelling instruction based on words chosen by the child have been gaining in popularity. Research suggests that children's self-selected words are usually longer and more complex than those chosen by the teacher but are retained to at least the same degree (Michael, 1986). Similarly, Gettinger (1985) found that children with specific spelling problems made better progress when they were actively involved in a self-selected learning strategy than when similar routines were imposed by teachers.

Schunk (1987) stressed the motivational importance of students' setting their own learning goals. In the United Kingdom, Moseley (1987) reported a teaching approach

Photo by Robert Finken

involving child self-selection of spelling words. He noted that many existing spelling programmes suffered from three main weaknesses: (a) a lack of generalisation of skills from mere study of spelling patterns, (b) introduction of skills in teaching sequences based on opinion and average developmental sequences rather than analyses of children's actual errors, and (c) a lack of flexibility, so students found little interest or relevance in the tasks presented. Individualised self-managed learning could help to resolve these problems.

Cued spelling is a simple, straightforward, and easy to use procedure designed for two individuals working together. The pairs might be parent and child working at home or two children working together in school. In the latter case, the children can be of the same or different age and spelling competence.

Cued spelling: A powerful technique

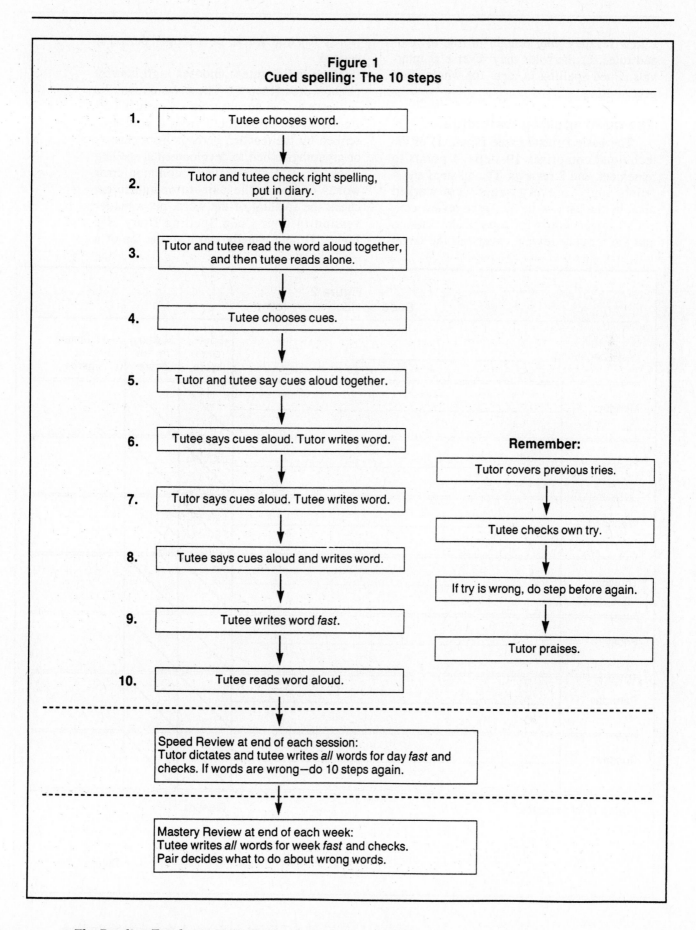

Figure 1
Cued spelling: The 10 steps

1. Tutee chooses word.

2. Tutor and tutee check right spelling, put in diary.

3. Tutor and tutee read the word aloud together, and then tutee reads alone.

4. Tutee chooses cues.

5. Tutor and tutee say cues aloud together.

6. Tutee says cues aloud. Tutor writes word.

7. Tutor says cues aloud. Tutee writes word.

8. Tutee says cues aloud and writes word.

9. Tutee writes word *fast*.

10. Tutee reads word aloud.

Remember:

Tutor covers previous tries.

Tutee checks own try.

If try is wrong, do step before again.

Tutor praises.

Speed Review at end of each session:
Tutor dictates and tutee writes *all* words for day *fast* and checks. If words are wrong—do 10 steps again.

Mastery Review at end of each week:
Tutee writes *all* words for week *fast* and checks.
Pair decides what to do about wrong words.

Likewise, they may remain in role as tutor and tutee, or the roles may reverse at intervals. Cued spelling is ideal for whole-class peer tutoring.

The cued spelling technique

The basic structure (see Figure 1) of the technique comprises 10 steps, 4 points to remember, and 2 reviews. The 10 steps and 4 points apply to every target word worked upon by the pair, while the speed review covers all target words for a particular session and the mastery review covers all the target words for one week, or a longer period if desired.

One child (tutee) chooses high interest target words (Step 1). These words may be collected by the student from a variety of curricular areas or selected from a pool prescribed by the teacher, perhaps from clusters or groupings allied to developmental spelling stages or of high frequency common error words or both. The pair, tutor and tutee, check the spelling of the word, put a master version in their Cued Spelling Diary (see Figure 2), and usually add it to the top of a

Figure 2
Cued spelling diary form

Week beginning: _____	Speed review score	Mastery review score	Comment or grade
Monday			
Tuesday			
Wednesday			
Thursday			
Friday			
Saturday			
Sunday			

Professional comment: Signed:

                                                          Date:

piece of paper on which subsequent attempts will be made (Step 2). The pair then reads the word out loud together and the tutee reads the word aloud alone, ensuring proper articulation (Step 3).

The tutee then chooses cues (prompts or reminders) to enable him or her to remember the written structure of the word (Step 4). These cues may be phonic sounds, letter names, syllables, or other fragments or chunks of words, or they may be quite idiosyncratic. Tutees are encouraged to consider and choose cues that fit well with their own cognitive structures (i.e., make sense and are memorable to them). Thus, although a parent or peer tutor might make suggestions or stimulate imagination, the decision on cueing rests wholly with the child. The nature of the chosen cues may sometimes reflect recent class spelling instruction, but if it does not, so be it. A handout elaborating cueing methods is reproduced in Figure 3.

Once cues are decided upon, the pair says the cues aloud simultaneously (Step 5). The tutee then says the cues aloud while the tutor writes the word on scrap paper to this dictation (Step 6). Thus the tutee is provided with a demonstration or model of the required behaviour. At Step 7, the tutor says the cues aloud while the tutee writes the word. At Step 8, the tutee says the cues and writes the word simultaneously.

At Step 9, the tutee writes the word as fast as possible (the tutee may or may not decide to recite the cues aloud at this step but may well recite them subvocally). At Step 10, the tutee again reads the word aloud as a reminder of the word as a meaningful whole.

The 4 points cover aspects of the technique relevant to its practical application. At every attempt at writing a target word, the tutor should ensure previous attempts on the work paper are covered in order to avoid the possibility of direct copying. Every time there is a written attempt on a target word, the tutee checks the attempt. The tutor only intervenes if the tutee proves unable to check his or her own attempt accurately in order to emphasize the importance of self-correction (Miller, 1987). If the tutee has written a word incorrectly, she or he should cross it out vigorously. When an attempt on a word is incorrect, the correction procedure is merely that the

pair return to the previous step. The tutor should praise the tutee's work at various junctures.

A speed review concludes each tutoring session. The tutor dictates all the target words for that session in random order and the tutee writes them as fast and accurately as possible. The tutee then self-checks all words with the master version in the Cued Spelling Diary. The 10 steps are applied again for incorrect words, perhaps with the choice of different cues. In fact, few errors are generally made at speed review, so the requirement to reapply the 10 steps is not as onerous as it may sound.

At the end of each week, the tutee writes all the target words for the whole week as fast and accurately as possible from dictation in random order. At this Mastery Review the pair negotiates for themselves what they wish to do about errors. Many pairs choose to include failed words in the next week's target words.

While the method may seem complex on first reading, 7-year-old children have been successfully trained in its use in about an hour. The technique has been designed and structured to be highly interactive. In operation it is democratic rather than didactic and provides a framework to scaffold self-managed learning.

Children do not have worries about cued spelling before they try it. They are always receptive to something new. Once they have tried it they may voice two main difficulties: finding words and finding cues. Promoting the collection of words is important. If the teacher chooses the difficulty level of the words, the most competent pairs may soon feel they can spell everything, and frustration can set in. All pairs will have difficulty finding effective and interesting cues for some words. Occasional whole-class sessions on cueing can be held for brainstorming effective cues and relating cueing to school spelling instruction. Good cues are effective in scaffolding retention of the chosen word in the long term and help the tutee develop predictive concepts about regularities in the English language. This may not be the same as how teacher would remember it.

Cued spelling should not, of course, be used in isolation; it is intended to be one possible strand in a multifaceted programme of

Figure 3
Cued spelling: Mnemonic strategies

Rules	Some spellings do follow logical rules (like "i before e, except after c," which most people remember). The learner may be helped by rules like this, but (a) make sure you've got them right, and (b) keep them simple and few in number.
Words in words	Just breaking words into bits like syllables helps us to remember them, but if you can break them into smaller words that mean something, it's even easier to remember them. Words like shep/herd, care/taker and water/fall are examples.
Fronts and backs	Many words have the same sort of start or finish. Starts and finishes can be looked at closely in a set of words that start or finish the same. Starts (e.g., *sta-*, *pre-*, *un-*) are often not as hard as finishes (e.g., *-tion*, *-ate*, *-ous*, *-ght*).
Families	Words that have the same start and finish can be put in groups or families. Sorting words into families can be a game. This can be done with words that have the same middles or other families or categories.
Make a picture	Making a picture in your mind about the word will help you remember it (like thinking up a picture of two people getting married [wed] on a Wednesday to remind you how to spell the name of that day). Some mind pictures or visual images will seem really silly, but this is good, because if they are funny you will remember them better.
Shrink and grow	You can remember a short hard bit of a word or just some initials for each part (e.g., *par* in separate). Often it helps to grow the initials into new words, to give you a saying or rhyme to remember. Like: - b / e / a / u / tiful big elephants aren't ugly n e c e s s ary one *collar* and two *socks*
Fix and stretch meaning	It helps if you really understand what those hard words mean. You might choose them because they seem interesting. Talking about meaning and use will make the word even more interesting and help fix it in your mind.
Funnies	Work jokes and other silly and comic things into what you do with cued spelling. Funny things are much more likely to be remembered.
Rhyme and rhythm	Rhyme is very good for helping you remember, like in "i before e, except after c." If finding a rhyme is too hard, try to get some rhythm into the mnemonic so it is easier to say. You could even try singing some of the words!
Highlight	We usually get only one bit of a hard word wrong. Try highlighting the hard bits with colours (green for easy bits, red for hard bits). Or like this: stationEry

Your must try these out to see what will work best for you. Different learners find different ways more helpful.

Cued spelling will not do much good if you don't get lots of practice with writing as well. To become a better speller, you need to practise writing, wherever you are.

This list may give you some ideas, but it's better if you think of your own ideas. You will have to remember your strategies quickly and easily when writing, so the ideas must be short and sweet. Remember—1. Keep it simple. 2. Do what's easy for you. 3. Find reasons to write.

spelling instruction. Its flexibility allows teachers to link it closely with other strands of the spelling programme. It does have advantages not necessarily shared by other forms of instruction.

Advantages

Cued spelling contains little that is new. It incorporates well known methods and aspects of accepted good practice. The assembly is as important as the components; it was designed as a coherent package, structured and flexible at the same time.

The technique is failure-free. Swift error correction and support procedures eliminate student anxiety and promote self-confidence. The technique is also very flexible; it is useful to students of a wide range of age and ability with word sets of infinite variety and complexity. Students are encouraged to self-select interesting and motivating individualised material; some both want and need to master quite specialised vocabulary. Addi-

tionally, students largely control the procedure, deciding themselves about the degree of support they require at any moment.

Modelling is included to give students an example of correct performance. Being left to work everything out by oneself often results in a high error rate, frequent correction, and considerable faulty learning.

The strong emphasis on understanding is essential for the task to be purposeful for the tutee. Tutees have individual attention and immediate feedback from their tutors, unlikely to be otherwise obtainable. With improved support, motivation, and concentration, students can work on a larger number of words than in more traditional approaches, increasing the amount of practice and learning.

The technique promotes fluency by eliminating stopping and starting and pondering at length about particular words. The steps in the technique are very small and incremental. A pair should be able to work through the steps reasonably quickly on all words.

Figure 4
Training for cued spelling

- Training is essential, and tutors and tutees are trained together in their pairs. Give a talk on the method and also a demonstration, preferably on video for ease of group viewing.

- Give pairs a 10 steps chart (see Figure 1) for reference . (You may also wish to use overheads.) Give cued spelling diaries (see Figure 2) to each pair. Each page includes space to write the master version of up to 10 words on all days of the week, boxes to record daily speed review and weekly mastery review scores, and spaces for comments from tutor (daily) and teacher (weekly).

- Use a chalkboard and solicit different words and different cueing strategies for each word. Make the point that there are many different cueing strategies and no right ones, only those effective and ineffective for the individual concerned. Have pairs practise directly with the tutee's own words (chosen before the meeting), using paper, pencils, and dictionaries you provide. Provide individualised feedback and further coaching as necessary.

- Ask each pair to use the technique on about five words per day (minimum time 15 minutes) for 3 days per week for the next 6 weeks. Let them do more if they like! Suggest that tutees create collecting books, so they always have a pool of suitable words from which to choose. Keep a watch on the words chosen for their long-term utility. A simple initial rule is three words for everyday use and two just for fun.

- If you use cued spelling in a reciprocal peer tutoring format where both members of the pair are of equal spelling ability, make sure that the master versions of words are checked in the dictionary and copied correctly into the CS Diary. In reciprocal tutoring, the fact that everyone gets to be a tutor is good for the self-esteem of both members of the pair. Of course, both end up learning their partner's words as well as their own.

- You might have a further class session on cueing, elaborating different approaches (see Figure 3). Encourage comparing and contrasting to help students perceive, relate, and map regularities. Check any creative adaptations a pair starts making to the method very carefully for effectiveness and mutual acceptability.

- Partners can be changed after a few weeks to increase novelty and widen the social effects of the tutoring.

Last, and perhaps most important, the technique is clear, straightforward, and enjoyable. Both tutor and tutee are easily trained in its use (see Figure 4).

Many of these advantages are in line with research on self-efficacy and motivated learning (Schunk, 1987). Regularity and frequency of success is as important as amount of success. Students with difficulties may over-attribute failure to their own inadequacy rather than to deficiencies in teaching. Students need to see that success is the result of their own efforts rather than an excess of support or random chance. Verbalisation by the student has been shown to facilitate strategic encoding and retention in learning. Regularity, frequency, and immediacy of feedback are particularly important when students are faced with very complex tasks or handicapped by learning disabilities.

Naturally, the method is not just intended to help children remember lists of words. As students create their own cues they must think about the auditory and visual structure of the word. It may well be that this self-directed interaction, rather than the cue itself, improves retention of the word. With experience and by making connections with taught spelling knowledge, students more readily perceive consistencies in word structures.

Cued spelling thus provides a framework within which students can make sense of spelling their *own* sense of it. Spelling is, of course, conceptual as well as perceptual, and students need to form predictive concepts about how words work. As the interactive procedures of cued spelling involve them in comparing and contrasting, they may organise and integrate these concepts for themselves more effectively.

There is a wide gulf between learning to write a word accurately during a tutoring session and being able to write it at a different time in a totally different context. The emphasis in cued spelling on speeded performance, drawn from the concept of fluency in precision teaching (Formentin & Csapo, 1980), promotes generalisation to other contexts.

Effectiveness

The initial reports on cued spelling were descriptive. Emerson (1988) used the technique with four parents who tutored their own children at home. Scoble (1988) described how an adult literacy student was tutored by his wife; he subsequently reported on the progress of 14 similar pairs (Scoble, 1989). All three reports noted excellent results at mastery review. Harrison (1989) described the extension of the method to peer tutoring between adult literacy students in a class situation.

The most popular application of cued spelling became peer tutoring. Oxley and Topping (1990) described how eight 7- and 8-year-old pupils were tutored by eight 9-year-old pupils in the same class in a small rural school. Striking social benefits were noted, and the children spontaneously generalised peer tutoring to other curricular areas. Subjective feedback from both tutors and tutees was very positive, and tutees' and tutors' self-concept as spellers showed a marked positive shift compared to nonparticipant children. Results on norm-referenced tests of spelling (the 1981 Diagnostic Spelling Test and the SPAR Reading and Spelling Test) were equivocal. Scores of both tutees and tutors were strikingly improved at posttest as were the scores of nonparticipant children.

Peer-tutored cued spelling in a classwide, same-age, same-ability, reciprocal tutoring format was reported by Brierley, Hutchinson, Topping, and Walker (1989). In all, seventy-five 9- and 10-year-old children in three classes participated. Tutor and tutee roles changed each week. All the children were trained in a single group meeting. Mastery Review scores averaged 80% and the average norm-referenced test gain was 0.65 years of spelling age after 6 weeks of participation. Subjective feedback from the children was very positive. Improved spelling self-concept was reported on a questionnaire by 84% of the children.

A study of parent-tutored cued spelling with 8-year-old mixed-ability children was carried out by France, Topping, and Revell (1993). On the norm-referenced test the 22 cued spellers gained at 2.8 times the rate of a comparison group of more able spellers. The children felt that cued spelling was easy to learn and improved their spelling.

Cued spelling: A powerful technique

Subsequent research (Oxley & Topping, 1970) looked increasingly at whether cued spelling resulted in generalised improvements in spelling beyond the specific words studied (i.e., whether students showed evidence of developing more effective predictive concepts about how English spelling was structured).

To control for the possible effects of extra attention and time on task, Watt and Topping (1993) compared cued spelling with traditional spelling homework (involving equal tutor attention and equal time on spelling tasks). They also compared parent- and peer-tutored cued spelling and assessed the generalisation of cued spelling effects to continuous free writing. Cued spellers gained over 2 months of spelling age per calendar month of cued spelling on the Graded Word Spelling Test, while the comparison group gained only half a month. Mastery Review scores averaged 93% correct. Parent and peer tutoring seemed equally effective. Improved spelling self-concept was reported on a questionnaire by 85% of the cued spellers, and 91% reported a higher rate of self-correction. Better self-correction was also reported by 88% of the parents and three of the four teachers. In samples of writing collected before and after the project, the average number of spelling errors per page reduced from 8.5 to 4.6 for the cued spellers and from 3.7 to 2.1 for the comparison children. Writing samples were also analysed for changes in writing style. On the categorical system employed, the cued spelling group averaged 1.7 specific improvements in free writing per child while the comparison group averaged 1.2.

Conclusion

Teachers sometimes worry about the cued spelling method before trying it out. They wonder if the method promotes mere memorization or supports spelling exclusively by cues. In practice, the children end up remembering the words but not usually the cues. As they become more familiar with the method, their cues become more systematic and reflective of the regularities in language as well as their own favoured learning style. Their powers of prediction of regularities in new words are certainly increased as has been demonstrated in previous research on cued spelling.

Learning to spell can be dreary, mechanical, and unmotivating, but it need not be. Spelling can also be absorbed in a learner-managed and socially interactive way that is enjoyable. Your can teach spelling by providing a high degree of supportive surface structure for students within which they generate self-directed individualised learning. Cued spelling is such a method. Cued spelling frees students to follow their own favoured pathways and evaluate the success of their metacognitive strategies on a word-by-word basis.

Author notes

The Paired Reading and Paired Learning Bulletins are available from ERIC (1985 ED285 124, 1986 ED 285 125, 1987 ED 285 126, 1988 ED 298 429, 1989 ED 313 656).

Topping directs school psychology training at the University of Dundee where he also specializes in parent and peer tutoring. He can be contacted at the Centre for Paired Learning, Department of Psychology, University of Dundee, Dundee, Scotland DD1 4HN.

References

Brierley, M., Hutchinson, P., Topping, K., & Walker, C. (1989). Reciprocal peer tutored Cued Spelling with ten year olds. *Paired Learning, 5*, 136-140.

Cummings, D. (1988). *American English spelling.* Baltimore, MD: Johns Hopkins University Press.

Emerson, P. (1988). Parent tutored Cued Spelling in a primary school. *Paired Reading Bulletin, 4*, 91-92.

Formentin, T., & Csapo, M. (1980). *Precision teaching.* Vancouver: Centre for Human Development and Research.

France, L., Topping, K., & Revell, K. (1993). Parent tutored Cued Spelling. *Support for Learning, 8*(1), 11-15.

Gable, R.A., Hendrickson, J.M., & Meeks, J.W. (1988). Assessing spelling errors of special needs students. *The Reading Teacher, 41*, 112-117.

Gentry, R. (1982). An analysis of developmental spelling in GYNS at Work. *The Reading Teacher, 36*, 192-200.

Gettinger, M. (1985). Effects of teacher-directed versus student-directed instruction and cues versus no cues for improving spelling. *Journal of Applied Behavior Analysis, 18*, 167-171.

Harrison, R. (1989). Cued Spelling in adult literacy in Kirklees, *Paired Learning, 5*, 141.

Henderson, E. (1990). *Teaching spelling.* Boston, MA: Houghton Mifflin.

Henderson, E., & Beers, J. (Eds.). (1980). *Developmental and cognitive aspects of learning to spell: A reflection of word knowledge*. Newark, DE: International Reading Association.

Hepburn, J. (1991). Spelling categories and strategies. *Reading*, 25(1), 33-37.

Michael, J. (1986). Self-selected spelling. *Academic Therapy*, 21, 557-563.

Miller, L. (1987). Spelling and handwriting. In J. Choate, T. Bennet, B. Enright, L. Miller, J. Poteet, & T. Rakes (Eds.), *Assessing and programming basic curriculum skills* (not paginated). Boston, MA: Allyn & Bacon.

Moseley, D. (1987). Words you want to learn. *British Journal of Special Education*, 14(2), 59-62.

Oxley, L., & Topping, K. (1990). Peer-tutored Cued Spelling with seven- to nine-year-olds. *British Educational Research Journal*, 16(1), 63-78.

Pressley, M. (1990). *Cognitive strategy instruction*. Cambridge, MA: Brookline.

Read, C. (1975). *Children's categories of speech sounds in English*. Urbana, IL: National Council of Teachers of English.

Scheid, K. (1993). *Helping students become strategic learners*. Cambridge, MA: Brookline.

Schlagel, R. (1989). Constancy and change in spelling development. *Reading Psychology*, 10, 207-229.

Schunk, D.H. (1987). Self-efficacy and motivated learning. In N. Hastings & J. Schwieso (Eds.), *New directions in educational psychology: Volume 2. Behaviour and motivation in the classroom* (pp. 233-252). Lewes, Sussex, UK: Falmer Press.

Scoble, J. (1988). Cued Spelling in adult literacy—A case study, *Paired Reading Bulletin*, 4, 93-96.

Scoble, J. (1989). Cued Spelling and paired reading in adult basic education in Ryedale, *Paired Learning*, 5, 57-62.

Scruggs, T.E. & Laufenberg, R. (1986). Transformational mnemonic strategies for retarded learners. *Education & Training of the Mentally Retarded*, 21(3), 165-173.

Slavin, R.E. (1990). *Co-operative learning: Theory, research and practice*. Englewood Cliffs, NJ: Prentice Hall.

Templeton, S., & Bear, D. (Eds). (1992). *Development of orthographic knowledge and the foundations of literacy*, Hillsdale, NJ: Lawrence Erlbaum.

Topping, K.J. (1988). The peer tutoring handbook: Promoting co-operative learning. London: Croom Helm; Cambridge, MA: Brookline.

Turner, I.F., & Quinn, E. (1986). Learning English spellings: Strategies employed by primary school boys. *Educational Psychology*, 6, 231-241.

Veit, D.T., Scruggs, T.E., & Mastropieri, M.A. (1986). Extended mnemonic instruction with learning disabled students. *Journal of Educational Psychology*, 78, 300-308.

Watt, J.M., & Topping, K.J. (1993). Cued Spelling: A comparative study of parent and peer tutoring. *Educational Psychology in Practice*, 9, 95-103.

Wong, B.Y.L. (1986). A cognitive approach to teaching spelling. *Exceptional Children*, 53(2), 169-173.

"Cued spelling: A powerful technique for parent and peer tutoring," Keith J. Topping, *The Reading Teacher*, February 1995. Reprinted with permission of Keith Topping and the International Reading Association.

Parent-Teacher Unity

I dreamed I stood in a studio and watched two sculptors there,
The clay they used was a young child's mind
And they fashioned it with care.
One was a teacher, the tools he used
Were books, and music and art.
One, a parent with a guiding hand
And a gentle loving heart.

For the things they had molded into the child
Could neither be sold nor bought.
And each agreed he would have failed
If he had worked alone.
For behind the parent stood the school
And behind the teacher, the home.

— Author Unknown

The Uses and Abuses *of* Invented Spelling

By REGIE ROUTMAN

Invented spelling does not mean "anything goes,"
says teacher, author, and nationally recognized expert
on whole language Regie Routman.
In this article, she shows how you can get the best
results from invented spelling in your own classroom.

Regie Routman models conferencing for third-grade teacher Dana Bulan. Regie prefers to write conference notes on Post-it notes, which she later gives to the student. This simple technique keeps the child's draft clean of teacher markings.

Invented spelling has gotten a bad name in many classrooms—mainly, I think, because of certain misconceptions surrounding its use. Too many well-intentioned teachers have been operating under the assumption that in a whole language classroom, they are not *allowed* to interfere with children's writing. As a result, students may be writing more and writing more often, but much of their work is illegible, sloppy, and filled with misspellings of basic words. Teachers are growing increasingly frustrated, while some parents have been left to wonder if we are teaching spelling at all. How did all this happen?

In the early stages of the whole language movement, as educators and parents were beginning to understand the developmental nature of all language learning, many believed that kids would learn to spell through immersion in reading and writing with lots of opportunities for practice and experimentation. As with reading, this approach worked fine for some kids—but not for all. Many students still needed strategies to be made explicit for them. When teachers didn't continually model reading and writing processes, provide lots of opportunities for guided practice, and help kids discover and notice features of words, some kids had trouble with reading and spelling despite the use of real literature and the writing process.

As I see it, invented spelling was never meant to be "anything goes." Its purpose was to free kids up to write. In a class of 25 to 30 students, children who are dependent on the teacher to spell every word correctly are unable to freely express themselves. Invented spelling (and with it, the teacher saying, "Do the best you can. That's fine for now. Spell it like it sounds.") allows

REGIE ROUTMAN *is a language arts resource teacher in the Shaker Heights, Ohio, City School District. She is the author of* Transitions: From Literature to Literacy *(Heinemann, Portsmouth, New Hampshire, 1988) and* Invitations: Changing as Teachers and Learners K-12 *(Heinemann, 1991).*

kids to concentrate on their messages without overconcern for correctness. That has allowed even kindergarten children to see themselves as writers early in the school year—and that's a wonderful thing.

But I also believe that we must hold kids accountable for basic standards so they can take pride in their work. Even in daily journal writing, we should have expectations such as legible handwriting, skipping every other line (at least for primary grade children), spelling high-frequency words correctly, and rereading to check for meaning, spelling, and punctuation.

When I am in a classroom in which writing looks a mess and the teacher accepts all invented spellings (even basic words), the students usually do not take writing seriously. The good news, of course, is that it doesn't have to be this way. It is possible to teach spelling and still remain true to the philosophy of whole language. The following strategies and ideas may help you rethink your use of invented spelling.

Use Core Word Lists

Invented spelling recognizes that learning to spell, like learning to talk, is developmental. Children are not expected to get it right immediately. Promotion of invented spelling recognizes and respects that language develops gradually and that learners need lots of time and practice to take risks, make mistakes, and do plenty of reading and writing.

At the same time, while it is unrealistic to expect a first grader to spell all words correctly, it is realistic to expect *some* words to be spelled correctly all

Yesterday we had a snowday. First I ant breakfast, then I got grest. We woched a movie called Annie. She was an orfine and the onwper said at the end I got your nomber you want to rombere. it was funny. And at the real real end some badguys said they were her parints. But the realey wert. And at the real real real end someone adoped her. And the badguys were put in

Typical journal writing from a first-grade class in which children write daily, expectations are high, and spelling strategies are taught in context of reading and writing.

It is possible to teach spelling and still remain true to the philosophy of whole language.

the time. Even most kindergarten children can be expected to spell a very small group of often-used words by the end of the school year (words such as *I, me, my,* and *to*). Older children should be inventing only new vocabulary words, uncommon words, and words we wouldn't expect them to be able to spell correctly

Regie saved all of her drafts of this article for INSTRUCTOR and brought them to school so kids could see the many stages that precede a published piece of writing.

at their age or grade level.

In the K–4 elementary building where I am based, teachers in grades 1–4 have worked together to develop core lists of words that we expect students to be able to spell by the time they leave each grade. We developed these core lists because we were concerned about children's misspellings of common words. The lists include words culled from our students' daily writing in addition to days of the week, months, the name of our school and city, and other common words such as *social studies, science, because, enough, through, two, too,* and *to.*

Many words are on more than one grade-level list. We make these core lists available to all parents and students.

Don't Accept Sloppy Drafts

I place the same expectations on children as writers that I place on myself as a writer. I would never expect a colleague to respond to my writing draft without first making sure it was in good form—and that includes legibility, standard spelling, and neatness. Out of respect for the reader, whom I want to focus on the content of the piece, I make sure the draft is easily readable. We should expect no less from our students.

That's one reason why I no longer use the term "sloppy copy" to refer to a draft. Some students have taken the term too literally and use "sloppy copy" as an invitation to turn in messy work with numerous misspellings.

I will not conference with a child until he or she has reread the paper and checked it for basic spelling and punctuation. Also, the paper must be legible, even in the first draft; that is, the writer must be able to read it easily, which brings me to the next strategy.

Make Conferences Count

Recently, I was in a third-grade classroom during writing workshop, modeling conferencing for the teacher. This teacher was exhausted by conferencing because she was assuming most of the responsibility for improving her students' writing. When Damien came up for his conference, I began as I always do. "How can I help you? What would you like out of this conference?"

"Spelling," he said without hesitation. "I want to work on my spelling." (His teacher had already told me he was the poorest writer in the classroom.)

Usually, in a first conference on a piece of writing, students want feedback on content. They might say something like, "I want to know if the beginning brings the reader in," or "I want to know if there are any confusing parts." But Damien was only interested in improving his spelling.

"Read me your piece," I said, while I wondered to myself how he could possibly read it. It was a mess—illegible, very few letters in many words, no punctuation. He began and stumbled along. When he came to the word *president,* he had written only *pt.*

"Damien," I said, "say the word *presi-*

dent slowly. What sound do you hear after the *p*? Good. That's right. Now what do you hear next? Say it slowly."

With continued modeling and questioning, Damien was able to write "prsdnt." Now we could both read it easily. I told Damien I would be glad to help him with his spelling, but first he needed to go back to his seat, reread, and make sure his spelling was his reasonable best and that he had punctuation at the end of his sentences. Even though he was a poor speller, not enough had been expected of him. He knew his teacher would correct his misspellings, so there was no need for him to put forth his best effort.

After the conference, his teacher was relieved. "I thought I had to do it all. It would have taken me 30 minutes to go through his piece, and then I wouldn't have seen any other students. I see that by placing the responsibility on Damien, I will be able to help him more effectively and have more time for other conferences."

Don't Be Afraid To Teach Spelling

While whole language teachers may choose not to teach spelling formally as a separate subject, they *do* teach spelling. They expect their students to spell high-frequency words correctly, to utilize reliable rules and patterns, and to apply spelling strategies in their daily writing. A classroom environment that encourages children to be good spellers provides:

◆ lots of opportunities to write and talk about words;

◆ lots of opportunities to read and talk about words;

◆ lots of spelling references for children (wall charts, personal dictionaries, other children to talk to, classroom dictionaries, print around the classroom, word walls, and so on);

◆ daily writing time, usually as part of writing workshop or journal writing;

◆ a posted core list of words that children and parents know must be spelled correctly;

◆ lots of mini-lessons to see word patterns, develop rules, notice unusual features of words (these lessons arise from what the teacher notices the children need);

◆ lots of playing around with language and noticing special features of words, for example, noticing and commenting on surprising letters found in a word; and

◆ opportunities to share and publish writing.

Underlying all of this is a teacher whose philosophy of how children learn to spell is consistent with the principles of language learning, and who takes the time to effectively communicate the research on learning to spell to parents.

Strive for Balance

Several years ago, most of the K–4 buildings in our school district used a common writing prompt in an attempt to get a handle on what constituted "good" writing across the grades. In an informal look at the invented spelling of students in grades 1–4, I noticed that by the beginning of fourth grade, almost all students were spelling a core of high-frequency words correctly. The message is clear: While students should use invented spelling freely during the primary years, we need to expect most words to be spelled correctly as they get older.

We need to strive for a balance. By over-attending to spelling, students may feel too constrained to write. But by accepting all spelling, even when we know the student can do better, we give the message that spelling is not important.

I believe that everything in writing matters. Of course, we want to emphasize content first, but spelling, handwriting, and general legibility are also important. We need to let our students and their parents know that and keep our expectations for students reasonable and high. Invented spelling is a marvelous tool, as long as we use it appropriately.

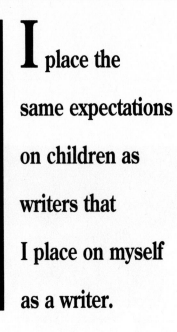

I place the same expectations on children as writers that I place on myself as a writer.

LOOK-COVER-WRITE-CHECK

1. Student **LOOKS** at word in middle column.

2. Student visualizes word in mind.

3. Student **COVERS** word by folding over right hand flap.

4. Student tries to **WRITE** the word from visual memory in left column.

5. Student **CHECKS** and corrects if necessary by looking at original word.

HAVE-A-GO

Jean Mann

Exploring Words

Word Blends
chortle
telethon
motel
brunch
bookmobile
electrocute
heliport
modem
moto-cross
splotch
smog
twiddle
twirl
sitcom

Acronyms
scuba
NASA
rem
radar
NATO
sonar
UNICEF

Abbreviations
ad
cafe
disco
gym
dorm
bag
burger
co-ed
demo
exam
fax
hippo
lab
math
photo
rad
ref
sax
ump
vet

Homophones
hour   our
air   heir
allowed   aloud
ate   eight
berry   bury
brake   break
creak   creek
blew   blue
cent   scent   sent
eye   I
to   two   too
its   it's
sun   son
tail   tale

Jean Mann

Semantic Spelling Activities

Flip Book

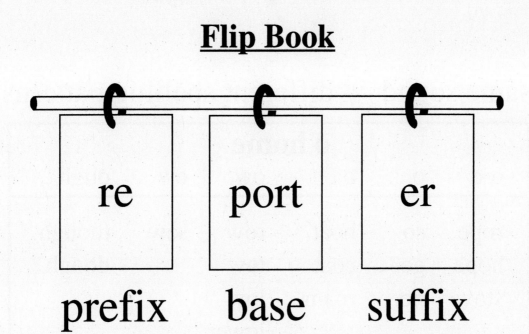

re   port   er

prefix   base   suffix

Word Web

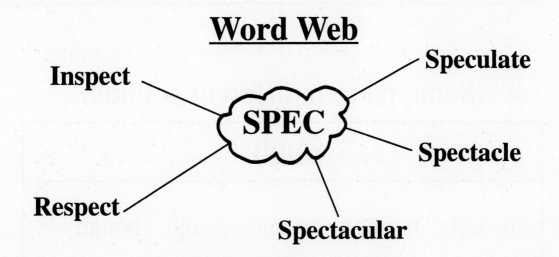

Inspect

Speculate

SPEC

Spectacle

Respect

Spectacular

Word Meanings

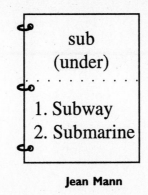

sub
(under)

1. Subway
2. Submarine

Jean Mann

Individual Spelling Books

(same sound — different spelling patterns)

ō home					
o-e	o	oa	ow	ew	ough
rope	so	boat	row	sew	though
hope	go	coat	tow		dough
stove	no	roam	low		
			lower		

(Same pattern different sounds)

ough
though   through   rough   cough   bough

Jean Mann

Word Banks / Wall Charts

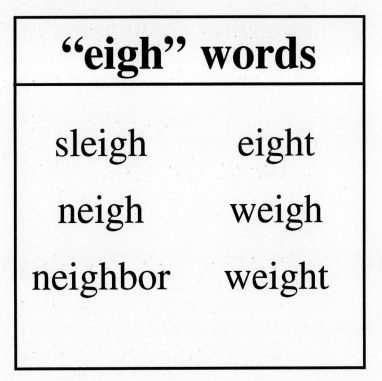

"eigh" words

sleigh	eight
neigh	weigh
neighbor	weight

Wall charts can be put together and made into a big book

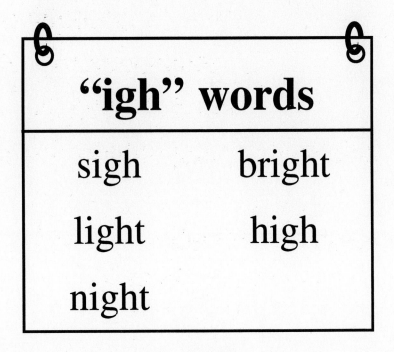

"igh" words

sigh	bright
light	high
night	

Jean Mann

Spelling

Pattern:
Goal

Mini-lesson:

Independent time:

Sharing:

Word list:

Activities:

Writing:

Jean Mann

Reading and Writing Workshop

Minilesson: Whole or small group together with teacher. (In beginning of year can be used to establish procedure.) Teacher-centered, orally-based group instruction where teacher models a lesson for a skill, strategy or convention. Provides a common frame of reference.

Independent time: Students have the opportunity to practice what was taught in the minilesson in the context of meaningful content, providing an immediate follow-up. Teacher has the chance to see how lesson is used by students and can plan for effective follow-up.

Sharing: Closure to reading or writing time. Coming back together as a group to talk, see how things went, discuss problems, and share what students did.

Jean Mann

Developmental Stages of Spelling

(Richard Gentry)

Pre-communicative:

Semi-phonetic:

Phonetic:

Transitional:

Conventional:

Developmental	Sight
back	the
sink	to
mail	it
dress	are
picking	they
lake	from
rice	words
peeked	were
stamp	said
light	which
seed	if
dragon	out
stick	so
side	like
feet	look
bed	see
gate	people
test	been
	now
	did

Jean Mann

DEVELOPMENTAL CHANGES IN SPELLING

PREPHONEMIC	EARLY PHONEMIC	PHONETIC	TRANSITIONAL	CONVENTIONAL
Random Letters Print Holds Message	"Practical Phonics" Letters Represent Sounds/Words Left to Right Direction Initial Consonants	Initial and Final Consonant Vowels A Place Holds	Initial, Medial, Final Sounds Visual Spellers Vowels in Every Syllable	Close to Standard Spelling
_____	_____	_____	_____	_____

DEVELOPMENTAL STAGES IN READING

PREREADER	BEGINNING READER	EMERGENT READER	DEVELOPING READER	INDEPENDENT READER
Story from Pictures Patterns	Retelling Word for Word	Retelling Some Word Recognition Uses Picture Cues Initial Consonants	Reading Simple Books	Reading More Challenging Books Chapter Books
_____	_____	_____	_____	_____

Adapted from Gentry, 1981; Graves, 1983; Temple, Nathan, Burris, Temple

Jean Mann

Developmental Ages and Stages

- 5's — Calm, Cool and Coordinated

- 5 ½'s — Wild and Wooly

- 6's — Teething, Teasing, Temper Tantrums, and Tattling

- 7's — Slow and Sensitive

- 8's — Fast and Sloppy

- 9's — Independent and Competitive

- 10's — Golden Age

Kathryn L. Cloonan

135

Stages of Reading Development

Stage 1

Displays an interest in handling books.
Listens to print read to him for extended periods of time.
Begins to notice print — signs, labels.
Letters may appear in her drawings.
Likes to "name" pictures.

Stage 2

Engages in reading-like activities.
"Reads" or reconstructs content of familiar stories.
Recognizes his name and some other words in environmental context.
Writing may show some letter/sound connection.
Can construct story meaning from pictures.
Cannot pick words out of print consistently.
Can do oral cloze activities.
Rhymes words.
Gives words orally that begin similarly.
Can recall key words.
Begins to internalize story grammer, i.e., "Once upon a time . . . "

Stage 3

Can write and read back her own writing.
Can pick out individual words and letters.
Can read familiar stories. Uses pictures as clues to print.
Words in one context may not be read in another.
Enjoys chants and choral reading.
Can match or pick out words of poems.

Independent Reading Stages

Stage 1

Excited about reading.
Wants to read to you often.
Can read words in new situations.
Reads aloud lots of environmental print.
May focus too much on letters and sounds.
Oral reading may be word-centered rather than meaning-centered.

Stage 2

Understands author's meaning.
Enjoys reading to himself for pleasure.
Reads orally with meaning and expression.
Reads in word-meaning clusters.
Has internalized several genres.
Brings her own experiences to print.

Stage 3

Processes material further removed from his own experiences.
Can use a variety of print forms for pleasure.
Can discuss various aspects of a story.
Can read at varying and appropriate rates.
Can focus on or use varying forms of genre and print.

Adaptation from Whole Language Evaluation for Classrooms. © 1992 Orin & Donna Cochrane.

Kathryn L. Cloonan

Components of a Balanced Literacy Curriculum

Reading to Children

Language Experience

Shared Reading

Guided Reading

Independent Reading

Writing

Sharing Responses

Kathryn L. Cloonan

Daily Schedule

8:50 Welcome

"Base Groups" — Getting Organized
Teacher — attendance / lunch money, etc.
Managers — Book check, snack table
Independent Writing / Independent Study

9:20 Morning Meeting

9:35 Super Readers

9:45 Literature Block   **Writer's Workshop**

Shared Reading   mini-lesson
                                              writers' write
                                              teacher conferencing

10:15 Guided Writing

10:30 Recess

10:45 Language Arts Block

Small Group Instruction   Morning Centers   Literature
Interest or needs or skills   Buddy Reading   Extension

11:45 Story / Songs / Book Talk

12:00 Lunch / Recess

12:30 Read Aloud

12:45 Math   **Math Centers**

                                             and small group instruction

1:15 Thematic Study   Science / Social Studies

2:00 Art / Music / P.E.

2:30 Open Centers

3:00 Clean Up / Songs / Story / Discuss the Day

3:20

Kathryn L. Cloonan

WHOLE LANGUAGE — THE COMPLETE CYCLE

By Kathryn L. Cloonan

WHOLE LANGUAGE STEPS

1. **Share a piece of literature . . .**
   Story — oral as well as written
   Song
   Flip Chart
   String Story
   Big Book
   Flannel Board Story
   Student Made Book

2. **Personalize It**   **READ IT!**

3. **Put It Into Print**   **READ IT!**

4. **Model It**   **READ IT!**

5. **Make a Big Book**   **READ IT!**

6. **Expand It — Recreate It**
   Mini Books
   Puppets
   Bulletin Board Stories
   Mobiles
   Wall Stories
   Overhead Transparency Stories
   Tutorette Stories
   Masks, Plays, Etc.
   Innovations

7. **Make the Writing Connection**
   Slot Stories
   Signs
   Posters
   Letters to a Character in the Story
   Letter to the Author
   "News" Article
   Adding Another Chapter
      Different Ending, etc.
   Writing Their Own Stories

Kathryn L. Cloonan

Concepts of Print

1. Displays book handling skills
2. Can tell letters from words
3. Has left to right directionality
4. Has some letter / sound connection
5. Knows where to start on a page
6. Can do one-to-one matching

Reading Strategies

1. **Semantic — meaning**
   Illustrations
   Prior knowledge
   Context of the sentence

2. **Syntactic — the structure of our language**

3. **Graphophonics — phonics**
   Letter / sound connections
   Rhyming words

Supportive Features of Text

Emergent Reading Materials

1. Consistent placement of text
2. Illustrations clearly match text
3. Simple vocabulary using children's natural language
4. Rhythm, rhyme, and repetition
5. Text parallels developmental stages of writing

Early Reading Materials

1. Longer sentence length
2. Book language
3. Variety of genres
4. Pictures enhance but do not consistently match text
5. Less repetition

Fluent Reading Materials

1. Short chapters
2. Increased variety of genres
3. Encourage integrating / utilizing many strategies
4. Encourage development of reading interests
5. Move the reader toward greater independence

Kathryn L. Cloonan

Julie's Picture

Julie painted a picture.

paints
She painted a face.

She painted eyes.

mouth
She painted a big smile.

like
She painted long hair.

Julie looked at her picture.

painting
It was a picture of her mom!

Julie took the picture home
after school.

That
"This is for you, Mom," said Julie.

"It's me!" said Mom. "Thank you, Julie!"

Kathryn L. Cloonan

141

DIFFERENT KINDS OF WRITING

Shared Writing

- Model Writing

- Daily News

- Morning Mystery Message

- Language Experience

- Labelling / Captioning

Children's Writing

- Guided Writing
  — Closed & Open-ended Guided Writing
  — Structure Writing
  — Content Writing

- Independent Writing
  — Book Publishing
  — Authors' Tea

Benefits	Process	Purpose

Writing

Encourages self-expression

Makes letter-sound connections

Builds fluency in ideas

Getting great ideas down on paper

Conference I

Makes the connection between their ideas and the printed word

Supports inventive spelling /corrective spelling

Communicating ideas

Learning new skills in
- phonics
- decoding skills
- grammar
- spelling
- punctuation
- sight words

Conference II

Builds self-confidence by acceptance

Enhances creativity

Increases communication skills through making choices and decisions

Creating, planning, and expressing ideas for a finished product

Publishing

Encourages further efforts

Builds self-respect and self-concept

Modeling correct spelling, punctuation, sentence formation, and publishing

Illustrating

Builds the connection between print and ideas

Encourages sight vocabulary

Increasing comprehension

Encouraging creativity

Reading

Builds sight vocabulary

Enhances decoding strategies

Builds reading fluency

Encourages a love for reading and writing

Building sight vocabulary

Decoding through meaningful context and phonetic clues

Celebrating

Celebrating with an Authors' Tea

Encourages a love for reading and writing

Enhances acceptance of others

Increases awareness of "presenting" to others

Enriches sight vocabulary

Builds a collection of readable materials

Encourages learning more about a subject

Builds self-confidence

Enriches organizational and planning skills

Models respect and love for literature

Gives *all* children an arena for success

Offers a completed reading and writing cycle that is relevant to children

Kathryn L. Cloonan

AUTHOR'S PLANNING PAGE

Name:_____

Title:_____

Dedicated to:_____

Because:_____

About - Me - The Author:_____

_____

_____

I would like my book:

    Handwritten

    or   _____

    Typed   _____

I would like the words this size:

VERY LARGE   LARGE   SMALL

I would like the color of the cover to be:_____

1. I have chosen my paper: _____

2. I have talked with my Publisher:_____

3. I have a picture of me: _____

4. I have done my illustrations:_____

5. My book is all put together:_____

I DID IT!!!

Kathryn L. Cloonan

144

Especially Honoring

Author of

Autograph

Especially Honoring

Author of

Autograph

Kathryn L. Cloonan

Success

Modeling   **Matching**

Confidence
Interest
Motivation

READING FOR MEANING
Comprehension and Achievement

I. Strategies

Understanding the author / editor's plan
Inferring from illustrations
Personalizing
Summing up information
Selective underlining / highlighting
Recording information
Presenting facts

II. Structures

Two column notes

Main idea — supporting details
Fact — proof
Opinion — proof
Fact — fiction
Problem — solution

Literature Matrix

Content Matrix

Graphic Organizers

Semantic mapping
Venn diagrams
Literature sociograms
Story grammars

Paragraph forms

III. Skills

Comprehension and Achievement
SUCCESS

Kathryn L. Cloonan

146

Steps in a Literature Block
for Intermediate Grades

1. Set up / Background / Semantic Mapping

2. Share a Piece of Literature
A. Whole Group
B. Book groups / Buddy reading / Individual reading
C. Author's Study
D. Thematic Units
E. Historical Collections

3. Personalize it
Retell chapter / segment in their own words and illustrate
   or
Select a favorite section

4. Put it into print
A. Overhead
B. Chart
C. Individual sheets

5. Expand it — Recreate it
Individual copies, talking books, group book
Video reports, advertisements
Slide stories, bulletin board stories
Readers' theatre, dramatizations, plays, masks

6. Making a Writing Connection
A. Response log, story journal
B. Adding another chapter, different ending
C. Writing and publishing their own stories

Kathryn L. Cloonan

Progressive Approximation Form

MOVING TOWARD STANDARD SPELLING

STUDENT NAME _____   ROOM_____

	TEXT	1st		2nd		3rd		4th	
1.									
2.									
3.									
4.									
5.									
6.									
7.									
8.									
9.									
10.									

KEY TO SYMBOLS: + = moving toward standard spelling
                    N = no change
                    − = moving away from standard spelling

Adaptation from *Whole Language Evaluation for Classrooms.*© 1992 Orin and Donna Cochrane.

Kathryn L. Cloonan

SING ME A STORY — READ ME A SONG

INTEGRATING MUSIC INTO THE WHOLE LANGUAGE CLASSROOM
By Kathryn L. Cloonan

PURPOSE

1. Instill a love for reading and music.
2. Make use of simple, delightful materials that have rhythm, rhyme, repetition.
3. To give children early successes in reading.
4. Give children an opportunity to make the connection between print and what they say and sing.
5. Build sight vocabulary by frequently seeing words in meaningful, predictable context.
6. Enrich decoding/reading skills through meaningful print.

STEPS

SHARE IT — Sing Lots of Songs Often
PRINT IT — Print a Favorite on Chart Paper
ILLUSTRATE IT — Make a Big Book, Make Mini Books
READ IT — Let the Children Read It

RESOURCES

Record and Tapes
Sing Me a Story, Read Me A Song, Kathryn Cloonan
Whole Language Holidays — Stories, Chants and Songs, Kathryn Cloonan
Peter, Paul and Mommy, Peter, Paul and Mary
Elephant Show Record, Sharon, Lois and Bram
Special Delivery, Fred Penner
The Cat Came Back, Fred Penner
Learning Basic Skills Through Music, Hap Palmer
We All Live Together, Volumes 1, 2, 3 & 4, Greg Scelse and Steve Millang
Doing the Dinosaur Rock, Diane Butchelor
You'll Sing a Song and I'll Sing a Song, Ella Jenkins
Singable Songs for the Very Young, Raffi
More Singable Songs for the Very Young, Raffi

Resource Books
Sing Me a Story, Read Me a Song, Book I, Kathryn Cloonan. Rhythm & Reading Resources, 1991.
Sing Me a Story, Read Me a Song, Book II, Kathryn Cloonan, 1991.
Whole Language Holidays, Books I and II, Kathryn Cloonan. Rhythm & Reading Resources.

SONGS

WE HAVE A FRIEND
We have a friend and
her name is Amy
Amy is her name
Hello, Amy-Hello, Amy
Hello, Amy
We're so glad you're here.
Innovation:
 Change names of children

TWINKLE TWINKLE LITTLE STAR
Twinkle, twinkle little star
How I wonder what you are.
Up above the world so high.
Like a diamond in the sky.
Twinkle, twinkle little star
How I wonder what you are.

HICKORY, DICKORY DOCK
Hickory, Dickory Dock
The mouse ran up the clock
The clock struck one
The mouse ran down
Hickory, Dickory Dock
Innovations:
 The clock struck 2, 3, 4, etc.

BAA, BAA, BLACK SHEEP
Baa, Baa Black Sheep
Have you any wool?
Yes sir, yes sir three bags full.

One for my master
One for the dame
One for the little boy
that lives down the lane.

Baa, Baa, Black Sheep
Have you any wool?
Yes sir, yes sir three bags full.
Innovation:
 Color Words
 Baa, Baa, Purple sheep, etc.

BINGO
There was a farmer
Had a dog and Bingo was his name-o.
B I N G O
B I N G O
B I N G O
And Bingo was his name-o.

ON A SPIDER'S WEB
One elephant went out to play
On a spider's web one day.
He had such enormous fun
He asked another elephant to come.

Two elephants went out to play
On a spider's web one day.
They had such enormous fun
They asked another elephant to come.

Three elephants, four elephants,
Five elephants, six elephants,
Seven elephants, eight elephants,
Nine elephants................

Ten elephants went out to play
They had such enormous fun
They asked everyone to come.
Innovations: Change with theme or holidays — black cat, Christmas elf, leprechaun, dinosaur, Panda bear, etc.

FIVE SPECKLED FROGS
Five green and speckled frogs
Sat on a speckled log
Eating the most delicious bugs.
 YUM! YUM!
One jumped into the pool
where it was nice and cool
Then there were four green speckled frogs.
Four...etc., Three...etc.,
Two...etc., One...etc.
Then there were NO green speckled frogs.

HOLIDAY SONGS

TRICK OR TREAT

They'll be Trick or Treating here on
  Halloween, **Trick or Treat!**
They'll be Trick or Treating here on
  Halloween, **Trick or Treat!**
They'll be Trick or Treating here,
They'll be Trick or Treating here,
They'll be Trick or Treating here on
  Halloween, **Trick or Treat!**

2. They'll be knocking at our doors on
   Halloween, **Knock! Knock!**
3. Ghosts will all go "Boo!" on Halloween, **Booooooooo!**
4. Black cats all meow on Halloween,
   Meeeeeeeeeeow!
5. We will all have fun on Halloween,
   Hurray!

ONCE I HAD A PUMPKIN

Once I had a pumpkin, a pumpkin, a
  pumpkin
Once I had a pumpkin with no face at all.
With no eyes and no nose and no mouth
  and no teeth.
Once I had a pumpkin with no face at all.

Then I made a Jack-o-Lantern, Jack-o-
  Lantern, Jack-o-Lantern.
Then I made a Jack-o-Lantern . . . with
  a big funny face.
With big eyes and a big nose and a big
  mouth and big teeth.
Then I made a Jack-o-Lantern . . . with
  a big funny face.

DOG HAIR STEW
© 1991 Kathryn L. Cloonan

Ten black cats were left by themselves
on Halloween night with nothing to do.
So they decided to make their own
Dog Hair Stew.

First they got a very large pot
And filled it with water that was
  extremely hot.
Their goal was to make a horrible brew
More horrible even, than last year's stew.

Cat #1 flicked his tail in a wave
And said, "Here's some slime from a
  nearby cave."
"And here's some juice from a
  skunkweed plant."
Said Cat #2 as he joined in the chant.

Cat #3 said, "Heh, Heh, wait till you see
  what I brought.
The eyes of two dead fish I finally got!"
"Let me add some bat liver oil,"
  meowed Cat #4,
A skinny cat named "Skin and Bones."

Cat #5 said, "Here's a couple of frogs
  and a snake.
This is my very favorite stew to make."
One by one the cats came by
Adding secret ingredients with a meow
  and a cry.

The oldest cat carefully stirred it round
  and round
While the fire crackled with an ominous
  sound.
The 10th cat hissed with eyes aglow,
"Here's the hair of a dog so stir it in
  slow."

Now the cats they pranced and danced
  around their Dog Hair Stew
Then drank every drop of their mysterious brew.
Then all at once the cats gave a very
  loud wail
And their hair stood up straight from
  their head to their tail.

"Happy spooky Halloween!", they said
  with a wink,
"Dog Hair Stew is our favorite drink!"
And for the rest of the year
They had nothing to fear . . .

For each time a dog was seen,
Their hair stood up straight and they
  looked so mean
Not a dog would dare
give them a scare.

And the cats would wink an eye and
  say,
A little Dog Hair Stew on Halloween
  day
Keeps even the meanest dogs away.

SCAT THE CAT
I'm Scat the Cat
I'm sassy and fat
And I can change my colors
Just like that! (Snap)

THIS IS THE CANDLE
This is the candle
This is the candle
That glowed in the jack-o-lantern.

This is the mouse
That lit the candle
That glowed in the jack-o-lantern.

This is the cat
That chased the mouse
That lit the candle
That glowed in the jack-o-lantern.

This is the ghost
That said "BOO!" to the cat
That chased the mouse
That lit the candle
That glowed in the jack-o-lantern.

This is the moon
That shown on the ghost
That said "BOO!" to the cat
That chased the mouse
That lit the candle
That glowed in the jack-o-lantern.
That shouted **"Happy Halloween!"**

ONE LITTLE SKELETON
One little skeleton, hopping up and
  down
One little skeleton, hopping up and
  down
One little skeleton, hopping up and
  down
For this is Halloween!

2. Two little bats, flying through the air.
3. Three little pumpkins, walking in a
   row.
4. Four little goblins, skipping down
   the street.♪
5. Five little ghosties, popping in and out.

FIVE LITTLE PUMPKINS
Five little pumpkins sitting on a gate.
The first one said, "My, it's getting late!"
The second one said, "There are bats in
  the air".
The third one said, "I don't care!"
The fourth one said, "Let's run, let's run."
The fifth one said, "Halloween is fun!"
OOOOOOOOOOOO went the wind.
Clap out went the lights.
And five little pumpkins rolled out of
  sight.

BRAVE LITTLE PILGRIM
The brave little Pilgrim went looking for
  a bear.
He looked in the woods and everywhere.
The brave little Pilgrim found a big bear.
He ran like a rabbit! Oh! what a scare!

FIVE FAT TURKEYS
Five fat turkeys are we.
We slept all night in a tree
When the cook came around
We couldn't be found

Let's fly to the tallest tree
There we'll be safe as safe can be.
From the cook and the oven you see
It surely pays on Thanksgiving days
To sleep in the tallest trees!!

Kathryn L. Cloonan

SING ME A STORY — READ ME A SONG
INTEGRATING MUSIC INTO THE WHOLE LANGUAGE CLASSROOM
by Kathryn L. Cloonan

✦ **GOOD MORNING!**
Leader: Good Morning!
Group: Good Morning!
Leader: How are you?
Group: How are you?
Leader: It's so nice to see you again.
With a one and a two and how-do-you-do. DING-DONG
It's so nice to see you again.

Leader: Here's _____.
Group: Hi _____.
Leader: Here's _____.
Group: Hi _____.
Leader: Here's _____.
Group: Hi _____.
Leader: Here's _____.
Group: Hi _____.

All Together: It's so nice to see you again.
With a one and a two and how-do-you-do. DING-DONG
It's so nice to see you again.

Leader: Here's _____.
Group: Hi _____.
Leader: Here's _____.
Group: Hi _____.
Leader: Here's _____.
Group: Hi _____.
Leader: Here's _____.
Group: Hi _____.

All Together: It's so nice to see you again.
With a one and a two and how-do-you-do. DING-DONG
It's so nice to see you again.
It's so nice to see you again.

* **WE HAVE A FRIEND**
We have a friend and
her name is Amy.
Amy is her name
Hello, Amy – Hello, Amy
Hello Amy
We're so glad you're here
Innovation:
  Change names of child

* **I'M BEING SWALLOWED BY A BOA CONSTRICTOR (Silverstein)**
I'm being swallowed by a boa constrictor
I'm being swallowed by a boa constrictor
I'm being swallowed by a boa constrictor
And I don't like it very much.

Oh no! Oh no! He's up to my toe
He's up to my toe. Oh gee! Oh gee!
He's up to my knee, he's up to my knee
On fiddle! Oh fiddle! He's up to my middle
He's up to my middle. Oh heck! Oh heck!
He's up to my neck, he's up to my neck
Oh dread! Oh dread! He's up to my _____ slurp!

* **TEN IN THE BED**
There were ten in the bed
And the little one said,
"Roll over, roll over"
So they all rolled over and one fell out
And they gave a little scream
And they gave a little shout

Please remember to tie a knot in your pajamas
Single beds were only made for
1,2,3,4,5,6,7,8,
Nine in the bed etc.
Eight etc., Seven etc.
Six-five-four-three-two . . . etc.
One in the bed and the little one said,
"I've got the whole mattress to myself"
(repeat last line three more times)
GOOD-NIGHT!

* **MICHAEL FINNAGIN**
There once was a man named Michael
  Finnagin
He had whiskers on his chin-again
The wind came along and blew them in-
  again
Poor old Michael Finnagin . . . begin-again.

There once was a man named Michael
  Finnagin
He went fishing with a pin-again
Caught a whale that pulled him in-again
Poor old Michael Finnagin . . . begin-again.

There once was a man named Michael
  Finnagin
He was fat and then grew thin-again
Ate so much he had to begin again
Poor old Michael Finnagin . . . begin-again.

* **LITTLE COTTAGE IN THE WOODS**
"Little cottage in the woods" (Touch fingertips of both hands together to form a triangle
shape for the house.) "Little man by the
window stood." (Form "glasses" shapes
with forefinger and thumb of each hand
making a circle — put hands up to eyes in
that shape, against face.) "Saw a rabbit hopping by" (Make rabbit "ears" by two fingers
held up on one hand and "hop" them
about.) "Frightened as could be." (Arms
held crossed across chest, "shake" in mock
fear.) "Help me, help me, help me," he said.
(Raise arms overhead and down several
times.) "Before the hunter shoots me dead."
(Form "guns" with forefingers and "shoot.")
"Come, little rabbit, come inside." (Beckon
with hand.) "And happy we will be."
(Stroke the back of one hand with the other
as though tenderly petting a rabbit.)

* *Sing Me A Story, Read Me A Song*, Kathryn Cloonan

✦ *Sing That Again*, Kathryn Cloonan

Kathryn L. Cloonan

"Sing That Again"

HEY THERE NEIGHBOR!
Hey there, neighbor!
What do you say?
It's going to be a wonderful day!
Clap your hands and boogie on down.
Give 'em a bump and pass it around!
> (or sit on down)

HI! MY NAME IS JOE!
Hi! My name is Joe and I work in the button
   (doughnut) factory.
I have a wife, a dog, and a family!
One day my boss came to me and said,
"Hey Joe, are you busy?"
I said, "No."
He said, "Well, then work with your right hand."
   • Repeat each time adding one more body part: left
     hand, right foot, left foot, head
   Last line, last time:
I said, "YES!!!"

TONY CHESTNUT
Toe knee chestnut
Nose eye love you.
Toe knee nose.
Toe knee nose.
Toe knee chestnut nose I love you . . .
That's what toe knee nose.

HI DE HAY! HI DEE HO!
Leader: *Hi dee hay! Hi dee ho!*
Group: **Hi dee hay! Hi dee ho!**
Leader: *Igglee wigglee wogglee wo!*
Group: **Igglee wigglee wogglee wo!**
Leader: *Raise your voices to the sky.*
Group: **Raise your voices to the sky.**
Leader: *Mrs. ____'s class is walking by*
Group: **Mrs. _____'s class is walking by.**
Leader: *Count off!*
Group: **1, 2, 3, 4, 5**
Leader: *Break it on down now!*
Group: **6, 7, 8, 9, 10 . . .**
Leader: *Let's do it all once again!*

RISE RUBY RISE!
Down in the valley two by two.
Down in the valley two by two.
Down in the valley two by two.
Rise Ruby Rise!

2nd verse:
We can do it your way two by two.
We can do it your way two by two.
We can do it your way two by two.
Rise Ruby Rise!

3rd verse:
We can do it my way two by two.
We can do it my way two by two.
We can do it my way two by two.
Rise Ruby Rise!

Mr. Rhythm and Rhyme
1. Mr. Jingle, Mr. Jangle, Mr. Rhythm and Rhyme
    I woke up this morning, I was feeling so fine.
    I went to my mother and my mother said,
    "You've got the rhythm in your head?"   tap tap
    I've got the rhythm in my head!   tap tap
    You've got the rhythm in your head!   tap tap
    We've all got the rhythm in our heads.   tap tap
2. hands   clap clap
3. hips   woo woo
4. feet   stamp stamp
5. Mr. Jingle, Mr. Jangle, Mr. Rhythm and Rhyme
    I woke up this morning, I was feeling so fine.
    I went to my mother and my mother said,
    "See if you can do it quiet instead."   shh! shh!
                                            stamp stamp
                                            woo woo
                                            clap clap
                                            tap tap
                                            shh! shh!
                                              shh! shh!

Sing That Again is available in both instrumental and vocals versions.

Kathryn L. Cloonan • 5125 N. Amarillo Drive • Beverly Hills, FL 34465

Kathryn L. Cloonan

Components of a Balanced Elementary Language Arts Program

CARROLLTON-FARMERS BRANCH INDEPENDENT SCHOOL DISTRICT

Reading	Writing	Materials/Activities
I. Reading Aloud to Students (READ TO): Teacher reads to class for enjoyment.	Writing to Students (WRITE TO): Teacher writes in front of students while verbalizing the task — the thinking, format, layout, spacing, handwriting, spelling, vocabulary used, etc. WRITE TO also occurs when the teacher models writing through written conversations with students, often in response to their entries in journals or Reader Response Logs.	Chapter books (novels), picture books, nonfiction selections, children's "published books," Big Books, class stories/charts, letters, poems, plays, newspapers, magazines. •••••••••••••••••••••••••••••••• Story time, author's chair, morning message, teacher/peer written response to journals/logs, campus or intracampus postal or pen pal programs.
II. Shared Reading (READ WITH): Purpose A: a pleasurable reading situation in which a learner or group of learners sees the text, observes an expert (usually a teacher) reading with fluency and expression, and is invited to read along. (This is the type of shared reading that occurs more frequently at pre-K-2.) Purpose B: a reading situation in which a learner or group of learners sees the text, and the teacher models specific strategies or skills. (This type of shared reading can occur at all grade levels.)	Shared Writing (WRITE WITH): A pleasurable writing situation in which an expert (usually the teacher) writes collaboratively with a learner or group of learners to demonstrate writing strategies such as: left to right, spacing, letter formations, letter-sound associations, conventions, etc.	Environmental/authentic print (signs, labels, lists, instructions, etc.) Big Books, regular-sized literature (fiction and nonfiction), basal texts, chart stories, poems, TAAS practice passages, letters, newspapers, etc. •••••••••••••••••••••••••••••••• Minilessons of reading or writing skills, interactive writing, sponge activities, class stories (shared experience stories), innovations on familiar texts, paired reading or writing, daily oral language exercises.
III. Guided Reading (STUDENTS READ WITH TEACHER GUIDANCE)** The teacher introduces a new book or story *that is at the child's or group's instructional reading level.* The student(s), each with his/her own copy of the text problem solves his/her way through the reading. If the student encounters a problem,* the teacher's role is to prompt using questions that spur the student's use of reading/thinking strategies. Guided Reading occurs in a reading group or one-on-one situation with a teacher. **THIS IS THE HEART OF THE INSTRUCTIONAL READING PROGRAM.**	Guided Writing (STUDENTS WRITE WITH TEACHER GUIDANCE): The teacher introduces or reteaches an aspect of writing *craft* (choosing topics, adding information, using logical sequence, etc.) or *conventions* (spelling, mechanics, grammar skills) as appropriate to the whole class or group and/or individuals. S/he then monitors student's application of that instruction through observation during writing time, in teacher/pupil conferences and through the analysis of drafts in pupil's writing folders. **THIS IS THE HEART OF THE INSTRUCTIONAL WRITING PROGRAM.**	INSTRUCTIONAL TEXTS: literature (fiction and nonfiction), basal and supplementary readers, content area texts, TAAS format reading passages for practice, students' "published" writing. •••••••••••••••••••••••••••••••• Teacher directed or monitored instructional activities such as: individual/group reading using instructional level text,** individual (or, occasionally, group) writing in appropriate modes, TAAS prompt writing for practice, whole class, group or individual minilessons of writing or reading skills.
IV. Independent Reading (READ ALONE): Self-selected or teacher recommended easy or familiar reading a child reads on his/her own. When reading is sent home, it should be at this level.	Independent Writing (WRITE ALONE): Student writes on self-selected or, occasionally, teacher recommended topics, without teacher intervention or evaluation.	A variety of reading material (fiction and nonfiction) including novels, picture books, informative text, poems, newspapers, magazines, peer "published" books, etc. •••••••••••••••••••••••••••••••• DEAR/SSR time, library center, diaries, journals, reading response logs kept for reflection or reaction only (not graded), letters to pen pals.

Susan Thomas

Sources of Information
Good Readers Use

(Dr. Marie Clay)

Meaning Cues:

Structure Cues:

Visual Cues:

Susan Thomas

What Can You Say Besides *"Sound it out"* ?

To help children *monitor* their reading:

- Wait time.
- Try that again.
- Are you right?

To help children *use meaning* (context or prior knowledge):

- Look at the picture to help yourself.
- Does that make sense?
- Think what would make good sense.
- Start that sentence again.
- Make a good guess then go on.

To help children *use language structure* (syntax):

- Does that sound right? Does it fit?
- Can we say it that way?

To help children *cross check* (use two or three sources of information):

- Check to see if what you said looks right and makes sense.
- Check to see if what you said makes sense and looks right.
- It could be _____ , but look at _____ .

To help children *use visual information* (print):

- Read all the words up to the tricky word and start it.
- Say more of the word.
- Does that look right to you?
- Get your mouth ready to say it.
- Look at how the word begins.
- Do you know another word that starts that way?
- If that was _____, what would you expect to see at the beginning? at the end?
- Do you know a word that looks/sounds like that?

To help children *problem solve independently*:

- What can you do to help yourself?
- I like the way you tried to help yourself.
- Good readers keep trying — good for you!
- I like the way you worked on the hard part.
- What can you try?
- Good readers . . . (praise the behavior).

Susan Thomas

What Do You Do When You're Stuck?

1. Go back and read it again.
2. Think what makes sense.
3. Look at the pictures.
4. Start the word.
5. Make a good guess.

That's what you do when you're STUCK!

Paulette Mansell — Carrollton-Farmers Branch I.S.D.

Susan Thomas

Word Attack Strategy

1. **Think** about what would make sense.

2. **Look** at the picture.

3. **Reread** the sentence.

4. **Crash** into the unknown word and say the beginning sound.

5. **Say** the word you think

   **makes sense,
   sounds right,
   looks right.**

6. **Read** on.

Susan Thomas

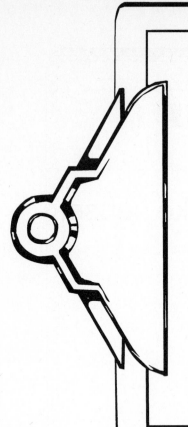

What to do when young readers make a mistake:

1. If the mistakes makes sense, don't worry about it.

2. If the mistake doesn't make sense, wait to see if the reader will fix it.

3. Say, "Try that again."

4. Say, "Did that make sense?"

5. Say, "Did what you read look right and sound right?"

6. Tell the correct response.

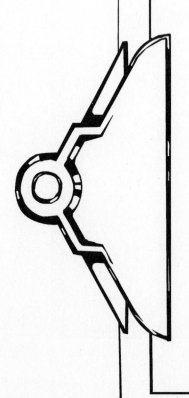

What to do when young readers get stuck:

1. Wait and see if they work it out.

2. Say, "Try that again."

3. Say, "Look at the picture."

4. Say, "Think about what would make sense."

5. Say, "Read the sentence again and start the tricky word."

6. Tell the word.

Susan Thomas

158

Home Reading Checklist

Date   **Title**

Please check all that apply:

— Child read independently.
— Child read with little assistance.
— Child read with great assistance.
— Parent read to child.
— Child uses "What if stuck?" strategies.
— Child points to words if needed.
—We discussed the story.

Comments:

Parent Signature:

Home Reading Checklist

Date   **Title**

Please check all that apply:

— Child read independently.
— Child read with little assistance.
— Child read with great assistance.
— Parent read to child.
— Child uses "What if stuck?" strategies.
— Child points to words if needed.
—We discussed the story.

Comments:

Parent Signature:

Home Reading Checklist

Date   **Title**

Please check all that apply:

— Child read independently.
— Child read with little assistance.
— Child read with great assistance.
— Parent read to child.
— Child uses "What if stuck?" strategies.
— Child points to words if needed.
—We discussed the story.

Comments:

Parent Signature:

How to Choose a Book
(from Dr. Patricia Hagerty, *Readers' Workshop   Real Reading*)

Consider the reading level:

Easy:

The book flows for you.
The ideas are easy to understand.
The words are easy for you to read.

Just right:

You understand most of the ideas.
You might not know some words, but
you can figure them out or skip
them.

Challenge:

The book is hard for you to read.
You don't understand a lot of the ideas.
Many of the words are hard for you.

Other things to think about:

Look at the cover.
Read the inside flap.
Do you know the characters?
Has the book won awards?
What size is the print?
Find someone who's read it.
Do you know the author?
How thick/thin is the book?
Use the five finger rule.

Susan Thomas

Books I've Read

Title

Author   **Date**

☺ ☹   **E   JR   C**

Title

Author   **Date**

☺ ☹   **E   JR   C**

Title

Author   **Date**

☺ ☹   **E   JR   C**

Title

Author   **Date**

☺ ☹   **E   JR   C**

Title

Author   **Date**

☺ ☹   **E   JR   C**

Title

Author   **Date**

☺ ☹   **E   JR   C**

Components of the Readers' Workshop

(from *Readers' Workshop Real Reading* by Patricia Hagerty)

Mini Lesson (5-10 minutes)

- Procedural
- Strategies and skills
- Literary
- Text responses

Activity Period (30-40 minutes)

Read

- Students read individually selected books
- Students may read alone, in pairs, heterogeneous or not

Respond

- Students write responses in a literature log
- Responses can be open or directed
- Write in literature log three times per week

Confer

- Discuss books with children individually
- Use a checklist or anecdotal records for assessment
- Teach one strategy, skill, etc. to individual/small group

Share (10-15 minutes)

- Large group-three or four students share
- Small groups of 3 or 4 members; each member shares

Susan Thomas

Name of Character

	Very	Some-what	Neither or Both	Some-what	Very	
clever						stupid
fair						unfair
agree-able						disagree-able
strong						strong
proud						embar-rassed
honest						dis-honest

Susan Thomas

Reader's Workshop Self-Evaluation

	👍	🤚	👎
1. I choose reading material at different levels (easy, just right, challenge).			
2. I am always trying to predict what the author will do next.			
3. I summarize my story when I tell my friends about it (setting, characters, problem and solution).			
4. I use different strategies to figure out words: • makes sense • sounds right • looks right			
5. I understand books that I read.			
6. I write about the books I read.			
7. I am learning new words with each book I read, like:			

I would give myself a grade of_____ for
this grading period because _____

Susan Thomas

Reading Profile

Date	Title/Level/p.	Reading Strategies Used					Comprehension/Retelling				Fluent	Comments
		Uses meaning/pictures tries to make it make sense	Uses visual — sounds out	Guesses	Skips	Rereads	Setting	Characters	Problem	Solution	Rate/reads punctuation/ makes it sound like talking	

Susan Thomas

GUIDED READING

1. Choose book/story

- Strategies children control/instructional level
- Interest
- Supportive text

2. Introduce the book/story

- Main idea statement
- Let children hear the language of the text.
- Locate one or two important words.

3. Children read simultaneously-may begin chorally.

- Teacher scaffolds individually
- Use strategy questions/statements

4. Re-read together chorally for fluency

5. Respond to text

- Orally
- Written

Susan Thomas

Literature Discussion Groups

How:

1. Select 4 or 5 texts. Selection criteria could be genre, common elements, theme, content area or topic study. Texts should have a range of readability.

2. Conduct book talks. Students browse and make a 1st and 2nd choice.

3. Assign books and discussion groups according to choice.

Schedule:

Day one: Read and write response to text in response journal.

Day two: Meet in literature discussion groups and discuss text read; use responses in journal to facilitate discussion.

Susan Thomas

Book Introductions for Guided Reading Groups

1. Encourage the students to **make predictions** or link the story to prior knowledge.

2. Give a brief (one or two sentence) **overview statement** about the story.

3. Allow students to **browse through the book**, looking at the pictures, and making predictions about the story. The teacher guides the students to the ideas in the story.

4. **Rehearse any unusual language** or repetitive phrases with the students.

5. **Locate one or two important words** in the story.

6. All students **read the whole story** with teacher prompting when necessary.

7. **Re-read** chorally for fluency.

Susan Thomas

SHARED READING

A. **Enjoy a good story, provide a reading model, and scaffold.**

B. **Model or teach specific strategies, skills, and literary devices.**

Strategies:

- What to do when you get stuck.
- How to check to see if you're right.
- Making reading sound like talking.
- Monitor comprehension.

Skills:

- Word attack (blends, ing, sh, etc.)
- Cause/Effect

Literary devices:

- Settings
- Similes
- How authors show instead of tell.
- How authors use varied vocabulary.

Susan Thomas

Whole Class Reading

- Introduce story / book

- Choose way to read story / book (levels of scaffolding)
    alone
    paired reading
    with the teacher

- Respond to story / book
    write letter to: character, author, teacher
    tell what you liked
    write the problem and solution
    tell how character was like/not like you
    sentence starters

- Read free-choice book(s)

- Literature discussion circle/response group(s)

Sample Schedule for Primary Grades

	Mon.	Tues.	Wed.	Thurs.	Fri.
8:30 - 8:40	——————— minilesson ———————				text innovations
8:40 - 9:00	——————— guided reading ———————				
9:00 - 9:20	small groups				
9:20 - 9:30	——— teacher conferring ——— one-to-one ———				special projects
9:30 - 9:45	——— share ———				

8:40 - 9:00	——— read self-selected books ———				
9:00 - 9:30	——— independent work/reader response ———				

Susan Thomas

Daily Language Arts Schedule

Shop for books

Warm-up
- Song
- Poem
- Chant
- Excellent piece of writing
- Newspaper article

Shared Writing
- Daily news
- Morning message

Read-to

Celebrate the book
- Respond orally
- Write on Language Chart
- Respond in writing
- Act it out
- Text innovation

Mini-lesson

Read/Respond
- Free choice books (independent)
- Read with teacher (guided)
- Write in literature log
- Celebrate a book
- Write a text innovation

Book/Literature log share

Susan Thomas

POSITIVE CHANGES FOR CHILDREN

Therese M. Bialkin

Third-grade teacher, Jackson Academy, East Orange, New 'ersey

Michele Giordano

Third-grade teacher, Jackson Academy, East Orange, New Jersey

Is that all there is? That song title, made famous decades ago, comes very close to summing up the way we felt about our teaching just a few years ago. As beginning, primary grade teachers, our enthusiasm and excitement could not be rivaled. We expected hard work and we approached it eagerly. We worked hard to learn all that we could about our students and their community, to acquaint ourselves with school and district expectations, and to establish ourselves as professionals. As graduates of local teacher education programs, we felt reasonably well prepared. Yet, as with most beginning teachers, those early years posed enormous challenges for us.

We both began teaching more than a decade ago, a time when school districts throughout the United States were heavily focused on the basics. Urban school districts, such as ours, were under tremendous pressure to improve student performance on standardized tests. Many felt that the surest and quickest way to raise test scores was to offer a curriculum that emphasized isolated skills and teacher-centered, direct instruction with strict time constraints for each curriculum area. It was not uncommon for us to leave school at the end of the day, loaded down with totebags full of worksheets and workbooks. We were working hard! Our students were working hard! Indeed, most of them *were* acquiring the skills that we presented. Unfortunately, much of the learning was devoid of a sense of purpose and joy—elements we knew were essential to the creation of lifelong learners. We knew there must be a better way.

Ironically, it was only after our routines settled into place and we felt a growing sense of confidence about ourselves as professionals, that we both—quite independently—began to question some of our teaching practices. We knew that our students were capable. Yet, the curriculum we were providing did not allow them to demonstrate their abilities to the fullest. We also knew that we were capable of more creative and inspired teaching. Yet, in many ways, the curriculum we had worked so hard to master seemed to discourage individual teacher creativity and initiative. We began to explore possibilities—together. Now, as third grade teachers, two years into our journey of change, the initial excitement and enthusiasm we felt as beginning teachers has returned, but in a very different way.

First Steps

It was easy to identify the first problem we would tackle together. We both had difficulty apportioning the time available in a typical school day among all the subjects we were required to teach. In order to reduce the time spent on some subjects without reducing the quality of the instruction, we devised a form of "semi-departmentalization." We divided the curriculum between us with one of us teaching science and math to both classes and the other teaching social studies and language skills. With classrooms right next door to each other, this was a relatively easy innovation.

After a year's experimentation, it was clear that our teaching had changed dramatically. Narrowing our focus gave us time to make our lessons more exciting and challenging. In general, we were better prepared. Moreover, teaching this way required us to communicate with each other frequently in order to coordinate our activities. Still, we were not satisfied. Our collaboration and discussion led us to realize that we could improve our lessons even further by working together to integrate the subjects we were teaching, rather than teaching them in isolation. Having some familiarity with whole language, we felt that this was the direction that would offer us the most help. We also knew that we had a lot to learn.

Moving toward Whole Language

Over the years, we had attended several workshops dealing with various aspects of whole language philosophy and practice. We continued to attend as many workshops as we could. We also shared articles with one another; and we talked with other professionals about what they were doing. We enlisted and received the administrative support of our principal, Gladys Calhoun. From the very beginning, her support has been an essential part of our success.

One of the most important activities affecting our change was the initiation of a whole language study group by our district reading and language arts supervisors, Norma Nichols and Ruth Gillman. The group was established to provide

support to teachers, like ourselves, who were interested in changing their teaching. We met once a month to discuss new insights, ideas, and problems encountered as we attempted to move toward the use of whole language. We read and discussed Regie Routman's *Invitations: Changing as Teachers and Learners*. These meetings helped us to know that the concerns we were experiencing were not unique to us. Our ideas about integrating the subject areas with the language arts were reinforced. During the summer of 1992, we began to do some serious planning.

Teaching through Themes

During our initial planning, we selected five theme topics, established goals for each theme, and brainstormed ideas for integrating subject areas and for establishing a learning environment that was natural and flowing, not forced. We decided to use a variety of children's literature (tradebooks), rather than a text-

---

book, as the major source of reading material. A story related to the theme would serve as the catalyst for framing our work.

Acquiring the literature we needed proved to be our first major challenge. We wanted a minimum of one book per child for each of the five themes. The challenge was met through a series of collaborative efforts. Our principal and the Office of Curriculum provided partial funding. Additional funds came through the use of monies allocated for the purchase of workbooks; a student-managed plant sale; and through the use of bonus points earned through student book clubs, such as Troll and Scholastic. Other teachers donated excess tradebooks and several publishers sponsored us through the donation of trial materials. Once we had obtained the necessary literature, we began each theme using a variety of instructional techniques.

Mapping the theme. We usually start each theme unit with a brainstorming activity. This involves the creation of a semantic map of the theme we are going to explore. We collaborate with students to list on the map the subjects and content we expect to cover in the unit. Copies of the map are distributed to students and referred to as we move through the unit.

Introducing the theme story. Each story is introduced with a prediction activity. For example, students may be asked to observe only the illustrations in the literature. A prediction list is then created from ideas that students volunteer, such as where they think the story takes place, what might occur in the story, and so on. These ideas are compiled on a chart. Students are required to justify their predictions with evidence gathered from the pictures or story title. After reading the story, the chart is used to evaluate all of the predictions made.

Reading the story. In order to accommodate the various reading abilities of individual students, we employ a number of different reading strategies. One of us may read the story aloud to the less proficient readers before they read it on their own. More able students may be initially assigned to read independently, while other students may be linked with a reading partner.

Reading is done in an informal setting with students lying on the carpet or gathered around the teacher in comfortable positions. After the reading, students respond to the story in their literature logs. These responses are later shared and discussed in small groups. The discussions focus on subject-area content, reading comprehension, and literary understandings in an integrated way.

Follow-through and follow-up. The brainstorming and story-reading activities serve as a commonly shared experience for all of the students. This is followed by a variety of lessons and experiences that may involve the whole group, small groups, and individuals. Here are three examples:

Extended reading and writing. Each day, we read aloud to students from materials related to the current theme. Students are also given time for independent reading in theme-related materials. The reading is followed by discussion as well as opportunities to write. Each child has a journal and a literature response log to write down their reactions to the reading, create a poem or story, or to record some interesting facts. Students are given time and assistance for the revision and editing of material that will eventually be published. Whenever possible, computers are used to publish books using different word-processing programs.

Cooperative learning. We use a variety of cooperative learning strategies throughout each unit. One cooperative learning technique we employ is called "Envelope." Varied levels of comprehen-

We collaborate with students to list on the map the subjects and content we expect to cover in the unit.

sion questions relating to the literature (or content) under study are written on the front of the envelopes. Students work together to discover the evidence in the story that supports the answer to the question written on the front of the envelope. The answers are written down and placed inside the envelope, which is then rotated to another group for evaluation. This is followed by a very high level class discussion, as students verify or challenge certain answers and return to the text for supporting evidence. Most often the questions are originated by the teacher, but as students become more familiar with the process, they enjoy developing questions themselves as a small-group or homework activity.

Grouping for specific strategies and skills. Strategies and skills, such as vocabulary or word analysis, are integrated into the various lessons. Based on our observation of student needs, skill groups in these areas are formed. Groups are changed daily as students progress. The literature always forms the nucleus of these lessons. For example,

one skill lesson originated from our observation that a number of students were having trouble recognizing and reading dialogue. A lesson addressing this problem consisted of helping children to identify specific lines of dialogue in the story. Having demonstrated that they could isolate the dialogue from the remaining text, we had them choose characters, identify all the dialogue for their character, practice reading it, and perform it as a play.

Pulling It All Together

Providing an integrated curriculum for students, while keeping track of the various disciplines, is a common dilemma for teachers using theme-based instruction. What follows are some examples of science, social studies, math, and language integration for a theme commonly taught in third grade. For purposes of record keeping and accountability, we labeled the activities in terms of specific subject areas. However, each activity overlapped into all the others.

Science. During our unit on Native Americans, students learned the importance of corn for the survival of many tribes. Students were shown real, fully grown corn plants. They learned the parts of the corn plant, grew their own corn, dissected corn seeds and looked at the baby plant under a microscope.

Language arts. After reading a number of Native American legends in class, students worked in groups to create their own legends, complete with illustrations. The stories were bound and made into books for everyone's reading enjoyment.

Social studies. Students investigated Native American homes, crafts, and tools. They created their own simulations using various materials and then wrote about them.

Mathematics. Students used corn seeds to conduct estimation activities.

All Day Learning Stations

Every Friday, we institute what we call our "All Day Learning Stations." Students are rotated through a series of learning stations, working cooperatively in small groups. They are grouped heterogeneously. This, in itself, is unusual in our school, where students are typically divided into groups according to academic ability. Our third grade classes contain a mixture of students with varying academic abilities, ranging from very fluent readers to several students who are more than a grade level behind in reading.

The make-up of each group is not absolutely fixed throughout the year. As we see fit, students are moved to different groups to allow them to gain experience working with other members of the class as well as to allow us to find the combination of students that produces the best results academically and socially.

Station assignments for the whole day are written on the board. Due to the size of each class, ten stations are required to keep group sizes to a maximum of six students.

At a station, each group is required to complete a task associated with our theme and requiring the use of children's literature. The tasks are designed so that they can be generally completed within the fifty minutes allotted to each group. While the students are working diligently at their stations, we act as facilitators, moving from station to station, monitoring progress, and offering assistance. After the time is up, groups rotate to the next station to begin a new task. Students are able to work through three stations in the morning, and then complete two more stations after lunch. On the following Friday, the remaining five stations are completed, using the same routine.

This scheduling leaves about thirty minutes at the end of the day to get together with the entire two classes and reflect on the day's progress. We use this time to discuss solutions to problems that may have occurred, share opinions of tasks assigned, listen to feedback from teacher observations, and sometimes use our journals to log personal evaluations. These sessions have proven to be invaluable in improving the listening skills of our students and ourselves.

A very bold innovation for us and for our school, the "All Day Learning Stations" have opened our eyes to what children can do when they are given greater control over their own learning. The children are learning more; they are thoroughly engaged in their tasks; and, contrary to what most teachers would think, there are virtually no discipline problems.

Assessment

Student evaluation is an ongoing process. As the need arises, students are given formal tests concerning information and skills taught within our theme. Daily classwork is also assessed by observing student behaviors and by measurable academic progress. In addition, we keep anecdotal records of academic and social progress for discussion in parent, student, and teacher conferences.

Reflections

These past two years have been enormously challenging and rewarding. It is true that our teaching has changed. But perhaps more importantly, we have changed the way we view ourselves as professionals. Taking greater control over what we do has meant that we work much harder, but we believe we also work much better. As we look back there are several things that really account for the success we have had so far. Our commitment to individual accountability and team planning is essential. We spend time together planning our weekly lessons and our Friday sessions so that we both understand the entire learning program and how it all fits together. Planning initially took a great deal of time. As the program developed, we found that less time had to be spent once the framework was in place.

Another key element is the support and talent of some of our colleagues. Gwendolyn Cottingham, our librarian, has proved to be an essential part of our program. She has created, at our request, a list of books available in our library covering our chosen theme. She also helps to provide literature for classroom read-alouds, silent reading, and student research projects. She even supplied her personal slides taken on her trip to Africa when we were studying African folktales.

The Music, Art, French, and Physical Education teachers also make themselves available to enhance the learning process. With advance notice, these professionals will develop their lessons specifically to relate to our current theme. The special talents of all these people are invaluable to our program.

We feel that we have progressed a long way toward achieving our goals and we are continuing to plan some interesting new activities for the upcoming school year. We are aware that research has shown that it can take as many as five years to develop a comprehensive whole language program. Keeping this in mind, we continue to monitor and adjust our learning environments to make them the best they can be for our student learners and for ourselves as professionals, continuing to learn. We are excited about what the future holds because we know that the change has been a positive one.

Friday Schedule for "All Day Learning Stations"

9:00–9:30   All students meet in one room for whole group conference (station directions, etc.). Each group is assigned to one of the ten areas.

9:30–12:00   Students rotate through three of the 40-minute stations with five-minute clean-up between each.

12:00–12:30   Lunch

12:30–2:00   Students rotate through two additional stations.

2:00–2:30   Whole group processing (discussions and reactions about the day's activities)

2:30–2:35   Dismissal

A repeat of the same ten stations will occur the following Friday in order for students to work through all of them. Below is an example of some possible station arrangements. Stations vary as they relate to our chosen theme.

1. Computer Station: Teacher selected integrated software
2. Listening Station with headphones
3. Arts & Crafts Station
4. Hands-On Science Lab Experiments
5. Writing and Publishing Center
6. Computer Station: Free choice from network menu
7. Social Studies Research
8. Math Manipulative Station
9. Reading/Language Strategies
10. Student/Teacher Writing Conferences

Classroom Floor Plans for "All Day Learning Stations"

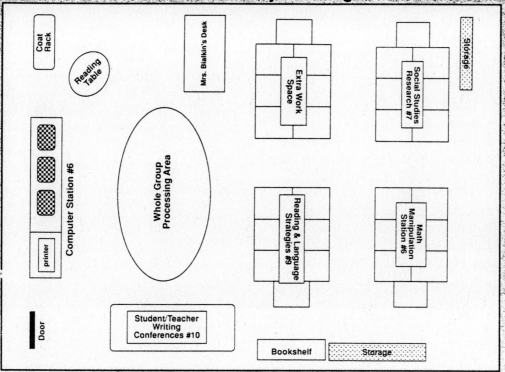

Mrs. Bialkin's Classroom

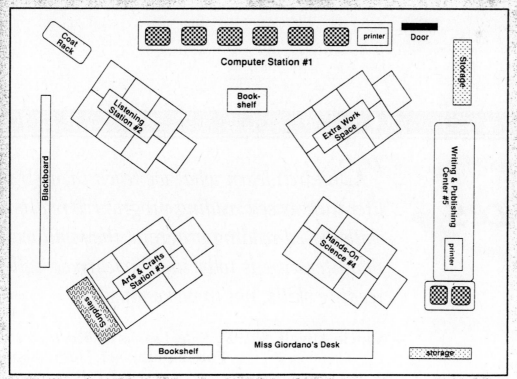

Miss Giordano's Classroom

Lingering Questions

1. Should a successful innovation created by classroom teachers be implemented across a school district? If so, under what circumstances and how?

2. How can children, who are only familiar with teacher-centered classrooms, be helped to adjust to the expectations of a whole language classroom?

3. How can teachers reconcile the need to encourage children to make their own choices with the need to maintain quality time on task during independent activities?

Resources That Supported Our Change

Glazer, S. (1992). *Reading comprehension.* New York: Scholastic Professional Books.

Goodman, K. (1986). Basal readers: A call for action. *Language Arts, 63* (4), 358–363.

Johnson, W., & Johnson, R. (1991). *Cooperating in the classroom.* Edina, MN: Interaction Book Company.

Newman, J., & Church, S. (1990). Myths of whole language. *The Reading Teacher, 44* (1), 1–7.

Routman, R. (1991). *Invitations: Changing as teachers and learners.* Portsmouth, NH: Heinemann.

Voices

"Children learn what we teach them. If the literature-based reading program is really a skills-based reading program, they will learn that literature is to be used to learn so-called reading skills, not to make music."

— Nancie Atwell, *Side By Side: Essays on Teaching to Learn,* Portsmouth, NH: Heinemann, 1991.

Writing in Math Class?

Absolutely!

How to enhance students' mathematical understanding while reinforcing their writing skills

By Marilyn Burns

For my first 20 years as an educator, I separated math and writing into opposing camps, convinced that they went together like oil and water. Now I can't imagine teaching math without making writing an integral part of it.

I've found that writing in math class has two major benefits. It supports students' learning because, in order to get their ideas on paper, children must organize, clarify, and reflect on their thinking. Writing also benefits teachers because stu-

A window on students' learning: Marilyn offers Lindsey feedback on her paper.

dents' papers are invaluable assessment resources. Their writing is a window into what they understand, how they approach ideas, what misconceptions they harbor, and how they feel about what they're discovering. Over the decade that I've been asking students to write about math, I've learned a great deal. In this article, I present nine important strategies, the answers to commonly asked questions, four different types of writing assignments for math, and math activities that lead to writing.

"Writing in Math Class? Absolutely!" by Marilyn Burns. From *Instructor*, 1995, vol. 104, number 7. Reproduced with permission.

As Elissa (left) uses manipulatives to investigate a problem, Ali and Darius write about their discoveries.

9 Math and Writing Strategies

1 **Talk with students about the purpose of their writing.** Make sure students understand the two basic reasons for writing in math class—to enhance and support their learning and to help you assess their progress.

2 **Establish yourself as the audience.** Explain to students how their writing helps you. Tell them, "What you write shows me what you're learning and what you understand. It helps me think about how to better teach you." During class it's hard to listen to all students describe their thinking, so point out that their writing should include as much detail as possible.

3 **Use students' writing in classroom instruction.** Children's papers are effective springboards for class discussions and activities. Using them in this way reinforces to the students that you value their writing. Hearing others' ideas shows children different ways to approach problems. Ask children to read their papers aloud. For example, when I asked fifth graders to trace one of their feet on centimeter-squared graph paper, figure out its area, and then describe the process they used, Nelson wrote that he had counted whole squares, added up partial squares that equaled whole ones, and used these numbers to calculate the area. Amy wrote that she had drawn a rectangle around the outline she'd traced and found its area. By listening to what others wrote, students learned about different methods they could have used. This inspired a few to revise their work.

4 **Have students discuss their ideas before writing them.** For most children, talking is easier than writing, and class discussions allow students to express their ideas and hear others. After a discussion, remind children that they may write about any idea they heard, as long as it makes sense to them and they can explain it.

For example, when a third-grade class read a book written in 1979, I asked, "How long ago was that?" (It was 1992 at the time.) Before having students write their responses, I had them share their thinking. Lisa said she counted from 1980 to 1992 and came up with 13 years. Leif started counting at 1979, and got 14. James said he knew it was 13 because his sister was born in 1979 and she was 13. Lauren argued that it depended on when in 1979 the book was written and when in 1992 we were reading it. After a 15-minute discussion, children wrote about the problem.

5 **Provide prompts.** To help students get started writing, put a prompt on the board, such as, "I think the answer is ___. I think this because ___." (Don't demand that students use the prompts. What's important is that their writing, no matter how they express it, relates to the problem and makes sense.)

Sometimes prompts may be more specific to the assignment. For example, I had fourth graders each take a handful of cubes, record the number of cubes they grabbed on a class graph, and use the graph to figure out how many cubes there were in all the handfuls. I wrote: "We have ___ altogether. We figured this out by ___. "

After I write a prompt, I remind students to describe their thinking with words, numbers, and, if they like, pictures.

6 **Give individual help to students who don't know what to write.** First, talk to students to make sure they understand the assignment. Then try additional prompts, such as: "What do you think?", "What idea do you have?", or "What do you remember about what others said?" Once children offer ideas, suggest that they repeat them in their heads before writing them down. I add: "Let the words go from your brain past your mouth, through your shoulder, down your arm, and out through your pencil onto your paper." It's graphic and it works!

7 **Post math word lists.** Post a list of the different areas of math you're studying—numbers, geometry, measurement, probability, and so on. Then start a word list that directly relates to each. Encourage students to consult the charts for vocabulary and spelling.

8 **Ask students to revise and edit.** If possible, when children hand in their papers, have them read their work aloud to you. Whenever their papers do not give complete or detailed information—which I find happens more often than not—ask students to revise. You might say, "That's a good beginning," and then give guidance by adding: "Write some more about why you're sure that's correct" or "Give some details or examples to help me better understand your idea."

Depending on the child and the assignment, you might ask a student to make spelling and grammatical corrections. My policy is that students should underline words they don't think they've spelled correctly. Because the purpose of their writing is to give me insights into their understanding—not to be published—sometimes I ask children to correct it and other times I don't. Making a decision in each case is part of the craft of teaching.

9 **Read students' work to evaluate your teaching and to assess progress.** Reading class sets of assignments gives you an overview of how the class responded to particular lessons and helps you evaluate the effectiveness of your instructional choices. It also gives you information on each child's understanding.

File students' papers in their individual folders. Keep the papers in order so you'll have a chronological set of work. Reading individual student work done over time gives you a sense of the child's progress.

"Writing in Math Class? Absolutely!" by Marilyn Burns. From *Instructor*, 1995, vol. 104, number 7. Reproduced with permission.

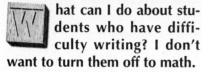**W**hat can I do about students who have difficulty writing? I don't want to turn them off to math.

Helping children learn to write is one of the basic responsibilities of school. In order for their writing abilities to improve, students need many different types of experiences, and incorporating writing into math class provides a ready source. What's important is that students understand that part of learning math is learning to communicate ideas.

What about my primary-grade students?

To help support emerging readers and writers, I tell students that what they put on their paper should help them remember their thoughts about a problem. I instruct children to use words, numbers, and pictures to record their ideas, and I make time to have them explain to me what they've written. At times, I'll take dictation for a child.

Is it appropriate for children to write in pairs or in small groups?

Yes. I often have students work and write cooperatively. Sometimes students talk together and then write their own papers. At other times, I have pairs or a small group of children collaborate on one assignment. In that case I make photocopies of the paper to put in the file folder of each child who contributed.

How often should I have students write?

My decision about how often students should write depends on the math they're studying, the purpose of their writing, and their comfort with writing. Sometimes I have students keep logs and write daily about what they do. Other times I have them write once or twice a week about problems they're solving or to respond to a question I've raised.

Math-Writing

When you write about your work, you ideas lead to other ideas, which lead to other ideas etc. and you can use that noledge for games which lead you to new thieries about the game, which solve problems nobody's ever thought of. Plus whos going to stop you? You can write so much, you can change your prespective about probability so you can use it every day.

Above, Dan explains why writing is beneficial. At right, students talk about their ideas. Later they'll write about them.

4 Ways to Have Students Write in Math Class

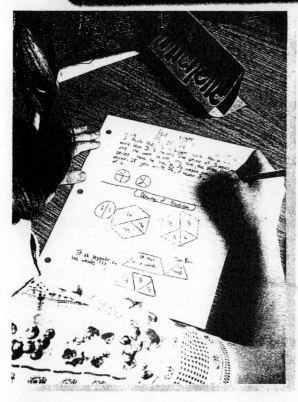

Michelle uses words, numbers, and pictures to explain why 1/3 is larger than 1/4.

riting the solutions to math problems. When writing solution to problems, students should not only present answers, but should also explain their thought processes.

riting math essays. From time to time, ask students to write about a mathematical concept. Their responses are excellent re-sources for assessing what they understand.

During a probability unit, for example, I asked third graders to write about *equally likely.* "Explain what it means," I said, "and give an example." At the end of a unit on division, I asked fourth graders to write about how multiplication and division were alike and different. In the middle of a unit on fractions I asked fifth graders to write "What I Know About Fractions So Far." (This title conveys to students that they're not expected to know everything yet.)

riting about learning. It's helpful occasionally to give a writing assignment that doesn't focus on a math concept or problem. but instead on some aspect of students' learning processes. For example. you might ask children to write about which was their most and least favorite activity in a unit and why. Or have them write about what makes a good partner or how well they worked with their partner or group. Sometimes you might have students write the directions for an activity or game they can teach to someone at home. →

riting in journals or logs. Journals or logs help students keep ongoing records of what they do in math class. When students begin to write in their logs, give them general reminders, such as, "Write about what you did, what you learned, and what questions you have"; "Include something you learned, you're not sure about, or you're wondering about"; or "Write about what was easy and what was difficult for you in solving this problem."

At times you may give guidelines that are specific to the lesson, such as: "Explain why Elissa's answer made sense," or "Write about why Lindsey and Daniel disagreed." It's helpful to some students if you write these suggestions on the board for them to refer to.

Math-Writing

What writing does for me is it unlocks my brain and it lets me think. But if I didn't write I would be getting nowhere. I wouldn't learn anything. I mean I wouldn't think so hard if I didn't write. I would just play the game even if I didn't know how because I wouldn't have to write But when you write it just makes you think.

Students agree with Marilyn—writing helps them better understand math.

"Writing in Math Class? Absolutely!" by Marilyn Burns. From *Instructor*, 1995, vol. 104, number 7. Reproduced with permission.

Math Activities to Write About

How Many Does it Take?
Grades: 1–4; for older students, vary the quantity of cubes to compare.

The Purpose: To help students build number sense and develop computational strategies by comparing quantities.

The Problem: Show children two identical jars, one filled to the top with blue cubes (or like objects, such as marbles) and the other half filled with white ones. Have students count the cubes in each jar, then ask them to figure out how many more white cubes

> The blue and white cube problem. We have to put in 17 more white cubes in the white jar because you got 19 white cubes in the white jar but how manny more to go up to 36? You got 19 white cubes plus 11 makes 30 plus six makes 17. So you need 17 more white cubes to fill the jar.

they'd need to fill the half-full jar.

The Writing Link: As with all writing assignments, ask children to explain—with words, numbers, and, if they like, pictures—how they arrived at the number of cubes needed.

MARILYN BURNS, Instructor's *math columnist, is the creator of Math Solutions, inservice workshops offered nationwide, and the author of numerous books for teachers and children.*

> ② Which is larger $\frac{3}{4}$ $\frac{2}{3}$ or $\frac{3}{4}$? Explain why.
>
> $\frac{2}{3}$ out of a circle leave $\frac{1}{3}$. $\frac{3}{4}$ out of a circle leave $\frac{1}{4}$. $\frac{1}{3}$ is bigger than $\frac{1}{4}$. If $\frac{1}{3}$ takes up more room than $\frac{1}{4}$ than $\frac{3}{4}$ is oviously bigger.
>
> ☐ Too Easy   ☒ Just right   ☐ Too hard

Comparing Fractions
Grades: 4–6

The Purpose: It's important that students' work with fractions involves explaining their understanding, not merely manipulating fractional symbols.

The Problem: Ask students to compare 2/3 and 3/4, or any other fractions.

The Writing Link: Have kids explain their reasoning and evaluate whether the problem is *too easy, just right,* or *too hard* for them.

How Much Is 21 Divided by 4?

Grades: 3–6; use larger numbers if appropriate.

The Purpose: To illustrate that the answer to a division problem is often dependent on the situation, especially when remainders are involved.

The Problem: Give students the problem

in four different contexts:
- divide 21 balloons among 4 people;
- divide 21 cookies among 4 people;
- divide $21.00 among 4 people; and
- divide 21 by 4 on a calculator.

The Writing Link: Ask students to explain why the answer they get for each situation makes sense.

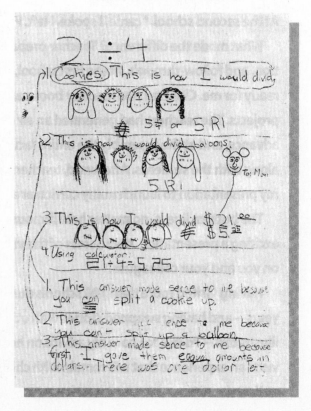

Excerpt from *Teaching Thinking and Problem Solving in Math*, by Char Forsten.

Getting Started by Investigating the Problem

What is a Problem, Exactly?

For many of us, the word *problem* has a negative connotation. Something is wrong that needs to be fixed.

Of course, there are many cases where this is true. When your car makes a suspicious noise, you see dollar signs. At school, when two students argue, you are likely to ask, "What's the problem?"

In mathematics, a problem can be a simple algorithm waiting to be computed or a complex situation with one or more steps and calculations needing to be solved.

I tell students problems are situations that require some kind of action or they go unresolved. If I am hungry, I must decide what to eat, then actually consume the food. If I want to take a vacation, I read about possible locations, then choose one to visit and take the trip. If I face a math problem, I must understand it, decide what to do, then solve it.

A variety of cultures exist in this world because societies solve the problems of food, clothing, shelter, and rules differently. Stop and think about it. An Inuit will solve the problem of needing shelter differently than an aborigine, because the conditions they face are so dissimilar. The fact that each situation reflects different conditions makes problem solving a fascinating adventure.

It is helpful for students to have an expanded view of what a problem is, whether it is a math riddle with one possible answer, or a social issue such as the solid waste program requiring in-depth analysis.

A Model for Problem Solving

Have you ever met someone who seems to know exactly what to do no matter how serious the problem? Such a person confronts an issue, sizes it up, and is at ease making a prompt decision. Most likely, he or she is well-trained or experienced in solving problems. We can help students feel comfortable with problem solving by starting to educate them in logical reasoning processes when they begin school.

In order to accomplish this, we must give students a sequence in which to analyze problems. Children face an overload when confronted with a task that requires them to do many things at once. Certainly complex problems can overwhelm them and leave the door open for a math block to form. That is why it is important to train students to approach problems in a step-by-step fashion.

The following is a problem solving model I use in my teaching:

1. Determine the problem.
2. Identify relevant facts and their relationships to each other.
3. Specify important conditions.
4. Choose a strategy.
5. Solve the problem.
6. Check your results.

Step 1: Determine the Problem

Have you ever walked around with a knot in your stomach and wondered what was bothering you? You know once you figure it out, you can work it through, and be rid of that gnawing feeling.

Determining what the problem is may seem like an easy step, but we should not take for granted that students will always recognize it. This skill requires concentration on the question and the ability to create a mental image of the situation. To help determine the problem:

1. Read, and, if necessary, reread the problem.
2. Create a mental picture of the problem.
3. Find the question and put it in your own words to show understanding.

Allow time for students to practice this skill of determining the problem. By starting out with simple problems, students will be better able to analyze more complex situations.

Step 2: Identify Relevant Facts and Their Relationships to Each Other

Math problems vary according to the amount of information they contain. Students must learn to sift through facts and decide which are necessary to solve the problem. They must also determine their relationships to each other and the order in which they will use them. We have all seen examples that contain too much information such as:

Terry, Larry, and Harry all collect baseball cards. Terry started with thirty-six, gave five to Larry, then bought three from her brother. Larry started with fifty-four. His brother, who collects stamps, gave him another thirteen for his collection. When Larry counted up his cards, he was very upset, because he was missing one of Reggie Jackson. He looked everywhere, but could not find it. Finally, there was Harry, who had the largest collection of seventy-two cards. Last Saturday, he went to a shop and traded three of his cards for five others. How many more cards did Harry have than Larry?

At first glance, this problem is confusing with its rhyming names and juggling of numbers. Students not trained in problem solving are overwhelmed. Those who learn the step-by-step approach would:

1. Determine the problem: In the end, how many more cards did Harry have than Larry?
2. Identify relevant facts and their relationships to each other:

Larry's cards: $54 + 5 + 13 - 1 = 71$
Harry's cards: $72 - 3 + 5 = 74$

Terry's role in this situation helps students create a mental picture of the problem, and the five cards she gave to Larry must be figured into the math equation. The other number facts about Terry are irrelevant to the solu-

tion — they contribute to an understanding of the whole picture, but are not necessary to solve the problem.

Much practice is needed to identify relevant facts correctly. Many students do not have a system for analyzing problems; they manipulate the numbers, come up with an answer which may or may not be reasonable, then move on to the next order of business.

Step 3: Specify Important Conditions

When choosing relevant facts, it is also important to identify conditions that might exist in a problem. In real life, if you want to buy a snack and only have fifty cents, you should immediately eliminate any snacks over this amount. You do not want to waste your time on solutions that are not feasible.

In Chapter Five of this book, I will explain how to do case studies with students. Recognizing conditions becomes a crucial step in these thinking activities. As children become more involved with real-life situations, they must not only look at the problem mathematically, but they also need to consider any conditions that could affect the solution.

If Billy, who is asthmatic, is groping with the dilemma of taking in a stray cat, he must consider both the cost factor of caring for the cat and the condition of his health when making his decision.

Step 4: Choose a Strategy

A variety of strategies used in problem solving are discussed at length in Chapter Three of this book. The ones I have included are: key words to operations; guess and check; make a table or an organized list; draw a picture or use real objects; work backwards

or make it simpler; find a pattern; and use logic.

I introduce each strategy separately in a large group setting, provide practice problems, then when all strategies have been taught, give students a variety of problems where they must decide what to do on their own or in their cooperative learning groups. Examples of teaching these applications are provided in Chapter Three.

Step 5: Solve the Problem

This is straightforward — students carry out the plan. Having determined the problem, identified relevant facts and their relationships, recognized conditions, and chosen a strategy, they should now be able to solve the problem mathematically and consider important factors to come up with a logical answer.

Step 6: Check the Results

A few years ago, I had a conference with a parent who is also a high school math teacher. When I discussed my concerns about students' ability to think and solve problems, he told me that if we could just get kids to ask this important question: "Does the answer make sense?," it would make a tremendous difference in their progress in math.

Thus the question, "Is the answer reasonable?" became a critical part of my math lessons. Students know I am going to ask this. In fact, I have a large poster hanging on a wall that constantly poses this evaluative question to the children.

When I ask if the answer is reasonable, I am really directing them to consider whether they used the correct computational approach and backed it up with logical reasoning.

A problem that will demonstrate

whether students are thinking logically is:

There are thirteen kids in an afterschool chess club. They have been invited to a tournament on the other side of the city, and must find adults to drive them. If only four students can ride in each car, how many cars will be needed?

I have seen answers such as 3R.1, which shows the student recognized division as the correct operation, but failed to determine the problem and understand what sort of answer was appropriate.

Other students might suggest only three cars are needed, because the one extra student could sit on someone's lap. This shows an understanding of the problem and creative thinking, but it also demonstrates the student did not recognize given conditions. The answer is not reasonable because the problem stated only four students could ride in each car.

Experience has taught me that many kids tend to use "if only" thinking. "If only the thirteenth student could sit on someone's lap, then only three cars would be needed." When this happens, I acknowledge their use of creative thinking in coming up with an alternative that would save gas and drivers, but I remind them that this problem gave the condition that only four students could ride in each car. There can be no "if only" in this case.

That is why, when dealing with logical thinking in math problems, I remind students they must recognize and adhere to given conditions.

Open-ended problems are another matter. There are times when altering conditions can be a problem. When students change variables in an experiment, they are altering conditions. In order to discover the effects of environmental factors on plant growth, students will vary the conditions in controlled experiments. Open-ended activities and real-life problems encourage students to develop all types of thinking. There are problems where conditions can be altered. Help students see how important conditions are when economists offer ways to control inflation, health workers discover cures for diseases, and environmentalists search for solutions to our solid and toxic waste problems.

When teaching problem solving to elementary students, I usually establish ground rules at the beginning of a session. Later, students are better able to determine which problems are open-ended and which require adherence to given information. When asked whether their answer is reasonable, students must be sure they have determined the correct problem, identified important facts, and recognized given conditions.

Checking results needs to become a habit. Reward students for questioning their answers and praise their movement through each step in the problem solving process.

How can you track the students' progress or identify their weak areas in the problem solving model? A chart that shows their thoughts at each step is a good way to observe growth.

Summary: Charting the Model

As you work through the model, students can fill in a chart to check their progress in problem solving and social skills. They can put the entire model to use with the following problem:

Jack and Jill went up the hill to fetch 2 liters of water. Along the way, they met Ms. Muffet who was collecting spiders. When they finally reached the top and filled their container with water, they turned around and began to run down the hill. Jack fell down and spilled the water everywhere. If Jack was 2 meters ahead of Jill, and Jill was 5 meters from the top, how far down the hill was Jack?

The sample chart on the following page (filled out in the name of John Doe) guides students through the six steps in the problem solving model and helps prevent them from getting stuck.

Learning Problem Solving Strategies

After examining the problem solving model as a whole, it is time to focus on the step of choosing a strategy. In Chapter 3, a variety of strategies will be presented and each will include warm-up activities, math applications, and extensions.

Problem Solving Chart

Name: John Doe   **Group:** Challengers   **Date:** June 1

Problem: How many meters from the top of the hill was Jack?

Relevant facts: 1.) Jill was 5 meters down the hill.

          2.) Jack was 2 meters farther than Jill.

Conditions: Jack was 2 meters farther down the hill than Jill. Jill was not in front of Jack.

Strategy: Draw a picture.

Jack———Jill———————top of hill

    2 m.   5 m.   = 7 m.

Solution: 2 m. + 5 m. = 7m.

Jack was 7 m. down the hill.

Reasonable answer? Yes. Jack was in front of Jill by 2 meters, which would mean he was farther down the hill.

SOCIAL SKILLS

Contributions to group: I drew the picture.

Encouraging words: I told Jill she did a great job of finding important facts.

Ways I cooperated: I let John determine the problem, even though I wanted to do it.

Neville J. Leeson

IMPROVING STUDENTS' SENSE OF THREE-DIMENSIONAL SHAPES

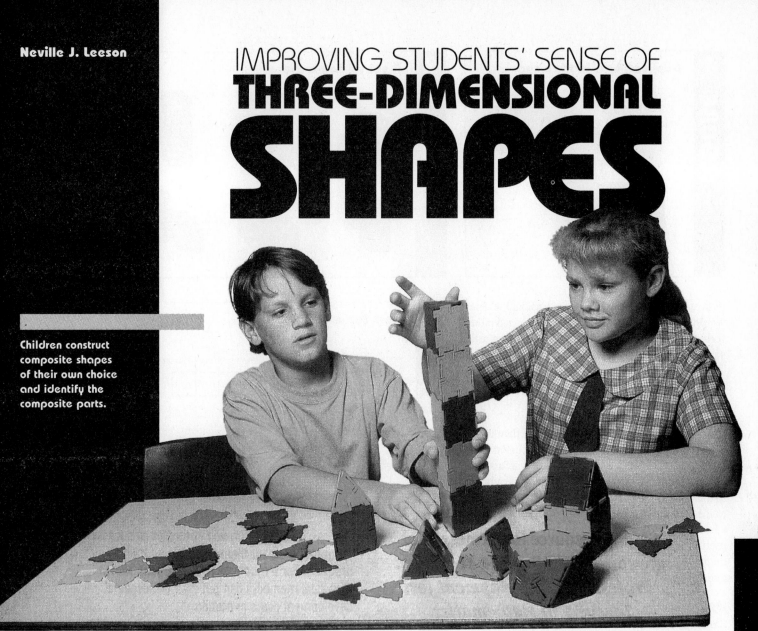

Children construct composite shapes of their own choice and identify the composite parts.

NCTM's *Curriculum and Evaluation Standards for School Mathematics* (1989) specifies that in grades 5–8 the mathematics curriculum should afford students opportunities to "visualize and represent geometric figures with special attention to developing spatial sense" (p. 112). Spatial sense is often referred to as spatial visualization (Wheatley 1990), which is the ability mentally to manipulate a pictorially presented stimulus object. This article describes activities that the author has used with fifth and sixth graders from a rural city in New South Wales, Australia. The intent of the activities is to improve the students' spatial sense with respect to three-dimensional shapes.

Neville Leeson teaches mathematics content and methods courses at the Southern Cross University, Lismore, NSW, Australia. He has regular contact with elementary school classrooms and has a special interest in teaching the concept of shapes.

If materials are not plentiful, teachers may wish to organize their students into three or four groups, so that each group rotates from one activity to the next over time. This approach could be particularly relevant for the third and fourth of the following six activities.

Visualizing nets

The teacher should display within the classroom a variety of three-dimensional shapes, including a cube, a triangular prism, a square pyramid, and a tetrahedron. Depending on classroom organization, each student or group of students should be supplied with plastic interlocking triangles and squares. Students are requested to make and then check arrangements that they predict are nets for a cube, a square pyramid, a triangular prism, and a tetrahedron. The teacher then displays, one at a time, nets for each of these shapes, at the same time asking students to

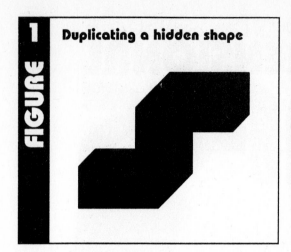

FIGURE 1 Duplicating a hidden shape

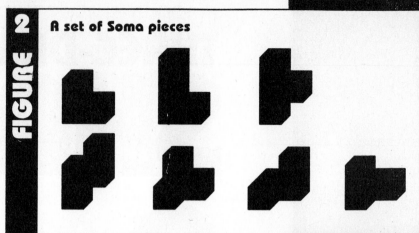

FIGURE 2 A set of Soma pieces

FIGURE 3 Nets for a cube

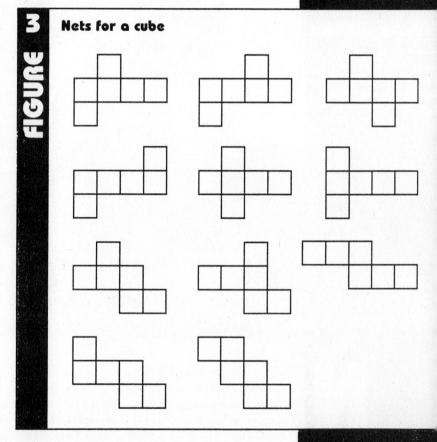

indicate which of the three-dimensional shapes would be made from that net. The teacher can either form the display nets from the interlocking plastic shapes or draw them on an overhead transparency.

Composite shapes

The teacher requests that students work either individually or in groups to make a "house" from interlocking plastic shapes; students are then asked to indicate and name the basic three-dimensional shapes of which it is composed–possibly a cube and a triangular prism. Students are afforded free choice to make other composite shapes and then are asked to identify the component parts. An outdoor observation tour or a search through magazines can be used to identify composite shapes in the environment (e.g., cylindrical-conical-shaped silos and cylindrical-hemispherical fuel containers).

Use of barriers

Students, working in pairs and separated by a small barrier, use interlocking cubes to complete this activity. One of the pair builds a structure from, say, six cubes and gives step-by-step instructions to the other student, who has to duplicate it. This activity helps to develop communication and listening skills as well as spatial visualization.

Further, the teacher can supply each student with a shape made by gluing together wooden cubes **(fig. 1)** or by assembling interlocking cubes. The shape is placed either behind a barrier or in a paper bag so that the student is not able to see it; the student, who is allowed to feel it as often as he or she likes, is asked to duplicate it using interlocking cubes.

Additional activities involving use of shape **(fig. 1)** include *(a)* requesting a student to look at it and duplicate it by feel behind a barrier so that he or she does not see the duplicate and *(b)* requesting a blindfolded student to feel it and duplicate it using interlocking cubes; in this variation the student sees neither the original nor the duplicate.

Soma cubes

The teacher furnishes each pair of students with a set of Soma pieces **(fig. 2)** and a sheet containing drawings of each piece. *(a)* To begin, students match each piece with the appropriate shape on the sheet. *(b)* Next one student from each pair closes his or her eyes while the partner removes one of the seven pieces; the first student then looks to determine which piece is missing by pointing to the correct shape on the sheet. *(c)* Again in pairs, students identify by feel a piece placed in their hands, which are held behind their backs; they point to a shape on the sheet to indicate their response. *(d)* A student from each pair selects by feel from behind a barrier a piece that the partner nominates from the list on the sheet. *(e)* Two or more of the Soma pieces can be used to construct solids; for details consult Izard (1990) and Leeson (1990).

Nets for a cube

Another activity involving spatial visualization requires students to find all the possible nets for a cube. Students work individually or in groups and record their answers by shading squares on a sheet of squared paper. The use of hands-on material may be permitted. Emphasize that two nets are similar if the first can be transformed into the second by flipping or turning it. The eleven possible nets are shown in **figure 3.**

Next the teacher presents on an overhead transparency a net with squares colored as in **figure 4a** and cubes numbered 1 to 4 as in **figure 4b.** Students are asked to state which cube can be formed from the net and to explain their reasoning.

Views of solids

On an overhead transparency, the teacher shows students three different views of the same cube and asks, "If each face is of a different color, what color is opposite *red?*" **(fig. 5).** When requested to indicate how they obtained their answer, many students explain that they "turned in their mind" the first cube to correspond to the third, or vice versa. A minority of students report using a process of elimination, by rejecting all colors that share an edge with red.

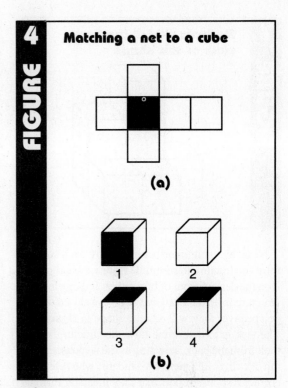

FIGURE 4

Matching a net to a cube

(a)

1 2 3 4

(b)

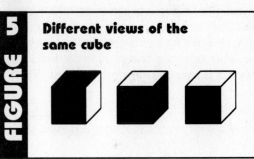

FIGURE 5

Different views of the same cube

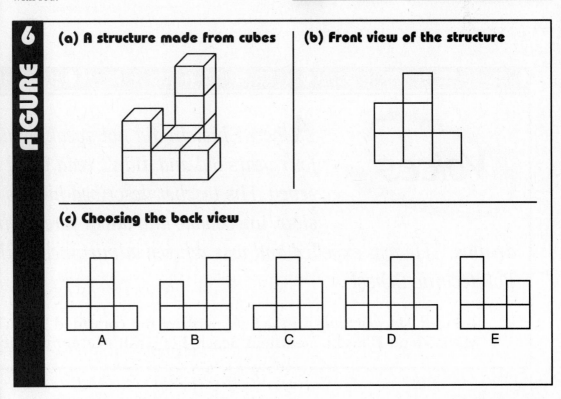

FIGURE 6

(a) A structure made from cubes

(b) Front view of the structure

(c) Choosing the back view

A   B   C   D   E

FIGURE 7

Students sketch the back view of this shape

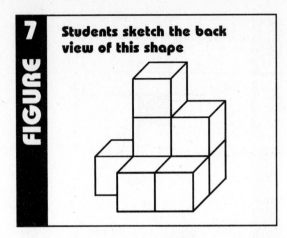

Next, by using interlocking cubes, each student forms a structure to resemble **figure 6a** and places it on the desk in front of him or her. If they view the structure from the front, with one eye closed to lose perspective, they will see the shape in **figure 6b**. The task is to determine how the structure would look from the back, selecting as the response one of the drawings in **figure 6c**. Students who select the correct response report that they mentally turn the object. This finding is in agreement with research, which indicates that when items are small in relation to the observer, the item is mentally turned, whereas for larger objects a change in orientation of the observer is imagined (Carpenter and Just 1986).

In the preceding activity students were asked to nominate the correct view from a number of choices. As a further activity, students again sight the front view of a structure, which they can create from interlocking cubes **(fig. 7)**; this time, however, they are requested to sketch the back view by shading in squares on squared paper, that is, to create rather than choose the correct response.

The hands-on spatial activities described in this article involve the use of a number of senses—sight, touch, and hearing. Such activities need to be experienced on a regular basis by students in fifth and sixth grades to aid in the development of their spatial sense.

References

Carpenter, Patricia A., and Marcel A. Just. "Spatial Ability: An Information Processing Approach to Psychometrics." In *Advances in the Psychology of Human Intelligence,* vol. 3, edited by R. J. Stenberg, 221–53. Hillsdale, N.J.: Lawrence Erlbaum Assoc., 1986.

Izard, John. "Developing Spatial Skills with Three-Dimensional Puzzles." *Arithmetic Teacher* 37 (February 1990):44–47.

Leeson, Neville. *Shapes Alive: Exploring Shapes with Primary Pupils.* Mount Waverley, Victoria: Dellasta Proprietary, 1990.

National Council of Teachers of Mathematics. *Curriculum and Evaluation Standards for School Mathematics.* Reston, Va.: The Council, 1989.

Wheatley, Grayson H. "Spatial Sense and Mathematics Learning." *Arithmetic Teacher* 37 (February 1990):10–11. ♥

Which drawing looks like the back view?

Voices

*A*lbert Einstein did not speak until he was four years old and didn't read until he was seven. His teacher described him as "mentally slow, unsociable and adrift forever in his foolish dreams." He was expelled and was refused admittance to the Zurich Polytechnic School.

— **From *Chicken Soup for the Soul*, written and compiled by Jack Canfield and Mark Victor Hansen. Deerfield Beach, FL: Health Communications, Inc., 1993.**

Hands-on

The Private Eye is a program to develop higher order thinking skills, creativity, and scientific literacy - across subjects. It's based on a simple set of "tools" that produce "gifted" results.
K-12 through life, all levels.

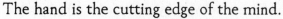

The hand is the cutting edge of the mind.
> - Jacob Bronowski
> Mathematician and poet

First, before everything else comes the seeing of nature with your own eyes, that is, experiencing it yourself.
> - Abraham H. Maslow
> Psychologist

Go back to the sources. You will see how far away we have got from them.
> - Auguste Renoir
> Painter

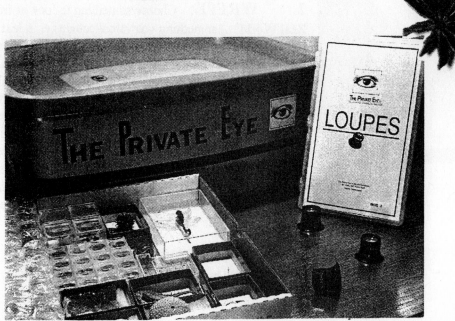

Preview... The Process

The Private Eye is... about the drama and wonder of looking closely at the world, thinking by analogy, changing scale, and theorizing.

1. TO BEGIN The Private Eye: Take a loupe (5X magnification). Press its wide end to bones around eye (typically take off glasses if you wear them). Hold your free hand about 2" from the lens-end of loupe. Focus on hand - until image is sharp. Plenty of light helps. (The loupe cuts out visual distractions!)

As you explore your hand - back, palm, nails, knuckles, dirt - ask the Question: "What else does it [my skin] remind me of? What else does it look like?" (This is thinking by analogy - main tool of scientist, poet, visual artist. It also keeps the eye/mind looking.)

2. WRITE: Choose something to look at from the Real World ....something you've collected (i.e., a leaf, a bug, a shell) and explore it with The Loupe-plus-Question: "What else does it remind me of?" Make up 5 to 10 analogies for each object. WRITE them down: the analogies become the Bones-for-a-Poem, the beginnings of short stories, naturalist essays, etc. (Metaphors and similes are compressed analogies.) Nest two loupes and you get 10X. Later, for a further change of scale, try the 50X kit microscope on the same items. Repeat the steps for things you find on your person, in your yard, in your refrigerator, at the beach, in the woods.

If you have The Private Eye Kit, you can choose something from "The World in a Box™" (See page 69).

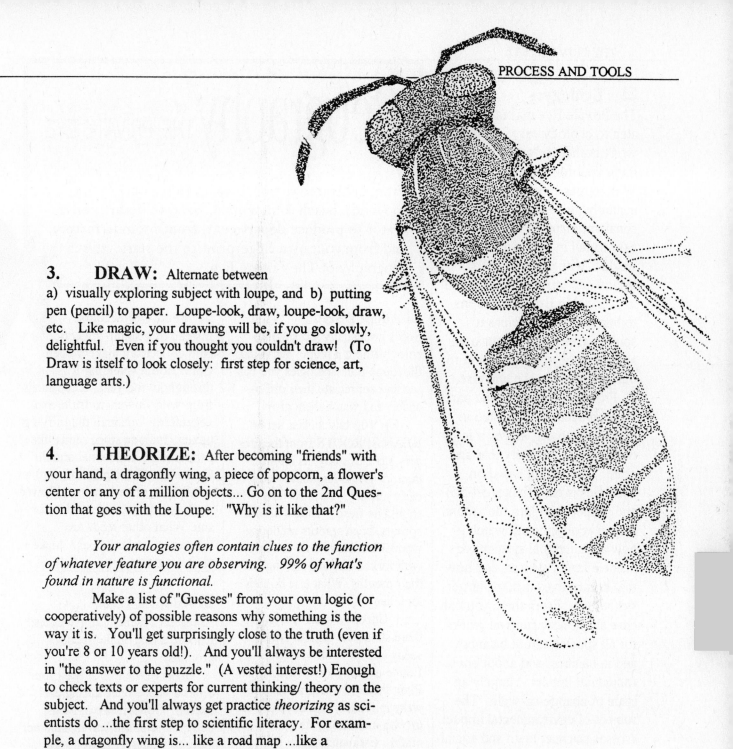

3.   DRAW: Alternate between
a) visually exploring subject with loupe, and b) putting pen (pencil) to paper. Loupe-look, draw, loupe-look, draw, etc.   Like magic, your drawing will be, if you go slowly, delightful.   Even if you thought you couldn't draw! (To Draw is itself to look closely: first step for science, art, language arts.)

4.   THEORIZE: After becoming "friends" with your hand, a dragonfly wing, a piece of popcorn, a flower's center or any of a million objects... Go on to the 2nd Question that goes with the Loupe: "Why is it like that?"

Your analogies often contain clues to the function of whatever feature you are observing.   99% of what's found in nature is functional.
Make a list of "Guesses" from your own logic (or cooperatively) of possible reasons why something is the way it is.   You'll get surprisingly close to the truth (even if you're 8 or 10 years old!).   And you'll always be interested in "the answer to the puzzle." (A vested interest!) Enough to check texts or experts for current thinking/ theory on the subject.   And you'll always get practice *theorizing* as scientists do ...the first step to scientific literacy.   For example, a dragonfly wing is... like a road map ...like a stained-glass window ...like a veined leaf.   "Why is it like that?   What is the design's function?"

5.   THINK first of how you would use these materials to boost your curriculum.

The Basics

❑ **Ecology:**

The Private Eye makes the first step to ecology easy. You won't bother to "save" something you don't first *care* about. With loupes-plus-analogies you instantly make the world personal, intimate, "a friend" - it's easy to fall in love with the world... with the enormous beauty and intrigue to be found in everything from dandelions to barnacles, sea urchins to spiders, tree bark to your own skin - and beyond this world to our neighbors in the universe.

From an interest in one part you can become interested in the whole object, in *why* it is the way it is, its every fold and point. Theorizing based on analogies is easy (pages 54-56) and propels you into the second step in ecology: you watch how an individual system lives inside a larger system, and how that in turn lives in some larger system yet. From there you can *care* about how survival works for all species, about balance and imbalance, and about environmental impact - largely an issue of change-of-scale. The subject of environmental impact crosses science, math and social studies.

> The Private Eye World is Inside/Outside. A small-scale object is a door to a large world.

Geography of THE PRIVATE EYE

From classroom to home, backyard to park, empty lot to woods, beach to mountain, pond to desert, refrigerator to produce department, front room to factory, and from your own fingerprint to the stars - this is the geography of The Private Eye.

❑ **Adopt a Seed:**

Seeds are usually too small to enjoy without a loupe, but using the loupe-plus-analogies you can see and appreciate their differences, and watch them grow.

For 10¢ buy a class set of BEAN SPROUTS from the grocery store to study, as an introductory visual map of a seed's early journey. Bean sprouts should be fresh. Unlike alfalfa sprouts, bean sprouts are loupe-wonderful: hairy little dragons with forked tongues coming out their mouths. What else do they look like?

Choose a seed. Perhaps there should be several types of seeds in a class for variety. Loupe-analogy look, write, draw. Plant the seed. Keep a journal: write in it every two days (tie in growth measurements with math). Estimate/predict how much it will grow over next two weeks based on growth after sprouting. Compare to other growing things: how fast does a baby grow? A tree?

Consider the Eyewitness book, *Plant* (Knopf, 1989), for this activity and all others on plants - all ages through adult.

❑ **Seed Collections:**

Instead of a stamp collection or a coin collection, make a Seed Collection, expanding it throughout the year. Keep seeds - from wild flowers to fruits and vegetables - in small magnifying boxes. Include spice seeds like peppercorns and fennel and dill. Consider collecting (or buying) a small pack of assorted wildflower seeds for shade, and another for sun. What other seeds are interesting under loupes? Make a Seed Art Gallery - Poem Gallery.

❑ **Adopt a Tree:**

*Suggests Teacher Carolyn Gates: Choose a tree on the school's grounds.

Observe the tree at least four times a year - once during each season. Collect leaves, twigs, buds, insects; fall leaves, summer leaves - whatever samples are available to bring in to the classroom to use with The Private Eye analogies and drawing. Lead to vocabulary development, stories and studies about the seasons.

Study the tree as a *community, as a kind of apartment house.* All kinds of Tree Math possible.

In *The Amateur Naturalist*, by Gerald Durrell, you will find on page 110, how to take the "vital statistics" of a tree - and much more to make the above activity, and many others, rich.

❑ Seed Pods Pop:

In the fall begin a study of the life of seeds and seed travel from the point of view of *seed pods*. Start a collection of seed pods - which are often as "artistic" and sculptural as they are fascinating models of nature's evolved efficiency. Seed travel is tied to seed pod structure. Some seed pods pop open when dry enough, usually in summer and fall, and act like cannons shooting the "next generation" out. Some are borne on feather wings like the tiny dandelion fruits. Some hook onto fur. Explore other ways that seeds travel. As always, loupe-look, write, draw and theorize.

● You might collect/buy some seed pods from around the world, or from countries you may be studying.

Some seed pods and seed heads to look for:

alpine poppy
oriental poppy
sunflower
magnolia
cone flower
columbine
pincushion flower pod
burrs
maple wings
alder cones
small pine cones
pin oak acorns
allium (onion family)
queen anne's lace
dandelions
sweet gum
plane tree pods
star anise

Look for the book *Seeds Pop, Stick, Glide,* by Patricia Lauber and Jerome Wexler (Crown, 1981)

● How many seeds are produced in these factory pods? How many seeds will reproduce? These questions are handled in a unit called "Foxglove Towers in Math/Social Studies, p.180.

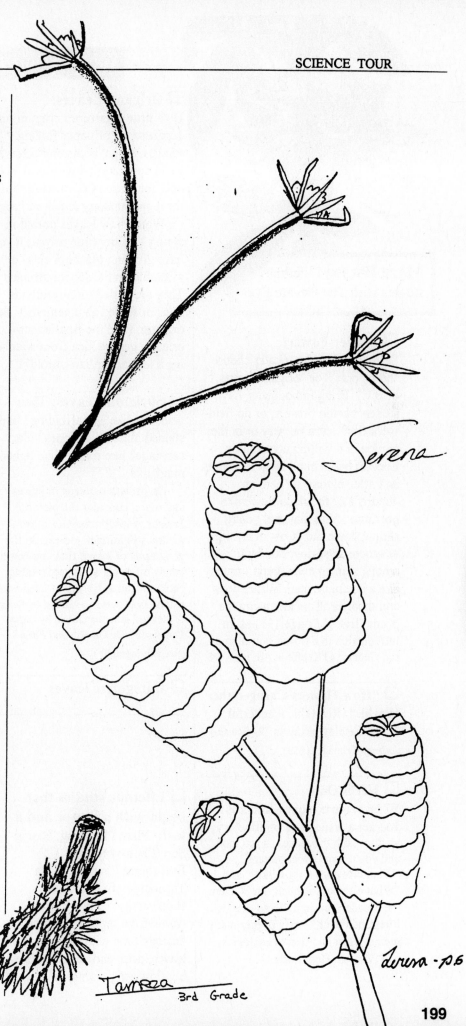

199

More Botany: lifetime studies with The Private Eye

☐ Flower Power!

Study just flowers. (Later choose "herbs only," or "origami leaves," below.) Bring in bouquets, have students bring flowers, or do field-work first... at a nursery or in the garden of a willing contributor. Look at buds, in all stages, blooms and after-blooms. There are hundreds of fabulous flowers to peer into. You may feel you're sliding down the throat of a tulip or crocus in spring, climbing among stamen and stigma - much like a bee must feel! Write, draw and theorize. Consider using the poem "Irises" (page 111) as an introduction to a flower power study, and Georgia O'Keeffe in Art, page 128.

☐ "How Flowers Changed the World." Read this wonderful Loren Eiseley essay in *The Immense Journey* (Vintage, 1959).

☐ Herbs Only

When you use loupes-on-herbs you get a visual and an olfactory wallop. Rub the leaves as you look and you'll have sweet breezes. "What else does it *look* like?" and "What else does it *smell* like?" Here, the broader question "What else does it remind me of?" may trigger many memories in addition to analogies.
  * Visit an Herb Farm.

☐ Origami Leaves:

Do a little classroom origami, the Japanese art of paper folding (cranes, frogs, boats and boxes) - as an appreciation warm-up, not only for masters of origami, but for loupe-analogy *leaf-watching*.

Watch how leaves unfold in spring - or any time of year if you have growing plants in class or available on the school grounds. They are furled as carefully as flags or folded as ingeniously as origami. (Did the first inventor of origami get the idea from watch-ing a leaf accordian-unfold?)

☐ Skeleton Leaves: Their veins are like... scaffolding? like stained glass? like bones? like cartilage? like rivers? like light-ning? like.....???

On growth patterns in leaves and more: consider the pictorial *Leaves, 199 Photographs*, by Andreas Feininger - to extend the geography of leaves that you begin hands-on in class. A remarkable book, to find at library or used book stores, is *Patterns in Nature*, by Peter S. Stevens; read the classic by Darcy Thompson, *On Growth and Form* (See Bibliography).

☐ Categorize leaves

☐ Lifetime studies that begin with a flower and a leaf: Plant Plumbing; Eating Sun (Photosynthesis); Evolution; Pharmaceutical Technology from Plants; Biodiversity. Work back-wards from repeated loupe-analogy time with flowers and leaves, pods and roots (trees are big flowering plants) to a life-time study of the remarkable plumbing and photosynthesis facto-ry that a plant is... and from there to the age-old or the new pharma-ceutical factories that trees and plants offer. It's an easy leap to the necessity of biodiversity. Along in here comes the subject of Global Warming.

It is necessary to become ex-tremely "friendly" with plants and trees to learn their secrets, includ-ing their pharmaceutical, cure-us-of-our-ills secrets. Study Chinese herbal medicine, or study research on the new cancer drugs made from the Pacific Yew's bark and from an English Yew's needles. (See *Sci-ence News*, 2/22/92, Vol. 141, No. 8; and *The New York Times*, 5/21/91, B10.) From here you can study the evolution of plants, and the role of branching systems and sub-systems seen in trees and throughout nature.

● Consider a subscription to *Science News*. It allows you to keep up weekly with subjects that will have a profound impact on your students' futures - and you'll enjoy this magazine's hearty use of analo-gies in reporting.

☐ Nursery Fieldtrip:

Visit a nursery with your class. Divide class into perhaps five groups of six each in fieldwork pairs, each pair having loupes and clipboard and using the Tove Andvik fieldwork approach described on page 75. Assign groups in staggered schedules to:
* the perennial shed
* the annuals
* the shade plants
* the trees
* the shrubs
* the ground covers
* the herbs

❏ Beautiful Weeds:

Many weeds are beautiful, in addition to being "smart" survivors. Start with the dandelion. If you loupe-write, draw and theorize with "just weeds" you can study their extraordinary survival strategies. They are like the "Marines" of the plant world.

❏ Dusty Miller and Cousins:

Meet Dusty Miller leaves with loupes, analogies - and theorize on the function of all that webby, furry, sweatery tangled hair on the leaves. See model lesson on pages 54-55. Find all of Dusty Miller's relatives - near and distant. First guess who's related. Arrange a sort of family reunion in class. Visit the Artemesia family at a Nursery.

❏ Plant Defense:

Study and compare how Dusty Miller survives versus Holly. Note the outside edge of Holly: Like needles? Like bone? "Like cartilage in your nose," as one student suggests. Use analogies, as always, from which to theorize: *"Why is it like that?"* Compare cactus, etc.

❏ Old & New:

To reveal that the "old" - the autumnal side of life is as beautiful as the "new" ...

Make up two boxes with 12 or so divisions. (Clear polyurethane fishing tackle boxes are good.)

● Box 1: Clip and put into compartments a variety of dried pods, seed heads, skeleton leaves to explore with loupes-plus analogy writing, drawing, theorizing.

● Box 2: Clip, as winter thaws and spring comes on, a variety of tiny emerging buds, unfurling leaves, blooms from crocus to cornflower, and lay in compartments to study with The Private Eye.

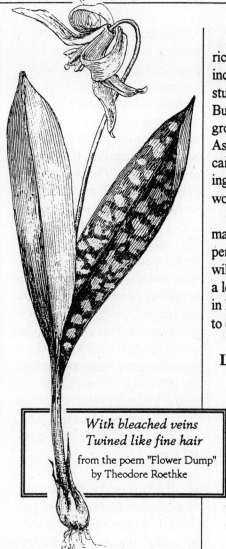

*With bleached veins
Twined like fine hair*
from the poem "Flower Dump"
by Theodore Roethke

❏ A Loupe Garden

Plant a loupe garden at home - so you'll have a good supply of cut flowers, seed pods, sedums and the insects they attract - to bring in to class for table-top fieldwork.

If possible, plant a School Garden - so students can loupe-analogy look at plants and critters and soil as they live and breathe and change throughout the seasons. The Garden is its own wild place - made exciting and personal by the loupe-analogy process.

If there *were* National Curriculum requirements, they should include such loupe-gardens for all students across-the-curriculum. Bulldoze some of the asphalt grounds! Dig up some of the lawn! Ask for retired volunteers to help in care, monitoring. George Washington Carver (see next page) would approve.

With loupes and analogies making the world close-up and personal, a garden, even an easy, wild, perennial garden - would go a long way to helping students fall in love with the world - first step to ecology.

●

Loupe-Garden Suggestions:

(No-work perennials are easy to get *free, as* starters, from neighbor gardeners)

Lenten Rose
Crocus
Bluebell
Forget-me-nots
Tulip
Oriental and Alpine Poppy
Iris
Foxglove
Daylily & Peruvian Lily
sedums and succulents
herbs like sages and mints
berries
Globe thistle
Sea holly
Allium
Cone flower
Pincushion flowers
Dusty Miller
Montana Cornflower
Daisies and Gallardia

Visit a Nursery with your loupe for more ideas.

●

Note: Teacher Libby Sinclair suggests making garden art based on loupe-drawings of plants and flowers to line a garden path: clay tiles, outdoor plant signs, and more.

> *I wanted to know every strange stone, flower, insect, bird, or beast.*
> - George Washington Carver

□ George Washington Carver's Garden and Collections:

George Washington Carver might as well have had a loupe in his eye. He had the combined habits of scientist, poet, artist - of looking closely, thinking by analogy, changing scale and theorizing - when exploring the woods and the garden from childhood and throughout his life.

As a boy he made non-stop collections of rocks, plants, insects, frogs and reptiles. "He even began a little garden of his own in the woods. There he transplanted and cultivated plants of various sorts, carefully observing the conditions that enabled them to grow and be healthy," writes biographer Gene Adair in *George Washington Carver, Botanist* (Chelsea House, NY 1989, p.21).

He became known around town as the "plant doctor." He drew and painted plants, insects, birds, reptiles. He "talked" with them all. Eventually he looked closely at the peanut (goober), considered only carnival food back in 1915. He became friendly with its ways. Out of such depth inventors are born. He invented over 300 uses for the peanut and sweet potato - from milk to dye - with enormous food, health, economic and manufacturing implications.

George Washington Carver is a timely model for the type of problem solver most needed in our immediate future. With worldwide human population increasing exponentially, even now unable to feed itself, the habits and impulses of Carver are a beacon. *"The primary idea in all of my work was to help the farmer and fill the poor man's empty dinner pail,"* said Carver. *"My idea is to help the 'man farthest down.' This is why I have made every process just as simple as I could to put it within his reach."* (*ibid*, p. 79) Carver's goals were not only humane, they model the best economic and manufacturing sense and imitate the efficiency of nature, mirroring Einstein's remark that "Everything must be made as simple as possible, but not one bit simpler."

Read a biography of George Washington Carver linked particularly to garden-louping and inventing. You and your students will be imitating his ways using The Private Eye across-the-curriculum.

(For younger readers see also *A Pocketful of Goobers*, by Barbara Mitchell, (Carolrhoda Books, Minneapolis, 1986).

Loupe-look, write and draw peanuts in the shell. And then eat!

> *...begin now to study the little things in your own door yard, going from the known to the nearest related unknown....*
> - George Washington Carver

□ **Visit A Botanical Garden and an Arboretum** with loupes and analogy-questions.

□ **Plant Parts**

□ **Pigments from Plants**

□ **Lichens and Liverworts**

□ **Fungus as Biomass**

□ **Write the Biography of a Plant**

□ **A Yard of Yard:** Explore on hands and knees a square yard of land outside your door. Make a Pocket Museum, suggests teacher Gregg Onewein, page 76.

□ **A Plot of Grass:** Teacher Diane Paulson suggests you examine a plot of grass in the spirit of the film *Honey, I Shrunk the Kids*, imagining you are ¼" tall... and go on an adventure. Slide down the blade of grass, climb up the twig, crawl under the stick and see what there is to see. Write your story.

□ **A Cup of Soil:** Teacher Melisa Garcia-Carrington suggests: Collect individual clumps of soil, perhaps in a paper cup. Take back to classroom. Have students look with eyes to see what they see. Discuss and draw.

Then pass out loupes and have students examine their clump. Discuss what they see now, using analogies. Draw. Discuss the differences between exploring without a loupe and with a loupe.

Do a "soil profile."

If a student finds a worm, start a study of worms and why worms are important. *If no student finds a worm, have a worm "planted" in your own soil sample.

❏ The Energy in Your Brain Was Once Sunlight:

Why bother to think about photosynthesis? Isn't that something just between the sun and the green growing things?

Not at all. We rely quite intimately on photosynthesis to read this very sentence. "The chemical energy and electrical energy used by brain cells... were once sunlight that was absorbed by the chlorophyll in green plants." (*The New Encyclopedia Britannica*, 1984, Vol. 14, p. 366) When you're eating a carrot or spinach or a salad or an animal that ate the grass - you're eating sunlight. As you walk and breathe and think about this, you are running on a kind of solar power yourself.

As you discuss with your students the interdependent relationship between sunlight, plants and people, consider the following points - and discuss their implications:

❶ "If plant photosynthesis were to stop, most living things would disappear from the earth in a few years." and ❷ "Increasing requirements for food in a world in which human population is increasing exponentially requires... an increase in the amount of photosynthesis on earth..." In short, "life and the quality of the atmosphere today depend on photosynthesis..." (*ibid*, Encyclopedia Britannica, 1984)

❏ Photosynthesis by Analogy

Philip Morrison, physicist and educator, says we probably don't understand something until we can make a visual model of it. Analogies are the equivalent of visual models.

Challenge: Re-study photosynthesis and see if you can explain to yourself, in analogies, exactly how a plant uses sunlight.

Challenge your students to do the same. Have students draw pictures and diagrams to illustrate the process of photosynthesis.

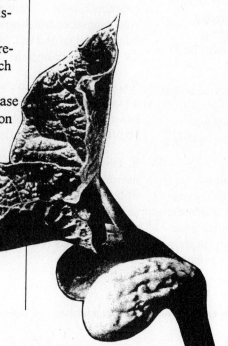

...it may be doubted if there are any other animals which have played such an important part in the history of the world as these lowly organized creatures.

- Charles Darwin,
The Formation of Vegetable Mold through the Action of Worms

❏ A Winding of Worms:

Study earthworms under loupe then **50X microscope.** Even with a loupe you can see the pulsations of the worm and its blood vessels. The worm's inner workings, suggests teacher Earl Wilson, are like plumbing.

In Richard Headstrom's *Adventures with a Hand Lens* (substitute a loupe for a hand lens and add the analogy-making process to get 50 loupe activities) - you'll find a wonderful lesson on worms. *"The worm," he writes, is "not only a mere tiller of the soil, it is also an agriculturist, for it plants fallen seeds by covering them with soil and cares for the growing plants by cultivating the soil around the roots. Furthermore, it enriches the soil by burying the bones of dead animals, shells, leaves, twigs, and other organic matter that, upon decaying, furnishes the necessary minerals to the plants. It even provides drainage by boring holes to carry off the surplus water, and by so doing also promotes aeration."*

Collect a worm in a cup of soil. In a clear cup you can watch it work. Start a worm farm. Discover how worms made great compost piles for intensified gardening. Love a worm!

Science Concepts

The National Center for Improving Science Education recommends that elementary schools design curricula that introduce nine scientific concepts. Many of the activities described in this handbook teach these concepts, which are drawn from the center's recent report, *Getting Started in Science: A Blueprint for Elementary School Science Education*. The nine concepts are:

1. Organization. Scientists have made the study of science manageable by organizing and classifying natural phenomena. For example, natural objects can be assembled in hierarchies (atoms, molecules, mineral grains, rocks, strata, hills, mountains, and planets). Or objects can be arranged according to their complexity (single-celled amoeba, sponges, and so on to mammals).

Primary grade children can be introduced to this concept by sorting objects like leaves, shells, or rocks according to their characteristics. Intermediate grade children can classify vegetables or fruits according to properties they observe in them, and then compare their own classification schemes to those used by scientists.

2. Cause and effect. Nature behaves in predictable ways. Searching for explanations is the major activity of science; effects cannot occur without causes. Primary children can learn about cause and effect by observing the effect that light, water, and warmth have on seeds and plants. Intermediate grade children can discover that good lubrication and streamlining the body of a pinewood derby car can make it run faster.

3. Systems. A system is a whole that is composed of parts arranged in an orderly manner according to some scheme or plan. In science, systems involve matter, energy, and information that move through defined pathways. The amount of matter, energy and information, and the rate at which they are transferred through the pathways, varies over time. Children begin to understand systems by tracking changes among the individual parts.

Primary children can learn about systems by studying the notion of balance — for example, by observing the movements and interactions in an aquarium. Older children might gain an understanding of systems by studying the plumbing or heating systems in their homes.

4. Scale refers to quantity, both relative and absolute. Thermometers, rulers, and weighing devices help children see that objects and energy vary in quantity. It's hard for children to understand that certain phenomena can exist only within fixed limits of size. Yet primary grade children can begin to understand scale if they are asked, for instance, to imagine a mouse the size of an elephant. Would the mouse still have the same proportions if it were that large? What changes would have to occur in the elephant-sized mouse for it to function? Intermediate grade children can be asked to describe the magnification of a microscope.

5. Models. We can create or design objects that represent other things. This is a hard concept for very young children. But primary grade children gain experience with it by drawing a picture of a cell as they observe it through a microscope. Intermediate grade children can use a model of the earth's crust to demonstrate the cause of earthquakes.

6. Change. The natural world continually changes, although some changes may be too slow to observe. Rates of change vary. Children can be asked to observe changes in the position and apparent shape of the moon. Parents and children can track the position of the moon at the same time each night and draw pictures of the moon's changing shape to learn that change takes place during the lunar cycle. Children can also observe and describe changes in the properties of water when it boils, melts, evaporates, freezes, or condenses.

7. Structure and function. A relationship exists between the way organisms and objects look (feel, smell, sound, and taste) and the things they do. Children can learn that skunks let off a bad odor to protect themselves. Children also can learn to infer what a mammal eats by studying its teeth, or what a bird eats by studying the structure of its beak.

8. Variation. To understand the concept of organic evolution and the statistical nature of the world, students first need to understand that all organisms and objects have distinctive properties. Some of these properties are so distinctive that no continuum connects them — for example, living and nonliving things, or sugar and salt. In most of the natural world, however, the properties of organisms and objects vary continuously.

Young children can learn about this concept by observing and arranging color tones. Older children can investigate the properties of a butterfly during its life cycle to discover qualities that stay the same as well as those that change.

9. Diversity. This is the most obvious characteristic of the natural world. Even preschoolers know that there are many types of objects and organisms. In elementary school, youngsters need to begin understanding that diversity in nature is essential for natural systems to survive. Children can explore and investigate a pond, for instance, to learn that different organisms feed on different things.

From *Helping Your Child Learn Science*, U.S. Department of Education, 1992.

Assessment

Portfolio Research: A Slim Collection

Joan L. Herman and Lynn Winters

Although initial findings favor portfolio assessments, the challenges lie in assuring technical quality, equity, and feasibility for large-scale assessment purposes.

Ms. Jackson is implementing portfolios in her classroom. Every month or so, she gives her students a new writing assignment. Sometimes the assignment is creative; sometimes it asks students to use information from their science or social studies work; sometimes it involves research in the community. First, the students engage in a variety of pre-writing activities and write drafts. Often, to supplement Ms. Jackson's routine feedback, students convene in small groups for peer review.

Students keep all their writing in a folder, periodically identifying the best pieces for their "showcase" portfolios. Students then take home their portfolios to discuss their progress and favorite pieces with their parents. At the end of the year. Ms. Jackson sends the portfolios to a central scoring site where she and other teachers participate in a statewide scoring effort. The state then plans to make the results public to show how well the schools prepare students in writing.

• • •

What will Ms. Jackson and her students gain from this innovative assessment program? Professional literature and national conference agendas extol the potential benefits of portfolios for teaching, learning, and assessment—particularly compared with traditional multiple-choice tests. Although initial findings favor portfolio assessments, the challenges lie in assuring technical quality, equity, and feasibility for large-scale assessment purposes.

Well-designed portfolios represent important, contextualized learning that requires complex thinking and expressive skills. Traditional tests have been criticized as being insensitive to local curriculum and instruction, and of assessing not only student achievement but aptitude. Portfolios are being heralded as vehicles that provide a more equitable and sensitive portrait of what students know and are able to do. Portfolios encourage teachers and schools to focus on important student outcomes, provide parents and the community with credible evidence of student achievement, and inform policy and practice at every level of the educational system.

And what of the evidence for these claims? Surprisingly, a dearth of empirical research exists. In fact, of 89 entries on portfolio assessment topics found in the literature over the past 10 years, only seven articles either report technical data or employ accepted research methods. Instead, most articles explain the rationale for portfolio assessment; present ideas and models for how portfolios should be constituted and used; or share details of how portfolios have been implemented in a particular class, school, district, or state. Relatively absent is attention to technical quality, to serious indicators of impact, or to rigorous testing of assumptions.

Technical Quality

Why worry about technical quality? Many portfolio advocates, bridling against the measurement experts who, they believe, have long defined assessment practice and used it to drive curriculum and instruction, do not seem to give much weight to technical characteristics. These advocates accept

Bobby Gear/Adelphi, Maryland

Technical quality will continue to be a critical issue if portfolio assessment results are used to make important decisions about students, teachers, and schools.

We need to know that an assessment provides accurate information for the decisions we wish to make. Are

at face value the belief that performance assessments in general and portfolio assessments in particular are better than traditional multiple-choice tests, are better matched to new theories of curriculum and learning, and are more suitable for the thinking and problem-solving skills that students will need for future success.

Although such concerns for curriculum, instruction, and student learning can and should remain paramount in the design of new assessments, technical quality will continue to be a critical issue if results are used to make important decisions about students, teachers, and schools.

the results of portfolio assessment reliable, consistent, and meaningful estimates of what students know and can do? If not, the assessment will produce fickle results. For students, teachers, schools, districts, or even states, adequate technical quality is essential.

And just what is technical quality? Many of us are familiar with two core elements—reliability and validity. These terms encompass a variety of technical questions and require a variety of evidence (see fig. 1). When available evidence is compared with the evidence needed to certify the soundness of portfolios for making high-stakes decisions about students,

we find that much work remains to be done before claims as to the accuracy and usefulness of these assessments can be supported.

Interrater agreement. Raters who judge student performance must agree regarding what scores should be assigned to students' work within the limits of what experts call "measurement error." Do raters agree on how a portfolio ought to be scored? Do they assign the same or nearly similar scores to a particular student's work? If the answer is no, then student scores are a measure of who does the scoring rather than the quality of the work. Interrater agreement is accepted as the foundation upon which all other decisions about portfolio quality are made. But out of 46 portfolio assessments listed in the *CRESST Alternative Assessments in Practice Database*, only 13 report data on rater agreement (CRESST 1993).

Further, the technical data that exist show uneven results. On one hand, results from Vermont's statewide portfolio assessment program, perhaps the most visible example in the country, have been disappointing. Here, 4th and 8th graders kept portfolios in both writing and mathematics. Writing portfolios contained six to eight pieces representing various writing genres, with one designated as a best piece. Mathematics portfolios contained five to seven papers, each a best piece of three types: puzzles, math applications, and investigations. Although scoring criteria and procedures for the two types of portfolios differed, both used analytic scoring that rated students' work on a number of different dimensions.

In both subjects, the students' classroom teachers were the first to rate the work. Based on the first year of full implementation, Koretz, Stecher, and Deibert (1993) report interrater reliability of .28 to .60, depending on how the scores were aggregated. This level of agreement was not sufficient to permit reporting many of the aggregate statistics the state had planned to use: The state could not accurately report the proportion of students who achieved each point on the dimensions on which student work was scored, and it could not provide accurate data on the comparative performance of districts and schools.

In Pittsburgh, however, the districtwide assessment obtained high inter·ater agreement for its writing portfolios (LeMahieu et al. 1993). The Pittsburgh portfolio system grew out of ARTS PROPEL, a five-year project funded by the Rockefeller Foundation to design instruction-based assessment in visual arts, music, and imaginative writing (Camp 1993). Pittsburgh students in grades 5–12 developed their portfolios over a year, a process that required them to compose, revise, and reflect upon their writing. The reflection component was especially extensive and included student comments about the processes they used, their choices and writing purposes, the criteria they used in assessing their writing, and their focus for future work.

The portfolio contained at least six selections that met such general categories as "a satisfying piece," "an unsatisfying piece," "an important piece," "a free pick," and so on. Students included drafts and reflections with their finished work. District raters—including both ARTS PROPEL and other teachers—were free to select any evidence in a student's portfolio. The work was rated on: accomplishment in writing, use of process and resources, and growth and engagement. Despite the amount of latitude that raters had in selecting pieces to rate and the broad

Figure 1

A Map of the Technical Territory of Portfolio Assessment

Technical Issue: Reliability	Data Needed to Assure Quality
Are the scores consistent or stable?	■ Scorer or rater agreement ■ Interrater consistency ■ Score stability for the same student on different occasions ■ Score stability of papers/entries given different contexts or "portfolio sets" in which a portfolio is scored ■ Score consistency across "like" tasks
Technical Issue: Validity	**Data Needed to Assure Quality**
What do the scores mean?	■ What are the scoring criteria based upon (what standards, what definition of "excellence")? ■ How were tasks selected? What view of "achievement" do the portfolio contents present?
Do inferences from the scores lead to accurate decisions about students? programs? schools?	■ Are the scores diagnostic? When students score "high," what can be said about their performance? What standards are met? What other things do students know or can they do? How do we know? ■ When students score "low," what directions for improving performance do the scores provide? How do we know that the diagnosis will lead to improved performance? ■ Is the assessment fair? Are portfolios a disadvantage to any group of students? If so, how? ■ What are the consequences of portfolio use on individual students? programs? schools? Do results lead to improvement in students and programs?

scope of the scoring criteria, interrater agreement correlations ranged from .60 to .70, and the generalizability estimate of interrater agreement when two raters reviewed each piece was in the .80 range.

In a third example (Herman et al. 1993), an elementary school-based study of writing portfolios found similarly high levels of interrater agreement. In this case, student portfolios contained final drafts of writing that had been assigned over the last half of the school year, composed mainly of narrative and, to a lesser extent, summaries and poems. Raters were recruited from outside the school, from a district that has a long and strong history in analytic writing

assessment. Drawing on essentially the same dimensions used in their regular district writing assessment, raters gave each portfolio a single, overall quality score. Average correlations between scores given by pairs of raters was .82, and percentage of absolute agreements for all pairs of raters averaged .98.

These three examples demonstrate the possibility of achieving interrater reliability for classroom-based portfolios in a variety of configurations. While such reliability is probably easiest to achieve when the contents of portfolios are relatively uniform and when experienced scorers use well-honed rubrics (as in Herman et al. 1993), the Pittsburgh example shows that reliability is also possible when contents are loosely structured. However, consensus among raters, as the Vermont case shows, is not easily achieved. Available data suggest that such consensus depends on clearly articulated criteria, effective training, and rubrics that reflect shared experience, common values, and a deep understanding of student performance. In the Pittsburgh case, such consensus evolved over time through close collaboration.

Further, despite the promising results reported in Pittsburgh and study by Herman and colleagues (1993), little work has been done to examine other, equally important sources of portfolio score reliability, such as score stability over time, stability across different rater groups or pairs, and the effect of task or "context" (the portfolio set in which a particular portfolio is rated). Without this information, decisions about individual student portfolio scores are limited to the one occasion, particular raters, and specific tasks comprising a particular portfolio assessment.

Validity and meaning of scores. Though reliability in all its forms is necessary, it is not a sufficient prerequisite to the core issue in technical quality: validity. When we assess students, what we really want to know is, do the scores of a portfolio assessment represent some enduring and meaningful capability? Are scores good indicators of what we think we're assessing? Beyond claims that portfolio work "looks like" it captures important learning, validity issues have been very sparsely studied.

One useful approach in determining what portfolio scores mean is to look for patterns of relationships between the results of portfolio assessments and other indicators of student performance. Score meaning becomes supported when portfolio scores relate highly to other, valued measures of the

same capability and show weak or no relationship to measures of different capabilities. Of course, this approach to verifying score meaning assumes we have good "other" measures for comparison. If, for example, we have no good measures of mathematics problem solving, how do we know whether portfolios are good measures of this capability? This is a vexing

> Advocates say that portfolios are more likely to elicit the true capability of most students, not just those motivated to do well on decontextualized, on-demand, one-shot tests.

problem for validity studies—especially because one of the reasons for the popularity of alternative and portfolio assessments has been our waning trust in the value of existing measurement techniques.

Using this general approach, Koretz and colleagues (1993) investigated score relationships between measures of both similar and different capabilities in the Vermont program. The researchers found moderate correlations ranging from .47 to .58 between writing portfolio scores and direct writing assessments. When comparing writing portfolios with an "unlike capability," in this case multiple-choice mathematics test scores, however, they found essentially the same level of correlation, rather than no or a very weak relationship.

The researchers state: "More grounds for pessimism occurred when mathematics portfolio scores were compared to ... uniform tests in both writing and mathematics"

(Koretz et al. 1993, p. 85). Whereas Koretz and colleagues expected the two measures of mathematics to be highly correlated and the math portfolio to be, at most, weakly related to writing scores, in fact the relationships among all three measures were at a similarly low level.

Similarly, Gearhart and others (1993) found virtually no relationship when comparing results from writing portfolios with those from standard writing assessments. In fact, two-thirds of the students who would have been classified as "masters" based on the portfolio assessment score would *not* have been so classified on the basis of the standard assessment. When portfolios were scored in two different ways—one giving a single score to the collection as a whole and the second as the average of the scores for all the individually scored pieces in the portfolio—correlations between the two sets of scores were moderately high (in the .6 range). Even so, half the students who would have been classified as "masters" on the basis of the single portfolio score would not have been so classified when scores for individual pieces were averaged. Thus, a student classified as a capable writer on the basis of the portfolio would not necessarily do well when given a standard writing prompt. Further, students classified as capable on the basis of an overall quality score were not always so classified when each piece in the portfolio was scored separately.

Which assessment best represents an enduring capability, a generalizable skill? Does one context overestimate or another underestimate students' skills? These questions are unanswerable with available data, but are important validity issues, particularly for large-scale assessment purposes.

Fairness: Whose Work Is It?

Portfolio advocates firmly believe that classroom tasks are the better indicator of student capability because they are likely to reflect an authentic purpose, perhaps a more stimulating or relevant topic, an opportunity to engage in an extended writing process, and so on. They say that portfolios are more likely to elicit the true capability of most students, not just those motivated to do well on decontextualized, on-demand, one-shot tests.

This argument, however, may have another side. Rather than motivating better performance and providing a more supportive context than traditional tests, portfolios actually may overestimate student performance. Students often get support in planning, drafting, and revising writing that is part of a classroom assignment; in fact, this support is a hallmark of good instruction. But does this additional support from peers, teachers, or others constitute learning for an individual student, or does it simply make an individual student's work look better? This question is not a major issue when portfolios are used for classroom assessment. Teachers, after all, have many indicators of student capability and are aware of the conditions under which work is produced. In large-scale assessment settings where the question is "What can an *individual* do?" the issue becomes important indeed.

If some students get more help and support than others, are they not given unfair advantage during the assessment? The study by Gearhart and others (1993) in a small sample of elementary school classes raises this issue. The researchers asked teachers how much structure or prompting they provided individual students, what type of peer or teacher editorial assistance occurred, and what were the available resources and time for portfolio compilation. Results showed

> Most educators believe that the use of portfolios encourages productive changes in curriculum, instruction, and student learning.

differences in the amount of support given to individual students within classrooms as well as differences between classrooms participating in the study. When students have different levels of assistance, how do we assess their work to determine what they actually can do individually? And how do we provide equitable assessment settings?

The popularity of group work and recommendations to include it in portfolios add additional complications to the "Whose work is it?" question. Webb (1993), for example, found substantial differences in students' performances when judged on the basis of cooperative group work compared with individual work. Not too surprisingly, low-ability students had higher scores on the basis of group work than on individual work. This, in fact, is an important reason for group work—groups may develop better solutions than individuals working alone. What is important to remember, however, is that the group product doesn't necessarily tell us about the capabilities of individuals.

Additional complications arise when class work merges with homework. The amount of help students get from family and friends becomes an additional threat to the validity of interpretations about individual scores. Consider the student whose screenwriter parent embellishes a composition compared with the student who receives no assistance. Will portfolio assessments put the latter student at a disadvantage? And what of the school in a community of highly educated professionals who are involved in their children's schooling? If portfolios are used for school accountability, does this school represent a better environment for educating students than one where students receive substantially less outside help? Differential support issues become important when student work is scored remotely and scores are used to make high-stakes decisions about students or schools.

The equity of portfolio assessment deserves continuing scrutiny. Research to date suggests that patterns of performance on portfolios mirror those on traditional measures in terms of the *relative* performance levels of disadvantaged or minority groups. LeMahieu and colleagues (1993), for example, in a study of writing portfolios, found that females do better than males and that white students show higher levels of performance than African-American students. Hearne and Schuman (1992) similarly found the same demographic patterns of performance for traditional standardized and portfolio assessments.

Effects of Implementing Portfolios

Based on self-reports from teachers and others, implementing portfolio assessment does appear to have positive effects on instruction. The majority of teachers queried in

Catherine Aldridge/Patterson, New York

Vermont, for example, reported that the implementation of mathematics portfolios led them to devote more classroom time to teaching problem-solving strategies, and about half indicated that they spent more time than before helping their students to deal with mathematical patterns and relationships (Koretz et al. 1993). More than two-thirds noted an increase in emphasis on mathematical communication, and approximately half reported engaging students in more small group work than in prior years. Principals also confirmed these changes. The majority of principals interviewed affirmed that Vermont's portfolio assessment program had beneficial effects on curriculum and instruction, citing as examples specific changes in curriculum content and instructional strategies. Additionally, more than half the principals suggested that portfolios had value as an educational intervention to promote change.

Similarly, Aschbacher's action research (1993) suggests that involve-ment in the development and implementation of alternative assessments influences teachers' instructional practices and their attitudes toward students. Two-thirds of the teachers in her study, who received training and follow-up technical support in assessment development and scoring, reported substantial change in the ways they thought about their own teaching. As one teacher explained:

> The portfolios seem to mirror not only the students' work but the teacher's as well. As a result, I have found the need to re-work, re-organize, and re-assess my teaching strategies (p. 22).

The Aschbacher study also noted that using portfolios had influenced teachers' expectations for their students. Two-thirds reported at least some increase in expecting more thinking and problem solving, and higher levels of performance. These findings mirror those in Vermont, where more than 80 percent of the teachers surveyed reported changes in their views of their students' mathe-matical ability on the basis of portfolio work. As Koretz and colleagues (1993) put it, "Although the amount of change reported by most teachers was small, the pervasiveness of change was striking" (p. 23).

Feasibility Issues

While the literature is promising regarding potential effects of portfolios on curriculum and instruction, it also indicates the substantial time and challenges that portfolio use entails. For example, a majority of principals interviewed in Vermont believed that portfolio assessment generally had salutary effects on their schools' curriculum, instruction, and effects on student learning and attitudes, but almost 90 percent of these principals characterized the program as "burden-some," particularly from the perspective of its demands on teachers (Koretz et al. 1993).

All studies reviewed reported substantial demands on teachers' time (Aschbacher 1993, Koretz et al., 1993; Wolf and Gearhart 1993): time for teachers to learn new assessment practices, to understand what should be included in portfolios and how to help students compile them, to develop portfolio tasks, to discern and apply criteria for assessing students' work, to reflect upon and fine-tune their instructional and assessment practices, and to work out and manage the logistics. The Vermont study, for example, asking about only some of these demands, found that teachers devoted 17 hours a month to choosing portfolio tasks, preparing portfolio lessons, and evaluating the contents of portfolios; and 60 percent of the teachers surveyed at both 4th and 8th grades indicated that they often lacked sufficient time to develop portfolio lessons (Koretz et al. 1993).

...ram Vara El Centro California

The time Vermont teachers spent developing tasks is indicative of another, even more significant challenge—helping teachers to change their teaching practices. Prior to the statewide assessment program, problem solving apparently wasn't a regular part of instruction in Vermont's classrooms. For example, many of the mathematics portfolios from the pilot year were unscorable because they did not contain work that required problem-solving skills. Have teachers been prepared to develop good assessment tasks? Have they been prepared to teach problem solving and to help students develop deep understanding of subject matter? The weight of evidence suggests not (Aschbacher 1991, 1992; Brewer 1991; Myers et al. 1992; Plake et al. 1992).

What is required is a paradigmatic shift not only in assessment, but in how teachers approach teaching. Teachers are being asked to engage students in deeper levels of cognitive involvement, rich content, and disciplinary understandings. They are also being asked to employ different instructional strategies—such as cooperative group work, extended assignments, discussion of portfolios,

students' self reflection. And they are being asked to engage in different instructional roles—monitoring, coaching, and facilitating students' performances. Yet teachers' preparation for making such shifts is meager at best. Without such preparation, the quality of implementation looms as a very large issue. Reflecting on the ARTS PROPEL experience, Roberta Camp notes:

> The portfolio is far more than a procedure for gathering samples of student writing. Portfolio reflection has changed the climate of the classroom and the nature of teacher/student interactions. Reflection has become part of an approach to learning in which instruction and assessment are thoroughly integrated. Assessment is no longer an enterprise that takes place outside the classroom: it is one in which teachers and students are actively engaged on a recurring basis as they articulate and apply criteria to their own and one another's writing (1993).

Many people rightly worry about the costs of implementing large-scale portfolio assessment programs. While the direct and indirect costs of portfolios have had little study, Catterall and Winters (in press) report the cost ingredients are many: staff training,

development of task specifications and prompts, administration of portfolio records and their storage, and scoring. For example, how are "one-shot" performances, such as speeches and dramatic presentations, recorded and stored in a portfolio? These costs pale, however, compared with those required to help teachers develop the skills necessary to realize the benefits of portfolio assessment. Needed are opportunities for professional development, ongoing support, technical expertise and time for teachers to develop, practice, reflect upon, and hone their instructional and assessment expertise.

The Future

What will the future bring for portfolio assessment? Will portfolio use benefit schools and children? Clearly there exist substantial challenges in the area of technical quality and feasibility if portfolios are to be used for large-scale assessment for high-stakes purposes. Evidence suggests that one basic requisite for technical quality—interrater reliability—is achievable. The conditions and costs of achievability, however, remain an open issue. More important to resolve are the validity of inferences about individual performances and a range of equity issues. On the one hand, some of these technical issues can probably be most easily solved if portfolio tasks are closely specified and highly standardized. But, in seeking technical rigor, we need to be sure not to lose the appeal of the portfolio concept.

Evidence about the impact of portfolio assessment on curriculum and instruction is weak, but provocative. Most educators believe that the use of portfolios encourages productive changes in curriculum, instruction, and student learning. Although this evidence is based solely on self-report data (with their well-known limitations), teachers and principals seem to think that portfolio assessment has encouraged them to rethink and to change their curriculum and instructional practices.

However, change alone is not enough—*the quality of change and the efficacy of the new practices must be subjected to inquiry*. For example, small group work alone, if not thoughtfully structured and if students are inadequately prepared, probably cannot facilitate students' learning. Similarly, the more frequent act of giving students extended assignments does not assure that they will be instructed effectively in how to complete such assignments or will receive effective feedback to help them hone their performance (Cohen and Ball 1990, Herman 1994).

Thus far, the literature is silent regarding how well new practices are being implemented. We know that student performance judged on the basis of large-scale portfolio assessments tends to be relatively low (Koretz et al. 1993, LeMahieu et al. 1993). We can infer from these findings that we have considerable room for improvement in both instructional practices and the quality of students' accomplishments. We cannot yet expect the relatively recent portfolio assessment projects to have influenced student outcomes, the ultimate indicator of effective practice. But we can cultivate appetites for research to address these and other issues that should guide educational assessment policy. ■

References

Aschbacher, P. R. (1991). "Performance Assessment: State Activity, Interest, and Concerns." *Applied Measurement in Education* 4, 4: 275–288.

Aschbacher, P. R. (1992). "Issues in Performance Assessment Staff Development." *New Directions in Education Reform* 1, 2: 51–62.

Aschbacher, P. R. (1993). *Issues in Innovative Assessment for Classroom Practice: Barriers and Facilitators* (Tech. Rep. No. 359). Los Angeles: University of California, CRESST; Center for the Study of Evaluation.

Brewer, R. (June 1991). "Authentic Assessment: Flagship, Fad or Fraud?" Paper presented to the ECS/CDE Assessment Conference, Breckenridge, Colo.

Camp, R. (1993). "The Place of Portfolios in Our Changing Views of Writing Assessment." In *Construction Versus Choice in Cognitive Measurement: Issues in Constructed Response, Performance Testing, and Portfolio Assessment*, edited by R. E. Bennett and W. C. Ward. Hillsdale, N.J.: Erlbaum.

Catterall, J., and L. Winters. (In press). *Economic Analysis of Tests: Competency, Certification, and Authentic Assessments* (technical report). Los Angeles: University of California, CRESST; Center for the Study of Evaluation.

Center for Research on Evaluation, Standards, and Student Testing (CRESST). (1993). *Alternative Assessments in Practice Database* [Machine-readable data file]. Los Angeles: University of California, CRESST.

Cohen, D. K., and L. D. Ball. (Fall 1990). "Policy and Practice: an Overview." *Educational Evaluation and Policy Analysis* 12, 3: 347–353.

Gearhart, M., J. L. Herman, E. L. Baker, and A. Whittaker. (1993). *Whose Work Is it? A Question for the Validity of Large-Scale Portfolio Assessment* (Tech. Rep. No. 363). Los Angeles: University of California, CRESST; Center for the Study of Evaluation.

Hearne, J., and S. Schuman. (1992). *Portfolio Assessment: Implementation and Use at an Elementary Level* (Tech. Rep. No. 143). (ERIC Document Reproduction Service No. ED 349 330)

Herman, J. L. (1994). "Evaluating the Effects of Technology in School Reform." In *Technology and Education Reform*, edited by B. Means. San Francisco: Jossey-Bass.

Herman, J. L., M. Gearhart, and E. L. Baker. (Summer 1993). "Assessing Writing Portfolios: Issues in the Validity and Meaning of Scores." *Educational Assessment* 1, 3: 201–224.

Koretz, D., B. Stecher, and E. Deibert. (1993). *The Reliability of Scores from the 1992 Vermont Portfolio Assessment Program* (Tech. Rep. No. 355). Los Angeles: University of California, CRESST; Center for the Study of Evaluation.

LeMahieu, P., D. H. Gitomer, and J. T. Eresh. (1993). "Portfolios in Large-Scale Assessment: Difficult but Not Impossible." Unpublished manuscript, University of Delaware [principal author].

Myers, M., U. Treisman, and D. Wolf. (June 1992). "In the Hands of Teachers: The Demands of Performance Assessment on Teaching, Training, School Practices and the Involvement of Teachers in Assessment Programs." Paper presented at the ECS/CDE Assessment Conference, Boulder, Colo.

Plake, B., J. Impara, B. Kapinus, and H. Kruglanski. (June 1992). "Performance Assessment, Teacher Training, and Teacher Change." Paper presented at the ECS/CDE Assessment Conference, Boulder, Colo.

Webb, N. (1993). *Collaborative Group Versus Individual Assessment in Mathematics: Group Processes and Outcomes* (Tech. Rep. No. 352). Los Angeles: University of California, CRESST; Center for the Study of Evaluation.

Wolf, S., and M. Gearhart. (1993). *Writing What You Read: Assessment as a Learning Event* (Tech. Rep. No. 358). Los Angeles: University of California, CRESST; Center for the Study of Evaluation.

Joan L. Herman is Associate Director and **Lynn Winters** is a Project Director at the National Center for Research on Evaluation, Standards, and Student Testing (CRESST), University of California, Los Angeles, Graduate School of Education, 405 Hilgard Ave., Los Angeles, CA 90024-1522.

Assessment and Reporting: A Natural Pair

Doris H. Sperling

Since the Ann Arbor, Michigan, school district created its K–2 assessment process and matching report form, both students and teachers have shown improved performance.

Three years ago, the Ann Arbor Public School district began developing an alternative way to measure student learning and to report the results to parents. The process took time and effort, but it appears to be paying off. Early data

Photos courtesy of Doris H. Sperling

revealed that kindergartners' performance, based on the school district's expectations for children their age, has risen over the past year.

These promising results have led us to three convictions: First, a performance assessment program and meaningful parent report form, like twins, must be conceived together; second, teachers must take a lead role in their

ongoing development (Stiggins and Conklin 1992); and third, by systematically monitoring students' progress, teachers can more effectively meet the children's individual needs.

Toward a Better Learning Yardstick

The impetus to design a new way to evaluate student performance came about six years ago when a group of 1st grade teachers petitioned the administration to stop administering the California Achievement Test. They viewed this standardized test—and indeed any achievement test—as academically inappropriate for 1st graders. Clifford Weber, our school system's executive director of instruction and research, agreed. He had already been searching for better ways to measure learning, and found Richard Stiggins' research (1988) on performance assessment convincing.

We began with a pilot project limited to mathematics learning goals. We asked a group of kindergarten, 1st, and 2nd grade teachers, to develop, under the direction of the district's math coordinator, limited performance outcomes for each grade, together with tasks and criteria to gauge students' progress toward these goals. We then trained a core group of teachers to put the assessment to the test. They inter-

viewed a sampling of students across the district, evaluating their proficiency in each of the tasks. This "Primary Mathematics Assessment Tryout" convinced us that we could develop a districtwide assessment program.

Benchmarks of Progress

Our goal was to develop student performance assessments tied directly to the outcomes the school district had established for each grade. In the first year, the language arts consultant, the math coordinator, and I worked with the kindergarten teachers to develop criteria and assessment methods. Over the next two years, we expanded the assessment to the 1st and 2nd grades.

Because children develop at different rates, arriving at specific outcomes that all the students could be expected to learn by the end of the year was a challenge. We also struggled with deciding which of these outcomes were most critical to assess. For language, for example, we agreed on the following reading outcomes:

- demonstrates knowledge of books and print;
- demonstrates knowledge of story structure;
- identifies words/logos within the classroom and outside of school; and
- exhibits positive attitude toward reading.

Articulating clear criteria for teachers to use in evaluating and documenting mastery of each outcome was even more difficult. The teachers delved deeply into different academic and developmental expectations before arriving at basic criteria. Along with the criteria, we also established a continuum of three performance levels: (1) *Not Yet*, (2) *Developing*,

and (3) *Achieving. Achieving* means the student has reached the stated goal. For example, for *Demonstrates knowledge of books,* children would be rated as *Achieving* if they met the following criteria:

- holds book in ready-to-read position;
- locates words in books;
- finds beginning and ending of story;
- can point to the title;
- knows left page is read before the right one;
- knows words carry meaning of story.

Students rated in the *Not Yet* category may hold books improperly or show no interest in them, while those identified as *Developing* may sometimes hold books properly, or point to some words on the cover, but not the title. Teachers also note any *Extended* activities children have mastered. A child may, for example, be able to recognize authors' and illustrators' styles or be aware of chapters and tables of contents. Teachers observe students during regular language instruction to assess their language skills, but use specific tasks to evaluate mathematics skills (see fig. 1).

Coordinating the Parent Report

As the kindergarten teachers were developing the performance assessment, they let us know it was incomplete without a matching parent report form. The existing form, they realized to their distress, bore no relationship to the extensive outcome-based assessment they had created. To remedy this mismatch, six kindergarten and 1st grade teachers informally and independently designed their own individual forms and tried them out. They were pleased to discover that their hard work in delineating outcomes made this task much easier. The report would merely present the assessment format the teacher used, accompanied by an explanation of the process. The following year, the six forms were consolidated into two alternative formats that teachers could choose between—a short checklist and a longer, more detailed report. The new formats worked: given the option, virtually all 100 district kindergarten and 1st grade teachers chose to use a new form in lieu of the old one. The format has been further modified and now combines elements of the long and short versions (see fig. 2).

The new report goes out to parents three times a year. It states the reading, writing, and math outcomes, the assessment criteria, and the children's progress in meeting these goals. The *Developing* section has three boxes, allowing teachers to show gradual growth for students who remain in this category most of the year.

The parents' reaction to the new form was mixed. They appreciated knowing exactly what was expected of their children. Knowing this enabled them to work cooperatively with the

Figure 1

Sample of Arithmetic Criteria for Kindergarten

Outcome: Counts by rote to 20

Not Yet	Developing	Achieving	Extending →
Criteria:	*Criteria:*	*Criteria:*	*Criteria:*
Counts only from 1 to 5.	Counts from 1 to 10 but cannot count from 11 to 19 without errors.	Counts orally from 1 to 20 without any errors.	Counts beyond 20.
Counts to 10 but skips one or more numbers.	Counts to 20 but skips one or more numbers.	(Automatically knows the next number.)	Counts by 2s, 5s, and/or 10s.
(May be able to count along with someone else.)	(When asked for next number, may need to start counting from 1.)		Counts backwards.

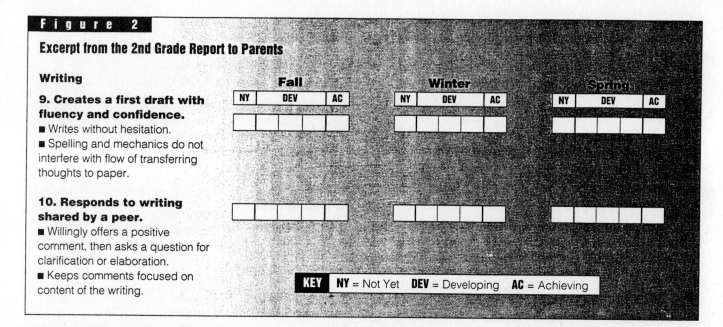

Figure 2

Excerpt from the 2nd Grade Report to Parents

Writing

9. Creates a first draft with fluency and confidence.
■ Writes without hesitation.
■ Spelling and mechanics do not interfere with flow of transferring thoughts to paper.

10. Responds to writing shared by a peer.
■ Willingly offers a positive comment, then asks a question for clarification or elaboration.
■ Keeps comments focused on content of the writing.

Fall — NY | DEV | AC
Winter — NY | DEV | AC
Spring — NY | DEV | AC

KEY NY = Not Yet DEV = Developing AC = Achieving

---

teacher and take a more active role in their children's education. They did, however, need a number of concepts explained. One source of confusion was the performance continuum over the school year. In the fall, most students perform somewhere between the *Not Yet* and *Developing* categories for their grade levels. (By June, however, they should reach *Achieving*.) But some parents interpreted these fall ratings as the equivalent of a *D* or *E*. On the other hand, parents of students who had in fact reached the *Achieving* level in the fall for most outcomes had a different concern. They wondered whether teachers would go on to meet their children's advanced academic needs the rest of the year.

Clearly it was important to supplement the report forms with further explanation and written materials. Teachers need to explain that performance assessment is an ongoing process, and that the outcomes assessed on the report form reflect only part of the curriculum. Teachers provide each family with a booklet detailing the criteria they use to evaluate students' progress.

A recent survey of parents revealed an overwhelmingly favorable response to the new format. They told us the reports took a lot of the guesswork out of report cards, and they appreciated the emphasis on observable and concrete behaviors and the individual attention their children received. Only a small minority felt otherwise, regarding the booklet as too detailed and complicated.

Coaching Teachers

Inservice teacher training has been critical. In the first year, teachers spent a total of three days at mandated language and mathematics inservices, examining outcome criteria and methods of collecting information to evaluate student progress. To improve interrater reliability, teachers watched videos of students being assessed, then used the criteria to assign a rating to their performance. If some teachers' ratings differed significantly from those of their colleagues, we reviewed the criteria to better understand what children look like when they're achieving that particular outcome.

As a result of the new assessment strategies, teachers have been monitoring students more closely and refining their teaching techniques. We have encouraged teachers to assess students in the course of classroom instruction, but this is difficult if their traditional teaching methods do not match the outcomes and/or the assessment criteria. Accordingly, our fourth-year inservices will focus heavily on new teaching strategies that are consistent with the outcomes. Teachers themselves say they want to know more about current research and philosophy for teaching language and mathematics.

Early on, our assessment practices ran up against the reality of time constraints; many teachers felt hard pressed to teach, assess students, and also record a tremendous amount of information. To give them more time to talk to and observe individual students, we have provided them with substitute teachers for seven half-days each school year. After three years, the kindergarten teachers report feeling more comfortable with the process. They say they have internalized the criteria and are learning to observe and assess student performance as they teach.

Teachers also are experimenting with more efficient record-keeping systems. The very process of filling out the new report forms requires teachers to review their ongoing assessment and record-keeping techniques. Said one teacher: "With the old form and its vague language I was not really accountable to be very specific, but now I feel obligated to provide the most accurate and up-to-date information possible."

Patience Pays Off

What else have we learned about implementing a new performance assessment process? For one thing, you cannot mandate skills, creativity, and a commitment to continuous improvement (McLaughlin 1991). You must have patience. Teachers need many opportunities to share their successful strategies with colleagues, and to receive support as they work through their problems. Administrators need to listen well while teachers relate what does and doesn't work. Following Glatthorn's "11 maxims of the change process (1992)," we were flexible, blended "top-down and bottom-up processes," had a plan, but were "ready to learn by doing" (Fullan 1993).

For their part, many teachers have found that the new system becomes more valuable and less stressful each year. It forces them to reflect on the needs of each student and consequently to gear their instruction to meet those individual needs. And as they stop to take stock of their students' progress, they often are surprised and inspired to discover clear improvement. In March, for example, one 1st grade teacher said she was startled to realize that "the students' growth was amazing!"

We will continue to question and improve this complex assessment process, never losing sight of our ultimate goal: success for all students. ■

References

Fullan, M. (1993). *Change Forces: Probing the Depths of Educational Reform.* New York: The Falmer Press.

Glatthorn, A. A. (1992). *Teachers as Agents of Change: A New Look at School Improvement.* Washington, D.C.: National Education Association.

McLaughlin, M. W. (1991). "Enabling Professional Development: What Have We Learned?" In *Staff Development for Education in the '90s*, edited by A. Lieberman and L. Miller, 3rd ed., pp. 61–82. New York: Teachers College Press.

Stiggins, R. J., (January 1988). "Revitalizing Classroom Assessment: The Highest Instructional Priority." *Phi Delta Kappan*: 363-368.

Stiggins, R. J., and N. F. Conklin. (1992). *In Teachers' Hands: Investigating the Practices of Classroom.* Albany, New York: State University of New York Press.

Doris H. Sperling is a Classroom Assessment Specialist who retired recently after 35 years with the Ann Arbor Public Schools. She now works as an independent consultant at 1265 Lincolnshire Lane, Ann Arbor, MI 48103.

Voices

To gain parental support for new practices, ask your parents to keep you posted on how their children like the new system and to keep track of instances in which they see their child doing more and better work than before. A Quality School teacher not only completely eliminates the adversarial relationship with students that is universal in the old system but makes sure that parents are well informed that this is what is going on. The best way to do this is to ask students to tell you in class discussions what they have learned that they believe is useful. It may take a while, but when they are able to do this, give them a homework assignment to tell their parents what they learned. Nothing will gain you more parental support than parents hearing from an enthusiastic child that he or she has learned something useful in school.

— From *The Quality School Teacher*, by William Glasser, M.D.
New York; HarperPerennial, 1993.

◆〜〼〜〼〜〼〜〼〜〼◆

Teaching All Children

Letting the Children Take Over More of Their Own Learning:
Collaborative Research in the Kindergarten Classroom

Kathy H. Barclay with Camille Breheny

C an we trust kindergarten children to make valid choices about some of what they need and want to learn? Can they assume responsibility for constructing appropriate extension activities to enhance their own construction of knowledge? Yes—through the use of cooperative learning, parent involvement, sixth-grade "buddies," and independent/collaborative research and writing.

Various educators and researchers have addressed the importance of promoting student choice and decision making and of providing ample time for students to pursue their own inter-

Kathy H. Barclay, *Ed.D., is a professor of early childhood education at Western Illinois University in Macomb. She teaches undergraduate and graduate courses in early literacy development and family/community involvement and recently coauthored a book,* Supporting the Move to Whole Language: A Handbook for School Leaders.

Camille Breheny, *B.S., a kindergarten teacher at St. Paul School in Macomb, Illinois, provides inservice for local school districts and often consults with preservice and inservice kindergarten teachers who wish to implement a child-centered, whole language curriculum.*

Do you have cooperative learning, parent involvement, upper-grade children as buddies, and children doing independent/collaborative research and writing? This teacher tried it all—and was pleased with the results!

ests. Teachers have been advised to "find out and verify what students already know about the topic" and to "include questions students want to explore" (Routman 1991, 279). Developmentally appropriate early childhood classrooms are those that evidence, among other important characteristics, maximum interaction among children as they pursue a variety of independent and small-group tasks. The teacher's role is one of facilitator or guide (Piaget 1972; Forman & Kuschner 1983; Lay-Dopyera & Dopyera 1986). The teacher "sets" the environment with challenging and interesting materials and activities and then steps back to observe, encourage, and

deepen children's use of them; teachers ask thought-provoking questions and make comments.

© Kathy H. Barclay

Each day the children met with members of their study groups to share the information they had learned from the book(s) they brought home the previous evening.

© Kathy H. Barclay

As early childhood teachers strive to implement developmentally appropriate programs—programs that represent integrated learning experiences based on the interests and needs of children, it is important for them to realize that they need not be the ones doing all of the theme planning. That is, children, even at the kindergarten level, can and will assume a reasonable degree of responsibility for selecting themes or topics that are worthy of study, for planning literature extension activities and other learning experiences, and for collecting, sorting, and preparing various resources and materials needed for the unit. This is not to say, of course, that the teacher can sit back and relax while the children carry forth completely on their own initiative; however, the teacher **will** be freed of many "planning" tasks that she previously carried out in the absence of the learners' involvement.

Prior to the "takeover"

The children in Camille Breheny's kindergarten classroom had been involved in a number of thematic units, including a study of "bugs" at the beginning of the school year, followed by a study of "seeds" in October. During the holiday season the unit centered on "homes," which led into a winter unit on "bears" and their winter homes. Early in March the children gained a new class pet—Lester, a white mouse—so naturally a study of mice evolved during the early springtime.

The daily schedule, one that Camille and I had adapted from Don Holdaway (1979), included (1) a morning "warm-up," which consisted of several poems, songs, chants, or rhymes related to the theme; (2) the rereading of one or two "old favorites," stories that the children had previously read and enjoyed; (3) the sharing of a new story; and (4) an independent-work period.

They could read from an interesting array of books and materials and write about the theme or about anything else that interested them. They could also choose to spend some of their time participating in block or dramatic play, or working

with paints, clay, or other art materials, to name a few activities that were routinely available.

Clearly, the children already had had the opportunity to direct a great deal of their own learning. They had learned to make choices and to spend their time wisely. They had participated in many units, and they knew how their room "worked" with respect to the various learning materials and resources available to them.

As the "mice" unit was drawing to a close, the children began to inquire about what they were going to study next. Ashley announced, "I want to study dogs!" The other children who were overhearing this conversation quickly jumped in with their preferences—cats, oceans, ducks, and so forth. "How about 'pets'?" Camille asked. "No, I only want to study dogs!" Ashley insisted.

Planning for the "takeover"

When Camille shared with me the conversation that had taken place regarding the next theme study, we began almost imme-

© Kathy H. Barclay

diately brainstorming ways to make a project of children taking over more of their own learning work in Camille's kindergarten. Although we had a number of questions and concerns about the children's ability to select "worthy" topics, to construct their own extension projects, and to engage in "research," we decided to let the children take over for the last three to four weeks of school.

We identified potential problems, such as the availability of resources, books, and materials relating to a wide variety of topics. The possibility of having all of the children involved in different topics of study concerned us, so we decided to have the children brainstorm a list of topics. We would then select the three or four topics that seemed to generate the most interest, and individuals would sign up to work in a study group. This would help us address one of our other concerns—that of whether or not all of the children were capable of constructing their own extension activities. With the support of a group, we really felt that all of the children would be able to handle this responsibility.

Of major concern were the logistics of transmitting information about the topics to the members of each study group. Because few of the kindergarten children were reading at a level required for most of the "good"

© Kathy H. Barclay

nonfiction books, such as those in the Eye Witness Books series published by Knopf, we knew that much of the information would have to be shared orally. To overcome this problem

• we enlisted the help of sixth-grade "buddies," a parent classroom volunteer, and the principal to "visit" with the study groups during their small group sharing periods; and

• we designed a home-study component that would involve parents and family members in sharing a variety of books based on the topic and in "taking dictation" as the kindergarten child recalled important facts about the topic from the listening experience.

We also arranged for a class "Share Fair" on the last day of school, at which the children in the various study groups would "exhibit" the products of their learning process—art projects, individual- and group-authored books, and so forth. This activity

would be planned in more detail by the children once our "takeover" project was underway.

The "takeover" takes shape

Toward the end of the "mice" unit, the children brainstormed numerous topics that they wanted to know more about. Their list was narrowed to five topics, and we gathered approximately 20 to 25 books relating to each. The selected books represented a variety of genres and reading levels. We purposefully included fiction and nonfiction, picture books and nonpicture books. Camille shared several of the books from each category during her class read-aloud times. She called attention to whether the books she selected were fiction or nonfiction. With nonfiction books, particularly those that were "text heavy," she modeled how to use the book to find answers for specific information, reading captions under interesting pictures and so forth. When sharing a fiction book, she asked the children to listen for new information about the topic, and she reinforced the idea that we can gain "true" information from a book with a "made-up" story.

The children had ample opportunity for free exploration of the new books during the independent-work periods and silent-reading times held throughout

---

The children were allowed a great deal of choice during the independent-work period. They could work alone or with a partner or small group of their choice. They could select from among a wide variety of activities related to the theme.

---

that week. After several days of book/topic exploration, the children signed up as members of one of the study groups. The topics that generated the most interest were three of the ones mentioned first—dogs, cats, and oceans. Over the next few days, Camille met with each group to record "What We Already Know About ___ " and "What We Want To Know About ___ " information on charts, which were then typewritten for inclusion in each child's home-study packet. In addition to these sheets, a sheet for jotting down new information from the books shared at home each evening and a letter to the parents (shown below) explaining the project were placed in "take-home packets"—large, brown envelopes that had been laminated—along with one book from the group collection.

In order to assure that each child brought home a variety of literature, Camille and I drew up lists containing five book titles. Before the children went home each day, the parent volunteer would remove the books from the envelopes and put in the next title from each child's list. Each evening, for a week, the children brought home in their "take-home packets" a different book, a list of what they thought they already knew about the topic for verifying with information from the book, a new sheet for recording answers to their group-study questions, and a new sheet for recording new information located about the topic. An example of one of the "What We Want To Know About ___ " sheets, filled out by a member of the "cat" study group, is shown on page 37. Notice the questions that were generated by the study group and the answers that were found in the book the child brought home that particular evening. Many of the kindergartners brought books and other resources from home about their study topic. One child even brought in her pet cat! An example of new information being recorded about the topic also appears on page 37. The information came from two different books that were shared that evening—the one from school that was sent home in the "take-home packet" and one that the child had at home.

It was during these group meetings that the parent volunteer and principal helped out by meeting with two of the groups while Camille met with a third group. The adult's role was simply to assist individual children in reading or recalling the information that had been recorded on their take-home sheets and, sometimes, to move the discussion along by asking questions that helped the children to clarify and summarize the information they were learning about their topic.

Dear Parents,

During these last two weeks of school, the kindergarten class will be working on group projects based on a self-selected topic. **This project will be a collaborative home-school project.** The topics chosen by the children are oceans, cats, and dogs.

*Your child will be bringing home one book each night **this week** in this special envelope.* Some of the books will be nonfiction, but some will be fiction since the children are learning that some fiction books do contain true information. *Please share the books with your child.* If the book is lengthy, you need not share the entire book. You may want to just read the captions, discuss the pictures, look up specific information, etc.

In addition to the book, each envelope contains several sheets of paper for you and your child to use together:

"What We Already Know About ___ " is a list of what the children already know (or think they know) about the topic. As you share the books, please help your child note any information that is *different* from that on this sheet.

"What We Want To Know About ___ " is a list of questions the children asked about their topic. Please write your child's name and the name of the book you read each night on the top of this sheet. If you find the answers to any of the children's questions, please record the answers on this sheet as your child dictates them to you. Some books may not contain any information related to these questions.

"New Information I Learned About ___ " is a blank sheet for recording your child's name and the title of the book(s) from which she gains new information that is not related to any of the questions. You may also use this sheet to record information from other books such as encyclopedias, library books, etc. that you may have at home.

*Since the children will be sharing their books and information on a **daily** basis with the other children in their "research" group, it is **very important** that your child brings the envelope and completed sheets back to school each morning.*

The children are very excited about their "research" projects! They will be sending you an invitation to visit their kindergarten "Share Fair" during the last week of school so that you can see the many writings, drawings, and creative projects that they have completed.

Thanks so much for your help with this home-school project!

Sincerely,

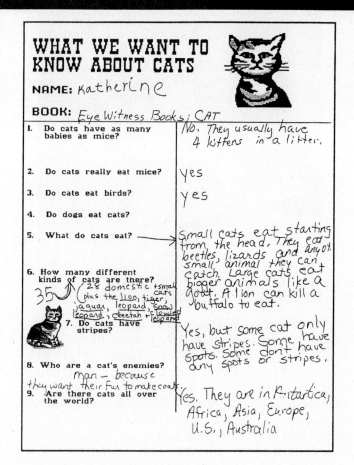

WHAT WE WANT TO KNOW ABOUT CATS

NAME: Katherine

BOOK: Eye Witness Books: CAT

1. Do cats have as many babies as mice? — No. They usually have 4 kittens in a litter.

2. Do cats really eat mice? — yes

3. Do cats eat birds? — yes

4. Do dogs eat cats?

5. What do cats eat? — Small cats eat starting from the head. They eat beetles, lizards and any other small animal they can catch. Large cats eat bigger animals like a goat. A lion can kill a buffalo to eat.

6. How many different kinds of cats are there? — 35 (28 domestic + small cats plus the lion, tiger, jaguar, leopard, snow leopard, cheetah + clouded leopard)

7. Do cats have stripes? — Yes, but some cat only have stripes. Some have spots. Some don't have any spots or stripes.

8. Who are a cat's enemies? — Man — because they want their fur to make coats.

9. Are there cats all over the world? — Yes. They are in Antartica, Africa, Asia, Europe, U.S., Australia

NEW INFORMATION I LEARNED ABOUT Cats

Name: Katherine

Book(s): The I.F.H. Book of Kittens + Peter Spier's Little Cats

New Information:

Feline is another word for cat.

Cats like to explore new places and things.

Most cats like to travel in cars.

Some cats and dogs can make friends very quickly, especially if they are kittens and puppies.

Spicy foods make cats sick

Cats are smart.

The sixth-grade buddies had been working with the children on various projects conducted throughout the year; therefore, the kindergarten children looked forward to their participation in the unit. After five books from the group collection had been shared at each child's home, the study groups were charged with the task of writing a group "research report." The sixth graders assisted primarily by helping the children in each group synthesize the information they found most important or interesting about their topic. As the children in a group shared their information, the older student wrote each fact on one strip of card stock. The sixth-grade students, along with the adult volunteers in the room, assisted in helping children categorize and arrange their information. One kindergarten child from each group then numbered the strips in the order they were to be typed. Each report was typed, and students were provided both an enlarged group copy and a smaller individual copy for illustrating in any way they each desired. Each report was also typed using a "report format" with all of the information on one or two pages, without room for illustrations.

We needn't have worried about the children's ability to design their own extension projects. Given an almost free rein, they came up with more ideas than we could have ever thought of!

Give them an inch . . .

At first, their enthusiasm for constructing elaborate art projects—cat puppets, submarines, dogs, and dog biscuits—made us wonder whether or not they were going to branch out into other areas, such as writing, as a vehicle both for constructing knowledge about their topic and for sharing that knowledge with others. We decided to give each child a "Research Contract" for stamping the date each time she (1) wrote about her topic, (2) constructed something about the topic, and (3) shared something about the topic. As it turned out, most of the children freely participated in a wide variety of learning experiences; however, the few children who didn't were made more aware of the need for "balance" in their study.

As we anticipated, the children responded enthusiastically to the idea of having a "Share Fair." In preparation for the culminating event, each group arranged an exhibit area to showcase its creations. Individuals were responsible for labeling their items and the group was responsible for creating a banner or sign to identify its area. Each child had decorated a pocket folder to collect all of the "take-home sheets" and other written work completed during the unit. The folders, housed in decorator bags with pictures of cats, dogs, and fish, were placed in each exhibit area. Finally, on the day before the "Share Fair," the children in each group concocted a special, edible-food recipe related to their topic to share with visitors.

The "Share Fair" was held on the last day of school, following an all-school picnic to which the parents were invited. The parents were impressed with the work that the children had done, and so were we.

In closing . . .

Not surprisingly, this experience has taught us many things. Although we did not really encounter any major problems, next time we would like to see each group limited to six children. The "ocean" group, with eight children, was a little too large for one volunteer or "buddy" to facilitate during the cooperative-group discussions and report-writing activities. Also, we recognize the importance of having the support and involvement of parents, classroom volunteers, and "buddies."

© Kathy H. Barclay

Without this outside help, the project would need to be conducted over a longer period of time, thus allowing each group to do more of the reading and "research" during the school day with support from Camille and a teaching aide.

Through our involvement in this project, we did gain satisfying answers to the questions we posed during the planning phase. The question, "Can kindergarten children make valid and appropriate choices regarding what they will study?" has been answered with a resounding "Yes!" The topics the children selected provided meaningful, important

---

The Range of Activities Ongoing at Any One Time in the Room Was Staggering!

During one two-hour time period, we observed children involved in the following activities:

1. block playing with toy replicas of "big cats";

2. constructing submarines from Styrofoam, plastic 2-liter bottles, and paper cups;

3. constructing a "lifeline" for scuba divers;

4. writing about a visit to an uncle's house to see new baby kittens;

5. writing facts learned about cats;

6. creating a large cat from boxes and wallpaper samples;

7. painting "dog biscuits" for dog puppets constructed out of paper bags;

8. creating a play about mermaids—and props to use in pre-

senting the play to the class during the sharing period to follow;

9. writing a poem about a cat;

10. making a cat from a paper cup and an old Christmas-tree ornament;

11. constructing an anchor for a submarine;

12. writing about a submarine going to look at a boat that sank; and

13. writing facts about sharks.

concepts that enabled them to learn more about their world and its inhabitants. To a second question, "Can kindergarten children be trusted to construct their own extension activities related to a topic of study?", again the answer is "Yes!" Not only did the children in this classroom participate in a wide variety of activities, they took responsibility for making decisions concerning materials, work partners, and procedures to be followed.

Perhaps the most important lesson for us lies in our realization that the children can, when provided the opportunity, be trusted to know what it is they want and need to learn. And they can be trusted to participate actively in the construction of that knowledge.

As Schwartz and Pollishuke stated in *Creating a Child-Centered Classroom*,

When the planning of an integrated, child-centered curriculum is done with the children and by the children, the curriculum, the themes, the activities, and the active learning experiences become more relevant, because they are built on the backgrounds, interests and everyday life experiences of each individual student. (1991, 50)

References

Forman, G.E., & D.S. Kuschner. 1983. *The child's construction of knowledge: Piaget for teaching children*. Washington, DC: NAEYC.

Holdaway, D. 1979. *The foundations of literacy*. Portsmouth, NH: Heinemann.

Lay-Dopyera, M., & J. Dopyera. 1986. Strategies for teaching. In *Early childhood curriculum: A review of current research*, ed. C. Seefeldt. New York: Teachers College Press.

Piaget, J. 1972. *Science of education and the psychology of the child*. New York: Viking.

Routman, R. 1991. *Invitations*. Portsmouth, NH: Heinemann.

Schwartz, S., & M. Pollishuke. 1991. *Creating the child-centered classroom*. Katonah, NY: Richard C. Owen Publishers.

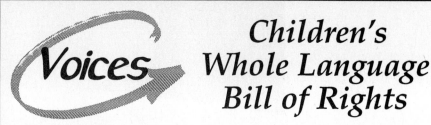

Children's Whole Language Bill of Rights

Every child has the right to:

1. Be literate.

2. A child-centered classroom where the development of language and literacy results from integrated reading, writing, listening and speaking.

3. Teachers who understand the whole language approach, who actively involve parents, and who are empowered by their administrators to be **key** decision makers.

4. A curriculum that meets the individual's needs and that is organized around broad themes integrating language arts with mathematics, science, social studies, music, art and physical education.

5. High interest, language-rich, meaningful reading material such as trade books, which take the place of workbooks and worksheets in the practice of reading skills.

6. Write about subjects that interest him or her without fear of criticism, and to scribble, reverse letters, and to invent spelling and punctuation as a part of his or her growth in literacy.

7. Speak and be heard in the classroom as an important step toward reading, writing and thinking.

8. Active involvement in learning through interaction with other children, manipulatives, toys and appropriate materials.

9. Abundantly supplied libraries, both school and classroom, that include predictable, printless, and pop-up books, poetry, fiction and non-fiction.

10. Progress assessment based on appropriate measurements such as writing portfolios, miscue analysis, book lists, peer reports and student-teacher interviews rather than norm-referenced, standardized tests.

The Society For Developmental Education / Robert L. Johnson ©

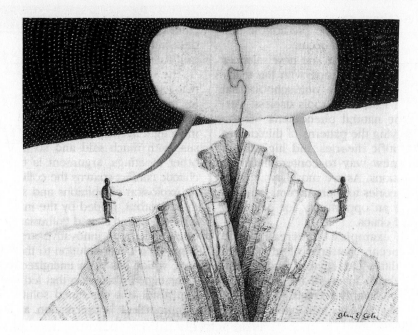

Alan Cober/SIS

RESEARCH REPORT

BRIDGING THE GAP

By Stan Friedland

*Cooperative learning, the research suggests, can help children
learn to understand and accept children of other races*

YOUR FIRST SIGN OF TROUBLE IS A RACIAL SLUR
scrawled across the door of a bathroom stall
or some name-calling at the football game,
and your first thought is, "Maybe we need an
ethnic food festival or a workshop on prejudice reduction."

Before you do either, consider: Attitudes such as tolerance and respect cannot be taught in a short time. Instead, you have to work at them continuously in your
school. And because the main focus of schools is on
academics, your most powerful leverage point for
change is not a festival or a workshop but the classroom itself. That's where both learning and human relations can become high priority goals. And that's where
cooperative learning comes in.

Developed over the past 25 years, cooperative learning has a strong research base. (Some 140 studies have

Stan Friedland, *a former teacher and high school principal, is an
education consultant in Syosset, N.Y.*

appeared to date.) A number of those studies have
dealt with the link between cooperative learning techniques and prejudice reduction. These findings are
worth noting.

For example, in a 1985 study on classroom bias, researchers from the University of California, Riverside,
showed that social contact in a classroom setting between students of unequal academic status does not improve relationships, while social contact in a classroom
where students can interact with and benefit from each
other, regardless of academic status, significantly does
improve relationships between students. In the traditional classroom, where students are expected to be responsible only for themselves and work in isolation
from each other, academic differences make for a de
facto academic and social segregation. When those academic differences parallel the ethnic or racial makeup
of your student body, then the experience often is one
of increased polarization and alienation, which is frequently the case today.

In other words, this study and others suggest that cooperative learning not only increases academic achievement but enables students to experience and develop tolerance, fair play, and mutual respect for all of their classmates.

Five positive steps

Today's schools generally use three kinds of instructional formats: the traditional (or competitive) format, which is used more than 90 percent of the time; the individualized format, used primarily in learning resource centers for students with learning disabilities or in remedial education; and the cooperative format, used barely 7 percent of the time.

In the competitive format, students are expected to do their own work and avoid helping or seeking help from others (actions often regarded as cheating). The result: Students quickly learn to work against each other, in terms of both grades and classroom activities. For example, when the teacher asks a question, six students might raise their hands in response. And when the teacher calls on one student, the other five generally root for a wrong answer so they can supply the right one. Under these circumstances, bright students often are disliked because they make the others feel inferior, and marginal students settle into the lowest perches of the pecking order, where they're subject to the indifference or disrespect of their peers.

In cooperative learning, on the other hand, students work in small teams with students of differing abilities. Each student is responsible, not only for learning the material being taught, but also for helping teammates to master the material. The format is highly structured and requires five specific elements, each of which is essential to the success of cooperative learning:

1. *Positive interdependence.* Every cooperative learning team has specific goals to achieve—goals that make students believe they need each other to complete the required tasks. In other words, in cooperative learning, the group sinks or swims together.

2. *Face-to-face interaction.* Each cooperative learning task also is structured so that students must interact with each other in a positive, task-oriented way.

3. *Individual and team accountability.* Team makeup is heterogeneous, both academically and socially. Students earn their own individual grades but are responsible for the improvement of the team as a whole and receive additional credit when the whole team improves. In addition, every team member is assigned one of four roles, each of equal importance so that everyone has 25 percent ownership of their four-person team. (The roles—whose titles are self-explanatory—are those of coordinator, praiser-encourager, recorder, and gatekeeper; the last one ensures that everyone understands his or her role, has a chance to ask questions, and avoids any temptation to let others do all the work.)

Students exchange these roles frequently, so everyone has a chance to experience each role. The teams themselves also are changed periodically. During the course of a school year, students have the chance to work with virtually every one of their classmates.

4. *Interpersonal and small-group skills.* Each task involves specific skills, taught by the teacher and then included as part of the total team task and evaluation. (One example of such skills might be praise or encouragement.)

5. *Team processing and evaluation.* Team members are expected to evaluate their efficiency in terms of both what they learn and the specific skills they acquire at the end of each task. (For instance, they might answer the question, "How good were we with encouraging others rather than putting them down?")

Each of these five elements must be in place or the cooperative learning structure is incomplete. These five parts complement each other and induce in students positive social behavior and a wide variety of learning skills.

Becoming 'color-blind'

Of course, cooperative learning won't replace traditional approaches to teaching in the classroom; instead, proponents of the method advise using it for between one-third and one-half of class time.

When used with this frequency, the results can be appreciable. For example, in a typical team setting, students who learn quickly will help other students keep pace. The slower-learning students, in turn, will contribute to the team's record by improving their performance from the last test or measurement, thereby helping earn bonus points for the entire team. This dynamic creates a considerable degree of equal status among team members, because each one can contribute to meeting the team's "improvement" goals, benefiting each team member. With this team interaction taking place both in and out of the classroom, students get to know, understand, and appreciate each other far better than they would in the traditional classroom.

Indeed, when Robert Slavin, who pioneered the use of cooperative learning in his work at Johns Hopkins, and his colleague Eileen Oickle looked at the effects of classroom experience on race relations, they found that when students were in traditional classrooms, second-graders were still relatively "color-blind," but sixth-graders had identifiable prejudices and eighth-graders had pronounced ones. However, students who had substantial experience in cooperative learning at these grade levels showed significantly higher levels of tolerance and understanding (as measured by standardized instruments given to both groups). Furthermore, the academic achievement levels of the latter group were better, across the board.

Other researchers report similar findings. For example, probably no one ever has looked at prejudice more intensely than the late Gordon W. Allport, a well-known social scientist and the foremost pioneer in sociological research dealing with race relations. In his 1975 pamphlet, *The ABC's of Scapegoating*, Allport described social relationships on his famous continuum, the friendliest behavior of which is cooperation; the most hostile, "scapegoating, discrimination and prejudice."

In that publication and elsewhere, Allport suggested that young people could develop much stronger positive social attitudes if they had a chance to work with different types of people in the pursuit of common goals. The more time and experience they had in doing this, he said, "the stronger they would become in their overall attitudes of tolerance and social appreciation."

Another strong advocate of team learning is psychiatrist and educator William Glasser. In his 1986 book, *Control Theory In The Classroom*, Glasser had researchers ask hundreds of students of all ages, "What has been your most beneficial or enjoyable experience in your school career?" Virtually all of the students cited the athletic team, school newspaper, chorus, band, or other extracurricular group. When asked about their classroom experiences, the majority of respondents were negative and mentioned boredom and the lack of personal attention as key turnoffs.

In other words, team activities turned kids on; yet, Glasser observes, "The only place where teaming is absent is in the classroom, where it is needed the most."

In his latest book, *The Quality School,* Glasser raises another issue as well: power. Because schools continue to use the "stimulus/response" method in the classroom—telling children what, where, and how to learn and expecting them to respond accordingly—schools control and direct behavior, he says. When students don't respond favorably, schools "coerce" them in varied ways, which, in turn, leads to alienation and disciplinary problems. "Students will do [high] quality work," says Glasser, "when they perceive that the process and product will meet their needs. No amount of coercive adult behavior will get them to do so." The only instructional format that will stimulate students to do high-quality work on a consistent basis, concludes Glasser, is cooperative learning.

Research on tracking underscores that argument. The most recent substantive studies of tracking suggest that average and below-average students don't learn more in homogeneous groups. In fact, says tracking researcher Jeannie Oakes, research shows that "nearly all students can learn as well in heterogeneous groups as in tracked classrooms [and that] . . . lower track programs often are detrimental to students in them." Furthermore, says Oakes, because disproportionately high numbers of poor and minority students tend to be placed in lower-track classes, tracking results not only in academic inequities but also in a significant degree of social segregation. The critics of tracking, and they are many, almost unanimously recommend cooperative learning as the format most able to provide the best instruction for any mixed-ability grouping.

In short, cooperative learning stresses the similarities of teammates and the commonality of team goals. It stresses getting along. It encourages students to think less of what's in it for them and more of what others need.

And the end result of all that can only be more teamwork—and more tolerance, which young people today so badly need. ▣

SELECTED REFERENCES ON COOPERATIVE LEARNING

Allport, Gordon W. *The ABC's of Scapegoating.* New York: Anti-Defamation League, 1975.

Brandt, Ron. "On Cooperative Learning: A Conversation with Spencer Kagan." *Educational Leadership,* 47, December-January 1989-90, pp. 8-11.

Davis, Bruce. "Effects of Cooperative Learning on Race/Human Relations: Study of a District Program." *Spectrum,* 3, Winter 1985, pp. 37-43.

Jules, Vena. "Interaction Dynamics of Cooperative Learning Groups in Trinidad's Secondary Schools." *Adolescence,* 26, Winter 1991, pp. 931-49.

Kagan, Spencer, et al. *Classroom Structural Bias: Impact on Cooperative and Competitive Structures.* San Juan Capistrano, Calif.: Resources for Teachers, 1985.

Ladestro, Debra. "Teaching Tolerance." *Teacher Magazine,* 2 February 1991, pp. 26-27.

Mabbutt, Richard. *Prejudice Reduction: What Works.* Boise, Idaho: Idaho Human Rights Commission, 1991.

Oakes, Jeannie. "Keeping Track, Parts 1 and 2: The Policy and Practice of Curriculum Inequality." *Phi Delta Kappan,* September and October 1986.

Parrenas, Cecilia, and Parrenas, Florante. "Cooperative Learning, Multicultural Functioning, and Student Achievement." In *Proceedings of the National Association for Bilingual Education Conferences,* Washington, D.C., 1993, pp. 181-89.

Piel, John A., and Conwell, Catherine R. *Differences in Perceptions between Afro-American and Anglo-American Males and Females in Cooperative Learning Groups.* Charlotte, N.C.: North Carolina University, 1989.

Sharan, S.L. "Cooperative Learning: Effects on Achievement, Attitudes, and Race Relations." *Review of Educational Research,* 1980.

Slavin, Robert E., and Oickle, Eileen. "Effects of Cooperative Learning Teams on Student Achievement and Race Relations: Treatment by Race Interactions." *Sociology of Education,* 54, July 1981, pp. 174-80.

Slavin, Robert E. "Cooperative Learning and Desegregation." *Journal of Educational Equity and Leadership,* 1, Spring 1981, pp. 145-61.

Slavin, Robert E. "Cooperative Learning." *Review of Educational Research,* 50, Summer 1980, pp. 315-42.

Slavin, Robert E. "How Student Learning Teams Can Integrate the Desegregated Classroom." *Integrated Education,* 15, November-December 1977, pp. 56-58.

Wells, Amy Stuart. *Middle School Education: The Critical Link in Dropout Prevention.* New York: ERIC Clearinghouse on Urban Education, 1989.

Two Dozen-Plus Ideas That Will Help Special Needs Kids

Valuable tips for all teachers – especially teachers with special needs children mainstreamed in their classroom

BY MARTHA BOYLE AND
SARAH KORN-ROTHSCHILD

" When giving instructions, stand close to the student. That way, your voice will stand out among other noises. "

With the increased number of students with special needs in our schools, we thought it would be helpful to put together a list of easy activity adaptations to help these students be successful. Inclusion teachers have been using these "tricks" successfully for several years. They can be used with equal success by all classroom teachers

These techniques are especially helpful for students with visual and auditory perceptual difficulties and poor motor skills.

Martha Boyle (left) and Sarah Korn-Rothschild *sit for a "group portrait" in a classroom at Smallwood Drive School.*

Location of Teacher

• When giving instructions, stand close to the student. That way, your voice will stand out among other noises. In addition, the student will be able to see your facial expressions and body gestures. This will also improve the student's comprehension and attending abilities. Students with receptive language difficulties often misinterpret language, tone of voice and body postures. A touch on the arm, shoulder, etc., may re-focus a student quicker and more successfully than verbal prompts.

Step-by-step Directions

• Avoid giving multiple directions; or, when repeating directions, give simple one-step cues.
• Have a model of a completed project or a model of various stages of a project readily accessible. Use this with hands-on demonstration.
• Have pre-cut pieces available.
• Complicated projects could be pre-started (measuring, using straight edge, folding, tracing, etc.).
• Pre-count materials or provide all of the necessary materials needed for the lesson. (Number concepts may not be developed and sequencing may be disorganized. For some children, just getting up out of their seats to get materials is disrupting to their organizational abilities.)

Visual Cues

• Using a highlighter pen, highlight a specific line that is to be cut. The student cuts only that line. Continue highlighting lines until the project is complete.

- Mark with an "X" the side or the area to be glued, using a pencil or piece of chalk.
- Help students visualize an image by sketching an outline of their chosen ideas. Demonstrate how simple shapes and lines create pictures. Verbalize the name of the shape or line, draw it lightly and have the student trace it. Using common objects, tell the student what shapes to use to draw the picture, i.e., "make a square; now put a triangle on top" … "a tree looks like a tall rectangle with a big circle on top" … "make a 3 with a fat tummy, fat tummy."

Verbal Cues
- Talking a student through a task (even from across the room) can be helpful.
- Use phrases such as, "use two hands," "start at the top," "turn your paper," "get closer to your work," "cut on the highlighted line."

Special Tools & Equipment
- Special scissors (provided by parents or occupational therapist).
- Pencil grips.
- Slant boards, clipboards or stabilize paper with tape. Children with low muscle tone have difficulty converging their eye muscles as they look down on materials on their desktop. Elevating the materials allows the student's eyes to gaze more comfortably, thus reducing fatigue and distractibility.
- Materials box so that project materials don't get lost, mixed up with others, etc.
- Supported seating either for the feet or back, to prevent muscle fatigue. When seated at a desk, the student should be able to rest his or her forearms comfortably on the desktop. Try different heights of chairs or desks until you find the best fit for your student. Fidgeting, falling out of chair and fatigue will be reduced. Handwriting and attention will be improved.
- Heavier-weight paper is easier for some children to cut. If heavier paper is not

available, use a glue stick or spray adhesive on the back of the paper and adhere the coated paper to construction paper just before cutting.

Directionality/Position in Space
- Terms such as right/left, top/bottom, between, next to, middle, etc. are often not established due to perceptual and/or language problems. Demonstrate these locations on the completed project, or simply point to or mark the correct places on a child's paper. Emphasize the words as you are showing the student direction.
- Left-right tracking, reversals, inversions can be minimized by simply pointing out or lightly marking where to start when drawing, cutting or writing.
- Copying is usually easier from a near point than a far point. It often helps a child to "copy" from a sample placed in front of him or her. Avoid seating arrangements that require the student to "turn" in his or her seat to view the board and then "turn" to return to work.

Computers
- Locating the correct key on the keyboard builds visual memory, matching of upper and lower case letters and symbol recognition.
- Dictation of letters to be typed builds auditory memory with a motor response, sequencing skills; develops visual images for symbols.
- Keyboarding itself develops fine motor dexterity and visual motor coordination.
- Math problems can be solved on the computer calculator.
- Use of mouse develops eye-hand coordination, controlled motor speed and positional concepts such as, *top, bottom, left, right.*
- Watching what is typed on the monitor improves visual tracking from left to right and helps in following the sequence of a written page.

Other
- Do not hesitate to consult with the occupational therapist or special educator before beginning new projects or when difficulty is noted. ↓

" These techniques are especially helpful for students with visual and auditory perceptual difficulties and poor motor skills."

Martha L. Boyle is a Registered Occupational Therapist and Sarah Korn-Rothschild is a Special Education Teacher at Smallwood Drive School, Snyder, NY.

What Are the Outcomes for Nondisabled Students?

Debbie Staub and Charles A. Peck

Although the research is limited, the consistency with which available studies indicate that inclusion does not harm nondisabled children—and in fact may benefit them—is encouraging.

Inclusion is receiving a lot of attention, both in school districts across the country and in the popular media. Most of that attention, however, is devoted to the effects of inclusion on students with disabilities. Here we want to consider the effects of inclusion on students who do not have disabilities.

We define *inclusion* as the full-time placement of children with mild, moderate, or severe disabilities in regular classrooms. This definition explicitly assumes that regular class placement must be considered as a relevant option for *all* children, regardless of the severity of their disabilities. This definition, however, does not preclude the use of pull-out services or instruction in a self-contained setting, when appropriate.

Three Common Concerns

In discussions about the effects of inclusion on nondisabled students, three fears commonly surface.

1. Will inclusion reduce the academic progress of nondisabled children? Unfortunately, only a limited research base exists documenting the impact of inclusion on the academic or developmental progress of nondisabled children. A few studies have used quasi-experimental designs to compare the progress of nondisabled children in inclusive classrooms to that of matched children enrolled in classrooms that do not include children with disabilities. These studies have consistently found no deceleration of academic progress for nondisabled children enrolled in inclusive classrooms. For example, when Odom and colleagues (1984) compared the progress of matched groups of nondisabled children in inclusive and noninclusive classrooms on standardized measures of cognitive, language, and social development, they found no significant differences in developmental outcomes (see also Cooke et al. 1981).

> Many nondisabled students experienced a growth in their commitment to personal moral and ethical principles as a result of their relationship with students with disabilities.

Other studies have tracked the developmental progress of nondisabled children enrolled in inclusive preschool programs over one or more years—again finding no evidence of developmental harm (Bricker et al. 1982). In one of the few studies carried out at the elementary level, Hunt and colleagues (in press) compared the academic achievement of nondisabled students in cooperative learning groups that either did or did not include a classmate with severe disabilities. The authors found no statistically significant differences between these groups on math achievement pre- and post-test scores.

Surveys conducted with parents and teachers who have been directly involved in inclusive settings generally show that both parties have positive views about inclusive programs and do not report any harm to the developmental progress of nondisabled children (Bailey and Winton 1989, Giangreco et al. 1993, Green and Stoneman 1989, Peck et al. 1992).

2. Will nondisabled children lose teacher time and attention? Although many have voiced their concern that classroom teachers will be forced to devote too much time to dealing with children with disabilities (Peck et al. 1989, Shanker 1994), only one study has directly investigated this issue in depth.

Hollowood and colleagues (in press) compared allocated and actual instructional time for six randomly selected nondisabled students in classrooms that included at least one student with severe disabilities, with a comparison group of nondisabled students in noninclusive classrooms. They also collected data on the rate of interruptions to planned instruction. Their findings indicated that the presence of students with severe disabilities had no effect on levels of allocated or engaged time. Further, time lost to interruptions of instruction was not significantly different in inclusive and noninclusive classrooms.

These findings are supported by survey responses from teachers and parents who have direct experience with inclusive classrooms (for example, Peck and colleagues 1992). In a related study, Helmstetter and colleagues (1993) surveyed a sample of 166 high school students who had been involved in inclusive classrooms in rural, suburban, and urban areas of Washington State. These students did not believe that their participation in inclusive classrooms had caused them to miss out on other valuable educational experiences.

3. Will nondisabled students learn undesirable behavior from students with disabilities? Observations of young children in inclusive classrooms suggest that this seldom occurs. In one survey, both parents and teachers indicated that nondisabled children had not picked up undesirable behavior from children with disabilities (Peck et al. 1992).

Another research effort conducted follow-along case studies of nondis-

abled students in inclusive elementary and middle school classrooms (Staub et al. in press, 1994). Interviews with parents and teachers, as well as direct observational data collected over two successive school years, indicate that nondisabled students do not acquire undesirable or maladaptive behavior from peers with disabilities.

Some caveats. The research about the impact of inclusion on children who do not have disabilities is limited in several ways. First, most studies have been carried out at the early childhood level—relatively few studies of elementary and secondary age children have been reported. Second, the existing research has been primarily descriptive or quasi-experimental in nature. Results of these studies must be interpreted with caution because of the ambiguity inherent in such designs.

It is also important to note that contextual variables, particularly the amount and nature of direct support provided to the classroom teacher, are

almost always considered critical to the ability of the classroom teacher to maintain adequate attention to the needs of all children (Giangreco et al. 1993, Peck et al. 1989, Salisbury et al. 1993).

Potential Benefits of Inclusion

Although teachers and parents often express concerns *before* experiencing inclusion, those who are familiar with inclusion indicate that nondisabled students benefit from their relationships with individuals with disabilities (Biklen et al. 1987, Murray-Seegert 1989, Peck et al. 1989). From our review of the available research, we identified five positive themes.

1. Reduced fear of human differences accompanied by increased comfort and awareness. On surveys and in interviews, high school students often attributed their reduced fear of people who looked or behaved differently to having had interactions with individuals with disabilities (Peck et al. 1992). For example, one student commented,

> If I had one thing to say to everybody, I would say, 'Don't be scared of students with disabilities—get to know them even if it takes a long time because it really is worth it' (Peck et al. 1990).

After interviewing 20 parents of nondisabled elementary-aged students attending inclusive classes, we found that not only did parents report that their children had less fear of people who looked and acted differently, but that they themselves had experienced a similar effect vicariously through their children's experiences (Staub et al., in press). In addition to feeling more accepting of others, students said that they came to value the contributions that all individuals make (Biklen et al. 1989, York et al. 1992).

2. Growth in social cognition. Murray-Seegert (1989), who conducted a yearlong ethnographic study in an inclusive high school, found that nondisabled students learned to be more tolerant of others as they became more aware of the needs of their peers with disabilities. She also found that these students demonstrated more positive feelings about themselves after spending time helping classmates with severe disabilities. In addition, researchers have found that elementary school children learn skills that enable them not only to communicate more effectively with their peers with disabilities, but also to be more supportive of them in daily interactions (Staub et al. 1994).

3. Improvements in self-concept. Many nondisabled students have experienced an increase in self-esteem as a result of their relationships with individuals with disabilities (Peck et al. 1992, Peck et al. 1990, Voeltz and Brennan 1983). Studies have shown that some students perceived that their relationship with a classmate with disabilities had elevated their status in class and school (Staub et al., in press).

© Susie Fitzhugh

A nondisabled junior high school student, who served as a peer tutor for a school mate with severe disabilities, explains it this way:

> Yeah, it's kind of rewarding if she [a student with disabilities] makes progress—you feel good about yourself because you've helped her to do it. I like that.

Teachers have also reported that for some students, having a role as a caretaker or peer tutor for a classmate with disabilities gives them a sense of belonging:

> Some kids reach out to everybody, but I've seen a few kids who have been saved by having somebody to care for in almost an unconditional way (Staub et al. 1994).

4. Development of personal principles. Many nondisabled students experienced a growth in their commitment to personal moral and ethical principles as a result of their relationship with students with disabilities. (Peck et al. 1990). Parents also reported that their children showed less prejudice toward people who behaved, acted, or looked differently from themselves (Peck et al 1992).

Helmstetter and colleagues (in press) noted that with the development of personal principles came an increased responsiveness on the part of nondisabled secondary school students toward the needs of other people. A high school student, commenting on his experience as a tutor for peers with severe disabilities, responded:

> I thought [my friends] wouldn't accept me interacting with the handicapped kids. I don't think it would have changed my mind if they wouldn't accept it because I don't care, you know—friends are friends but they are not going to stop me from doing something that I think is important (Peck et al. 1990).

Often nondisabled students assume an advocacy role toward their peers and friends with disabilities (Bogdan and Taylor 1989).

5. Warm and caring friendships. In many cases, the relationships that have

> The development
> of all children is
> enhanced by the
> extent to which
> they feel a sense
> of belonging,
> caring, and
> community in
> school.

emerged between students with and without disabilities have developed into meaningful, long-lasting friendships (Amado 1993, Strully and Strully 1985, Voeltz and Brennan 1983).

Many nondisabled students have commented on the value of the personal acceptance they have experienced from their peers who have disabilities, as well as the relaxed nature of their interactions with them:

> Like a lot of times he'll be sitting there and I won't feel like, should I say something, should I say something? ... It's a really nice connection, not to talk but to feel comfortable.

Bogdan and Taylor (1989), in their interviews with nondisabled people who do not "stigmatize, stereotype, or reject" those with disabilities, found that most of them mentioned deriving pleasure from their relationships with peers with disabilities. A mother, describing her son's relationship with a peer with severe disabilities, put it this way:

> Aaron's friendship with Cole is a caring, teaching relationship. I get the feeling that Aaron wants to let Cole experience the things he has experienced.... He gets a lot of joy from being able to do that (Staub et al. 1994).

Reflections on the Research

Although the research is quite limited, we are encouraged by the consistency with which existing studies indicate that inclusion does not harm nondisabled children. Even more encouraging is the evidence of potential benefits of inclusion.

We also agree with the majority of teachers and administrators we have interviewed that realizing the benefits of inclusion for all students will require active mediation of the experience by teachers, as well as the transfer of resources from traditional special education programs to support children placed in regular classes (Peck et al. 1993).

A central assumption underlying our interpretation of the studies reviewed here is that the purposes of inclusion are highly relevant to the needs of all children. The development of all children is enhanced by the extent to which they feel a sense of belonging, caring, and community in school (Noddings 1984). The values of belonging, caring, and community that underlie the inclusive schools movement represent a substantive shift from those that have traditionally dominated American life (Bellah et al. 1985). We interpret many aspects of the current controversies about inclusion to reflect the kinds of struggles that are inherent in such a shift in values and priorities. We suggest that including children with disabilities in regular public school classrooms is stimulating exactly the kind of experience in the lives of children, and the kind of reflective dialogue among adults, that is necessary to achieve change in the values and ethics underlying public education policy. ∎

References

Amado, A. N. (1993). *Friendships and Community Connections Between People With and Without Developmental Disabilities.* Baltimore: Paul H. Brookes.

Bailey, D., and P. Winton. (1989). "Friendship and Acquaintance among Families in a Mainstreamed Day Care Center." *Education and Training of the Mentally Retarded* 24: 107–113.

Bellah, R., R. Madsen, W. Sullivan, A. Swindler, and S. Tipton. (1985). *Habits of the Heart: Individualism and Commitment in American Life.* Berkeley, Calif.: University of California Press.

Biklen, D., C. Corrigan, and D. Quick. (1989). "Beyond Obligation: Students' Relations with Each Other in Integrated Classes." In *Beyond Separate Education: Quality Education for All,* edited by D. Lipsky and A. Gartner, pp. 207–221. Baltimore: Paul H. Brookes.

Bogdan, R., and S. J. Taylor. (1989). "Relationships with Severely Disabled People: The Social Construction of Humanness." *Social Problems* 36, 2: 135–148.

Bricker, D. D., M. B. Bruder, and E. Bailey. (1982). "Developmental Integration of Preschool Children." *Analysis and Intervention in Developmental Disabilities* 2: 207–222.

Cooke, T. P., J. A. Ruskus, T. Apolloni, and C. A. Peck. (1981). "Handicapped Preschool Children in the Mainstream: Background, Outcomes, and Clinical Suggestions." *Topics in Early Childhood Special Education* 1, 1: 73–83.

Giangreco, M. F., R. Dennis, C. Cloninger, S. Edelman, and R. Schattman. (1993). " 'I've counted Jon': Transformational Experiences of Teachers Educating Students with Disabilities." *Exceptional Children* 59, 4: 359–373.

Green, A., and Z. Stoneman. (1989). "Attitudes of Mothers and Fathers of Nonhandicapped Children." *Journal of Early Intervention* 13, 4: 292–304.

Helmstetter, E., C. Peck, and M. F. Giangreco. (1993). "Outcomes of Interactions with Peers with Moderate or Severe Disabilities: a Statewide Survey of High School Students." Unpublished manuscript, Washington State University.

Hollowood, T. M., C. L. Salisbury, B. Rainforth, and M. M. Palombaro. (In press). "Use of Instructional Time in Classrooms Serving Students with and Without Severe Disabilities." *Exceptional Children.*

Hunt, P., D. Staub, M. Alwell, and L. Goetz. (In press). "Achievement by All Students Within the Context of Cooperative Learning Groups." *The Journal of the Association for Persons with Severe Handicaps.*

Murray-Seegert, C. (1989). *Nasty Girls, Thugs, and Humans Like Us: Social Relations Between Severely Disabled and Nondisabled Students in High School.* Baltimore: Paul H. Brookes.

Noddings, N. (1984). *Caring: A Feminine Approach to Ethics and Moral Education.* Berkeley, Calif.: University of California Press.

Odom, S. L., M. Deklyen, and J. R. Jenkins. (1984). "Integrating Handicapped and Nonhandicapped Preschoolers: Developmental Impact on Nonhandicapped Children." *Exceptional Children* 51, 1: 41–48.

Peck, C. A., P. Carlson, and E. Helmstetter. (1992). "Parent and Teacher Perceptions of Outcomes for Typically Developing Children Enrolled in Integrated Early Childhood Programs: A Statewide Survey." *Journal of Early Intervention* 16: 53–63.

Peck, C. A., J. Donaldson, and M. Pezzoli. (1990). "Some Benefits Adolescents Perceive for Themselves from Their Social Relationships with Peers Who Have Severe Handicaps." *The Journal of the Association for Persons with Severe Handicaps* 15, 4: 241–249.

Peck, C. A., L. Hayden, M. Wandschneider, K. Peterson, and S. Richarz. (1989). "Development of Integrated Preschools: A Qualitative Inquiry into Sources of Resistance among Parents, Administrators, and Teachers." *Journal of Early Intervention* 13, 4: 353–364.

Peck, C. A., L. Mabry, J. Curley, and M. Conn-Powers. (May 1993). Implementing Inclusion at the Early Childhood Level: A Follow-Along Study of 54 Programs." Paper presented at the annual Washington State Infant and Early Childhood Conference, Seattle.

Salisbury, C. L., M. M. Palombaro, and T. M. Hollowood. (1993). "On the Nature and Change of an Inclusive Elementary School." *The Journal of the Association for Persons with Severe Handicaps* 18, 2: 75–84.

Shanker, A. (January 23, 1994). "Where We Stand." New York State United Teachers and the American Federation of Teachers. Column in the *New York Times.*

Staub, D., I. Schwartz, C. Gallucci, and C. Peck. (In press). "Four Portraits of Friendship at an Inclusive School." *The Journal of the Association for Persons with Severe Handicaps.*

Staub, D., C. Peck, I. Schwartz, and C. Gallucci. (1994). "Multiple Case Studies of Friendships at Inclusive Schools." Unpublished manuscript.

Strully, J., and C. Strully. (1985). "Friendship and Our Children." *The Journal of the Association for Persons with Severe Handicaps* 10, 4: 224–227.

Voeltz, L. M., and J. Brennan. (1983). "Analysis of the Interactions Between Nonhandicapped and Severely Handicapped Peers Using Multiple Measures." In *Perspectives and Progress in Mental Retardation, Chapter VI: Social Psychology and Educational Aspects,* edited by J. M. Berg. Baltimore: University Park Press.

York, J., T. Vandercook, C. MacDonald, C. Heise-Neff, and E. Caughey. (1992). "Feedback about Integrating Middle-school Education Students with Severe Disabilities in General Education Classes." *Exceptional Children* 58, 3: 244–258.

Authors' note: This research was supported in part by a U.S. Department of Education Grant and Cooperative Agreement. The opinions expressed herein do not necessarily reflect the position or policy of the U.S. Department of Education, and no official endorsement should be inferred.

Debbie Staub is Project Coordinator, Inclusive Education Research Group, University of Washington, Emily Dickinson School, 7040 - 208th Ave., N.E., Redmond, WA 98053. **Charles A. Peck** is Associate Professor of Special Education, Washington State University at Vancouver, 1812 E. McLoughlin Blvd., Vancouver, WA 98663.

♦ ≋ Ж ≋ Ж ≋ Ж ≋ Ж♦Ж ≋ Ж ≋ Ж ≋ Ж ≋ ♦

Voices

A Thanksgiving Day editorial in the newspaper told of a school teacher who asked her class of first graders to draw a picture of something they were thankful for. She thought of how little these children from poor neighborhoods actually had to be thankful for. But she knew that most of them would draw pictures of turkeys or tables with food. The teacher was taken aback with the picture Douglas handed in . . . a simple childishly drawn hand.

But whose hand? The class was captivated by the abstract image. "I think it must be the hand of God that brings us food," said one child. "A farmer," said another, "because he grows the turkeys." Finally when the others were at work, the teacher bent over Douglas's desk and asked whose hand it was. "It's your hand, Teacher," he mumbled.

She recalled that frequently at recess she had taken Douglas, a scrubby forlorn child by the hand. She often did that with the children. But it meant so much to Douglas. Perhaps this was everyone's Thanksgiving, not for the material things given to us but for the chance, in whatever small way, to give to others.

— *Source Unknown*

From *Chicken Soup for the Soul,* written and compiled by Jack Canfield and Mark Victor Hansen. Deerfield Beach, FL: Health Communications, Inc., 1993.

Suggested books to use with acceptance activities:

Be Good to Eddie Lee
   By Virginia Fleming

Big Al
   By Andrew Clements Yoshi

Boastful Bullfrog
   By Keith Faulkner

Chrysanthemum
   By Kevin Henkes

Crowboy
   By Taro Yashima

Do I Have To Go To School Today?
   By Larry Shles

Elephant and the Rainbow
   By Keith Faulkner

I Like Me
   By Nancy Carlson

I Wish I Were A Butterfly
   By James Howe

Josh: A Boy with Dyslexia
   By Caroline Janover

Kids Explore the Gifts of Children with Special Needs
   By Westridge Young Writers Workshop

Kittens Who Didn't Share
   By Keith Faulkner

Little Rabbit Who Wanted Red Wings
   By Carolyn Sherwin Bailey

Mama Zooms
   By Jane Cowen-Fletcher

Me First and the Gimme Gimmes
   By Gerald G. Jampolsky & Diane V. Cirincione

My Buddy
By Audrey Osofsky

My Sister is Different
by Betty Ren Wright

Original Warm Fuzzy Tale
By Claude Steiner

Our Brother Has Down's Syndrome
By Shelley Cairo

Owl and the Woodpecker
By Brian Wildsmith

People
By Peter Spier

Rainbow Fish
By Marcus Pfister

Reach for the Moon
By Samantha Abeel

Santa's Book of Names
By David McPhail

Stellaluna
By Janell Cannon

Table Where Rich People Sit
By Byrd Baylor

That's What a Friend Is
By P.K. Hallinan

What Do You Mean I Have a Learning Disability?
By Kathleen M. Dwyer

When Learning is Tough
By Cynthia Roby

Tacky the Penguin
By Helen Lester

We Can Do It
By Laura Dwight

Patricia Pavelka, M. Ed.

Desk Clean

☐☐☐☐☐ 1. Take everything out.

☐☐☐☐☐ 2. Put back hard cover books.

☐☐☐☐☐ 3. Pile the loose papers.

☐☐☐☐☐ 4. Put loose papers in colored folders.

☐☐☐☐☐ 5. Put colored folders back in desk.

☐☐☐☐☐ 6. Put back pencils, markers, etc.

☐☐☐☐☐ 7. Put back assignment notebook.

☐☐☐☐☐ 8. Bring everything else up to Mrs. Pavelka.

Organizing Students For Success

Organizational Tips for Students

1. Color coding subjects
2. Pocket folder for "Take Home Papers"
3. Pocket folder for "Keep at School Papers"
4. "Desk clean" every day
5. Assignment notebook signed by teacher and parent every day

Organizational Tips for Teachers

1. Daily schedules posted
2. Monthly calendar posted
3. Ten minute "organizational time" at the end of each day
4. Check in time each morning
5. Seating arrangements

Not only do students need to be physically organized, everything in its place, they also need to be <u>mentally organized.</u> They need to be able to organize their thoughts in order to set them up for success.

Strategies to Help Organization Students' Thoughts

1. KWL
2. Concept mapping
3. Categorizing concepts and vocabulary
4. Eliciting background knowledge and prior experiences
5. Brainstorming
6. Think-Alouds
7. Set for flexibility (What do I do when I don't know a word?)
8. Purpose setting
9. Webbing
10. Story maps

Patricia Pavelka, M.Ed.

Flexible Grouping

One of the most challenging undertakings teachers of reading and language arts face is having to organize students for instruction: group them. In most classrooms this is accomplished by ability grouping, which simply means grouping students according to ability and achievement. This often leads to ability level tracks, lowered expectations on the teacher's part and poor self esteem on the child's part. We need to look at restructuring our classrooms in order to provide effective instruction for all students. There is no right or wrong way. Here are some alternatives to ability grouping.

Whole Group

All students are reading the same novel. Information is presented to all students at the same time.

Needs-Based Groups

Needs-based groups are formed when there are students who would benefit from additional instruction and support. Most times needs-based groups are formed from the whole group.

Interest Groups

Interest groups form when students place themselves together according to their interests.

Cooperative Groups

Cooperative groups are formed by the teacher or by students as a forum for sharing or completing a task.

Adapted from Paratore's Flexible Grouping: Why and How (Leadership Letters)

Patricia Pavelka, M.Ed.

Whole Group

What are students doing during independent work time?

Not Proficient Readers

Written responses are expected at least two days from students.

Responses may include:
  Free responses
  Assigned questions
  Vocabulary
  Literature Extensions

These responses may be modified. For example, instead of answering six questions students may choose two or three.

Proficient Readers

Daily written responses are expected from students.

Responses may include:
  Free responses
  Assigned questions
  Vocabulary
  Literature Extensions

Day 5
Because this has been a whole class book a real 'family feeling' has taken place this week. We usually end with some cooperative learning experience.

Drama
interviews, short plays, favorite parts, debates

Free Choice

Cooperative Learning Experiences

ART
illustrations, sculptures, murals, dioramas

Literature Extensions
compare/contrast charts, character maps

How does the reading get done?

Day 1
New vocabulary and concepts are introduced. Predictions are made based on the title, genre etc. Prior knowledge and background knowledge are discussed. Motivation is established. Some or all of the book is read together. Reading assignment is given.

Not Proficient Readers

Collaborative Teaming

Home

School

Reads with classroom teacher

Reads with support teacher

Pair reads with a friend

Books on tapes

Proficient Readers

1. Silent reads during SSR
2. Reads for homework
3. Reads with a friend during L.A.

Days 2-4
The whole class (both needs-based groups) are together and a discussion of the story takes place. Students retell what has happened and then respond. Story events and characters are analyzed. Do students like/dislike what has been happening? Do they agree/disagree with the way characters behave? Predictions about what will happen next also occur, etc.

Patricia Pavelka, M.Ed.

238

Home and School Reading Contract

Independent   Home

Monday	☐	☐
Tuesday	☐	☐
Wednesday	☐	☐
Thursday	☐	☐
Friday	☐	☐
Saturday	☐	☐
Sunday	☐	☐

Patricia Pavelka, M.Ed.

Collaborative Teaming Planning Sheet

Week of _____

Reading

Writing

Math

Science / Social Studies

Misc.

Patricia Pavelka, M.Ed.

Name _____ Date _____

1. How do you feel about reading?

2. Do you think you are a good reader? Why?

3. What was the last book you read?

4. What kinds of books do you like to read?

5. Do you think it is important to be a good reader?
   Why?

6. What do you do when you come to a word you can't read?

7. Do you read at home?

8. What do you usually do after school when you get home?

9. Do you like to read? Why?

10. Is there anything you would like me to know that would help you have a good year at school?

Patricia Pavelka, M.Ed.

Get rid of that line!

* Model and Demonstrate

* Brainstorm

* One Minute Partner Share

* Ask Two Before Me

* Directions on Board

* Assignments on Board

  1st   First
  2nd Second

Three Cueing Systems

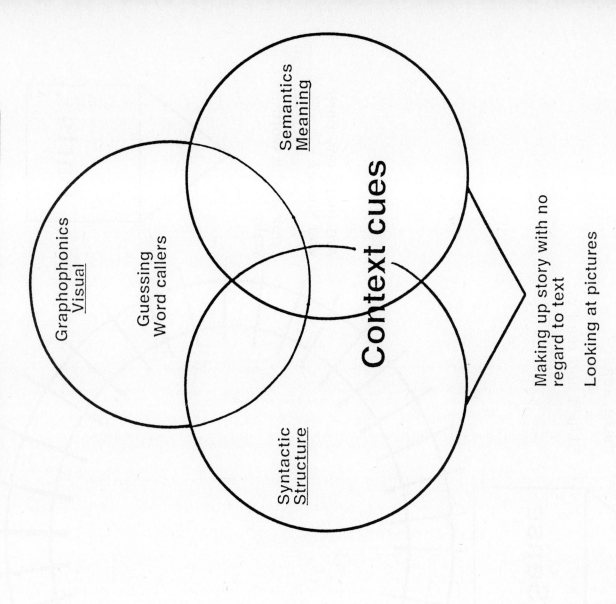

Graphophonics
Visual

Semantics
Meaning

Syntactic
Structure

Guessing
Word callers

Context cues

Making up story with no
regard to text

Looking at pictures

Patricia Pavelka, M.Ed.

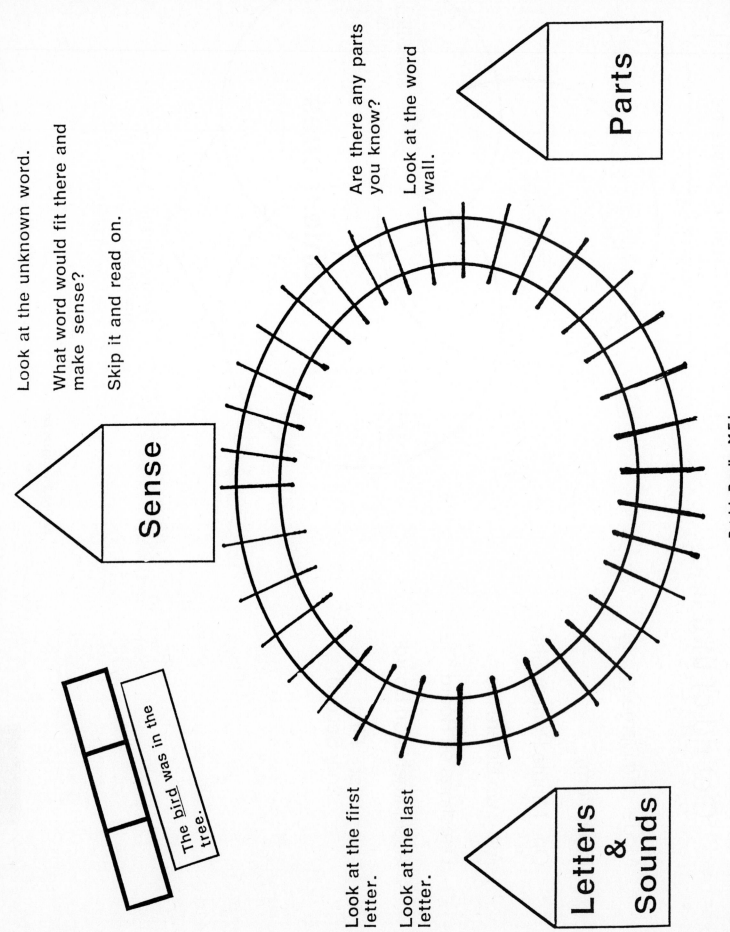

Look at the unknown word.

What word would fit there and make sense?

Skip it and read on.

Sense

Are there any parts you know?

Look at the word wall.

Parts

The <u>bird</u> was in the tree.

Look at the first letter.

Look at the last letter.

Letters & Sounds

Patricia Pavelka, M.Ed.

244

Think-Alouds

Proficient Readers Good Readers Mature Readers	Not Proficient Readers Poor Readers Immature Readers
Activate prior knowledge	Start reading without preparation
Understand task and set purpose	Read without knowing why
Monitor comprehension	Do not know they do not understand
Anticipate and predict	Read to get done
Have fix-up strategies	Do not know what to do
Use text structure	Do not see any organization
Organize and integrate new information	Add on, rather than integrate new information
Reflect	Stop reading and thinking
Summarize	Stop reading and thinking
Seek additional information	Stop reading and thinking
Success is a result of effort	Success is a result of luck

Prior to Reading

What are my purposes for reading?
What do I already know about the topic?
What do I think I will learn?
What are my predictions?
Look at titles and chapter headings.

During Reading

Am I understanding?
Does this make sense?
Do I have a clear picture in my head?
Is this what I expected?
What can I do to increase my understanding?

After Reading

What are the most important points?
What new information did I learn?
How does it fit with what I already know?
Were my predictions correct?
Should I go back and reread?
How do I feel about the book?

Adapted from Strategic Learning in the Content Areas: Wisconsin Dept. of Public Instruction

Patricia Pavelka, M.Ed.

Characteristics of Differently Abled Readers

Proficient Readers	Not Proficient Readers	How can we help?
Actively monitor comprehension	Do not see view reading as a meaning making process. Do not know they do not understand	Model the reading process. Activities: shared book experience, language experience stories, read alouds, retelling, charting directions, labeling
Possess strategies to use when comprehension breaks down or unfamiliar words are encountered	Have no strategies, use inappropriate strategies or do not see the need for strategies	Develop a set for flexibility, use think-alouds
Possess a positive self image and have a sense of control regarding their reading achievements.	Possess a poor or negative self image and have a sense of no control regarding their reading achievements.	Build self esteem and self worth, focus on strengths not weaknesses, utilize cooperative learning, keep "Books I've Read" charts, repeated reading
Attribute success to themselves	Attribute success to luck	
Set a purpose before reading and activate prior knowledge	Read without preparing or knowing why	Brainstorming, previewing purpose setting
Utilize the three cueing systems simultaneously (graphophonics, semantics, syntactic)	Rely on one system	Model using the three cueing systems simultaneously, masking
After reading reflect, summarize and seek more information	Stop reading Stop thinking	Meaningful literature extensions, book shares, writing process

Patricia Pavelka, M.Ed.

Free Responses

I. Characters

Who is the main character?

Do you like the main character? Why or why not?

Who are the minor characters?

Do you know anyone like the characters in the books?

What problems do the characters have?

Who was your favorite character? Why?

What does the main character want?

Do any of the characters change?

Do any of the characters do things you feel are good? Bad?

Compare and contrast the characters.

II. Setting

Where does this story take place?

Do you know a place like this?

How is the setting important to the story?

Why do you think the story takes place in . . . ?

How would the story be different if it took place in _____ at _____ ?

When does the story take place?

III. Plot

What is happening in the story?

How did the story end?

What was the climax of the story?

What events led to the climax?

What might have happened if a certain action did not take place?

IV. Theme

What is the theme of the story?

V. Personal Reactions

What is your favorite part of the story? Why?

What was the funniest part? Saddest? Happiest? Scariest?

What would happen if . . . ?

What would you have done if you were . . . ?

Why do you think the book is titled _____ ?

Patricia Pavelka, M. Ed.

Name _____   **Date** _____

Title of Book _____

Author _____

What was your favorite part? _____

Patricia Pavelka, M.Ed.

Why use learning centers?

No Levels

Active Participation

Independence:
  making decisions
  following directions
  working independently
  self-directed

Responsibility and Organization

Individualized Learning

Social Skills
  sharing
  taking turns
  respecting each other
  helping each other
  cooperative learning

Community of learners

Information about Students

Learning Styles

Resources

Teachers relinquish control...
Students take ownership

Child-centered

Stimulates self-discovery

Risk taking

Individual and Group Instruction
  less interruptions
  peer interactions

Review, Reteach and Enrich

Three-Four Groups

Group 1	Teacher
Group 2	Centers
Groups 3&4	Assignment

Whole Group

All students go to centers.
One of the centers is me.
I assign students to my center.

All students go to centers with no assignments.

Whole Group

An assignment is given.
Students go to centers after the assignment is completed

September/October

Center activities require a minimum of teacher direction.

* Routines & Responsibilities

  Appropriate use of materials

  Time Frames

  Clean up

* What ifs...

* Social Skills

* Independence

Patricia Pavelka, M.Ed.

Science/Social Studies Center

Activities

Climate of Inquiry
investigating
observing
collecting data
gathering information
hypothesizing
making connections

Materials

maps
globe
magnifying glasses

items related to what is being studied

Art Center

Activities

Follows the art curriculum
See your art teacher for the weekly project

'creative designs'
posters
pictures & murals
dioramas & mobiles
puppets for drama
costumes
collages
paper mache

Materials

paper
scissors
glue
writing utensils
  pencils markers
  crayons colored pencils
stencils
paint
recyclables & crafts
  boxes   cotton balls
  buttons paper plates
  cans
  egg cartons
yarn and string

Writing Center

Activities

shape books
  informational
  creative writing
stories and books
writing letters
labeling pictures
book responses
acronyms
mobiles
theme related
  writing
  pictures

Materials

patterns for shape books
writing paper
  lined
  unlined
  story paper
envelopes
writing utensils
  pencils
  markers
  colored pencils
stencils
pictures
  magazines
scissors

Listening Center

Activities

listening to a new story
revisiting an old story
following along in a book

record student reading

Materials

headphones
tape recorders
walkmans
cassettes
cassettes with matching books
filmstrips

Patricia Pavelka, M.Ed.

Math

Follows math curriculum

Creative Play

Connects to our theme

Computer

Reading Center

Activities

reading
retelling stories through
props

Materials

books
magazines
student-created
books
poetry

carpet
beanbag chairs
cushions

puppets
storyboards
flannel boards

Blocks

Activities

Materials

building blocks
attribute blocks
pattern blocks
architecture books
graph paper
carpenter apron

Patricia Pavelka, M.Ed.

A good discipline program for a multiage classroom is one that reflects the following:

1. Students experience themselves as a community of learners, supporting one another's success in the classroom.

2. Students have opportunities to demonstrate that they are responsible and capable people.

3. Students learn to respect their own and others' humanity in the classroom.

4. Students are treated with respect and dignity even when they are being disruptive.

Q.

What kind of discipline program would be appropriate for a multiage classroom?

In this classroom, the teacher may involve students in setting up the discipline program. Students are given opportunities to offer suggestions for the kinds of rules or agreements they will create. There may be a "Responsible Citizen" committee that offers or recommends support systems needed by students who have chronic problems in the classroom. A "pay back" system can be set up where students are made aware of the contribution each of them makes to a successful classroom environment. When an individual has threatened the safety or success of the classroom, she is required to give something back — some action that will contribute to classmates to make up for what she took away.

The teacher reads stories and has discussions about anger, frustration, and fears that children have, both in and out of the classroom. Systems are set up to support students who have problems with these issues. A "cooling off" area can be made available with drawing materials, journals, clay, teddy bears, pillows to punch, toy telephones, puppets, etc.

Some children require more structure and support than others. Some are very distractible and impulsive and require systems that assist them in developing the ability to focus and wait for what they want and need. Others have learned that whining, temper tantrums, or defiance are ways to get what they want. These children need to learn from a supportive and nurturing teacher how to communicate their needs appropriately.

Discipline programs for the multiage classroom must be consistent with the overall philosophy of developmentally appropriate education. Students express themselves differently and require a teacher who is aware and able to accept and work with each child wherever she is in her growing process.

A classroom can offer a safe and nurturing learning environment if behavior issues are thought of as a learning process. The three questions every teacher must ask are:

- What does this child need (i.e., attention, power, motivation)?
- What does this child need to learn (i.e., to communicate, to be responsible)?
- How can I provide what this child needs in a loving and supporting manner?

Discipline programs that support this kind of philosophy are reflected in books such as *Loving Discipline A to Z, Cooperative Discipline, Positive Discipline,* and *Discipline with Dignity* (see bibliography.)

A. Without effective intervention techniques for the difficult child, this would be a valid concern. Looked at from another angle, however, it's an opportunity for more time to apply effective interventions and encouragement to make a long-term, positive change in this child's life.

All children need to belong, and to feel connected to their classmates and teacher. Being in the same class for two or three years gives a child a sense of security, continuity, and stability.

Difficult students sometimes have issues of trust. A multiyear placement gives these childen more time to bond with the teacher and build that trust. In return, the teacher can provide consistent acceptance, affection, and discipline in a caring environment, which will help a child feel valued and secure.

If a teacher consistently uses encouragement and applies effective discipline interventions, there's a good chance the difficult student will become cooperative before the first year is over; then the teacher can enjoy a good relationship with the child.

In *Cooperative Discipline*, Linda Albert talks about the three C's of encouragement: helping the child feel capable, connected, and contributing. In a multiage classroom, there are many more opportunities to apply these than in a regular classroom. Older kids helping younger students get all three C's at the same time! Cooperative learning activities and classroom meetings also provide them simultaneously.

Consider the possibility that the difficult child is a child with special needs. This child may or may not qualify for services. What better place can his learning style be honored than in a multiage setting, where kids have a better chance at having individual learning needs met? Many borderline or fall-through-the-cracks students will thrive in this environment.

Some techniques that frequently help a difficult child include individual conferences with the student, involving the child in making decisions that affect him, praise and encouragement, contracts, time-out, and behavioral consequences that are related, reasonable, and respectful.

Q. What if a teacher is concerned about having a difficult child for more than one year?

Using effective teaching practices and discipline interventions, honoring learning styles, and adding heavy doses of encouragement all help win over the difficult child. This, done on a consistent basis over a period of two or three years with the same teacher, has an even stronger chance of succeeding than if the child has a different teacher every year. What a gift for the child!

Q. What are our options for handling a personality clash between a child and her teacher?

A. First, what is meant by a personality clash? Is such a perceived clash caused by who the teacher is, who the student is, or by teacher and student behaviors that consistently lead to conflict? Often behaviors that continually lead to conflict are labeled personality conflicts.

The teacher and student should become involved in a conflict resolution process to establish the issues and try to arrive at a solution which is of mutual benefit to both. If, after sincere effort at problem solving, it is apparent that the problem is going to continue, the school should consider changing the class placement of the student. Neither the child's best interest nor the teacher's is served by continuing a situation in which there is a continuous, unsolvable conflict.

Excerpt from *Multiage Q&A: 101 Practical Answers to Your Most Pressing Questions*, by Jim Grant, Bob Johnson and Irv Richardson. Reprinted by permission of Crystal Springs Books, Ten Sharon Road, Peterborough, NH 03458. 1-800-321-0401.

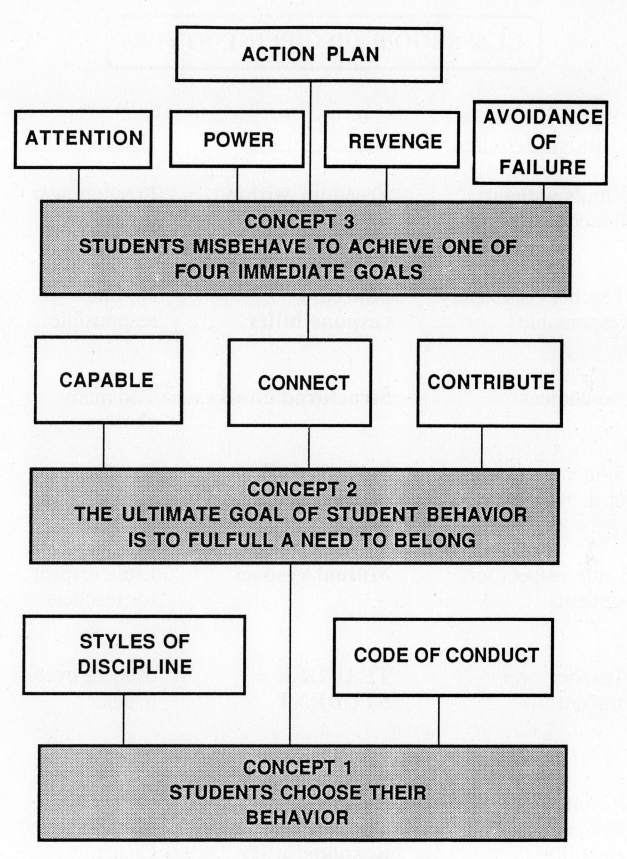

**CONCEPTUAL FRAMEWORK OF
LINDA ALBERT'S *COOPERATIVE DISCIPLINE***

Yvette Zgonc

257

CLASSROOM DISCIPLINE STYLES

Hands-Clenched	Hands-Joined	Hands-Off
Limits without freedom	**Freedom within limits**	Freedom w/o limits
Teacher completely responsible	**Shared responsibility**	No one responsible
No choices	**Structured choices**	Too many choices
Students threatened or demanded	**Self-discipline encouraged**	Conflicts avoided
Little respect for students	**Mutual respect**	Little respect for teachers
Teacher over student	**TEACHER = STUDENT**	Student over teacher
Result: Defiance and Hostility	**Result: Cooperation and Responsibility**	Result: Confusion and Chaos

Adaptation from Linda Albert's
Cooperative Discipline

Yvette Zgonc

DIRTY DOZEN DESTRUCTIVE DON'TS
(TOOLS OF TORTURE)

1. NAGGING

2. YELLING

3. LECTURING

4. THREATENING

5. FORCED APOLOGIES

6. SENDING TO PRINCIPAL TOO SOON

7. SARCASM

8. WRITING NAME ON CHALKBOARD

9. WRITING 100, 200, TIMES...................

10. SPANKING

11. SITTING OUTSIDE IN HALL

12. HUMILIATING

Yvette Zgonc

SAMPLE CODE OF CONDUCT

❶ I Will Treat Everyone With Courtesy And Respect.

❷ I Will Treat Personal And School Property With Respect.

❸ I Will Create And Maintain A Positive And Safe Environment.

❹ I Will Come To School Prepared For Learning.

❺ I Will Act Responsibly And Accept Consequences For My Actions.

❻ I Will Help Everyone In This School Feel Capable, Connected, And Contributing.

CODE OF CONDUCT

Yvette Zgonc

SAMPLE CODE OF CONDUCT

- ◆ **I WILL RESPECT OTHERS.**

- ◆ **I WILL RESPECT PROPERTY.**

- ◆ **I WILL BE SAFE.**

- ◆ **I WILL BE PRE-PARED.**

- ◆ **I WILL BE RE-SPONSIBLE.**

TEACHING THE CODE OF CONDUCT

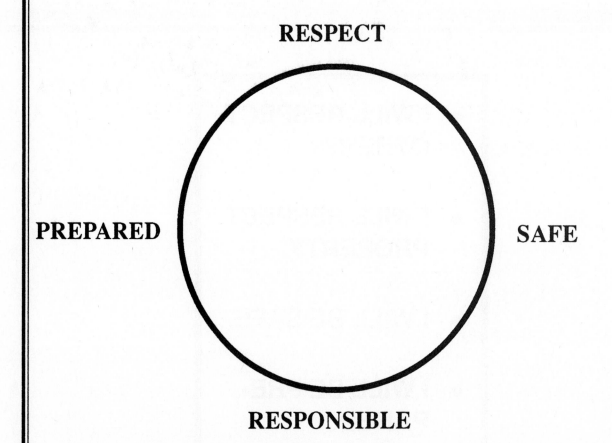

Honor all learning styles when teaching the Code of Conduct. Consider using Howard Gardner's Seven Levels of Intelligences:
- *Verbal/Linguistic
- *Logical/Mathematical
- *Visual/Spatial
- *Body/Kinesthetic
- *Musical/Rhythmic
- *Interpersonal
- *Intrapersonal

Yvette Zgonc

THE THREE C'S OF SELF-ESTEEM

♦ **CAPABLE**

Make mistakes okay.
Make learning tangible.
Recognize achievement.

♦ **CONNECT**

Give attention.
Show appreciation.
Use affirmations.

♦ **CONTRIBUTE**

Give students opportunities to have a say in decisions that affect them.

Encourage students to help other students.

Let students contribute to the well-being of the class.

Adaptation from *Cooperative Discipline* by Linda Albert

Yvette Zgonc

FOUR GOALS OF MISBEHAVIOR

Goal and Belief	How does teacher feel?	What does teacher do?	What does student do as a result?
Attention (I'm only OK when I'm being noticed or served)	Irritated Annoyed	Remind, nag	Stop temporarily Start again or do something else
Power (I'm only OK when I'm boss)	Angry	Confrontive Give in	Confrontive Passive aggressive
Revenge (I'm only OK when I'm getting even)	Angry Hurt	Retaliate	Retaliate
Avoidance-of-Failure (I'm only OK when I'm showing you I'm helpless)	Helpless (Professional concern)	Give up	Give up Continue to do nothing

Adaptation from the works of Linda Albert, Don Dinkmeyer, and Rudolf Dreikurs

Yvette Zgonc

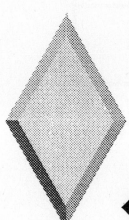

MAINTAIN YOUR SANITY WITH EFFECTIVE INTERVENTION TOOLS

◆ Ignore the behavior.

◆ Give "The Eye".

◆ Stand close by.

◆ Send a secret signal.

◆ Give written notice.

◆ Give an "I" message.

◆ Use a diminishing quota.

◆ Talk to the wall.

◆ Cease teaching temporarily.

◆ Use "Target, Stop, Do".

◆ Have a classroom meeting.

◆ Use humor.

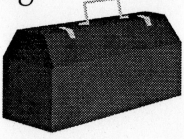

Yvette Zgonc

GRACEFUL EXIT STRATEGIES

☛ **Decide not to pick up the rope (Remain unimpressed.)**

☛ **Acknowledge student's power**

☛ **Remove the audience**

☛ **Table the matter**

☛ **Make a date to talk about it**

☛ **Take a "teacher time-out"**

☛ **Use a fogging technique**
   Agree with the student
   Change the subject

☛ **State both viewpoints**

☛ **Use humor (Aikido)**

☛ **Refuse responsibility**

☛ **Say an exit statement**

☛ **Call their bluff**

Yvette Zgonc

INDIVIDUAL CONFERENCE

1. **DEFINE THE PROBLEM OBJECTIVELY.**

2. **DESCRIBE THE FEELINGS AND NEEDS OF EACH.**

3. **DISCUSS ALTERNATIVES AND EVALUATE.**

4. **DECIDE ON A PLAN WITH A TIME FRAME.**

5. **DETERMINE EFFECTIVENESS.**

Yvette Zgonc

STUDENT CONFERENCING RESPONSES

STONEWALL--SINCE YOU'RE NOT READY TO TALK ABOUT IT, I WILL DECIDE.

UNWORKABLE SOLUTION--I'M UNWILLING TO TRY THAT BECAUSE_____. DO YOU HAVE ANOTHER IDEA?

PROMISES-PROMISES--THAT WILL HELP A LOT. WHAT CONSEQUENCE WOULD BE FAIR IF YOU SHOULD FORGET?

DISRESPECT--YOU MAY CONTINUE IF YOU TALK RESPECTFULLY OR YOU MAY GO TO TIME OUT. YOU DECIDE.

BLAMING OTHERS--I'M NOT INTERESTED IN FAULT-FINDING. I'M INTERESTED IN SOLUTIONS.

DENIAL--WHAT ARE YOUR IDEAS ON SOLVING THE PROBLEM?

Yvette Zgonc

RESPONSES TO BUTTON PUSHERS

1. I don't know why I have to be in this dumb class anyway.
   Which dumb class would you like to be in?
   Hey, just your luck.

2. You're the meanest math teacher I've ever had.
   I'm mean, cruel, and nasty and those are my good points.
   That was one of the requirements for this job.
   Great! I finally won something.

3. Who ever told you that you know how to coach a team?
   My father, my mother, Bo Jackson, God
   Instructions come with Reebok tennis shoes.

4. I can't learn anything the way you teach!
   (Turn backwards) How about if I teach this way?
   Well, this is my position on this. (Make Egyptian stance.)
   Don't learn anything. Learn science.

5. I hate it in this class. I want to be changed to a different teacher.
   Zap. You're a different teacher.
   Hate it quietly, OK?
   They don't get anymore different than I am.

6. I sure wish I didn't have to be doing this stupid science experiment right now.
   When would you like to do this stupid science experiment?
   Why waste a wish on that?
   Do a smart one.
   When would be a good time to do this stupid science experiment?

7. I can't wait for the bell to ring. This class is driving me bananas.
   When the bell rings, we'll have banana splits, but be careful how you peel out of here.
   That makes a whole bunch of us.
   Quit monkeying around.

8. Somebody ought to take away your teaching license.
   What license?
   I have to get one first.
   How else can I drive you crazy?

Yvette Zgonc

9. You never let us have any fun.
   Have a card with the word "fun" on it and give it to the student.

10. Why are you looking at me like that?
    (Make a ridiculous face) Is this better?

11. I think this class sucks.
    So does my Hoover, but it works.
    Here's a lollipop.
    Would you spell that "S" word. I'm not sure I know that word.
    If this class sucks, be sure not to slurp.

12. Why do we need this dumb stuff anyway?
    So you can win on Jeopardy.

13. This work is too hard.
    If you hold on a minute, I'll get you some soft work.
    See what you can do to soften it up?
    Not it's not. It's just right.

15. Why do we have to come to school anyway?
    So I won't be lonely.
    Because school can't come to you.

16. You make me sick.
    I thought you looked a little strange. I'll see if I can find an antidote.
    The color green looks good on you.
    I'm glad I'm having some kind of effect on you.

These responses came from teachers all over the country.

Yvette Zgonc

TIME-OUT TIPS

If students exhibit out-of-bounds behavior or repeat the same misbehavior over and over again, teachers may want to exclude the student from the rest of the students in a time-out area. Places might include a classroom location away from the other students, a colleague's classroom or a time-out room.

The student is sent to time out using the language of choice:

> You may keep your hands and feet to yourself or go to time out. You decide.
>
> You may participate in the discussion if you wait until you're called on, or go to time out. You decide.
>
> If you continue to _____, you'll need to go to time out. You decide.

Once the student is in time out, he/she is more likely to learn to make more appropriate choices if a plan of action is written. The plan should include such questions as:

> Why are you in time out?
> What did you want to happen?
> How did what you chose to do relate to our class Code of Conduct?
> What could you do differently next time?

Younger students may choose to draw what they are going to stop doing and draw what they will start doing. Students who have difficulty with writing may tape their plan with a tape recorder or discuss their plan with another student, volunteer, or teacher's assistant.

Some teachers allow their students to return to their seats when the students think they are ready and can show through their behavior they are ready to be part of the group. Other teachers like to make the decision when the time out is over.

If the student is asked to go to time out again, the plan should be taken home and signed by the parent. The time-out plan is also good documentation for an office referral and can be discussed with the principal. Time out should be used sparingly to gain the most effectiveness.

Yvette Zgonc

DIFFERENCES BETWEEN PUNISHMENT AND CONSEQUENCES

PUNISHMENT

- Expresses power of a personal authority
- Is usually painful and reminds student of the past
- Is not related to the misbehavior
- Is easy or expedient
- Has a "you'll pay for this" or "now I gotcha" attitude
- Concentrates on verbal embarrassment
- Creates a desire for revenge

CONSEQUENCES

- Are logically related to the misbehavior
- Concerned with the present or immediate future
- Are friendly, but firm
- Maintain dignity of both adult and student
- Are reasonable in terms of length of time
- Are respectfully given
- Give responsibility to the individual responsible for the misbehavior

Yvette Zgonc

Sample School Consequences
Using Categories of Consequences

Loss or delay of activity

Not following rules of the game	Remove from game
Talking out	Loss of free time
Disruptive at listening center	Loss of center time
Incomplete work	Loss of recess
Late to class	Make up work during free time
Too long on pass	Loss of pass privilege temporarily

Loss or delay of using objects/equipment

Throwing blocks	Loss of blocks temporarily
Playing with toy brought from home during seatwork	Loss of toy until after school
Misuse of manipulatives	Loss of own manipulatives
Swinging bat inappropriately	Loss of bat
Misuse of microscope	Loss of using microscope
Improper use of recorder	Loss of recorder temporarily

Loss or delay of access to school areas

Disruptive during story time	Removal from story area for the remainder of story
Misbehaving on bus	Temporary loss of bus privileges
Library misbehavior of student	Sent back to class
Continued misbehavior in lunchroom	Temporary loss of lunchroom privileges
Misbehaving in computer lab	Loss of computer room
Fighting on playground	Removal from playground

Denied interactions with other students

Hitting	Time out
Disrupting group activity	Finish work alone
Throwing food in cafeteria	Sit in separate section
Fighting on playground	Play alone
Looking at another person's paper	Finish work in isolated area
Teasing or put downs	Remove to isolated area

Yvette Zgonc

Required interaction with school personnel

Extreme disrespect to teacher   Send to principal
Inability to handle anger   Meet with counselor
Excessive swearing   Meet with dean
Continued refusal to do work   Send to In-School Suspension
Refusal to go to time out   Bring "Who Squad"
Violent behavior   Send to principal

Required interaction with parents

Biting/anything breaking skin   Contact parents
Student coming without materials on a regular basis   Phone call/letter home
Chronic tardiness or absenteeism   Contact parents
Failing   Contact parents
Disruptive behavior in class   Call parents
Sexual harassment   Call parents

Required interaction with police

Vandalism   Call police
Live ammunition brought to school   Call police
Drugs   Call police
Assault   Call police
Weapons   Call police
Sexual abuse   Call police and protective services

Restitution

Hurt child's feelings   Apologize
Rip a page of friend's book   Help child tape it
Destroy school property   Pay for or replace, or perform
                                                   school service

Loss of library book   Pay for book
Destruction of another person's property   Pay or replace
Milkshake "bomb"   Help custodian clean up

Note: These are actual consequences shared by K-12 teachers using them in schools throughout the country.

SCHOOL ACTION PLAN

Step 1:   **Pinpoint and describe the student's behavior.**

_____

_____

_____

Step 2:   **Identify the goal of misbehavior. (Attention, Power, Revenge, Avoidance-of-Failure)**

_____

Step 3:   **Choose intervention techniques.**

_____

_____

_____

Step 4:   **Select encouragement techniques.**

_____

_____

_____

Step 5:   **Involve parents as partners.**

Yvette Zgonc

Attention Deficit Hyperactivity Disorder

by Karen Durbin

Attention Deficit Hyperactivity Disorder (ADHD) has been defined as a collection of symptoms, all of which lead to disruptive behavior and are therefore expected to be seen in various combinations in most ADHD children.

The characteristic symptoms of ADHD are not abnormal in themselves. In fact, they are present in all children at one time or another, and only when excessive do they become disruptive behavioral problems. Three distinctions to keep in mind when examining the eight principal ADHD characteristics discussed here are their intensity, persistence, and patterning (Wender 1987). But also note that not all of these characteristics are present in every ADHD child.

1. Inattentiveness and Distractibility

ADHD children are nearly always easily distracted and have short attention spans. At home, these children don't listen to what their parents say to them; they don't mind; and they forget things. Their homework is never finished. When getting dressed, they may leave buttons unbuttoned and zippers unzipped, and even put shoes on the wrong feet. At school, their teachers notice that they have difficulty listening to and following directions, have trouble completing assignments, and often are off-task and out of their seats.

It is important to remember that inattentiveness and distractibility need not be present at all times. Many teachers report that these children do well when given one-to-one attention, and physicians and psychiatrists note good attention spans during brief office visits.

The paradox of ADHD children being attentive under specialized conditions, but unable to pay attention and complete tasks under normal conditions, is confusing to parents and teachers, especially when they see that these children are able to sit and watch television for long periods of time. But, as Pugliese (1992) has observed, television programming *reinforces* the way ADHD children think by switching rapidly from idea to idea and scene to scene, with numerous commercial interruptions. There is constant movement both on the screen and in the minds of the affected children.

2. Impulsiveness

ADHD children tend to speak and act first, and think later (Garber *et al.* 1990). They talk out in class and interrupt others. They rush across streets, oblivious to traffic, and have more than their share of accidents.

These children are often unable to tolerate delays, and become upset when people or things fail to respond as they wish. This may result in broken toys, as well as attacks on siblings and classmates (Wender 1987).

3. Hyperactivity

Hyperactivity, which involves such attributes as restlessness, excessive talking, difficulty awaiting turns in games, and shifting from one uncompleted activity to another (Garber *et al.* 1990), is not always exhibited by ADHD children. They may appear to be normally, or even less than normally, active until they have an important task to complete. It is then that these children, distracted by things that would barely be noticed by anyone else, display the classic symptoms of hyperactivity — constant motion, fidgeting, drumming fingers, and shuffling feet. In the classroom, hyperactive children talk constantly, jostle and annoy others, do a lot of clowning, and are generally disruptive.

4. Attention-Demanding Behavior

All children want and need adult attention, and ADHD children are no exception. The difference is in their insatiable desire for such attention. They have to have center stage, be the clown, monopolize the conversation, and show off. Wender (1987) explains the adult reaction to such behavior:

The demand for attention can be distressing, confusing, and irritating to parents. Since the child demands so much, they feel they have not given him what he needs. Since they cannot understand how to satisfy him, they feel deficient. Finally, because the child may cling and poke simultaneously and endlessly, they feel angry.

5. Learning Difficulties

While ADHD is in no way related to mental retardation, some ADHD children do have similar problems. Their intellectual development may be uneven — advanced in some areas and behind in others. For example, a child may be able to do fifth-grade mathematics, but only second-grade reading.

Problems in perception are more difficult to define and are more complex than simple vision or hearing limitations. ADHD children may be unable to distinguish between similar sights or sounds, or to connect sensations in a meaningful way.

Such difficulties in children of normal intelligence are called specific developmental disorders (SDDs), a term that is replacing "learning disabilities." While the most common SDDs are in reading and arithmetic, not all ADHD children have these disorders. Nevertheless, because most ADHD children have learning difficulties, they are often viewed as underachievers.

6. Coordination Difficulties

About half of all ADHD children have problems with various types of coordination. For example, trouble with fine muscle control may result in difficulties in coloring, writing, tying shoelaces, and buttoning. For many of these children, handwriting is perceived as an awesome chore, and the results are often illegible. They may also have difficulty learning to ride a bike and throwing and catching a ball. Such difficulties are especially detrimental for boys because these abilities help win social acceptance, and their importance as building blocks for self-esteem should not be taken lightly.

7. Unacceptable Social Behavior

Probably the most disturbing feature of ADHD, and the one most likely to be the initial cause of referral, is the difficulty that ADHD children have in complying with adult requests and prohibitions. While some may appear to forget what they are told, others may obstinately refuse to comply. Parents often describe their ADHD children as obstinate, disobedient, stubborn, bossy, sassy, and uncaring (Wender 1987).

While these children are often very adept at making initial friendships, they are unable to maintain them because they have to be the leaders, the first ones in line, the ones that make the rules. Unable to see the connection between how they treat others and the way others respond to them, they wonder why they have no friends.

8. Immaturity

It is important to remember that while all of these characteristics can be seen in all children from time to time, in ADHD children they appear to reflect the behavior of children four or five years younger. It may be helpful to consider the ac-

tions of a ten-year-old ADHD child as being much like those of a normal five-year-old (Wender 1987).

Diagnosis and Implications

The first step parents should take for a child suspected of having ADHD is a medical examination to rule out physical problems that may show similar symptoms. The second step is for a qualified physician or psychologist to diagnose the child's condition, based in part on a parent questionnaire and teacher assessments.

What are the implications of an ADHD diagnosis on a child's relationships with family and peers? This is an important area, minimized in the past, that may continue to hinder the development of self-esteem even after most or all ADHD symptoms have disappeared.

Because managing these children requires such energy, parents are likely to give more direct orders, feel they need to supervise more, and not allow the kind of freedoms that other children of the same age would be able to handle. Parents may also demonstrate unresolved anger toward their ADHD children. If self-esteem is formed on the basis of how others respond to us, it is easy to see why ADHD children often form low opinions of themselves (Wender 1987).

Peer Relationships

This attack on self-esteem occurs not only within the family, but in the ADHD child's relationships with peers. Because these children lack social skills, they often find themselves without friends. They are not invited to parties; in choosing up sides for games, they are chosen last — or not at all; and they are often teased because they react highly to teasing (Wender 1987). The area of peer relationships is one that continues to be troubling for ADHD children even when most or all of their symptoms respond to treatment. While the attitudes and reactions of adults may improve, studies have shown that

peers continued to reject ADHD children even after they had successfully learned social skills.

Treating ADHD: Medication

The most common treatment for ADHD children is stimulant medication, and the three most widely used stimulants are Dexedrine, Ritalin, and Cylert. All have been highly effective in improving attention span, impulse control, restlessness, and compliance with requests from parents and teachers (Anastopoulos and Barkley 1990). Also, by being less bossy, more obedient, and better students, these children are more readily accepted by the people around them at home and in school. They feel better about themselves and about their lives in general.

While treatment with stimulant medication alone makes ADHD children more manageable and attentive in the short term, it is not clear if it will have a long-term beneficial effect on learning. Studies have shown that this type of treatment is not always a panacea (Klein and Abikoff 1989).

Treating ADHD: Therapy

Other treatments that have shown some effectiveness in reducing ADHD symptoms are behavior therapy, cognitive therapy, and combinations of these, with and without medication.

At the Attention-Deficit Hyperactivity Disorder Clinic of the University of Massachusetts Medical Center, two of the most commonly recommended treatment services are parent training and parent counseling (Anastopoulos and Barkley 1990). Even when medication is used, parents must possess the knowledge and skills to manage their ADHD children on evenings and weekends, when medication is usually not taken, and medication-improved behavior may not be maintained.

Parents must also be aware that ADHD children often exhibit forms of psychosocial behavior that cannot be helped through medication, such as aggression, diminished self-esteem, depression, and lack of appropriate social skills (Anastopoulos and Barkley 1990).

Behavior Management

The use of behavior management principles is one way parents can minimize ADHD symptoms and establish positive new behaviors. Behavior therapy is based on the assumption that ADHD children need clear, consistent, and immediate consequences for their behavior (Gordon *et al.* 1991).

One approach for parents is the use of negative consequences. For example, simply ignoring an attention-seeking behavior is one effective way to eliminate it, particularly with younger children. There are a number of other effective behavior modification techniques, but of paramount importance is the coordination of such efforts between parents and educators.

How Educators Can Help

Because the problems of ADHD children spill over into school, effective classroom intervention is needed. Teachers should know and be able to use the same behavior modification principles used by parents. In addition, however, teachers can benefit from classroom management suggestions like these:

- Maintain a structured program for ADHD children.
- Have them practice positive behaviors repeatedly until they internalize them.
- Give them work paced to fit their capabilities.
- Keep a daily checklist to help them stay focused on their behavior. (Pugliese 1992).

The success of school interventions is dependent not only on the range of cognitive strategies used, but on a high level of communication and cooperation between parents and educators. The main goal is to instill self-control and reflective problem-solving skills in ADHD children.

However, behavior and cognitive therapies also have some limitations. Research has found, for example, that treatment focused on one academic or social skill does not tend to transfer to another area. It appears that behavior therapy needs to be instituted in each specific setting, and that the success of cognitive therapy is highly dependent on the ability of an adult to provide the needed learning cues and encouragement.

Because successful treatment of ADHD by medication and/or therapy has thus far been elusive, we are left with the realization that affected children need individualized, broadly based, and long-term intervention, and that those who help these children must sustain a high level of optimism, enthusiasm, and energy throughout their involvement (Pfiffner and Barkley 1990).

Is ADHD Curable?

There is no one-shot cure for ADHD. One theory is that treatment intervention is required until the brain matures and is able to produce adequate amounts of required chemicals (Wender 1987). Another theory is that ADHD is a lifestyle rather than an acute disorder and therefore cannot be completely eliminated (Whalen and Henker 1991).

Even though symptoms may diminish or disappear in over half of all ADHD children as they move into adolescence and adulthood, many of them will continue to have symptoms well into their adult years. Psychiatrists recognize an adult form of ADHD as Attention Deficit Disorder, Residual Type (ADD/RT).

For the present, research indicates that ADHD children will derive the greatest benefit from multimodal treatment strategies that combine various therapeutic approaches. But such treatment requires a long-term, consistent effort by both parents and educators.

Karen Durbin, a teacher at Southwest Elementary School in Belton, Texas, is working toward a master's degree in educational counseling at the University of Mary Hardin Baylor in Belton.

References

Anastopoulos, A. D., and Barkley, R. A. "Counseling and Training Parents." In R. A. Barkley (ed.), *Attention-Deficit Hyperactivity Disorder: A Handbook for Diagnosis and Treatment.* New York: Guilford Press, 1990.

Garber, S. W.; Garber, M. D.; and Spizman, R. F. *If Your Child Is Hyperactive, Inattentive, Impulsive, Distractible: Helping the ADD (Attention Deficit Disorder) / Hyperactive Child.* New York: Villard Books, 1990.

Gordon, M.; Thomason, D.; Cooper, S.; and Ivers, C. L. "Nonmedical Treatment of ADHD/Hyperactivity: The Attention Training System." *Journal of School Psychology* 29 (Summer 1991): 151-152.

Klein, R. G.; and Abikoff, H. "The Role of Psychostimulants and Psychosocial Treatments in Hyperkinesis." In T. Sagvolden and T. Archer (eds.), *Attention Deficit Disorder: Clinical and Basic Research.* New York: Lawrence Erlbaum Associates, 1989.

Pfiffner, L. J.; and Barkley, R. A. "Educational Placement and Classroom Management. In R. A. Barkley (ed.), *Attention-Deficit Hyperactivity Disorder: A Handbook for Diagnosis and Treatment.* New York: Guilford Press, 1990.

Pugliese, Frank. Lecture notes by author, March 10, 1992.

Wender, P. H. *The Hyperactive Child, Adolescent, and Adult: Attention Deficit Disorder through the Lifespan.* New York: Oxford University Press, 1987.

Whalen, C. K.; and Henker, B. "Therapies for Hyperactive Children: Comparisons, Combinations, and Compromises." *Journal of Consulting and Clinical Psychology* 59:1 (February 1991): 126-135.

Whalen, C. K.; and Henker, B. "Social Impact of Stimulant Treatment for Hyperactive Children." *Journal of Learning Disabilities* 24:4 (April 1991): 231.

Attention Deficit Disorders: A Guide for Teachers

Prepared by the Education Committee of CH.A.D.D. (Children With Attention Deficit Disorders)

Recommendations for Giving Instructions to Students:

1. Maintain eye contact with the ADD student during verbal instruction.
2. Make directions clear and concise. Be consistent with daily instructions.
3. Simplify complex directions. Avoid multiple commands.
4. Make sure ADD student comprehends before beginning the task.
5. Repeat in a calm, positive manner, if needed.
6. Help ADD child to feel comfortable with seeking assistance (most ADD children won't ask).
7. These children need more help for a longer period of time than the average child. Gradually reduce assistance.
8. Require a daily assignment notebook if necessary.
   a. Make sure student correctly writes down all assignments each day. If the student is not capable of this then the teacher should help the student.
   b. Parents and teachers sign notebook daily to signify completion of homework assignments.
   c. Parents and teachers may use notebook for daily communication with each other.

Recommendations for Students Performing Assignments:

1. Give out only one task at a time.
2. Monitor frequently. Use a supportive attitude.
3. Modify assignments as needed. Consult with special education personnel to determine specific strengths and weaknesses of the student. Develop an individualized educational program.
4. Make sure you are testing knowledge and not attention span.
5. Give extra time for certain tasks. The ADD student may work more slowly. Don't penalize for needed extra time.
6. Keep in mind that ADD children are easily frustrated. Stress, pressure and fatigue can break down the ADD child's self-control and lead to poor behavior.

Recommendations for Behavior Modification and Self-Esteem Enhancement
Providing Supervision and Discipline

a. Remain calm, state infraction of rule, and don't debate or argue with student.
b. Have pre-established consequences for misbehavior.
c. Administer consequences immediately and monitor proper behavior frequently.
d. Enforce rules of the classroom consistently.
e. Discipline should be appropriate to "fit the crime," without harshness.
f. Avoid ridicule and criticism. Remember, ADD children have difficulty staying in control.
g. Avoid *publicly* reminding students on medication to "take their medicine."

Recommendations for the Proper Learning Environment:

1. Seat ADD student near teacher's desk, but include as part of regular class seating.
2. Place ADD student up front with his back to the rest of the class to keep other students out of view.
3. Surround ADD student with "good role models," preferably students that the ADD child views as "significant others." Encourage peer tutoring and cooperative collaborative learning.
4. Avoid distracting stimuli. Try not to place the ADD student near:
   - air conditioner
   - heater
   - high traffic areas
   - doors or windows
5. ADD children do not handle change well so avoid:
   - transitions
   - changes in schedule
   - disruptions
   - physical relocations (monitor closely on field trips)
6. Be creative! Produce a "stimuli-reduced study area." Let all students have access to this area so the ADD child will not feel different.
7. Encourage parents to set up appropriate study space at home with routines established as far as set times for study, parental review of completed homework, and periodic notebook and/or book bag organized.

Using Medication in the Treatment of Attention Deficit Disorders

The use of medication alone in the treatment of ADD is *not* recommended. As indicated earlier, a multimodal treatment plan is usually followed for successful treatment of the ADD child or adolescent. While not all children having ADD are prescribed medication, in certain cases the proper use of medication can play an important and necessary part in the child's overall treatment.

Excerpt from prepared material. For more information on ADD, contact
CH.A.D.D., 499 NW 70th Ave., Suite 308, Plantation, FL 33317, 1-305-587-3700.

279

Getting Ready for Young Children with Prenatal Drug Exposure

Shirley Cohen and Christina Taharally

The appearance of crack cocaine in 1984 precipitated a dramatic increase in women of childbearing age who abuse drugs. Many of these women are poly-drug users, combining heroin, methadone, cocaine, marijuana and alcohol (Feig, 1990). As a result, the numbers of young children prenatally exposed to drugs are increasing. Moreover, for many of these young children, prenatal drug exposure is but one of multiple risk factors present before and after birth (The Future of Children, 1991).

While the effects of prenatal drug exposure appear to vary with the type of drugs used, the amount and timing of drug use and differences in fetuses, the research indicates mild-to-moderate developmental delays and behavioral differences in some young children (Rodning, Beckwith & Howard, 1989). Young infants with prenatal drug exposure often experience problems. Their sleep patterns may be irregular; they may cry frequently, appear agitated and be difficult to console. They may also be deficient in the social engagement skills (e.g., eye gaze and reciprocal smiling) necessary for early attachment (Schneider, Griffith & Chasnoff, 1989). Initial injury to the fetus from prenatal drug exposure and other risks may be compounded by environmental factors that inhibit sensitive and skilled caregiving.

The growing population of young children with prenatal drug exposure raises concern about special education referrals. In fact, referrals of 5-year-olds for special education evaluations are increasing in New York City and other urban areas, a phenomenon at least partially attributed to greater use of drugs by pregnant women during the '80s (Daley, 1991).

The authors take the position that the education of young children with prenatal drug exposure is not primarily the responsibility of special education. The behavior of such children varies greatly, and most do not appear to have severe disabilities. For the most part, their IQs are in the normal range (Rodning, Beckwith & Howard, 1989; Viadera, 1992), and generally they are not characterized by severe sensory, motor or health impairments. Moreover, the field of special education is moving toward integration of special needs children into the education mainstream, particularly at the early childhood level (Burton, Hains, Hanline, McLean & McCormick, 1992). An appropriate response, therefore, is to strengthen early childhood education and develop collaborative relationships with special education, allowing effective care without special placements. Only a small percentage of these children are likely to need or be better served in separate special education programs during the preschool years.

Although prenatal exposure to crack cocaine has attracted the greatest attention during the last few years, exposure to alcohol affects an even greater number of young children (Streissguth et al., 1991). Four-year-old children whose mothers engaged in even moderate social drinking during pregnancy were less attentive, less obedient and more fidgety than children of nondrinkers (Spohr & Steinhausen, 1987). Children identified as having fetal alcohol syndrome (1 of every 600-700 live births) and children with fetal alcohol effects (1 of every 300-350 live births) often display impulsivity, poor attention and difficulty in making transitions (Burgess & Streissguth, 1990). Many of these children are now in early childhood programs. To be effective, the programs require greater awareness of such children's needs, modifications in instructional strategies and additional supports for the children and their families.

Shirley Cohen is Professor, Department of Special Education, Hunter College, New York, New York. Christina Taharally is Associate Professor, Department of Curriculum and Teaching, Hunter College.

Issues in Practice

An *American School Board Journal* article asked: "When crack babies are ready for school (and the first cohort will arrive sooner than you think) will your schools be ready for them?" (Rist, 1990). Many teachers of pre-kindergarten and kindergarten classes, along with their colleagues in Head Start and day care, are answering "No." A veteran kindergarten teacher in the Bronx reported her recent experience: "The first few days of school . . . when I came home from work, I just fell down I was so tired. I kept thinking, 'What is going on here?'" (Daley, 1991).

Data on the characteristics of preschool children with prenatal drug exposure are scarce. Most research has focused on infancy. Information about preschool children comes largely from anecdotal reports by preschool personnel, parents and other caregivers. This anecdotal literature describes children who are having difficulty in selected areas of development, including relationships/attachments, communication, attention and play. Some of them may experience mood changes and distress more frequently than other children, and display aggressive behavior without apparent provocation.

One must remember, however, that the anecdotes focus on children presenting difficulties or causing problems, not on those who are developing satisfactorily and may constitute a large percentage of this population. Furthermore, anecdotal material does not distinguish between children exposed to other risk factors (e.g., low birth weight and inadequate or erratic caregiving during the first three years) and those who are not. Preschool personnel cannot wait for research results, however; they are confronting the problems now. The remainder of this article suggests ways of serving these children

> P reschool personnel cannot wait for research results, however; they are confronting the problems now.

without violating core early childhood principles and premises.

Developmentally Appropriate Practices

The National Association for the Education of Young Children guidelines for developmentally appropriate practices (Bredekamp, 1987) can serve as a framework for establishing preschool programs for children with prenatal drug exposure. The most relevant ones relate to adult-child interaction. Some of these guidelines are discussed here.

■ *Guideline: Adults respond quickly and directly to children's needs, desires, and messages and adapt their responses to children's differing styles and abilities* (Bredekamp, 1987, p. 9). Children with prenatal drug exposure may need extra help forming relationships. The literature (Rodning, Beckwith & Howard, 1989) suggests that some of these children may not have formed secure attachments to caregivers. Furthermore, anecdotal reports refer to lack of discrimination between familiar and unknown adults; some children show inappropriate interest and affection toward strangers. One appropriate response might be "specialing" by an adult in the classroom (not necessarily the teacher) whose style seems best suited to a particular child. The "specialing" adult would provide

physical proximity, instructional assistance and comforting.

Comforting may be important because some children appear to be difficult to console. Techniques developed to console drug-exposed infants include swaddling the infant in a blanket and rocking slowly (Schneider & Chasnoff, 1987). Preschoolers who are difficult to console might be calmed by age appropriate equivalents of these techniques; e.g., by enveloping children in their nap blankets and gently pushing them in a child-size rocking chair within a set-off, quiet area of the room. Teachers need to be aware of variation in children's responses to physical contact. Some children seek physical signs of affection and are comforted best by being held on a teacher's lap; others distance themselves and need to be comforted without close physical contact, at least while developing a relationship.

Children with prenatal drug exposure may be subject to mood changes or distress without easily recognizable catalysts. One such instance observed by the authors involved a 4-year-old girl who became distressed at the slight overlapping of two oaktag letters the teacher had placed in sequence to form the child's name. Even after the letters were separated, the child continued to whimper for several minutes. When offered the responsibility of distributing cups for juice, however, she quickly recovered.

■ *Guideline: Adults provide many varied opportunities for children to communicate* (Bredekamp, 1987, p. 10). One of the most commonly reported characteristics of children with prenatal drug exposure is poor language development. Some children acquire speech late, while others speak infrequently. To develop their communication skills, stimulation of conversation should take place throughout the day and in virtually every activity. Teacher directives do not usually encourage discourse, while questions that ask "what," "where," "who," "how" and "why" do—even in children with delayed language whose responses are partially gestural.

Some children may receive services from a speech therapist. Therapy, however, is no substitute for stimulation through natural classroom activities and interactions. Formal language development strategies should supplement peer modeling, peer interaction, teacher modeling and gentle encouragement. Care should be taken, however, not to bombard children with rapidly delivered speech or speech that has little communicative value.

■ *Guideline: Adults facilitate the development of self-control in children* (Bredekamp, 1987, p. 11). Another characteristic commonly attributed to children with prenatal drug exposure is aggressiveness, particularly unanticipated aggression. Thus, it is necessary to help the child gain an understanding of what constitutes both appropriate and inappropriate behavior and to develop controls that enable the child to act in accordance with these guidelines.

Clear limits, redirection, modeling of appropriate behavior and verbalization of feelings are the major tools for facilitating self-control. Children with particular difficulty in this area may require additional guidance in the form of more specific directions, a more limited range of choices at any one time, more clearly bounded play areas and more ongoing teacher assistance with peer interactions. Teachers must recognize that these children may not yet have developed skill in relating to peers in ways that support the forming of friendships. They may also require more private work space and materials than are commonly provided in early childhood programs. Some children will also need alternative activities during large group instructional periods.

One of the most commonly reported characteristics of children with prenatal drug exposure is poor language development.

■ *Guideline: Adults facilitate a child's successful completion of tasks by providing support, focused attention, physical proximity and verbal encouragement* (Bredekamp, 1987, p. 10). Children with prenatal drug exposure are often described as hyperactive and easily distracted. Some, however, have no difficulty concentrating on selected tasks. Those children who do will need extra support, attention, encouragement and proximity to an adult.

Early childhood teachers also have to reappraise the placement and storage of materials. Maintaining attention to a particular activity may be easier if irrelevant materials are not within the child's visual field or reach. Recently, the authors observed a class for children with prenatal drug exposure where the teacher had great difficulty holding children's interest during storytime. They were distracted by a nearby shelf with puppets, records and picture books. Many years ago, one of the authors installed "curtains" over open shelves in her classroom for emotionally disturbed children and found it helped the children focus their attention on the activity in progress.

Administrative Supports
Without administrative supports, early childhood programs will not be able to effectively serve the population of children whose pre-

natal drug exposure has left them at particular risk of developmental delay and educational failure. The NAEYC guidelines on "policies essential for achieving developmentally appropriate early childhood programs" recognize the significant role of administrative supports. Critical among these supports is adult-to-child ratios.

Implementation of developmentally appropriate early childhood programs requires limiting the size of the group and providing sufficient numbers of adults to provide individualized and age-appropriate care and education. (Bredekamp, 1987, p. 14)

For 4- and 5-year-olds, NAEYC recommends a ratio of 2 adults to 20 children. Yet some urban school systems, like that of New York City, often have kindergarten classes of 25 or more students, sometimes with only one teacher and no other adult. These same urban schools are most likely to include children with prenatal drug exposure in their kindergartens. School systems must restructure resources to provide at least two full-time adults for every kindergarten and lower-grade class and limit class size to a maximum of 20 children. Even this ratio is far too high; ways must be found to enlist the assistance of other adults. Without such restructuring, it will be impossible to effectively serve many drug-exposed or otherwise seriously at-risk children in the education mainstream.

Apart from the critical issue of adult-to-child ratios, administrators who want to serve drug-exposed children in mainstream programs need to become knowledgeable about new trends in using special education resources. They also need to encourage early childhood personnel to expand their knowledge and skill to include teaching children with special needs arising from prenatal drug exposure and other risk factors.

Accessing Special Education Services

Some young children with prenatal drug exposure may benefit from special education resources and supports. Many of these resources can be made available to children in mainstream early childhood programs, although a referral for special education evaluation and a determination that a child is in need of special education services may first be required. The Individualized Education Program (IEP) and Individualized Family Service Plan (IFSP) are the critical tools in determining services and in placing the child. The IEP or IFSP can mandate the services of a consultant teacher, resource teacher, speech/language therapist or assistant teacher to work with the child in the mainstream class, and other personnel to work with the parent or family.

With special education moving toward redefinition as a support system for mainstream education, newer administrative arrangements are appearing that combine special education and early childhood education staff. The New York City public school system is pilot-testing such a model at the Pre-K level. This model involves collaborative teaching teams of early childhood and special education staff serving groups of about 18 children, one-third of whom have been identified as needing special education services.

Another model was put into practice by an upstate New York nonprofit agency that formerly operated a special education preschool program. The agency placed its former students in mainstream early childhood settings, assigning its special education staff as consultant teachers, resource teachers and assistant teachers. These new administrative arrangements may be particularly advantageous for children with prenatal drug exposure needing more than an early childhood program.

Personnel Preparation Programs

Recently the authors were approached by an undergraduate interested in a program that prepared teachers to work with young drug-exposed children. This student verbalized an assumption that may be quite common; namely, young children with prenatal drug exposure are distinctly different from other young children, including those who have special needs or are at risk of developmental delay. The available data do not support this view.

A strong case can be made for preservice programs that combine special education with early childhood education, including special knowledge accumulated over two decades of experience with Head Start and other programs serving children of poverty (Miller, 1992; Schutter & Brinker, 1992). The goal of such preparation programs would be to serve the greatest possible percentage of children in early childhood mainstream programs, including children with prenatal drug exposure. While some universities have initiated such programs, most state certification systems do not support such preparation; they do not offer a certificate in early childhood special education.

Inservice education can serve as a lifeline for those early childhood educators who ask, as did the teacher quoted earlier, "What is going on here?" For such teachers, the focus of inservice activities would be to:

- Develop an understanding of developmental and functional changes in the kindergarten population
- Acquire additional strategies, some adapted from special education, for coping with behavior that doesn't respond to standard early childhood strategies
- Share and gain support from others who are also experiencing shock and searching for new answers.

After several sessions of observing 3- and 4-year-olds in a program for children with prenatal drug exposure, the authors selected six skills as examples of important points of focus for inservice programs:

- Skill in designing classroom environments that encourage independence and autonomy while supporting self-control and that respond to children's need for safety, personal space and quiet retreats to balance stimulating activities
- Skill in adapting and modifying the typical schedule and format of activities in early childhood classrooms to better meet the learning and behavioral needs of a particular group, and of individual students in that group
- Skill in recognizing nonverbal cues to children's emotions and determining when supportive intervention is needed
- Skill in responding to a wide spectrum of child behavior, including sudden mood changes and inappropriate attempts to engage other children
- Skill in recognizing "teachable moments" and selecting teaching strategies that match these opportunities
- Skill in working in supportive and complementary ways with assistant teachers, speech therapists, social workers and family assistants.

Conclusion

This is a time of challenge, a time to expand and seek new collaborations. Historically, early childhood education programs have responded most directly to student needs and, over the past 25 years, have focused increasingly upon children of poverty. The influx of children prenatally exposed to drugs, therefore, does not represent a change in direction; rather, it presents a heightened challenge. Early childhood educators need to seek new collaborations, joining forces with whatever support systems are available and redesigning administrative structures to respond more effectively to children with prenatal drug exposure.

References

Bredekamp, S. (Ed.), (1987). *Developmentally appropriate practice in early childhood programs serving children from birth through age 8*. Washington, DC: National Association for the Education of Young Children.

Burgess, D. M., & Striessguth, A. P. (1990). Educating students with fetal alcohol syndrome or fetal alcohol effects. *Pennsylvania Reporter, 22*(1), 1-3.

Burton, C. B., Hains, A. H., Hanline, M. F., McLean, M., & McCormick, K. (1992). Early childhood intervention and education: The urgency of professional unification. *Topics in Early Childhood Special Education, 11*(4), 53-69.

Daley, S. (1991, February 7). Born on crack, and coping with kindergarten. *The New York Times*, pp. A1, A13.

Feig, L. (1990). *Drug exposed infants and children: Service needs and policy questions*. Washington, DC: U. S. Department of Health and Human Services, Office of Human Services Policy, Division of Children and Youth Policy.

The Future of Children. (1991). Special Issue: Drug exposed infants, 1(#1).

Miller, P. S. (1992). Segregated programs of teacher education in early childhood: Immoral and inefficient practice. *Topics in Early Childhood Special Education, 11*, 39-52.

Rist, M. C. (1990). The shadow children. *The American School Board Journal, 177*(1), 18-24.

Rodning, C., Beckwith, L., & Howard, J. (1989). Characteristics of attachment organization and play organization in prenatally drug-exposed toddlers. *Development and Psychopathology, 1*, 277-289.

Schneider, J. W., & Chasnoff, I. J. (1987). Cocaine abuse during pregnancy: Its effects on infant motor development—a clinical perspective. *Topics in Acute Care and Trauma Rehabilitation, 2*(1), 59-69.

Schneider, J. W., Griffith, D. R., & Chasnoff, I. J. (1989). Infants exposed to cocaine in utero: Implications for developmental assessment and intervention. *Infants and Young Children, 2*(1), 25-36.

Schutter, L. S., & Brinker, R. P. (1992). Conjuring a new category of disability from prenatal cocaine exposure: Are the infants unique biological or caretaking casualties? *Topics in Early Childhood Special Education, 11*(4), 84-111.

Spohr, H. L., & Steinhausen, H. C. (1987). Follow-up studies of children with fetal alcohol syndrome. *Neuropediatrics, 18*, 13-17.

Streissguth, A. P., Aase, J., Clarren, S. K., Randels, S. P., LaDue, R. A., & Smith, D. F. (1991). Fetal alcohol syndrome in adolescents and adults. *Journal of the American Medical Association, 265*(15), 1961-1967.

Viadero, D. (1992, January 29). New research finds little lasting harm for 'crack' children. *Education Week, XL*(19), 1, 10.

In every task the most important thing is the beginning and especially when you have to deal with anything young and tender.

Plato, *The Republic*

Slow Learners: Students at Risk

by Kaye Johns, Founder and President
The Center for Success in Learning

The following is an address by Kaye Johns, founder and president of The Texas Center for Success in Learning before the Texas Commissioner of Education's Advisory Committee on the 1990-94 Long-Range Plan for Public Education. Johns, a well-known author and topic presenter on the subject of slower learners, has served on three TEA Advisory Committees during the development of rules for Alternatives to Social Promotion and frequently testifies before the State Board of Education.

We believe it is important for the State Board of Education, its Long-Range Plan, and individual school districts to clearly delineate slower learners as part of the at-risk student population.

When slower learners are not mentioned specifically, it is presumed that they should be able to do grade level work, to keep up academically with their peers — and when they don't, it is their fault because they are not motivated, or not trying hard enough. They are blamed because they don't learn as quickly as other children. They are set up to fail.

If they are not identified as a group with significant learning problems, there is no call to action, no reason to do anything differently in the classroom. The assumption is that all children with learning problems are served by special education, and all other students should be able to master nine months of information in nine months' time in a traditional classroom setting.

The basic presumption of "Alternatives to Social Promotion" is that being "at risk" is a temporary condition for students, who should be "remediated" or caught up, when placed in alternative programs or given modifications in classrooms. Slower learners have problems that are not temporary and that are not resolved in one year's time in the classroom. These students are likely to remain academically at risk from kindergarten through grade 12.

And yet, without an acknowledgment of the severity of their problems, slower learners are expected to maintain passing grades of 70, stay on grade level with their peers, earn 21 Carnegie Credits to graduate, and pass the TEAMS Exit Exam just like the other students. Is this realistic?

It didn't used to be. That's why slower learners were so often socially promoted before educational reform. They couldn't keep up and stay on grade level with their peers. If they were unable to keep up *before* educational reform raised the standards, *how will they keep up now?*

Slower learners have not changed. The world has changed. Education has changed, standards have risen — but these students, with their limited capacity to learn, are still the same.

Are we saying these students cannot learn? Cannot one day graduate?

Absolutely not! But we are saying that unless we change the way most of them are being taught, particularly in secondary schools, many of them may not have a chance.

Who is the Slower Learning Student?

We acknowledge that there is no agreed-upon definition of the slower learner. But in general, educators agree that these students are caught in that grey area between average and retarded, generally IQ 70-89.

We are talking about 22% of the population who fall within this IQ range, one in five.

We are the first to acknowledge that IQ scores are imperfect and can be biased. But IQ scores are used to qualify students for special education as well as gifted/talented programs, so they are respected in the educational community.

IQ does not measure a student's grit, drive, determination, ambition, tenacity or perseverance. It doesn't tell us whether the student is lazy or motivated, an under-achiever or an over-achiever — because slower learners are as individual as the rest of us. Nor does it tell us what kind of home students come from, what kind of love and support they receive.

IQ tests do not guarantee a student's success in life — *but they are one of the best predictors we have to indicate a student's likely difficulty in learning, in doing grade level work in school.*

Students Learn at Different Rates

Although the following chart illustrates how far behind slower learners typically are by the time they enter the ninth grade, we know this doesn't just happen in the 8th grade. These students are usually not fully on grade level at the end of their first or second grade, and they fall gradually further behind every year.

This chart is surely our challenge. What would happen if slower learners were picked up in kindergarten and given individualized instruction according to what we know works with these students? Examples are: multi-sensory teaching, peer tutoring, small group techniques, accommodations for learning styles and perceptual strengths, modifications to supplement textbooks with study guides and other materials on an appropriate reading level, tests adapted for clarity, and appropriate study

	9th Grade	12th Grade
IQ 75	5th grade, 5 months	7th grade, 7 months
IQ 80	6th grade, 2 months	8th grade, 6 months
IQ 85	6th grade, 9 months	9th grade, 5 months

skills. If so, might these students do much better than this chart predicts?

Still, this chart stands on historical data as an illustration of the frustration and sense of failure that is constantly reinforced as we expect these students to do grade level work — and their teachers to be able to "catch them up."

Here are educators' comments:

"Students whose mental ability places them in the slow learner range (IQ 70-90) are — because of their limited ability — low achievers. Yet the general public (including the press, state legislators, and members of boards of education) in the current push for minimum competency testing for high school graduation seems largely unaware that no amount of testing, no setting of competencies, and no establishment of standards and remedial programs can cause these students to achieve beyond the limits of their intellectual capacity.

"The public expects that students not in special education should achieve at grade level or at the national average. They do not realize that, by definition of the word 'average,' as many students must be below this mark as above it."

Howard G. Dunlap, "Minimum Competency Testing and the Slow Learner," *Educational Leadership*, Vol. 367, pp. 327-328.

Slower Learners — More Than Half of the Dropouts

If we accept that most slower learning students will be 2-4 years below grade level in their basic skills when they *enter* high school, it is easy to see how they fit into the at-risk population.

"The single best predictor of

whether or not a student will drop out of school is his or her level of academic achievement. The typical at-risk student has mathematics or reading skills two or more years below grade level and is not maintaining a scholastic average of 70%."

"Characteristics of At-Risk Youth," *TEA Practitioner's Guide*, Series No. One, p. 26.

"The most common reason for leaving school is poor academic performance . . . . A majority of all dropouts in the National Longitudinal Survey had basic skills in the bottom 20% of the score distribution."

Andrew Hahn, "Reaching Out to America's Dropouts: What to Do?" *Phi Delta Kappan*, Dec. 1987, pp. 256-263.

"It has been estimated that as many as one-third of all students attending school today will drop out before graduation. Of these, more than half could be described as slow learners."

H. Hodgkinson, "Today's Numbers, Tomorrow's Nation." *Education Week*, May 14, 1986, pp. 14-15.

Many Other At-Risk Programs

As at-risk students and their problems are studied, programs are springing up everywhere to help with identified problems — drug and alcohol abuse, teenage pregnancy, counseling for students who are abused, depressed, suicidal. We see a renewed emphasis on helping students with self-esteem; we are working with cultural issues; we are addressing students' needs when they have English as a second language.

When a problem is identified, we develop programs, policies, and strategies to deal with it. Every-

one — from the Legislature to the local school board to the district administrative staff, local campus administrators, teachers, parents — even the public — is aware of the need to do something to solve the problem.

When the problem is not identified, it is overlooked at best, or considered not to exist at worst.

This is the primary reason we feel it is imperative that we let parents, teachers and the public know that some children who are not served by special education still have significant problems learning.

We must do something to help teachers learn what works with these children — because research is showing us many things do.

What Works with Slower Learners, Works with Many Other At-Risk Students

Slower learners and other at-risk students do not do well in traditional classroom settings (straight rows, no moving, not talking) with a standard textbook/lecture format. They need multi-sensory teaching through high school.

It is clear from both research and classroom application that the following strategies work for slower learners and other at-risk students, and most students in general:
• Multi-sensory teaching
• Peer and cross-age tutoring
• Small group techniques
• Mixed ability classes, heterogeneous groupings
• Increasing the time spent on a single subject
• Teaching to students' perceptual strengths
• Informal classroom design
• Changing the time of day for testing
• Matching student's strongest period of day with testing time and major academic subjects
• Smaller student/teacher ratio
• Technology/media-assisted instruction
• Extending the classroom to the community

But Aren't Those Simply Good Teaching Principles, Period?

Of course they are. And based on the feedback received from teacher workshops, these techniques are much more likely to be utilized by elementary teachers, although by no means are all elementary teachers taking advantage of these strategies. Why not? Why do many classes still fall into the traditional textbook/lecture pattern at the fourth grade level, or sooner? Why are 95% of academic high school classes still taught in the traditional classroom setting with a textbook/lecture format?

> *We must have high expectations for all children, just as we must believe that all children can learn. But all children cannot learn in the same way, or at the same rate, or even with the same amount of information . . . . We must recognize, respect and support the learning differences in children.*

One reason is that even though most students will do better with the above techniques, they will not be hurt if these techniques are not used. Students with average, or above average intelligence have been making it through school academically for a long time. Some of them may not be excelling as they could and should and probably would if these strategies were used, but they haven't been pushed out of school because they weren't.

Slower learners, on the other hand, are students living on the edge. For them, the difference between a teacher who utilizes the previously mentioned techniques and one who doesn't can make the difference between passing and failing, graduating or not.

Let's identify slower learners specifically as students who have needs to be addressed. Otherwise, where will the impetus, the urgency, for changing what happens in the classroom come from?

But wait! We shouldn't label students!

And yet, we do. We have "labeled" students gifted and talented, honors, learning disabled, emotionally disturbed, visually, auditorily or physically impaired, mentally retarded, minority, transient, economically disadvantaged, non-English speaking, home ec, vocational, and so on.

Why do we have these labels? Because they provide access into services in the school. They describe the program that the student has which has been identified, or they describe the program where the student is placed.

Who says we haven't already labeled slower learners?
- Ask anyone who the "students who fall through the cracks" are.
- Or ask about "shadow children," slower learners in the shadow of the system.
- Or the students in the grey area.
- Or the "dull."
- Or the "borderline."
- Or the "marginal."

We prefer *slower learner* because it emphasizes a positive — these students learn, but they learn slowly.

Think of the cost to the students when we don't identify their problem. Parents often punish them for not trying. Teachers crack down because the children aren't paying attention. Other kids think they're dumb because they don't have any apparent problem. The students feel it's all their fault. If they were better, tried harder, worked longer, then they could learn.

Learning disabled and mentally retarded students don't have to face that. They know they have a problem that isn't their fault, that it is something they have to come to terms with.

All Children Can Learn

We must have high expectations for all children, just as we must believe that all children can learn. But all children cannot learn in the same way, or at the same rate, or even with the same amount of information. More time will not make a slower learner a brain surgeon. We must recognize, respect and support the learning differences in children.

And we must have high but realistic expectations. We do not expect our "C" students to win scholarships to Harvard or Yale, and we do not hold average students to the same goals and expectations as our gifted/talented students. Why then, must we insist that students with below average intelligence meet the same expectations as students with average and above average intelligence? Why do we set them up to fail over and over again? It doesn't take long until they don't even try.

As long as we don't use the term "slower learner" — or some other legitimate, identifying term — to describe these children, we leave them and their parents and their teachers shadow boxing. They can't attack the problem because they don't even know what it is.

When we don't say "slower learner," we're saying it isn't okay to be a slower learner. And it must be. It has to be, because all children are not alike. They cannot be the same.

Educating Children with Attention Deficits: A Call for Change

by Betsy Busch

Change is coming to education. Children with attention deficits comprise one of many groups for whom some educational changes are due. Classroom teachers have been given very little guidance about the approaches that can and should be taken when working with this population of children. This is unfair both to the children and the teachers. Attentional disorders are common; they are estimated to occur in 6-9% of our children. This means that the average class will have two or three students with attention deficits. These children need help to function well in school despite their attentional problems; and it is up to us to help them realize these expectations.

Most of us who chose to be teachers did so because of the importance of the mission of educating our nation's children. The children and we both have been dealt a challenging hand. We must meet the challenge.

Although attentional problems often masquerade as laziness, poor motivation, procrastination, or poor attitude, they are biologically determined, largely inherited. Children with attention deficits can be bright and talented in many ways, and have much to offer their teachers and peers. They can be funny, spontaneous, creative, curious, talented, energetic, eager, and empathetic.

Once they finish school, young adults with attention deficits may be quite successful. They often find that the adult world is more tolerant of their attentional problems than school was. How is this possible? Most adults can get up and sharpen their pencils whenever they wish, pace while talking on the phone, sit in desk chairs that rock and swivel, and stop for a coffee break now and then. But children may not be permitted to stand, nor fidget, nor take frequent breaks while working. In fact, they may be kept in class during recess if they have not completed their paperwork, although they may need a break more than any of their classmates! We must work to make school a less hostile environment for children with attentional disorders.

Children with attention deficits want to do well in school and get good grades, as do all children. They want to be liked and admired by their teachers and peers; they want to make their parents and teachers proud of them; they need to learn important academic concepts. We must find creative, constructive ways for them to achieve their goals, and not give up on themselves or their education.

These principles do not apply only to those who teach young children. Many of us learned that special help in the earliest grades would help children outgrow their need for special education. Therefore, special education services and classroom modifications tend to be phased out in the upper grades. What we now know, however, is that attentional disorders (and most other learning disorders) are chronic, lifelong conditions, and **new accommodations must be at every developmental stage,** as students strive for mastery of new and more complex tasks. Because there are fewer special education supports available in the upper grades, the responsibility for making these accommodations rests heavily on individual classroom teachers.

For most children with attentional problems, the majority of the school day will be spent in the mainstream. The basic assumption that needs to be made when designing adaptive techniques for the mainstream is that we can accommodate the child's difficulties with short attention span and impulsivity and teach to the child's strengths and abilities. Educational accommodations work best when used in combination with other therapies, especially medical therapy. It is important to note that, although medical therapy can be enormously helpful, it does not usually eliminate the need for academic modifications. The following approaches can be successful when assisting a child with an attention deficit in the mainstream.

1. Think flexibly about educational objectives and techniques: Each educational exercise and homework assignment has one or more main educational objectives. Children with attention deficits often are unable to achieve all objectives simultaneously when they are condensed into one such assignment. Successful academic modifications keep these objectives in mind. For example, students may be given a weekly homework assignment in which they copy their weekly spelling words five times, then write a grammatically correct sentence in which each word is used. The educational objectives of this assignment: a) spelling correctly, b) sentence formulation with grammatical usage of new vocabulary, and c) penmanship. If the teacher is willing to emphasize the first two objectives as the key objectives and can address the third objective elsewhere, an adaptation to this assignment easily can be achieved by decreasing the written work in this task.

In math, instead of solving 15 two-digit multiplication problems (the key educational objective: to practice newly-learned math skills), the child could be asked to solve three math problems at five different points during the day. Or, perhaps only eight problems could be assigned to our student, on the premise that eight well-done problems are a better educational exercise than 15 poorly-done problems.

2. Encourage frequent breaks from work and limit total working time: Students with attention deficits can get more work done if an assignment is broken up into several shorter tasks, separated by opportunities to move around the classroom. Most schools have guidelines for the length of time children are expected to work on homework. If children with attentional disorders are unable to complete their homework in a reasonable amount of time, their assignments should be modified. Similarly, if children cannot complete all their paperwork in class, they may need their in-class work demands decreased.

3. Decrease demands for written work and length of work: If a child is exhausted by copying ten math problems from the blackboard, he has no attentional energy left to solve the problems. Our key educational objective will not be met, for this is a math assignment, not a copying assignment. Therefore, certain children may be far more productive learners if they are given teacher-prepared papers. Children with attention deficits should be encouraged to do written homework on the word processor. Certain subjects may lend themselves to the development of innovative, challenging, hands-on assignments as alternatives to essays or papers. Alternate assignments should demand thinking and concept mastery, but not extensive writing. The more active and hands-on the learning, the more likely the student is to attend to maximal capacity.

Once they finish school, young adults with attention deficits may be quite successful. They often find that the adult world is more tolerant of their attentional problem than school was.

Older students with attention deficits may be helped greatly by having the teacher either hand out prepared lecture notes, or ask a good note-taker in each class to make a carbon copy of their notes from which other students can study.

4. Help with written language: Children with attention deficits characteristically find it difficult to put their ideas into written form. They have problems with the organization of their ideas, theme, and paragraph development. Many find it difficult to initiate the writing process and simply do not know what to say first. Others have problems expanding an idea into an elaborated paragraph. Some do not make the main point of a paper clear to the reader; others will state a thesis, but will not include enough detail to support their conclusions.

Before the written assignment is begun, students with attentional disorders can benefit from brainstorming, or discussing their ideas with the teacher. The teacher facilitates the writing process asking leading, open-ended questions. This can provide a framework on which the student can then hang his ideas. Notes should be kept to remind the student about the areas to be covered in the paper. Specific discussion of introductory and concluding paragraphs is helpful.

5. Reduce distractions: Seating children with attention deficits near quiet students is helpful. However, such arrangements must be done in a socially acceptable way. Also, many children find the amount of printed information on a worksheet on the page of a book to be distracting. Simple techniques, such as folding a worksheet in half, or using a 3" x 5" card to block out distractions and track accurately along a line of print can be very helpful.

6. Increase teacher supervision and support: The child with an attention deficit has a biological disorder. He pays attention as well as he can. We know that working one-to-one with a teacher or in small groups helps to maximize the child's attentional focus. In fact, it is because a child can work well with increased supervision that we may conclude, incorrectly, that the child "could do it if he tried." When we work individually with a child, we are lending the child the use of our organizational and initiation skills. When we walk away, however, we take those skills with us, and then the child's ability to work deteriorates again.

Therefore, an abrupt or premature decrease in teacher support must be avoided.

7. Work with students during each phase of a long-range assignment: Because students with attentional disorders have particular difficulty planning and organizing the six-to-eight week project term paper, teachers need to provide special assistance with these endeavors. Assistance should include a detailed analysis of the tasks necessary to complete the project, and the creation of a timeline that gives each task an appropriate amount of time.

Whenever possible, the teacher should work with the student to break down the long-term assignment into a series of intermediate products, each of which will have a schedule of completion. Part of the student's grade can be based on the completion of each step, under supervision. After a first draft is composed, it should be reviewed with the teacher, who can make suggestions about clarity, expanding introductory comments, or developing a theme further. The teacher must be quite explicit in explaining, describing, or giving examples of how the materials should be written.

8. Give students direct instruction in study skills: Students with attentional disorders often benefit from organizational techniques, such as making sure the correct books and papers are taken home each night for homework and budgeting time. They may benefit from help in keeping an assignment book or calendar and setting priorities (especially how to juggle both long-range and day-to-day assignments). Learning how to study for tests may include having the student compose test questions and their possible re-

sponses, or allowing the student to practice test-taking using another examination with a format similar to the upcoming test.

9. Devise ways to test what students really know: This is a tremendous challenge; it takes creativity, and certainly requires that the teachers understand the student's test-taking difficulties. There are two basic approaches that can be helpful. The first is to negotiate an alternative assignment, such as a project, diorama or poster, that would permit the student's research and mastery of the material covered in class to be demonstrated, in lieu of an examination. This may be an attractive option, because it allows the student to use imagination and creativity, attributes that are often well developed in students with attentional disorders.

The second approach is to modify the examination process or the examination itself. For example, if a student has difficulty getting his thoughts organized and on paper, an essay format test may become a multiple-choice examination or an oral examination. Students with attentional disorders may require untimed tests, so they can work carefully and avoid responding impulsively. Some students may benefit from taking examinations in a quieter, less distracting room than the classroom, while others should take tests with teacher supervision to discuss each question before the student writes down his answers.

10. Foster positive self-concept and better self-esteem: Students with attentional disorders are often frustrated and discouraged when they try to work, despite the fact that they want to do well in school. By the time they leave high school, many have suffered for years with

diminished self-esteem. Flexible teachers, who make it clear they understand a student's difficulties and will help to ensure that he is successful, can make a huge difference in a student's academic life.

Teachers should meet with students individually to discuss problems and to negotiate possible strategies for managing them. It is important that the student feels that he has an ally in each of his teachers, and that he and they will work together to help him to succeed. With perspective, the student will be more likely to leave school not only with better academic skills, but also with his self-esteem intact. The student's sense of competence and self-esteem appears to be a crucial factor in ultimate outcome. It is the combination of cognitive ability, educational attainment, and preserved self-esteem that allows individuals to succeed during the years beyond school.

If children with attentional disorders grow up in a more accepting and flexible educational environment, we may have an opportunity to influence outcome positively. Although it is difficult to change our traditional methods, we can and must do so. Each of us must be responsible for making these changes happen in our schools, in our classrooms, for our students. Our children need our help, and they need it now. We haven't a moment to waste.

Betsy Busch, M.D., is the Research Director, Learning and Attentional Disorders, Division of Pediatric Neurology, Department of Pediatrics, at The Floating Hospital, Boston, MA; and an Assistant Professor of Pediatrics, at Tufts University School of Medicine. She also serves on The Network's Council of Advisors.

Educating Children with Attention Deficits: A Call for Change. Reprinted with permission of *The Network Exchange*, Spring/Summer 1993, Vol. 11, No. 1. *The Exchange* is published by The Learning Disabilities Network, 72 Sharp St., Hingham, MA 02043.

Pro-Active and Responsive Discipline Interventions

Set up a classroom environment and instructional program designed to meet the needs of your students. If a child is exhibiting disruptive behaviors, implement one or more of the following interventions. Experiment until you find the ones that are effective. Remember that some behaviors are "habits" that may take time to change.

Physical Environment Interventions:
1. Seat the child in close proximity to the teacher.
2. Place the child away from other children who exhibit disruptive behaviors.
3. Place the child away from distractions (traffic areas, windows).
4. Provide the child with a study carrel to cut down on visual distractions.
5. Place masking tape around the floor near the child's desk to clearly indicate the child's boundaries during individual seatwork activities.
6. Play low volume classical music to set a relaxed tone in the classroom.
7. Make buttons and/or signs that say: "I am a good listener," or "I am a good friend." Have the student wear the button or tape the sign to his/her desk. Use illustrations for children who do not yet read.
8. Designate a small bulletin board section to display the child's work and encourage completion of assignments.
9. Try setting up room in a circle or semi-circle arrangement, or with all rows facing the center of the room. These arrangements sometimes result in improved student behavior.

Psychological Interventions:
1. Establish a friendly and positive relationship with each child.
2. Provide children with opportunities to make choices.
3. Provide opportunities for children to be responsible and self-sufficient.
4. Identify children's special interests and talents. Allow children to share these during class time.
5. Be respectful, calm, and confident when disciplining a child.
6. Teach children to be aware of their feelings and their needs.
7. Teach children how to express their feelings and needs appropriately.
8. Acknowledge effort and improvement.
9. Encourage children to support each other; establish a sense of community in the classroom.
10. Bring humor and fun into your classroom whenever possible.

Instructional Interventions:
1. Plan classroom activities that are developmentally appropriate.
2. Provide whatever support is needed to ensure that children experience success at least 80% of the time.
3. Use a multi-sensory approach. Offer opportunities for tactile-kinesthetic learning, especially for active boys.
4. Alternate activities frequently, including opportunities for students to change work/play locations.
5. Assign a "study-buddy" so that each student has a support system.
6. As much as possible, monitor the work of students by walking around the room. Provide support as necessary. Stay in proximity to students who have difficulty attending to their assignment.
7. Provide students with adequate time to complete assigned activities.
8. Give students choices regarding working independently, with a partner, or with a group.
9. Modify assignments for students who demonstrate attention deficits or have perceptual disabilities or fine motor delays.
10. Have mistakes (wrong answers) be OK.
11. Acknowledge effort and improvement.

Esther Wright

Temperament

Natural Disposition
> As many as 15% of all children are born with a difficult temperament

Learning Style

Sensory
Cultural
Perceptual

Developmental

Slower than average social/emotional growth

Unmet Needs

Love
Attention
Power
Stability/Security

Prenatal Conditions

Drug/Alcohol Exposed
> As many as 18% of America's children

Other Conditions

Attention Deficit/Hyperactivity
Learning Problems
Physical/Emotional Abuse

DISCIPLINE: PUNISHMENT OR TEACHING?

PUNISHMENT   =   Anger

Resentment

Revenge

Sadness

Negativity

TEACHING   =   Responsibility

Alternative Behaviors

Actions/Consequences

Good Judgment

Values

©1993 Esther Wright

Esther Wright

HELPING CHILDREN DEAL WITH ANGER

1. Read stories or show videos about children feeling and expressing anger.

2. Let children know that anger is a human emotion that can be expressed and resolved in *safe and appropriate* ways.

3. Have students make lists or draw pictures of situations that make them angry.

4. Have students brainstorm *appropriate* ways to express and resolve anger (i.e. physical activity, removing oneself from the situation, art or writing activities, etc.).

5. Have students role play appropriate and inappropriate ways of expressing anger.

6. Have students do art or writing activities that show examples of appropriate and inappropriate expressions of anger.

7. Set up a "cooling off" area in the classroom. Have writing materials, art materials, pillows for punching, stuffed animals for hugging, toy telephones, tape cassette player with relaxing music, etc.

8. Teach students a simple communication activity:
   a. Say what happened from your perspective.
   b. Say how you feel.
   c. Say what you need.

9 Set up a "special friend" or "study buddy" system so students have support when they're having a bad day.

Esther Wright, 1995

DO YOU *REACT* OR *RESPOND* TO DISCIPLINE PROBLEMS?

REACTIVE TEACHERS

Every teacher has expectations about themselves and their students:

We expect to be able to control student behavior.
We expect to be able to teach without disruption.
We expect students to be motivated and respectful.
We expect students to follow rules.

Although these appear to be reasonable expectations, there are very few classrooms where these expectations are met 100% of the time.

When our expectations aren't met, we often become:

- Angry
- Frustrated
- Resentful
- Disappointed
- Hurt

These emotional reactions to our unfulfilled expectations cause stress for the teacher and the students. Reactive teachers are not as effective as responsive teachers.

RESPONSIVE TEACHERS

Responsive teachers deal with all students and all behaviors in a calm and confident manner.

- They do not take students' behavior personally.
- They ask themselves, "What does the student or the class need at this moment?"
- They use humor (without sarcasm).
- They do not get into power struggles with students.
- They ignore minor infractions.
- They use eye contact or proximity before calling out a student's name.

Esther Wright, 1994

Building Partnerships with Parents

Teachers and parents ultimately want the same goals for children. We want them to be successful and happy, and we want them to reach their full potential. Parents of children with special needs hope their children will have as normal a life as possible. They want them to learn how to get along with people as well as develop the ability to become self-sufficient and independent.

In order for a classroom teacher to develop a partnership with the parent of a child with special needs, the teacher should appreciate the challenges inherent in raising a child who has physical, emotional, or learning disabilities. However, we must communicate to the parents that there is a great deal they can do to support their child's school success.

A positive and supportive relationship between teacher and parent established early in the school year will support the child's success in the regular classroom.

Tips for Establishing Effective Home/School Partnerships

• Communicate your commitment to the success of this student in your classroom.

• Let the parents know that their child's success is dependent on an effective parent/teacher partnership.

• Acknowledge the positive aspects of the child — his/her strengths and talents.

• Identify one or two specific behaviors that need to be improved.

• Work out a plan of support.

• Decide on the method and frequency of communication between you and the parents.

• Request that the parents practice the new behavior at home as much as possible.

• Jointly determine what additional support is needed (counseling, tutoring).

Esther Wright

Karen Morrow Durica

The labeled child

Durica teaches at Carl Sandburg Elementary School, Littleton, Colorado, USA.

I pray for the labeled child;
That child who is gifted and talented.
No longer can she be lazy and idle
Or a daydreamer.
So much more is expected
Of those as gifted and talented as she.

I pray for the labeled child;
That child who is learning disabled.
No longer will the world expect brilliance
No longer will someone tell him to reach for the
    stars
Because that is where greatness will be found.

I pray for the labeled child;
That child who is dyslexic.
Reading — oh, the joy of reading!
Will always be hard for her to find.
No matter that she can recite — no *sing* —
Mary Had a Little Lamb,
She won't be able to read it,
At least not without difficulty.
She will learn that all her friends
Who laugh and cry and wonder about books
Can do so because they are not dyslexic.

I pray for the labeled child;
That child who is A.D.D.
An unorganized bubble of hyperactivity.
No longer will someone teach him to cope in a
    world
That values compliance.
No longer will someone say "You can do this;
Oh, it may be hard, but it is within you to do this."
A dose of medicine now replaces the need for
    that inner effort
And eliminates the possible victory.

I pray for the labeled child;
That child who is emotionally handicapped.
That child who rebels
Because she *should* rebel.

The child who acts out
Because there is nowhere else
For the hurt and anxiety and fear to go.
The child who is diagnosed "sick,"
When perhaps her actions are the one true sign
    of sanity
In the demented world in which she is forced to
    live.

I pray for the child of no label.
In a system which marks so many special,
This child neither shines nor demands.
For this child life has been neither harsh nor
    generous.
This is the one who "makes" the teacher's day
Because there are so many children who need
    real attention.

I pray most of all for some magic day
When the tests, the labels, and the names
Will disappear — will be forgotten.
When each child who enters a classroom
Will be an apprentice of learning.
When each classroom will be a safe place
To discover — on your own —
What will be the struggles of your life,
And the victories.
When the feeble and the bright,
The gregarious and the shy
Will all find their place
In the great adventure of education.
When the only label that will be attached to
    anyone is
                LEARNER.

"The labeled child," Karen Morrow Durica, *The Reading Teacher,* March, 1994.
Reprinted with permission of Karen Morrow Durica and the International Reading Association.

Esther Wright

Call in the Troops

Some of your students will require one-to-one instructional or behavioral support. If paraprofessionals are not available, call upon community resources when you need additional adult support in your classroom. Some of these people are eager to volunteer an hour or more a week. In some cases, they may be able to support your classroom an hour or more a day.

• Parents (current or past)

• Local business people

• Graduate students from local universities (especially those majoring in psychology, counseling, or education)

• Retired teachers

• Special education resource staff

• ESL resource staff

• High school students (some schools give credit for community service)

• Social service personnel

• Off duty nurses or flight attendants

• Service club members (Lions/Kiwanis/Association of University Women, sororities, fraternities)

Local businesses and service clubs have been known to "adopt" a classroom or a school. They can sometimes contribute funding for special projects and materials, as well as provide volunteer tutors for needy students.

Although inviting members of the community to volunteer in your classroom does not require additional funding from your school district, it does take time to locate people who are available, set up schedules, and provide whatever training will be necessary. Once you have a routine established, however, it will be well worth the time invested.

ΙΝ ΤΗΙΣ ΩΕ ΜΥΣΤ ΧΟΝΘΥΕΡ

Don't worry.
Year-Round Education is a lot easier to understand.

Plan now to attend the

1996 NATIONAL CONFERENCE

of the
NATIONAL ASSOCIATION FOR YEAR-ROUND EDUCATION

February 17-22, 1996
Omni Rosen Hotel, Orlando, FL

Each year innovative educators from around the world gather to learn about year-round education and share their experiences with their colleagues.

What works? Why does it work? Find out.

Whether it's your first time or your fifth, remember...

With year-round education, the learning never stops

For further information contact Jeanne Walsh

NAYRE
P.O. Box 711386
San Diego, CA 92171-1386
(619) 276-5296 FAX (619) 571-5754

Early registration discounts available

The National Association for Year-Round Education (NAYRE) has a variety of professional resources available, including those listed below. To request a publication, or for information on a topic not addressed, contact NAYRE at P.O. Box 711386, San Diego, CA 92171-1386 or call (619) 276-5296.

FROM PARENT TO PARENT
By Sandy Hawkins
Provides a basic explanation of the year-round concept and addresses the special questions and concerns of parents. Available in English and Spanish.

TWENTY-FIRST REFERENCE DIRECTORY OF YEAR-ROUND EDUCATION PROGRAMS FOR THE 1994-95 SCHOOL YEAR
Compiled by NAYRE staff
A listing of school districts currently using a year-round calendar, includes addresses, phone numbers, contact persons, calendar type and implementation scope.

A REVIEW OF RECENT STUDIES RELATING TO THE ACHIEVEMENT OF STUDENTS ENROLLED IN YEAR-ROUND EDUCATION PROGRAMS
Prepared by Walter Winters
Reviews 19 recent studies dealing with the achievement of students in YRE programs.

YEAR-ROUND CALENDAR AND ENROLLMENT PLANS
By Don Glines
Detailed descriptions of year-round calendar plans.

CREATING EDUCATIONAL FUTURES: CONTINUOUS MANKATO WILSON ALTERNATIVES
By Don Glines
Focuses on 21st century learning systems and proposes the implementation of educational prototypes such as the Mankato-Wilson model to shift the idea from schooling to learning.

THE GREAT LOCKOUT IN AMERICA'S CITIZENSHIP PLANTS: PAST AS FUTURE
Supplemental Edition by William Wirt and Don Glines
This edition relates Gary, Indiana's designs of the past with the local realities of the present and discusses the national visions reflecting continuous learning systems for the future.

NATIONAL ASSOCIATION FOR YEAR-ROUND EDUCATION: A HISTORICAL PERSPECTIVE
By James Bingle and Don Glines
A record of the YRE movement in the United States from 1904 to present.

SCHOOL BY SCHOOL LISTING OF YEAR-ROUND EDUCATION PROGRAMS FOR THE 1994-95 SCHOOL YEAR
Compiled by NAYRE Staff
A listing of public and private schools currently on a year-round schedule complete with school address, phone number, principal's name and calendar used.

A COMPARATIVE STUDY OF MULTI-TRACK YRE AND THE USE OF RELOCATABLES
By Robert W. Coleman and Charles Freebern
A cost comparison of relocatables versus a four-track year-round program.

A HANDBOOK FOR IMPLEMENTING YRE IN THE HIGH SCHOOL
By Marsha Speck
Details how to implement single- or multi-track YRE in a high school.

YEAR-ROUND EDUCATION: HISTORY, PHILOSOPHY AND FUTURE
By Don Glines
Traces the evolution of YRE, details innovative programs, makes projections to year 2020.

National Association for Year-Round Education

P.O. Box 711386, San Diego, CA 92171-1386 • (619) 276-5296 • FAX (619) 571-5754

Year-Round Education
Where the Learning Never Stops

"If year-round education were the traditional school calendar and had been so for a hundred years and if someone came along to suggest a 'new' calendar wherein school students were to be formally educated for only nine months each year, with another three months free from organized instruction, would the American public allow or even consider such a calendar?"
— *Charles Ballinger, Executive Director of NAYRE*

The National Association for Year-Round Education (NAYRE) is a non-profit organization comprised of parents, teachers, administrators and other concerned individuals. NAYRE advocates the improvement of K-12 education by reorganizing the school year to foster continuous learning. Breaking up the long summer vacation into shorter, more frequent vacations reduces summer learning loss and corresponds to the manner in which students best learn. Year-Round Education (YRE) does not eliminate the summer vacation but merely reduces it. NAYRE also serves as a clearinghouse for information regarding YRE and provides guest speakers and expert guidance to districts interested in implementing YRE.

Over 1.6 million students are attending year-round schools during the 1994-95 school year. Currently, 37 states have one or more schools utilizing a year-round calendar. Within those states, 436 school districts and 2,252 public and private schools are on a year-round schedule.

YEAR-ROUND TERMINOLOGY

Track:
The designated time periods when students and teachers are either in school or on vacation.

Single-Track:
A configuration where all students and school personnel follow the same schedule.

Multi-Track:
A configuration where students and school personnel are divided between two or more tracks. The instructional and vacation periods of each track are staggered so that the tracks are on vacation at various times, thereby maximizing the use of available space.

Intersession:
Literally, time between sessions. Can be utilized for intervention, enrichment programs, or vacation.

WHAT YEAR-ROUND EDUCATION CAN DO

- Reduce summer learning loss
- Help raise test scores
- Reduce student overcrowding
- Combat teacher burnout
- Save taxpayers money by reducing the need to build new facilities, thus saving building costs and the interest on bonds used to finance new school construction
- Increase student and teacher attendance
- Reduce vandalism
- Allow families to take less-expensive, off-peak vacations

Multiage Organizations

National Alliance of Multiage Educators (N.A.M.E.)
Ten Sharon Road, Box 577
Peterborough, NH 03458
1-800-924-9621

N.A.M.E. is a networking organization for educators who want to share ideas, information, and experiences with others who have a similar interest in multiage and continuous progress practices. N.A.M.E. is also a source of information on books and audiovisual materials about multiage. Membership is open to those considering multiage as well as those already teaching and supervising it.

---

n.a.m.e.
NATIONAL ALLIANCE OF MULTIAGE EDUCATORS sm
Ten Sharon Road, PO Box 577
Peterborough, NH 03458

Membership Application

SB 8
1995-96

Name _____

Position _____

Grade/age levels taught _____

Home Address _____

Town/City _____ State _____ Zip _____

Home phone _____

School phone _____

Name of School _____

School Address _____

Town/City _____ State _____ Zip _____

N.A.M.E. membership will be under (circle one)   individual   school

___I want to join N.A.M.E. My membership fee is enclosed.($9 individual, $19 school)

For school membership, photocopy and complete this form for each of the 3 members.

International Registry of Nongraded Schools (IRONS)
Robert H. Anderson, Co-director (with Barbara N. Pavan)
PO Box 271669
Tampa, FL 33688-1699

IRONS is housed at the University of South Florida. It has been established to gather information about individual schools or school districts that are either in the early stages of developing a nongraded program or well along in their efforts. Its purpose is to facilitate intercommunication and research efforts. There is a phase one membership and a full membership.

Multiage Classroom Exchange
Teaching K-8
40 Richards Ave.
Norwalk, CT 06854

The Multiage Classroom Exchange puts teachers in contact with others who are interested in swapping ideas, activities, and experiences relating to the multiage, progressive classroom.

To join, send your name, address, age levels you teach, years of experience with multiage education, and a self-addressed, stamped envelope to the address listed. You'll receive a complete, up-to-date list of teachers who are interested in exchanging information.

California Alliance for Elementary Education
Charlotte Keuscher, Program Consultant
California Department of Education
721 Capitol Mall, 3rd Floor
Sacramento, CA 95814

The Elementary Education Office and the California Alliance for Elementary Education have published the second and third installments of The Multiage Learning Source Book.

The second installment is a guide for teachers, principals, parents, and community members who are involved and interested in multiage learning. It contains descriptions of what multiage learning is and is not, questions staffs and parents need to explore before and during the implementation stage, samples of how schools have communicated to their communities about multiage learning, classroom curriculum vignettes, anecdotes from schools that have successfully implemented multiage learning under a variety of conditions, descriptions of multiage programs throughout the state, and current and relevant research and articles.

The third installment deals with evaluation of a multiage program and assessment in multiage classrooms. Copies of the Source Book are distributed free of charge to California Alliance for Elementary Education members.

California Multiage Learning Task Force
(see California Alliance for Elementary Education)

Much of the multiage learning effort in California is guided by the Multiage Learning Task Force, which is made up of California Alliance for Elementary Education teachers, principals, parents, board of education members and university professors. The group has provided guidance and material for The Multiage Learning Source Book and are practitioners of multiage learning.

Networks supporting multiage education are being developed throughout California, coordinated by the Elementary Education Office, which assists the startup of the groups. Once started the groups operate independently.

NEWSLETTER

MAGnet Newsletter
805 W. Pennsylvania
Urbana, IL 61801-4897

The MAGnet Newsletter provides information about schools that have implemented multiage practices.

ERIC

ERIC (Educational Resources Information Center) is a clearinghouse or central agency responsible for the collection, classification, and distribution of written information related to education. If you need help finding the best way to use ERIC, call ACCESS ERIC toll-free at 1-800-LET-ERIC. If you need specific information about multiage education, call Norma Howard at 1-800-822-9229.

A Value Search: Multiage or Nongraded Education is available for $7.50 and can be ordered from Publication Sales, ERIC Clearinghouse on Educational Management, 5207 University of Oregon, Eugene, OR 97403-5207. A handling charge of $3.00 is added to all billed orders.

Workshops and Conferences

The Society For Developmental Education
Ten Sharon Road, Box 577
Peterborough, NH 03458
1-800-462-1478

The Society For Developmental Education (SDE) presents workshops and conferences throughout the year and around the country for elementary educators on multiage, inclusion education, multiple intelligences, character education, discipline, whole language, authentic assessment, and related topics.

SDE sponsors an International Multiage Conference each July. For information on dates and location, write or phone SDE at the address or number listed above.

Child Advocacy Organizations

Child Care Action Campaign
330 Seventh Ave., 17th Floor
New York, NY 10001

Children's Defense Fund
25 E. St. NW
Washington, DC 20001

Child Trends, Inc.
2100 M Street NW
Washington, DC 20037

Families and Work Institute
330 Seventh Ave., 14th Floor
New York, NY 10001

Inclusive Education Resources

A.D.D. Warehouse
300 Northwest 70th Ave. Suite 102
Plantation, FL 33317
1-800-233-9273
   *Books, tapes, videos on ADD
   and hyperactivity*

Paul H. Brookes Publishing Co.
   (catalog available)
P.O. Box 10624
Baltimore, MD 21285-0624
1-800-638-3775

Center for Success in Learning
17000 Preston Rd., #400
Dallas, TX 75248
1-800-488-9435
FAX (214) 407-9852

Centre for Integrated Education and Community
24 Thome Crescent
Toronto, Ontario M6H 2S5

CH.A.D.D. (Children with Attention Deficit Disorder)
499 NW 70th Ave., Suite 308
Plantation, FL 33317
1-305-587-3700

The Council for Exceptional Children
1920 Association Drive
Reston, VA 22091-1589
703-620-3660
      (publishes *Teacher Education and Special
      Education* and *Teaching Exceptional Children*)

Down Syndrome News
National Down Syndrome Congress
1605 Chantilly Dr., Suite 250
Atlanta, GA 30324
1-800-232-6372

Exceptional Children's Assistance Center
PO Box 16
Davidson, NC 28036

The Exchange

The Learning Disabilities Network
72 Sharp St., Suite A-2
Hingham, MA 02043
(617) 340-5605

Impact
Institute on Community Integration
University of Minnesota
6 Patte Hall
150 Pillsbury Dr. SE
Minneapolis, MN 55455
(612) 624-4848

Inclusion Press
24 Thome Crescent
Toronto, Ontario M6H 2S5

Kids on the Block Puppets
3509 M. Street, NW
Washington, DC 20007

Learning Disabilities Association (LDA)
4156 Library Rd.
Pittsburgh, PA 15234
(412) 341-1515

MPACT (Missouri Parents Act)
8631 Delmar, Suite 300
St. Louis, MO 63124
1-800-995-3160

National Center for Learning Disabilities (NCLD)
99 Park Ave.
New York, NY 10016
(212) 687-7211

The Orton Dyslexia Society
Chester Building, Suite 382
8600 LaSalle Rd.
Baltimore, MD 21286-0024
1-410-296-0232

PEAK (Parent Education and Assistance Program)
6055 Lehman Dr., Suite 101
Colorado Springs, CO 80918

Resurgens Press, Inc.
PO Box 12389
Atlanta, GA 30355-2389
1-800-556-6002
FAX (404) 457-0302
      Materials for LD and ADD, preschool through adult

The Safety Net
Schools Are For Everyone (SAFE)
PO Box 9503
Schenectady, NY 12309

Whole Language Hotline
In the fall of 1991, the Center for the Expansion of Language and Thinking (CELT) began sponsoring a crisis hotline to support teachers and administrators who come under attack for their child-centered practices.
For further information, contact:

The Center for Establishing Dialogue in Teaching and Learning (CED)
325 E. Southern Ave.
Suite 107-108
Tempe, AZ 85282
1-602-894-1333 • FAX 602-894-9547

Publications

Children's Literature

AAP Reading Initiative News
Association of American Publishers
220 East 23rd St.
New York, NY 10010

Booklinks: Connecting Books, Libraries and Classrooms
American Library Association
50 Huron St.
Chicago, IL 60611

The Bulletin
Council on Interracial Books for Children
1841 Broadway
New York, NY 10023

The Bulletin of the Center for Children's Books
University of Illinois Press
1325 S. Oak St.
Champaign, Il 61820

CBC Features
350 Scotland Rd.
Orange, NJ 07050

Chapters
Hodge-Podge Books
272 Lark St.
Albany, NY 12210

Children's Book Council
568 Broadway, Suite 404
New York, NY 10012

Children's Literature and Reading
(special interest group of the
International Reading Association)
Membership: Dr. Miriam A. Marecek
                10 Marchant Rd.
                Winchester, MA 01890

Children's Literature in Education
Human Sciences Press, Inc.
233 Spring St.
New York, NY 10013-1578

The Five Owls
2004 Sheridan Ave. S.
Minneapolis, MN 55408

The Horn Book Magazine
11 Beacon St.
Boston, MA 02105

Journal of the Children's Literature
226 East Emans St.
Middletown, PA 17057

Journal of Children's Literature
Membership: Marjorie R. Hancock
                2037 Plymouth Rd.
                Manhattan, KS 66502

The Kobrin Letter (reviews nonfiction books)
732 Greer Rd.
Palo Alto, CA 94303

The New Advocate
Christopher Gordon Publishers, Inc.
480 Washington St.
Norwood, MA 02062

Perspectives
College of Education and Allied Professions
The University of Toledo
Toledo, OH 43606

Reading is Fundamental (RIF)
600 Maryland Ave.
Suite 600
Washington, D.C. 20024

The WEB (Wonderfully Exciting Books)
The Ohio State University
Room 200 Ramseyer Hall
29 West Woodruff
Columbus, OH 43210

Early Childhood / Developmental Education

Childhood Education
Journal of the Association for Childhood
    Education International
Suite 315
11501 Georgia Ave.
Wheaton, MD 20902

Early Childhood News
Peter Li, Inc.
2451 E. River Rd.
Dayton, OH 45439

Early Childhood Research Quarterly
Ablex Publishing Corp.
355 Chestnut St.
Norwood, NJ 07648
1-201-767-8450

Early Childhood Today
Scholastic, Inc.
P.O. Box 54813
Boulder, CO 30323-4813

A Newsletter for Teachers
Northeast Foundation for Children
71 Montague City Rd.
Greenfield, MA 01301

Young Children
National Association for the Education of Young Children
    (NAEYC)
1509 16th St. NW
Washington, DC 20036-1426
1-800-424-2460

General Education — Classroom Focus

Creative Classroom
Children's Television Workshop
P.O. Box 53148
Boulder, CO 80322-3148

Instructor Magazine
Scholastic, Inc.
555 Broadway
New York, NY 10012-3999

Learning
1111 Bethlehem Pike
Springhouse, PA 19477

Teaching K-8
40 Richards Ave.
Norwalk, CT 06854

General Education — Issues/Research Focus

*The American School Board Journal /
    Executive Educator*
National School Boards Association
1680 Duke St.
Alexandria, VA 22314

Democracy and Education
The Institute for Democracy and Education
College of Education
313 McCracken Hall
Ohio University
Athens, OH 45701-2979

Education Week
P.O. Box 2083
Marion, OH 43305
Editorial:
4301 Connecticut Ave. NW #250
Washington, DC 20008

Educational Leadership
Journal of the Association for Supervision and
    Curriculum Development (ASCD)
1250 N. Pitt St.
Alexandria, VA 22314-1403

The Elementary School Journal
University of Chicago Press
P.O. Box 37005
Chicago, IL 60637

Phi Delta Kappan
Eighth and Union
P.O. Box 789
Bloomington, IN 47402

Principal
National Association of Elementary School
    Principals (NAESP)
1615 Duke St.
Alexandria, VA 22314-3483

The School Administrator
American Association of School Administrators
1801 North Moore St.
Arlington, VA 22209

Teacher Magazine
Subscription Services
P.O. Box 2091
Marion, OH 43305-2091

Teaching Voices
The Massachusetts Field Center for Teaching
    and Learning
University of Massachusetts
100 Morrissey Blvd.
Boston, MA 02125

TIP (Theory into Practice)
Subscription Dept.
The Ohio State University
174 Arps Hall
1945 N. High St.
Columbus, OH 43210-1172

Language *(See also Whole Language, this section)*

Language Arts
National Council of Teachers of English
1111 Kenyon Rd.
Urbana, IL 61801

Literacy
The International Institute of Literacy Learning
Box 1414
Commerce, TX 75429

Primary Voices K-6
National Council of Teachers of English
1111 Kenyon Rd.
Urbana, IL 61801-1096

The Reading Teacher
International Reading Association
P.O. Box 8139
Newark, DE 19714-8139

(IRA also publishes *Journal of Reading, Reading
Today, Reading Research Quarterly; lectura y
yida* — a Spanish language journal.)

Teachers As Readers Project
AAP Reading Initiative
Association of American Publishers
220 East 23rd St.
New York, NY 10010

Math and Science

Arithmetic Teacher
National Council of Teachers of Mathematics
1906 Association Dr.
Reston, VA 22091

NatureScope
National Wildlife Federation
1412 16th St.
Washington, DC 20036

Science and Children
National Science Teachers Association
1840 Wilson Blvd.
Arlington, VA 22201-3000

Whole Language

Spotlight on Whole Language
A Newsletter of the ASCD Whole Language Network
Hofstra University
Hempstead, NY 11550-1090

Teachers Networking
The Whole Language Newsletter
Richard C. Owen Publishers
P.O. Box 585
Katonah, NY 10536

Whole Language Assembly of NCTE
Paul Crowley
614 B Dufranedue
Sebastopal, CA 95472

The Whole Idea
The Wright Group
19201 120th Ave. NE
Bothell, WA 98011-9512

Whole Language Network
Teaching K-8
40 Richards Ave.
Norwalk, CT 06854

The Whole Language Teachers Association
  Newsletter
P.O. Box 216
Southboro, MA 01772

WLSIG Newsletter
Whole Language Special Interest Group of the IRA
Membership: Grace Vento Zogby
125 Proctor Blvd.
Utica, NY 13501

Whole Language Umbrella
President: Sharon Murphy
Faculty of Education
5876 Ross Building
York University
4700 Keele St.
North York, ON M3J 1T3
416/736-5009

Membership: Kathy Egawa
306 N. 79th #6
Seattle, WA 98103

Newsletter: Debra Goodman
P.O. Box 721326
Berkley, MI 48072

Sources of Multiage Materials

Crown Publications
521 Fort St.
Victoria, British Columbia
Canada V8W 1E7
Phone: 604-386-4636
Fax: 604-386-0221
   Distributes books and videos for the Province
   of British Columbia Ministry of Education.

Crystal Springs Books
Ten Sharon Road
Box 500
Peterborough, NH 03458
Phone: 1-800-321-0401
Fax: 603-924-6688

Big Book Publishers

Creative Teaching Press, Inc.
P.O. Box 6017
Cypress, CA 90630-0017
1-800-444-4287

Curriculum Associates, Inc.
5 Esquire Rd.
N. Billerica, MA 01862-2589
1-800-225-0248

Holt Impressions
6277 Sea Harbor Dr.
Orlando, FL 32887
1-800-782-4479

Modern Curriculum Press
13900 Prospect Rd.
Cleveland, OH 44136
1-800-321-3106

Richard C. Owen Publishers, Inc.
P.O. Box 585
Katonah, NY 01536
1-800-336-5588

Rigby Education
P.O. Box 797
Crystal Lake, IL 60039-0797
1-800-822-8661

Scholastic, Inc.
P.O. Box 7502
Jefferson City, MO 65102
1-800-325-6149

Sundance
P.O. Box 1326
Littleton, MA 01460
1-800-343-8204

Whole Language Consultants
Blue Frog Distributors
#6-846 Marion St.
Winnipeg, Manitoba
Canada R2J OK4
1-204-235-1644

The Wright Group
19201 12th Ave. NE
Bothell, WA 98011-9512
1-800-523-2371

Materials

Compiled by Kathryn Cloonan and Jay Buros

Big Book Materials

Sticky pockets, colored cotton balls — Demco Library
Supplies and Equipment, 1-800-356-1200

Velour paper — Dick Blick Art Supply,
1-800-345-3042

Grommets — Hardware stores

Alphabet stickers — Childcraft, 1-800-631-6100

"Scribbles" Glitter Glue — Arts and crafts stores or
Duncan Hobby, 1-209-291-2515

Binding Machines and Spiral Binding

Quill Office Products
P.O. Box 1450
Lebanon, PA 17042-1450
(717) 272-6100

General Binding Corporation
One GBC Plaza
Northbrook, IL 60062
(708) 272-3700

Scholastic, Inc.
1-800-325-6149

Book Racks/Easels

Fixturecraft Corp.
443 East Westfield Ave.
P.O. Box 292
Roselle Park, NJ 07204-0292
1-800-275-1145

Chart Paper/Sentence Strips

New England School Supply
P.O. Box 3004
Agawam, MA 01101-8004

J.L.Hammett Company
P.O. Box 9057
Braintree, MA 02184-9057
1-800-333-4600

Computer Programs

Magic Slate
Sunburst Communications
101 Castleton
Pleasantville, NY 10570
1-800-321-7511

Letters, Labels, Lists
MECC
6160 Summit Dr. N.
Minneapolis, MN 55430-4003
1-800-685-MECC

Print Shop
Broderbund
500 Redwood Blvd., P.O. Box 6121
Novato, CA 94947
1-800-521-6263

SuperPrint
Scholastic
P.O. Box 7502
Jefferson City, MO 65102
1-800-325-6149

Evaluation Tapes

5 minute tapes to evaluate oral reading
World Class Tapes
1-800-365-0669

Highlight Tape

Available through Crystal Springs Books
1-800-321-0401

Kinesiology

Techniques to help children make
right/left brain connections
Educational Kinesiology Foundation
P.O. Box 3396
Ventura, CA 93006
1-800-356-2109

Metal Shower Curtain Rings

Department Stores

Plastic Rings/Bird Bands

Farm Feed Stores

Plastic Slide Mounts

"Lott 100" — photo stores or
Arel Inc., St. Louis, MO 63110

Ribbons and Awards

Hodges Badge Company, Inc. — 1-800-556-2440

Stencil Machines

Ellison Educational
P.O. Box 8209
Newport Beach, CA 92658-8209
1-714-724-0555

Tutorettes

Audiotronics — 1-800-821-6104
Language Masters — 1-800-771-4466

Wikki Stix

Available through Crystal Springs Books
1-800-321-0401

More Than Books
Expanding Children's Horizons Through Magazines

Publication Subscription Address	Interest Area/Age Group
Big Book Magazine Scholastic, Inc. P.O. Box 10813 Des Moines, IA 50380-0813	General Interest 4-7
Boys' Life Boy Scouts of America P.O. Box 152079 1325 Walnut Hill Lane Irving, TX 75015-2079	General Interest 7-17
* *Chickadee* 25 Boxwood Lane Buffalo, NY 14227-2780	Science/ Nature 3-7
* *Child Life* P.O. Box 7133 Red Oak, IA 51591-0133 Submissions: P.O. Box 567 1100 Waterway Blvd. Indianapolis, IN 46206	Health/General Interest 9-11
* *Children's Album* P.O. Box 6086 Concord, CA 94524	Writing/Crafts 8-14
C.A.R.E. (Children's Authors Make Reading Exciting) Apple Peddler 25112 Woodfield School Rd. Gaithersburg, MD 20882	Children's Authors 5-10
* *Children's Digest* P.O. Box 7133 Red Oak, IA 51591-0133 Submissions: (*see Child Life*)	Health/General Interest 8-10
* *Children's Playmate* P.O. Box 7133 Red Oak, IA 51591-0133 Submissions: (*see Child Life*)	Health/General Interest 6-8
Classical Calliope 7 School St. Peterborough, NH 03458-1454	World History 9-16
Cobblestone 7 School St. Peterborough, NH 03458-1454	American History 8-14
* *Creative Kids* P.O. Box 637 Holmes, PA 19043 Submissions: P.O. Box 6448 Mobile, AL 36660	Student Art/Writing 8-14

Publication Subscription Address	Interest Area/Age Group
* *Cricket* P.O. Box 592 Mt. Morris, IL 61054-7904 Submissions: 315 5th St. P.O. Box 300 Peru, IL 61354	Literature/Art 9-14
Dolphin Log The Cousteau Society 870 Greenbrier Circle, Suite 402 Chesapeake, VA 23320	Science/Ecology 7-15
Faces 7 School St. Peterborough, NH 03458-1454	World Cultures 8-14
* *Highlights for Children* P.O. Box 269 Columbus, OH 43216-0269 Submissions: 803 Church St. Honesdale, PA 18431	General Interest 2-12
* *Humpty Dumpty's Magazine* P.O. Box 7133 Red Oak, IA 51591-0133 Submissions: (*see Child Life*)	Health/General Interest 4-6
Images of Excellence Images of Excellence Foundation P.O. Box 1131 Boiling Springs, NC 28017	Social Studies 10-13
* *Jack and Jill* P.O. Box 7133 Red Oak, IA 51591-0133 Submissions: (*see Child Life*)	General Interest 6-8
* *Kid City* Children's Television Workshop P.O. Box 10820 Des Moines, IA 50380-0820	General Interest 6-9
Kids City Big Magazine Children's Television Workshop P.O. Box 10820 Des Moines, IA 50380-0820	General Interest 5-7
KIDS Discover P.O. Box 54209 Boulder, CO 80321-4209	Science/General Interest 5-12

encourages children's submissions

Publication Subscription Address	Interest Area/Age Group	Publication Subscription Address	Interest Area/Age Group
Kids Life and Times Kids Life P.O. Box D Bellport, NY 11713 Submissions: Children's Television Workshop One Lincoln Plaza New York, NY 10023	Entertainment/Education 6-12	*School Mates* 186 Route 9W New Windsor, NY 12553	Beginning Chess 7 and up
Kidsports Venture Communications 60 Madison Ave. New York, NY 10160-0981	Sports 7-14	*Scienceland* 501 Fifth Ave. Suite 2108 New York, NY 10017-6165	Science 5-11
Koala Club News San Diego Zoo Membership Dept. P.O. Box 271 San Diego, CA 92112	Animals 3-15	*Seedling Short Story* International P.O. Box 405 Great Neck, NY 11022	Short Stories 9-12
Ladybug P.O. Box 592 Mt. Morris, IL 61054-7904	Literature 2-6	*Sesame Street Magazine* P.O. Box 52000 Boulder, CO 80321-2000	General Interest 2-6
* *The McGuffey Writer* 400 A McGuffey Hall Miami University Oxford, OH 45056	Student Writing 5-18	* *Skipping Stones: A Multi-Cultural Children's Forum* P.O. Box 3939 Eugene, OR 97403-0939	Multicultural Education/ Literary Arts, Social Studies, Environment 7-14
* *Merlyn's Pen* The National Magazine of Student Writing P.O. Box 1058 East Greenwich, RI 02818	Student Writing 12-16	*Sports Illustrated for Kids* P.O. Box 830607 Birmingham, AL 35283-0607	Sports 8-13
National Geographic World P.O. Box 2330 Washington, DC 20077-9955	Science/General Interest 8-14	**Stone Soup* The Magazine by Children P.O. Box 83 Santa Cruz, CA 95063	Student Writing/Art 6-13
* *Odyssey* 7 School St. Peterborough, NH 03458-1454	Space Exploration/ Astronomy 8-14	*Storyworks* Scholastic 555 Broadway New York, NY 10012-3999	Literature 8-11
Owl 25 Boxwood Lane Buffalo, NY 14227-2780	Science/Nature 8-12	*3-2-1 Contact* P.O. Box 51177 Boulder, CO 80321-1177	Science 8-14
Plays 120 Boylston St. Boston, MA 02116-4615	Drama 6-18	*Turtle* P.O. Box 7133 Red Oak, IA 51591-0133	Health/General Interest 2-5
Ranger Rick National Wildlife Federation 8925 Leesburg Pike Vienna, VA 22180-0001	Science/Wildlife Nature, Environment 6-12	*Voices of Youth* P.O. Box 1869 Sonoma, CA 95476	Student Writing / Art 14-18
* *Reflections* P.O. Box 368 Duncan Falls, OH 43734	Poetry 4-18	*The Wave: A Newspaper for Kids* 814 Amiford Drive San Diego, CA 92107	Student Writing / Art 6-12
		Your Big Backyard National Wildlife Federation 8925 Leesburg Pike Vienna, VA 22184	Animals/Conservation 3-5
		Zoo Books 9820 Willow Creek Rd. Suite 300 San Diego, CA 92131-1112	Wildlife 5-12

encourages children's submissions

Paperback Book Clubs

Scholastic, Inc.
P.O. Box 7502
Jefferson City, MO 65102
1-800-325-6149

The Trumpet Club
P.O. Box 604
Holmes, PA 19043
1-800-826-0110

Troll Book Club
2 Lethbridge Plaza
Mahwah, NJ 07430
1-800-541-1097

Weekly Reader Paperback Club
P.O. Box 16628
Columbus, OH 43216

Bibliography
Compiled by SDE Presenters

Anti-Hurrying

Elkind, David. *All Grown Up & No Place to Go*. Reading, MA: Addison-Wesley, 1984.

———.*The Hurried Child*. Reading, MA: Addison-Wesley, 1981.

———.*Miseducation: Preschoolers at Risk*. New York: Alfred A. Knopf, 1987.

Gilmore, June E. *The Rape of Childhood: No Time to Be a Kid*. Middletown, OH: J & J Publishing, 1990.

Healy, Jane. *Endangered Minds: Why Children Don't Think and What We Can Do About It*. New York: Simon & Schuster, 1990.

National Education Commission on Time and Learning. *Prisoners of Time*. Washington, DC: U.S. Government Printing Office, Superintendent of Documents, 1994.

Packard, Vance. *Our Endangered Children*. Boston: Little, Brown & Co., 1983.

Postman, Neil. *The Disappearance of Childhood*. New York: Dell, 1982.

Uphoff, James K. *Real Facts From Real Schools: What You're Not Supposed To Know About School Readiness and Transition Programs*. Rosemont, NJ: Modern Learning Press, 1990, 1995.

Uphoff, James, K.; Gilmore, June; and Huber, Rosemarie. *Summer Children: Ready (or Not) for School*. Middletown, OH: The Oxford Press, 1986.

Winn, Marie. *Children Without Childhood*. New York: Penguin Books, 1984.

Need a Book? Can't Find It?
Try Us First.

Crystal Springs Books can help you locate most of the books in this bibliography. Call us at 1-800-321-0401 if you need assistance.

Periodicals and information published by departments of education, school districts, and some educational associations generally must be obtained from their original source.

Attention Deficit Disorder (ADD) /
Attention Deficit Hyperactivity Disorder (ADHD)

Bain, Lisa J. *A Parent's Guide to Attention Deficit Disorders*. New York: Dell, 1991.

Copeland, Edna D., and Love, Valerie L. *Attention Without Tension: A Teacher's Handbook on Attention Disorders (ADHD and ADD)*. Atlanta, GA: 3 C's of Childhood, 1990.

Hartmann, Thom. *Attention Deficit Disorder: A Different Perception*. Penn Valley, CA, and Lancaster PA: Underwood-Miller, 1993. 186 pages.

Moss, Deborah. *Shelley, the Hyperactive Turtle*. Rockville, MD: Woodbine House, 1989.

Moss, Robert A., and Dunlap, Helen Huff. *Why Johnny Can't Concentrate: Coping with Attention Deficit Problems*. New York: Bantam Books, 1990.

Parker, Harvey. *The ADD Hyperactivity Handbook for Schools*. Plantation, FL: Impact Publications, 1992.

————. *The ADD Hyperactivity Workbook for Parents, Teachers, and Kids*. Plantation, FL: Impact Publications, 1988.

————. *The ADAPT Accommodation Planbook for Teachers*. Plantation, FL: Impact Publications, 1992.

————. *The ADAPT Student Planbook*. Plantation, FL: Impact Publications, 1992.

Quinn, Patricia O., M.D., and Stern, Judith M., M.A. *Putting on the Brakes: Young People's Guide to Understanding Attention Deficit Hyperactivity Disorder (ADHD)*. New York: Magination Press, 1991. 64 pages.

Rief, Sandra. *How to Reach and Teach ADD/ADHD Children*. West Nyack, NY: The Center for Applied Research in Education, 1993.

Assessment

Anthony, Robert. *Evaluating Literacy*. Portsmouth, NH: Heinemann, 1991.

Barrs, Myra et al. *The Primary Language Record: Handbook for Teachers*. Portsmouth, NH: Heinemann, 1988.

Baskwill, Jane, and Whitman, Paulette. *Evaluation: Whole Language, Whole Child*. New York: Scholastic. 1988.

Batzle, Janine. *Portfolio Assessment and Evaluation: Developing and Using Portfolios in the K-6 Classroom*. Cypress, CA: Creative Teaching Press, 1992.

Belanoff, Pat, and Dickson, Marcia, eds. *Portfolios: Process and Product*. Portsmouth, NH: Heinemann, 1991.

Clay, Marie. *An Observation Survey of Early Literacy Achievement*. Portsmouth, NH: Heinemann, 1993.

Clemmons, J.; Laase, L.; Cooper, D.; Areglado, N.; and Dill, M. *Portfolios in the Classroom: A Teacher's Sourcebook*. New York: Scholastic, Inc., 1993.

Cochrane, Orin, and Cochrane, Donna. *Whole Language Evaluation for Classrooms*. Bothell, WA: The Wright Group, 1992.

Daly, Elizabeth, ed. *Monitoring Children's Language Development*. Portsmouth, NH: Heinemann, 1992.

Eggleton, Jill. *Whole Language Evaluation*. Hong Kong: Applecross LTD, 1990.

Goodman, Kenneth, ed. *The Whole Language Evaluation Book*. Portsmouth, NH: Heinemann, 1988.

Goodman, Yetta et al. *Reading Miscues Inventory: Alternative Procedures*. New York: Richard C. Owen Publishers, 1987.

Graves, Donald, and Sustein, Bonnie, eds. *Portfolio Portraits*. Portsmouth, NH: Heinemann, 1992.

Harp, Bill, ed. *Assessment and Evaluation in Whole Language Programs*. Norwood, MA: Christopher Gordon Publishers, 1993.

ILEA/Centre for Language in Primary Education. *The Primary Language Record: Handbook for Teachers*. Portsmouth, NH: Heinemann, 1989.

Johnston, Peter. *Constructive Evaluation of Literate Activity*. New York: Longman, 1992.

Kamii, C., ed. *Achievement Testing in the Early Grades: The Games Grownups Play*. Washington, DC: National Association for the Education of Young Children, 1990.

Lazear, David. *Multiple Intelligence Approaches to Assessment: Solving the Assessment Conundrum*. IRI/Skylight Publishing, Inc., 1994.

Parsons, Les. *Response Journals*. Portsmouth, NH: Heinemann, 1989.

Picciotto, Linda. *Evaluation: A Team Effort*. Ont.: Scholastic, 1992.

Sharp, Quality Quinn. *Evaluation in the Literature-Based Classroom: Whole Language Checklists Grades K-6*. New York: Scholastic, 1989.

Tierney, Robert J.; Carter, Mark A.; and Desai, Laura E. *Portfolio Assessment in the Reading-Writing Classroom*. Norwood, MA: Christopher Gordon, 1991.

Traill, Leanna. *Highlight My Strengths*. Reed Publications, 1993.

Behavior/Discipline

Albert, Linda. *An Administrator's Guide to Cooperative Discipline*. Circle Pines, MN: American Guidance, 1989.

————. *A Teacher's Guide to Cooperative Discipline: How to Manage Your Classroom and Promote Self-Esteem*. Circle Pines, MN: American Guidance Service, 1989.

————.*Coping With Kids*. Tampa, FL: Alkhorn House, 1992.

————.*Responsible Kids in School and At Home: The Cooperative Discipline Way*. (six-video series). Circle Pines, MN: American Guidance Service, 1994.

Bluestein, Jane. *21st Century Discipline—Teaching Students Responsibility and Self-Control*. New York: Scholastic, 1988.

Burke, Kay. *What to Do with the Kid Who ... Developing Cooperation, Self-Discipline and Responsibility in the Classroom*. Palatine, IL: IRI/Skylight Publishing, 1992.

Canfield, Jack, and Siccone, Frank. *101 Ways to Devleop Student Self-Esteem and Responsibility*. Needham Heights, MA: Allyn & Bacon, 1993.

Charles, C.M. *Building Classroom Discipline*. New York: Longman, 1992.

Coletta, Anthony. *What's Best for Kids*. Rosemont, NJ: Modern Learning Press, 1991.

Curwin, Richard L., and Mendler, Allen N. *Discipline with Dignity*. Alexandria, VA: Association for Supervision and Curriculum Development, 1993.

————.*Am I in Trouble? Using Discipline to Teach Young Children Responsibility*. Santa Cruz, CA: Network Publications, 1990.

Fox, Lynn. *Let's Get Together*. Rolling Hills, CA: Jalmar Press, 1993.

Glasser, William, M.D. *Control Theory: A New Explanation of How We Control Our Lives*. New York: HarperPerennial, 1984.

————.*Control Theory in the Classroom*. New York: HarperPerennial, 1986.

————.*The Quality School: Managing Students Without Coercion*. New York: HarperPerennial, 1992.

————.*The Quality School Teacher: A Companion Volume to the Quality School*. New York: HarperPerennial, 1993.

Knight, Michael et al. *Teaching Children to Love Themselves*. Hillside, NJ: Vision Press, 1982.

Kohn, Alfie. *Punished by Rewards: The Trouble with Gold Stars, Incentive Plans, A's, Praise, and Other Bribes*. Boston: Houghton Mifflin, 1993.

Kreidler, William. *Creative Conflict Resolution: Strategies for Keeping Peace in the Classroom*. Glenview, IL: Scott, Foresman, & Co., 1984.

Kurchinka, Mary Sheedy. *Raising Your Spirited Child*. New York: Harper, 1991.

Kuykendall, Crystal. *From Rage to Hope: Strategies for Reclaiming Black & Hispanic Students*. Bloomington, IL: National Educational Service, 1992.

Mendler, Allen. *Smiling at Yourself: Educating Young Children About Stress and Self-Esteem*. Santa Cruz, CA: Network Publications, 1990.

————.*What Do I Do When? How to Achieve Discipline with Dignity in the Classroom*. Bloomington, IL: National Educational Service, 1992.

Nelson, Jane, Ed.D. *Positive Discipline*. New York: Ballantine Books, 1987 by Jane Nelson.

Redenbach, Sandi. *Self-Esteem: The Necessary Ingredient for Success*. Esteem Seminar Publications, 1991.

Reider, Barbara. *A Hooray Kind of Kid*. Folsom, CA: Sierra House Publishing, 1988.

Wright, Esther. *Good Morning, Class — I Love You!* Rolling Hills, CA: Jalmar Press, 1988.

————.*Loving Discipline A to Z*. San Francisco: Teaching From the Heart, 1994.

Cooperative Learning

Cohen, Dorothy. *Designing Groupwork: Strategies for the Heterogeneous Classroom*. New York: Teachers College Press, 1994.

Curran, Lorna. *Cooperative Learning Lessons for Little Ones: Literature-Based Language Arts and Social Skills*. San Juan Capistrano, CA: Resources for Teachers, Inc., 1992.

DeBolt, Virginia, with Dr. Spencer Kagan. *Write! Cooperative Learning and The Writing Process*. San Juan Capistrano, CA: Kagan Cooperative Learning, 1994.

Ellis, Susan S., and Whalen, Susan F. *Cooperative Learning: Getting Started*. New York: Scholastic, 1990.

Fisher, Bobbi. *Thinking and Learning Together: Curriculum and Community in a Primary Classroom*. Portsmouth, NH: Heinemann, 1995.

Forte, Imogene, and MacKenzie, Joy. *The Cooperative Learning Guide and Planning Pak for Primary Grades: Thematic Projects and Activities*. Nashville, TN: Incentive Publications, 1992.

Glover, Mary, and Sheppard, Linda. *Not on Your Own: The Power of Learning Together*. New York: Scholastic, 1990.

Johnson, David, and Johnson, Roger. *Cooperation and Competition: Theory and Research*. Edina, MN: Interaction Book Company, 1989.

————.*Learning Together and Alone*. Englewood Cliffs, NJ: Prentice Hall, Inc, 1991.

Kagan, Spencer. *Cooperative Learning*. San Juan Capistrano, CA: Resources for Teachers, Inc., 1994.

Reid, Jo Anne; Forrestal, P.; and Cook, J. *Small Group Learning in the Classroom*. Portsmouth, NH: Heinemann, 1989.

Shaw, Vanston, with Spencer Kagan, Ph.D. *Communitybuilding In the Classroom*. San Juan Capistrano, CA: Kagan Cooperative Learning, 1992.

Slavin, Robert. *Cooperative Learning*. Englewood Cliffs, NJ: Prentice-Hall, 1989.

————.*Cooperative Learning*. Boston: Allyn and Bacon, 1995.

Curriculum — Overview

Bredekamp, Sue, and Rosegrant, Teresa, eds. *Reaching Potentials: Appropriate Curriculum and Assessment for Young Children*, Vol. 1. Washington, DC: NAEYC, 1992.

Dodge, Diane Trister; Jablon, Judy R.; and Bickart, Toni S. *Constructing Curriculum in the Primary Grades*. Washington, DC: Teaching Strategies, Inc., 1994.

Fogarty, Robin. *The Mindful School: How to Integrate the Curricula*. Palatine, IL: Skylight Publishing, 1991.

Hall, G.E., and Loucks, S.F. "Program Definition and Adaptation: Implications for Inservice." *Journal of Research and Development in Education* (1981) 14, 2:46-58.

Hohmann, C. *Mathematics: High Scope K-3 Curriculum Guide.* (illustrated field test edition.) Ypsilanti, MI: High Scope Press, 1991.

Maehr, J. *Language and Literacy: High Scope K-3 Curriculum Guide.* (illustrated field test edition.) Ypsilanti, MI: High Scope Press, 1991.

National Association of Elementary School Principals. *Standards for Quality Elementary and Middle Schools: Kindergarten through Eighth Grade.* Alexandria, VA, 1990.

Short, Kathy, and Burke, Carolyn. *Creating Curriculum.* Portsmouth, NH: Heinemann, 1981.

Rowan, Thomas E., and Morrow, Lorna J. *Implementing the K-8 Curriculum and Evaluation Standards: Readings from the "Arithmetic Teacher."* Reston, VA: National Council of Teachers of Mathematics, 1993.

Stevenson, S. Christopher and Carr, Judy F. *Integrated Studies in the Middle School: Dancing Through Walls.* New York: Teachers College Press, 1993.

Whitin, D.; Mills, H.; and O'Keefe, T. *Living and Learning Mathematics: Stories and Strategies for Supporting Mathematical Literacy.* Portsmouth, NH: Heinemann, 1990.

Curriculum — Integrated Activities

Bauer, Karen, and Drew, Rosa. *Alternatives to Worksheets.* Cypress, CA: Creative Teaching Press, 1992.

Beierle, Marlene, and Lynes, Teri. *Book Cooks: Literature-Based Classroom Cooking (4-6).* Cypress, CA: 1992.

Brainard, Audrey, and Wrubel, Denise H. *Literature-Based Science Activities: An Integrated Approach.* New York: Scholastic, 1993.

Bruno, Janet. *Book Cooks: Literature-Based Classroom Cooking (K-3).* Cypress, CA: Creative Teaching Press, 1991.

Burns, Marilyn. *About Teaching Mathematics.* Sausalito, CA: Math Solutions Publications, 1992.

———.*A Collection of Math Lessons: From Grades 3 Through 6.* White Plains: Cuisinaire Company of America, 1987.

Burns, Marilyn, and Tank, B. *A Collection of Math Lessons: From Grades 1 Through 3.* White Plains: Cuisinaire Company of America, 1987.

Cherkerzian, Diane. *The Complete Lesson Plan Book.* Peterborough, NH: Crystal Springs Books, 1993.

Cochrane, Orin, ed. *Reading Experiences in Science.* Winnipeg, Man.: Peguis, 1985.

Forsten, Char. *Teaching Thinking and Problem Solving in Math.* New York: Scholastic Professional Books, 1992.

———.*Using Calculators is Easy!* Scholastic Professional Books, 1992.

Goin, Kenn; Ripp, Eleanor; and Solomon, Kathleen Nastasi. *Bugs to Bunnies: Hands-on Animal Science Activities for Young Children.* New York: Chatterbox Press, 1989.

Hiatt, Catherine; Wolven, Doug; Botka, Gwen; and Richmond, Jennifer. *More Alternatives to Worksheets.* Cypress, CA: Creative Teaching Press, 1994.

Huck, Charlotte, and Hickman, Janet, eds. *The Best of the Web.* Columbus, OH: Ohio State University, 1982.

Irvine, Joan. *How to Make Pop-ups.* New York: Beech Tree Books, 1987.

———.*How to Make Super Pop-ups.* New York: Beech Tree Books, 1992.

Johnson, Virginia. *Hands-On Math: Manipulative Activities for the Classroom.* Cypress, CA: Creative Teaching Press, Inc., 1994.

Jorgensen, Karen. *History Workshop.* Portsmouth, NH: Heinemann, 1993.

Kohl, MaryAnn, and Potter, Jean. *ScienceArts: Discovering Science Through Art Experiences.* Bellingham, WA: Bright Ring Publishing, 1993.

McCarthy, Tara. *Literature-Based Geography Activities: An Integrated Approach*. New York: Scholastic, 1992.

Ritter, Darlene. *Literature-Based Art Activities (K-3)*. Cypress, CA: Creative Teaching Press, 1992.

———.*Literature-Based Art Activities (4-6)*. Cypress, CA: Creative Teaching Press, 1992.

Steffey, Stephanie, and Hood, Wendy J., eds. *If This Is Social Studies, Why Isn't It Boring?* York, ME: Stenhouse Publishers, 1994.

Rothstein, Gloria Lesser. *From Soup to Nuts: Multicultural Cooking Activities and Recipes*. New York: Scholastic, 1994.

Ruef, Kerry. *The Private Eye. Looking/Thinking by Analogy: A Guide to Developing the Interdisciplinary Mind*. Seattle: The Private Eye Project, 1992.

Spann, Mary Beth. *Literature-Based Multicultural Activities*. New York: Scholastic, 1992.

———.*Literature-Based Seasonal and Holiday Activities*. New York: Scholastic, 1991.

Developmental Education

Ames, Louise Bates. *What Do They Mean I'm Difficult?* Rosemont, NJ: Modern Learning Press, 1986.

Ames, Louise Bates; Baker, Sidney; and Ilg, Frances L. *Child Behavior (Specific Advice on Problems of Child Behavior)*. New York: Barnes & Noble Books, 1981.

Ames, Louise Bates, and Chase, Joan Ames. *Don't Push Your Pre-Schooler*. New York: Harper & Row, 1980.

Ames, Louise Bates, and Haber, Carol Chase. *He Hit Me First (When Brothers and Sisters Fight)*. New York: Dembner Books, 1982.

———.*Your Seven-Year-Old (Life in a Minor Key)*. New York: Dell, 1985.

———.*Your Eight-Year-Old (Lively and Outgoing)*. New York: Dell, 1989.

———.*Your Nine-Year-Old (Thoughtful and Mysterious)*. New York: Dell, 1990.

Ames, Louise Bates, and Ilg, Frances L. *Child Behavior*. New York: Barnes & Noble Books, 1955.

———.*The Child from Five to Ten*. New York: Harper & Row, 1946.

———.*Your Two-Year-Old (Terrible or Tender)*. New York: Dell, 1980.

———.*Your Three-Year-Old (Friend or Enemy)*. New York: Dell, 1980.

———.*Your Four-Year-Old (Wild and Wonderful)*. New York: Dell, 1980.

———.*Your Five-Year-Old, Sunny and Serene*. New York: Dell, 1979.

———.*Your Six-Year-Old, Loving and Defiant*. New York: Dell, 1979.

———.*Your Ten-to-Fourteen Year-Old*. New York: Dell, 1981.

Ames, Louise Bates; Ilg, Frances L.; and Haber, Frances L. *Your One-Year-Old (The Fun-Loving 12-to-24-month-old)*. New York: Delacorte, 1982.

Ames, Louise Bates, et al. *The Gesell Institute's Child from One to Six*. New York: Harper & Row, 1946.

Bluestein, Jane. *Being a Successful Teacher—A Practical Guide to Instruction and Management*. Belmont, CA: Fearon Teacher Aids, 1988.

Bluestein, Jane, and Collins, Lynn. *Parents in a Pressure Cooker*. Rosemont, NJ: Modern Learning Press, 1990.

Boyer, Ernest. *The Basic School: A Community for Learning*. Ewing, NJ: Carnegie Foundation for the Advancement of Learning, 1995.

———.*Ready to Learn: A Mandate for the Nation*. Princeton, NJ: The Foundation for the Advancement of Teaching, 1991.

Brazelton, T. Berry. *Working and Caring*. Reading, MA: Addison-Wesley, 1985.

———.*To Listen to a Child: Understanding the Normal Problems of Growing Up*. Reading, MA: Addison-Wesley, 1986.

Bredekamp, Sue, ed. *Developmentally Appropriate Practice in Early Childhood Programs Serving Children From Birth Through Age 8*, expanded edition. Washington, DC: National Association for the Education of Young Children, 1987.

Elovson, Allanna. *The Kindergarten Survival Book*. Santa Monica, CA: Parent Ed Resources, 1991.

Grant, Jim. *Childhood Should Be a Precious Time*. (poem anthology) Rosemont, NJ: Modern Learning Press.

———.*"I Hate School!" Some Common Sense Answers for Parents Who Wonder Why, Including the Signs and Signals of the Overplaced Child*. Rosemont, NJ: Programs for Education, 1994.

———.*Jim Grant's Book of Parent Pages*. Rosemont, NJ: Programs for Education, 1988.

———.*Worth Repeating: Giving Children a Second Chance at School Success*. Rosemont, NJ: Modern Learning Press, 1989.

———.*Developmental Education in the 1990's*. Rosemont, NJ: Modern Learning Press, 1991.

Grant, Jim, and Azen, Margot. *Every Parent's Owner's Manuals. (Three-, Four-, Five-, Six-, Seven-Year- Old)*. Rosemont, NJ. Programs for Education.

Hayes, Martha, and Faggella, Kathy. *Think It Through*. Bridgeport CT: First Teacher Press, 1986.

Healy, Jane M. *Endangered Minds: Why Children Don't Think and What We Can Do About It*. New York: Simon and Schuster, 1990.

———.*Your Child's Growing Mind: A Guide to Learning and Brain Development From Birth to Adolescence*. New York: Doubleday, 1987.

Holt, John. *How Children Fail*. New York: Dell Publishing, 1964, 1982.

Horowitz, Janet, and Faggella, Kathy. *Partners for Learning*. Bridgeport, CT: First Teacher Press, 1986.

Lamb, Beth, and Logsdon, Phyllis. *Positively Kindergarten: A Classroom-proven, Theme-based Developmental Guide for the Kindergarten Teacher*. Rosemont, NJ: Modern Learning Press, 1991.

Mallory, Bruce, and New, Rebecca, eds. *Diversity and Developmentally Appropriate Practices: Challenges for Early Childhood Education*. New York: Teachers College Press, 1994.

Miller, Karen. *Ages and Stages: Developmental Descriptions and Activities Birth Through Eight Years*. Chelsea, MA: Telshare Publishing Co., 1985.

National Association of Elementary School Principals. *Early Childhood Education and the Elementary School Principal*. Alexandria, VA: NAESP, 1990.

National Association of State Boards of Education. *Right from the Start: The Report of the NASBE Task Force on Early Childhood Education*. Alexandria, VA: NASBE, 1988.

Northeast Foundation for Children. *A Notebook for Teachers: Making Changes in the Elementary Curriculum*. Greenfield, MA, 1991.

Reavis, George H. *The Animal School*. Rosemont, NJ: Modern Learning Press, 1988.

Singer, Dorothy, and Revenson, Tracy. *How a Child Thinks: A Piaget Primer*. Independence, MO: International University Press, 1978.

Wood, Chip. *Yardsticks: Children in the Classroom Ages 4-12*. Greenfield, MA: Northeast Foundation for Children, 1994.

Grade Replacement

Ames, Louise Bates. *What Am I Doing in This Grade?* Rosemont, NJ: Modern Learning Press, 1985.

———.*Is Your Child in the Wrong Grade?* Rosemont, NJ: Modern Learning Press, 1978.

Ames, Louise Bates; Gillespie, Clyde; and Streff, John W. *Stop School Failure*. Rosemont, NJ: Modern Learning Press, 1972.

Grant, Jim. *I Hate School*. Rosemont, NJ: Modern Learning Press, 1986.

————.*Worth Repeating*. Rosemont, NJ: Modern Learning Press, 1989.

Healy, Jane M., Ph.D. *Your Child's Growing Mind*. New York: Doubleday & Co., 1987.

Hobby, Janice Hale. *Staying Back*. Gainesville, FL: Triad, 1990.

Moore, Sheila, and Frost, Roon. *The Little Boy Book*. New York: Clarkson N. Potter, 1986.

Grade Replacement — Audio/Video
(All from Modern Learing Press, PO Box 167, Rosemont, NJ 08556. 1-800-627-5867)

Ames, Louise Bates. *Part I: Ready Or Not: Here I Come!* and *Part II: An Evaluation of the Whole Child*, video. 1983.

Gesell Institute of Human Development. *Ready or Not Here I Come!* Video/16 mm film. 1984.

Grant, Jim. *Jim Grant Live*. Audiotape. 1985.

————.*Grade Replacement*. Audiotape. 1988.

————.*Worth Repeating*. Video. 1988.

————.*Do You Know Where Your Child Is?* Video, 1985.

Inclusion / Differently Abled / Learning Disabilities

Dudley-Marling, Curtis. *When School is a Struggle*. New York: Scholastic, 1990.

Bailey, D.B, and Wolery, M. *Teaching Infants and Preschoolers with Handicaps*. Columbus, OH: Merrill, 1984.

Dunn, Kathryn B., and Dunn, Allison B. *Trouble with School: A Family Story about Learning Disabilities*. Rockville, MD: Woodbine House, 1993.

Fagan, S.A.; Graves, D.L.; and Tressier-Switlick, D. *Promoting Successful Mainstreaming: Reasonable Classroom Accommodations for Learning Disabled Students*. Rockville, MD: Montgomery Couny Public Schools, 1984.

Friend, Marilyn, and Cook, Lynne. "The New Mainstreaming." *Instructor Magazine*, (March 1992): 30-35.

Goodman, Gretchen. *Inclusive Classrooms from A to Z: A Handbook for Educators*. Columbus, OH: Teachers' Publishing Group, 1994.

Harwell, Joan. *Complete Learning Disabilities Handbook*. New York: Simon & Schuster, 1989.

Jenkins, J., and Jenkins, L. "Peer Tutoring in Elementary and Secondary Programs." In *Effective Strategies for Exceptional Children*, edited by Meyer, E.L.; Vergason, G.A.; and Whelan, R.J., 335-354, Denver, CO: Love Publishing Co., 1988.

Lang, Greg, and Berberich, Chris. *All Children are Special: Creating an Inclusive Classroom*. York, ME: Stenhouse Publishers, 1995.

McGregor, G., and Vogelsberg, R.T. *Transition Needs Assessment for Parents*. Philadelphia, PA: Temple University, 1989.

Perske, R. and Perske, M. *Circle of Friends*. Nashville, TN: Abingdon Press, 1988.

Phinney, Margaret. *Reading with the Troubled Reader*. Portsmouth, NH: Heinemann, 1989.

Rainforth, Beverly; York, Jennifer; and McDonald, Cathy. *Collaborative Teams for Students with Severe Disabilities*. Baltimore: Paul H. Brookes, 1992.

Rhodes, Lynn, and Dudley-Marling, Curtis. *Readers and Writers with a Difference: A Holistic Approach to Teaching Learning Disabled and Remedial Students*. Portsmouth: Heinemann, 1988.

Rosner, Jerome. *Helping Children Overcome Learning Difficulties*. New York: Walker and Co., 1979.

Society For Developmental Education. *Creating Inclusive Classrooms: Education for All Children*. Peterborough, NH: 1994.

Stainback, S., and Stainback, W. *Curriculum Considerations in Inclusive Classrooms: Facilitating Learning for All Students*. Baltimore: Paul H. Brookes, 1992.

———.*Support Networks for Inclusive Schooling*. Baltimore: Paul H. Brookes, 1990.

Stainback, S, Stainback, W., and Forest, M., eds. *Educating All Students in the Mainstream of Regular Education*. Baltimore: Paul H. Brookes, 1987.

Thousand, J., and Villa, R. "Strategies for Educating Learners with Severe Handicaps Within Their Local Home, Schools and Communities." *Focus on Exceptional Children*, 23 (3), 1-25, 1990.

Vail, Priscilla. *About Dyslexia*. Rosemont, NJ: Programs for Education, 1990.

———.*Smart Kids with School Problems*. New York: E.P. Dutton, 1987.

Vandercook, T., and York, J. "A Team Approach to Program Development and Support." In *Support Networks for Inclusive Schooling: Interdependent Integrated Education*, edited by Stainback, W. and Stainback, S., 95-122. Baltimore: Paul H. Brookes, 1990.

Villa, R., et al. *Restructuring for Caring and Effective Education: Administrative Strategies for Creating Heterogeneous Schools*. Baltimore: Paul H. Brookes, 1992.

Issues in Education

Ledell, Marjorie and Arnsparger, Arleen. *How to Deal with Community Criticism of School Change*. Alexendria, VA: Association for Supervision and Curriculum Development, 1993.

National Commission on Excellence in Education. *Nation at Risk: The Full Account*. USA Research Staff (ed.), 1984.

———.*Nation at Risk: The Full Account*. 2nd ed. USA Research Inc. Staff (ed.), 1992.

Language Arts

Allen, JoBeth, and Mason, Jana, eds. *Risk Makers, Risk Breakers*. Portsmouth, NH: Heinemann, 1989.

Andrasick, Kathleen. *Opening Texts*. Portsmouth, NH: Heinemann, 1990.

Atwell, Nancie. *Coming to Know: Writing to Learn in the Middle Grades*. Portsmouth, NH: Heinemann, 1990.

———.*In the Middle: Writing, Reading, and Learning with Adolescents*. Portsmouth, NH: Heinemann, 1987.

———.*Side by Side: Essays on Teaching to Learn*. Portsmouth, NH: Heinemann, 1991.

———.*Workshop 1: Writing and Literature*. Portsmouth, NH: Heinemann, 1989.

———.*Workshop 2: Beyond the Basal*. Portsmouth, NH: Heinemann, 1989.

———.*Workshop 3: The Politics of Process*. Portsmouth, NH: Heinemann, 1991.

Barrett, F.L. *A Teacher's Guide to Shared Reading*. Toronto, Ont.: Scholastic TAB, 1982.

Barron, Marlene. *I Learn to Read and Write the Way I Learn to Talk*. Katonah, NY: Richard C. Owen Publishers, 1990.

Barton, Bob. *Tell Me Another*. Portsmouth, NH: Heinemann, 1986.

Baskwill, Jane. *Connections: A Child's Natural Learning Tool*. Toronto, Ont.: Scholastic TAB, 1982.

Baskwill, Jane, and Steven. *The Language Arts Sourcebook: Whole Language, Grades 5 and 6*. Toronto: Scholastic, 1991.

Baskwill, Jane, and Whitman, Paulette. *A Guide to Classroom Publishing*. Toronto: Scholastic TAB, 1988.

———.*Moving On: Whole Language Sourcebook for Grades 3 and 4*. Toronto, Ont.: Scholastic TAB, 1988.

———.*Whole Language Sourcebook: Grades K-2*. Toronto: Scholastic TAB, 1986.

Beeler, Terri. *I Can Read! I Can Write! Creating a Print-Rich Environment*. Cypress, CA: Creative Teaching Press, 1993.

Beierle, Marlene, and Lynes, Teri. *Teaching Basic Skills through Literature: A Whole Language Approach for Teaching Reading Skills*. Cypress, CA: Creative Teaching Press, 1993.

Bird, Lois Bridge. *Becoming a Whole Language School: The Fair Oaks Story*. Katonah, NY: Richard C. Owen Publishers, 1989.

Bissex, Glenda. *GNYS AT WRK*. Cambridge, MA: Harvard University Press, 1980.

Bissex, Glenda, and Bullock, Richard, eds. *Seeing for Ourselves*. Portsmouth, NH: Heinemann, 1987.

Blake, Robert, ed. *Whole Language: Explorations and Applications*. New York: New York State English Council, 1990.

Bosma, Bette. *Fairy Tales, Fables, Legends, and Myths*. New York: Teacher's College Press, 1987.

Bromley, Karen. *Journalling: Engagements in Reading, Writing, and Thinking*. New York: Scholastic, 1993.

Brown, Hazel, and Mathie, Vonne. *Inside Whole Language: A Classroom View*. Portsmouth, NH: Heinemann, 1991.

Buchanan, Ethel. *For the Love of Reading*. Winnipeg, Man.: The C.E.L. Group, 1980.

Buncombe, Fran, and Peetoom, Adrian. *Literature-Based Learning: One School's Journey*. New York: Scholastic, 1988.

Buros, Jay. *Why Whole Language?* Rosemont, NJ: Programs for Education, 1991.

Butler, Andrea, and Turbill, Jan. *Towards a Reading-Writing Classroom*. Portsmouth, NH: Heinemann, 1984.

Butler, Dorothy. *Cushla and Her Books*. Boston: The Horn Book, 1980.

Calkins, Lucy M. *The Art of Teaching Writing*. Portsmouth, NH: Heinemann, 1986.

———.*Lessons from a Child: On the Teaching and Learning of Writing*. Portsmouth, NH: Heinemann, 1983.

———.*Living Between the Lines*. Portsmouth, NH: Heinemann, 1990.

Cambourne, Brian. *The Whole Story*. New York: Scholastic, 1988.

Cambourne, Brian, and Brown, Hazel. *Read and Retell*. Portsmouth, NH: Heinemann, 1990.

Cambourne, Brian, and Turbill, Jan. *Coping with Chaos*. Portsmouth, NH: Heinemann, 1988.

Clay, Marie. *Becoming Literate*. Portsmouth, NH: Heinemann, 1991.

———.*Sand* and *Stones: "Concepts about Print" Tests*. Portsmouth, NH: Heinemann, 1980.

———.*Observing Young Readers*. Portsmouth, NH: Heinemann, 1982.

———.*Reading Recovery: A Guidebook for Teachers in Training*. Portsmouth, NH: Heinemann, 1993.

———.*What Did I Write?* Portsmouth, NH: Heinemann, 1975.

Clifford, John. *The Experience of Reading: Louise Rosenblatt and Reader-Response Theory*. Portsmouth, NH: Heinemann, 1991.

Cloonan, Kathryn L. *Sing Me A Story, Read Me a Song* (Books I and II). Beverly Hills, FL: Rhythm & Reading Resources, 1991.

———.*Whole Language Holidays*. (Books I and II). Beverly Hills, FL: Rhythm & Reading Resources, 1992.

Collis, Mark, and Dalton, Joan. *Becoming Responsible Learners*. Portsmouth, NH: Heinemann, 1991.

Cochrane, Orin et al. *Reading, Writing, and Caring*. Katonah, NY: Richard C. Owen Publishers, 1985.

Crafton, Linda. *Whole Language: Getting Started, Moving Forward*. Katonah, NY: Richard C. Owen Publishers, 1991.

Cullinan, Bernice. *Children's Literature in the Reading Program*. Newark, DE: International Reading Association, 1987.

———.*Pen in Hand*. Newark, DE: International Reading Association, 1993.

Cutting, Brian. *Talk Your Way to Reading*. Auckland, New Zealand: Shortland Publications, 1985.

———.*Getting Started in Whole Language*. Auckland, New Zealand: Applecross, 1989.

Dakos, Kalli. *What's There to Write About?* New York: Scholastic, 1989.

Daniels, Harvey. *Literature Circles: Voice and Choice in the Student-Centered Classroom.* York, ME: Stenhouse Publishers, 1994.

Danielson, Kathy Everts, and Rogers, Sheri Everts. *Literature Connections Day-by-Day.* New York: Scholastic, 1994.

Davidson, Merrilyn et al. *Moving on with Big Books.* Auckland, New Zealand: Ashton Scholastic, 1989.

DeFord, Diane et al. *Bridges to Literacy.* Portsmouth, NH: Heinemann, 1991.

Department of Education, Victoria. *Beginning Reading.* Victoria: Department of Education, 1984.

Department of Education, Wellington, New Zealand. *Reading in Junior Classes.* New York: Richard C. Owen Publishers, 1985.

Dewey, John. *The Child and the Curriculum* and *The School and Society.* Chicago: Phoenix Books, combined edition, 1956.

Drutman, Ava Deutsch, and Huston, Diane L. *150 Surefire Ways to Keep Them Reading All Year.* New York: Scholastic, 1992.

Dudley-Marling, Curtis, and Searle, Dennis. *When Students Have Time to Talk.* Portsmouth, NH: Heinemann, 1991.

Edelsky, Carole; Altwerger, Bess; and Flores, Barbara. *Whole Language: What's the Difference?* Portsmouth, NH: Heinemann, 1990.

Eisele, Beverly. *Managing the Whole Language Classroom: A Complete Teaching Resource Guide for K-6 Teachers.* Cypress, CA: Creative Teaching Press, 1991.

Fairfax, Barbara, and Garcia, Adela. *Read! Write! Publish!* Cypress, CA: Creative Teaching Press, 1992.

Ferreiro, Emilia, and Teberosky, Ana. *Literacy Before Schooling.* Portsmouth, NH: Heinemann, 1979.

Fisher, Bobbi. *Joyful Learning: A Whole Language Kindergarten.* Portsmouth, NH: Heinemann, 1991.

Five, Cora Lee. *Special Voices.* Portsmouth, NH: Heinemann, 1991.

Fletcher, Ralph. *What a Writer Needs.* Portsmouth, NH: Heinemann, 1992.

Frank, Marjorie. *If You're Trying to Teach Kids How to Write, You've Gotta Have This Book.* Nashville, TN: Incentive Publications, 1979.

Freeman, Yvonne, and Freeman, David. *Whole Language for Second Language Learners.* Portsmouth, NH: Heinemann, 1992.

Froese, Victor, ed. Whole Language: *Theory and Practice.* Scarborough, Ont.: Prentice Hall, 1990.

Fulwiler, Toby, ed. *The Journal Book.* Portsmouth, NH: Heinemann, 1987.

———.*Programs That Work: Models and Methods for Writing Across the Curriculum.* Portsmouth, NH: Heinemann, 1990.

Furniss, Elaine, ed. *The Literacy Agenda.* Portsmouth, NH: Heinemann, 1991.

Garvey, Catherine. *Children's Talk.* Boston: Harvard Press, 1984. (Part of the Developing Child Series.)

Geller, Linda Gibson. *Word Play and Language Learning for Children.* Urbana, IL: National Council of Teachers of English, 1985.

Goodman, Kenneth. *What's Whole in Whole Language?* New York: Scholastic, 1986.

Goodman, Kenneth, et al. *Language and Thinking in School: A Whole-Language Curriculum.* Katonah, NY: Richard C. Owen Publishers, 1987.

———.*Report Card on Basals.* New York: Richard C. Owen Publishers, 1988.

Goodman, Yetta. *How Children Construct Literacy.* Newark, DE: International Reading Association, 1990.

Goodman, Yetta M.; Hood, Wendy J.; and Goodman, Kenneth S. *Organizing for Whole Language.* Portsmouth, NH: Heinemann, 1991.

Graves, Donald. *Build a Literate Classroom*. Portsmouth, NH: Heinemann, 1991.

———. *A Researcher Learns to Write*. Portsmouth, NH: Heinemann, 1984.

———. *Discover Your Own Literacy*. Portsmouth, NH: Heinemann, 1990.

———. *Experiment with Fiction*. Portsmouth, NH: Heinemann, 1990.

———. *Investigate Nonfiction*. Portsmouth, NH: Heinemann, 1989.

———. *Writing: Teachers and Children at Work*. Portsmouth, NH: Heinemann, 1983.

Graves, Donald, and Stuart, Virginia. *Write from the Start*. New York: New American Library, 1985.

Greenwood, Barbara. *The Other Side of the Story*. Toronto, Ont.: Scholastic Tab, 1990.

Gunderson, Lee. *A Whole Language Primer*. New York: Scholastic, 1989.

Haack, Pam, and Merrilees, Cynthia. *Ten Ways to Become a Better Reader*. Cleveland, OH: Modern Curriculum Press, 1991.

———. *Write on Target*. Peterborough, NH: The Society For Developmental Education, 1991.

Hall, Nigel, and Robertson, Anne. *Some Day You Will No All About Me: Young Children's Explorations in the World of Letters*. Portsmouth, NH: Heinemann, 1991.

Hancock, Joelie, and Hill, Susan, eds. *Literature-Based Reading Programs at Work*. Portsmouth, NH: Heinemann, 1988.

Hansen, Jane. *When Writers Read*. Portsmouth, NH: Heinemann, 1987.

Hansen, Jane; Newkirk, Thomas; and Graves, Donald, eds. *Breaking Ground: Teachers Relate Reading and Writing in the Elementary School*. Portsmouth, NH: Heinemann, 1985.

Harste, Jerome, and Short, Kathy. *Creating Classrooms for Authors: The Reading-Writing Connection*. Portsmouth, NH: Heinemann, 1988.

Harste, Jerome; Woodward, Virginia; and Burke, Carolyn. *Language Stories and Literacy Lessons*. Portsmouth, NH: Heinemann, 1984.

Hart-Hewins, Linda, and Wells, Jan. *Read It In The Classroom!* Portsmouth, NH: Heinemann, 1992.

Harwayne, Shelley. *Lasting Impressions: Weaving Literature into the Writing Workshop*. Portsmouth, NH: Heinemann, 1992.

Hayes, Martha. *Building on Books*. Bridgeport, CT: First Teacher Press, 1987.

Heald-Taylor, Gail. *The Administrator's Guide to Whole Language*. Katonah, NY: Richard C. Owen, 1989.

Heard, Georgia. *For the Good of the Earth and Sun: Teaching Poetry*. Portsmouth, NH: Heinemann, 1989.

Holdaway, Don. *The Foundations of Literacy*. New York: Scholastic, 1979.

———. *Stability and Change in Literacy Learning*. Portsmouth, NH: Heinemann, 1984.

Holly, Mary Louise. *Writing to Grow: Keeping a Personal-Professional Journal*. Portsmouth, NH: Heinemann, 1989.

Hopkins, Lee. *Pass the Poetry Please*. New York: Harper & Row, 1987.

Hornsby, David; Sukarna, Deborah; and Parry, Jo-Ann. *Read On: A Conference Approach to Reading*. Portsmouth, NH: Heinemann, 1986.

———. *Teach On*. Portsmouth, NH: Heinemann, 1984.

Hubbard, Ruth. *Authors of Pictures, Draughtsmen of Words*. Portsmouth, NH: Heinemann, 1989.

Hubbard, Ruth, and Power, Brenda. *The Art of Classroom Inquiry*. Portsmouth, NH: Heinemann, 1993.

Infant Education Committee. *Beginning Reading*. Victoria: Education Department, 1984.

Johnson, Paul. *A Book of One's Own*. Portsmouth, NH: Heinemann, 1992.

———. *Literacy Through the Book Arts*. Portsmouth, NH: Heinemann, 1993.

Johnson, Terry, and Louis, Daphne. *Literacy through Literature*. Portsmouth, NH: Heinemann, 1987.

———.*Bringing It All Together*. Portsmouth, NH: Heinemann, 1993.

Karelitz, Ellen Blackburn. *The Author's Chair and Beyond*. Portsmouth, NH: Heinemann, 1993.

Kitagawa, Mary, and Kitagawa, Chisato. *Making Connections with Writing*. Portsmouth, NH: Heinemann, 1987.

Kovaks, Deborah, and Preller, James. *Meet the Authors and Illustrators: 60 Creators of Favorite Children's Books Talk about Their Work*, Vol. 1. New York: Scholastic, 1991.

———.*Meet the Authors and Illustrators: 60 Creators of Favorite Children's Books Talk about Their Work*, Vol. 2. New York: Scholastic, 1993.

Lamme, Linda. *Highlights for Children: Growing up Reading*. Reston, VA: Acropolis Books, 1984.

———.*Growing up Writing*. Reston, VA: Acropolis Books, 1984.

Lloyd, Pamela. *How Writers Write*. Portsmouth, NH: Heinemann, 1987.

Lynch, Priscilla. *Using Big Books and Predictable Books*. New York: Scholastic, 1987.

Mann, Jean. *Literacy Labels* (six book set). Columbus, OH: Essential Learning Products, 1994.

McClure, Amy; Harrison, Peggy; and Reed, Sheryl. *Sunrises and Songs*. Portsmouth, NH: Heinemann, 1990.

McConaghy, June. *Children's Learning Through Literature*. Portsmouth, NH: Heinemann, 1990.

McCracken, Robert and Marlene. *Stories, Songs and Poetry to Teach Reading and Writing*. Chicago: American Library Association, 1986.

———.Reading, Writing and Language: A Practical Guide for Primary Teachers. Winnipeg, Man.: Peguis, 1995.

McKenzie, Moira. *Journeys into Literacy*. Huddersfield: Schofield & Sims, 1986.

McTeague, Frank. *Shared Reading in the Middle and High School Years*. Portsmouth, NH: Heinemann, 1992.

McVitty, Walter. *Children and Learning*. PETA (Heinemann), 1985.

———.*Getting It Together: Organizing the Reading-Writing Classroom*. Portsmouth, NH: Heinemann, 1986.

Meek, Margaret, ed. *Opening Moves*. London: University of London Institute of Education, 1983.

Miller, Joan. *Sharing Ideas: An Oral Language Programme*. Melbourne: Nelson Publishing Co., 1988.

Mills, Heidi, and Clyde, Jean Anne. *Portraits of Whole Language Classrooms*. Portsmouth, NH: Heinemann, 1990.

Moffett, James, and Wagner, Betty Jane. *Student-Centered Language Arts, K-12*, Fourth Edition. Portsmouth, NH: Boynton/Cook, 1991.

Mooney, Margaret. *Developing Life-Long Readers*. Katonah, NY: Richard C. Owen Publishers, 1988.

Murray, Donald. *Learning by Teaching*. Portsmouth, NH: Boynton-Cook, 1982.

Myers, Miles. *The Teacher-Researcher: How to Study Writing in the Classroom*. Urbana, IL: National Council of Teachers of English, 1985.

NCTE and IRA. *Cases in Literacy*. International Reading Association and National Council of Teachers of English, 1985.

Newman, Judith, ed. *Whole Language: Theory in Use*. Portsmouth, NH: Heinemann, 1985.

———.*The Craft of Children's Writing*. Portsmouth, NH: Heinemann, 1985.

———, ed. *Finding Our Own Way*. Portsmouth, NH: Heinemann, 1990.

Newkirk, Thomas. *More Than Stories*. Portsmouth, NH: Heinemann, 1989.

———.*Nuts and Bolts*. Portsmouth, NH: Heinemann, 1993.

Nova Scotia Department of Education. *Language Arts in the Elementary School*. Curriculum Development Guide No. 86, 1986.

Olsen, Janet. *Envisioning Writing*. Portsmouth, NH: Heinemann, 1992.

Paley, Vivian. *Molly Is Three*. Chicago: University of Chicago, 1986.

———. *Wally's Stories*. Boston: Harvard Educational Press, 1981.

Parsons, Les. *Poetry, Themes, and Activities*. Portsmouth, NH: Heinemann, 1992.

———. *Writing in the Real Classroom*. Portsmouth, NH: Heinemann, 1991.

Peetboom, Adrian. *Shared Reading: Safe Risks with Whole Books*. Toronto, Ont.: Scholastic TAB, 1986.

Peterson, Ralph, and Maryann Eeds. *Grand Conversations: Literature Groups in Action*. New York: Scholastic, 1990.

———. *Life in a Crowded Place: Making a Learning Community*. Portsmouth, NH: Heinemann, 1992.

Picciotto, Linda Pierce. *Managing an Integrated Language Arts Classroom*. Ontario: Scholastic, 1995.

Pigdon, Keith, and Woolley, Marilyn. *The Big Picture: Integrating Children's Learning*. Portsmouth, NH: Heinemann, 1993.

Pinnell, Gay Su. *Teachers and Research: Language Learning in the Classroom*. Newark, DE: International Reading Association, 1989.

Raines, Shirley C., and Canady, Robert J. *Story Stretchers*. Mt. Ranier, MD: Gryphon House, 1989.

———. *More Story Stretchers*. Mt. Ranier, MD: Gryphon House, 1991.

———. *Story Stretchers for the Primary Grades*. Mt. Ranier, MD: Gryphon House, 1992.

———. *The Whole Language Kindergarten*. New York: Scholastic, 1993.

Rief, Linda. *Seeking Diversity: Language Arts with Adolescents*. Portsmouth, NH: Heinemann, 1992.

Romano, Tom. *Clearing the Way*. Portsmouth, NH: Heinemann, 1987.

Routman, Regie. *Transitions: From Literature to Literacy*. Portsmouth, NH: Heinemann, 1988.

———. *Invitations: Changing as Teachers and Learners K-12*. Portsmouth, NH: Heinemann, 1991.

Roy, Susan, ed. *Young Imagination*. New South Wales: Primary English Teaching Association, 1988.

Sampson, Michael. *Pathways to Literacy*. New York: Holt, Rinehart & Winston, 1991.

Schell, Leo. *How to Create an Independent Reading Program*. New York: Scholastic, 1991.

Schickedanz, Judith. *Adam's Righting Revolutions*. Portsmouth, NH: Heinemann, 1990.

Schlosser, Kristin G., and Phillips, Vicki L. *Beginning in Whole Language: A Practical Guide*. New York: Scholastic, 1991.

———. *Building Literacy with Interactive Charts*. New York: Scholastic, 1991.

Schwartz, Susan. *Creating the Child-Centered Classroom*. Katonah, NY: Richard C. Owen Publishers, 1991.

Shannon, Patrick. *Becoming Political*. Portsmouth, NH: Heinemann, 1990.

———. *The Struggle to Continue*. Portsmouth, NH: Heinemann, 1990.

Shedlock, Marie. *The Art of the Storyteller*. New York: Dover Press, 1951.

Short, Kathy, and Pierce, Kathryn, eds. *Talking About Books*. Portsmouth, NH: Heinemann, 1990.

Silko, Leslie Marmon. *Storyteller*. New York: Seaver Books, 1981.

Sloan, Peter and Ross Latham. *Teaching Reading Is...* Melbourne: Nelson, 1981.

Smith, Frank. *Essays into Literacy*. Portsmouth, NH: Heinemann, 1983.

———. *Insult to Intelligence*. Portsmouth, NH: Heinemann, 1986.

———.*Joining the Literacy Club*. Portsmouth, NH: Heinemann, 1988.

———.*Reading Without Nonsense*. New York: Teachers College Press, 1978.

———.*Understanding Reading*. Hillsdale, NJ: Lawrence Erlbaum Publishers, 1986.

Sobut, Mary A., and Bogen, Bonnie Neuman. *Whole Language Literature Activities for Young Children*. West Nyack, NY: The Center for Applied Research in Education, 1993.

Somerfield, Muriel. *A Framework for Reading*. Portsmouth, NH: Heinemann, 1985.

Stephens, Diane. *What Matters? A Primer for Teaching Reading*. Portsmouth, NH: Heinemann, 1990.

Strickland, Dorothy. *Emerging Literacy: Young Children Learn to Read and Write*. Newark, DE: International Reading Association, 1989.

Sunflower, Cherilyn. *75 Creative Ways to Publish Students' Writing*. New York: Scholastic, 1993.

Taylor, Denny. *Family Literacy*. Portsmouth, NH: Heinemann, 1983.

———.*Learning Denied*. Portsmouth, NH: Heinemann, 1990.

Taylor, Denny, and Dorsey-Gaines, Catherine. *Growing Up Literate*. Portsmouth, NH: Heinemann, 1990.

Turbill, Jan, ed. *No Better Way to Teach Writing!* Portsmouth, NH: Heinemann, 1982.

Van Manen, Max. *The Tone of Teaching*. Portsmouth, NH: Heinemann, 1986.

Ward, Geoff. *I've Got a Project*. Australia: PETA, 1988. (Distributed in the United States by Heinemann, Portsmouth, NH.)

Watson, Dorothy. *Whole Language: Inquiring Voices*. New York: Scholastic, 1989.

Weaver, Constance. *Reading Process and Practice*. Portsmouth, NH: Heinemann, 1988.

———.*Understanding Whole Language*. Portsmouth, NH: Heinemann, 1990.

Weaver, Constance, and Henke, Linda, eds. *Supporting Whole Language*. Portsmouth, NH: Heinemann, 1992.

Wells, Gordon. *The Meaning Makers*. Portsmouth, NH: Heinemann, 1986.

Wilde, Jack. *A Door Opens: Writing in Fifth Grade*. Portsmouth, NH: Heinemann, 1993.

Wollman-Bonilla, Julie. *Response Journals*. New York: Scholastic, 1991.

Language Arts — Bilingual

Whitmore, Kathryn F., and Crowell, Caryl G. *Inventing a Classroom: Life in a Bilingual, Whole Language Learning Community*. York, ME: Stenhouse Publishers, 1994.

Language Arts — Spelling and Phonics

Bean, Wendy, and Bouffler, Christine. *Spell by Writing*. Portsmouth, NH: Heinemann, 1988.

Bolton, Faye, and Snowball, Diane. *Ideas for Spelling*. Portsmouth, NH: Heinemann, 1993.

Booth, David. *Spelling Links*. Ontario: Pembroke Publishers, 1991.

Buchanan, Ethel. *Spelling for Whole Language Classrooms*. Winnipeg, Man.: The C.E.L. Group, 1989.

Fry, Edward, Ph.D. *1000 Instant Words*. Laguna Beach, CA: Laguna Beach Educational Books, 1994.

———.*Phonics Patterns: Onset and Rhyme Word Lists*. Laguna Beach Educational Books, 1994.

Gentry, J. Richard. *Spel . . . Is a Four-Letter Word*. New York: Scholastic, 1987.

Gentry, J. Richard, and Gillet, Jean Wallace. *Teaching Kids to Spell*. Portsmouth, NH: Heinemann, 1993.

Lacey, Cheryl. *Moving on in Spelling: Strategies and Activities for the Whole Language Classroom*. New York: Scolastic, 1994.

Powell, Debbie, and Hornsby, David. *Learning Phonics and Spelling in a Whole Language Classroom*. New York: Scholastic, 1993.

Trisler, Alana, and Cardiel, Patrice. *My Word Book*. Rosemont, NJ: Modern Learning Press, 1994.

———.*Words I Use When I Write*. Rosemont, NJ: Modern Learning Press, 1989.

———.*More Words I Use When I Write*. Rosemont, NJ: Modern Learning Press, 1990.

Vail, Priscilla. *Common Ground: Whole Language and Phonics Working Together*. Rosemont, NJ: Programs for Education, 1991.

Wagstaff, Janiel. *Phonics That Work! New Strategies for the Reading/Writing Classroom*. New York: Scholastic, 1995.

Wittels, Harriet, and Greisman, Joan. *How to Spell It*. New York: Putnam, 1982.

Learning Centers

Cook, Carole. *Math Learning Centers for the Primary Grades*. West Nynack, NY: The Center for Applied Research, 1992.

Poppe, Carol A., and Van Matre, Nancy A. *Language Arts Learning Centers for the Primary Grades*. West Nynack, NY: The Center for Applied Research in Education, 1991. 234 pages.

———.*Science Learning Centers for the Primary Grades*. West Nyack, NY: The Center for Applied Research in Education, 1985.

Wait, Shirleen S. *Reading Learning Centers for the Primary Grades*. West Nynack, NY: The Center for Applied Research, 1992.

Waynant, Louise, and Wilson, Robert M. *Learning Centers, A Guide for Effective Use*. Paoli, PA: Instructo Corp., 1974. 130 pages.

Learning Styles / Multiple Intelligences

Armstrong, Thomas. *In Their Own Way: Discovering and Encouraging Your Child's Personal Learning Style*. New York: Putnam, 1987. 212 pages.

———.*Multiple Intelligences in the Classroom*. Alexandria, VA: Association for Supervision and Curriculum Development, 1994. 198 pages.

Banks, Janet Caudill. *Creative Projects for Independent Learners*.

Bloom, Benjamin S. *All Our Children Learning: A Primer for Teachers and Other Educators*. New York: McGraw-Hill, 1981.

———,ed. *Developing Talent in Young People*. New York: Ballantine, 1985.

Carbo, Marie. *Reading Styles Inventory Manual*. Roslyn Heights, New York: National Reading Styles Institute, 1991.

Carbo, Marie; Dunn, Rita; and Dunn, Kenneth. *Teaching Students to Read Through Their Individual Learning Styles*. Needham Heights, MA: Allyn & Bacon, 1991.

Gardner, Howard. *Frames of Mind: The Theory of Multiple Intelligences*. New York: Basic Books, 1985.

———.*Multiple Intelligences: The Theory in Practice*. New York: Basic Books, 1990.

———.*The Unschooled Mind: How Children Think and How Schools Should Teach*. New York: Basic Books, 1990.

Gilbert, Labritta. *Do Touch: Instant, Easy Hands-on Learning Experiences for Young Children*. Mt. Ranier, MD: Gryphon House, 1989.

Lazear, David. *Multiple Intelligence Approaches to Assessment: Solving the Assessment Conundrum*. IRI/Skylight Publishing, Inc., 1994. 205 pages.

———.*Seven Pathways of Learning: Teaching Students and Parents About Multiple Intelligences*. Tucson, AZ: Zephyr Press, 1994. 241 pages.

———.*Seven Ways of Knowing: Teaching for Multiple Intelligences*. Palatine, IL: IRI/Skylight Publishing, Inc., 1991. 254 pages.

————.*Seven Ways of Teaching: The Artistry of Teaching With Multiple Intelligences*. 190 pages.

Vail, Priscilla. *Gifted, Precocious, or Just Plain Smart*. Rosemont, NJ: Programs for Education, 1987.

————.*Learning Styles: Food for Thought and 130 Practical Tips for Teachers K-4*. Rosemont, NJ: Modern Learning Press, 1992. 133 pages.

Learning Theory

Bailey, D.B.; Burchinal, M.R.; and McWilliam, R.A. "Age of Peers and Early Childhood Development." *Child Development* 64: 848-62, 1993.

Hart, Leslie. *Human Brain, Human Learning*. New York: Longman Press, 1983.

Rogoff, Barbara. *Apprenticeship in Thinking: Cognitive Development in Social Context*. New York: Oxford University Press, 1990.

Vygotsky, Lev. S. *Mind in Society: The Development of Higher Psychological Processes*. Michael Cole et al, eds. Cambridge, MA: Harvard University Press, 1978.

————.*Thought and Language*. Alexey Kozulin, ed. Cambridge, MA: MIT Press, 1986. 256 pages.

Multiage Education

American Association of School Administrators. *The Nongraded Primary: Making Schools Fit Children*, Arlington, VA, 1992.

Anderson, Robert H., and Pavan, Barbara Nelson. *Nongradedness: Helping It to Happen*. Lancaster, PA: Technomic Press, 1992.

Banks, Janet Caudill. *Creating the Multi-age Classroom*. Edmonds, WA: CATS Publications, 1995. 136 pages.

Bridge, Connie A.; Reitsma, Beverly S.; and Winograd, Peter N. *Primary Thoughts: Implementing Kentucky's Primary Program*. Lexington, KY: Kentucky Department of Education, 1993. 254 pages.

Chase, Penelle, and Doan, Joan. *Full Circle: A New Look at Multiage Education*. Portsmouth, NH: Heinemann, 1994. 184 pages.

Davies, Anne; Politano, Colleen; and Gregory, Kathleen. *Together is Better*. Winnipeg, Canada: Peguis Publishers, 1993. 77 pages.

Crystal Springs Books. *Multiage Handbook: A Comprehensive Resource for Multiage Practices*. Peterborough, NH: CSB. Available in January, 1996.

Fogarty, Robin, ed. *The Multiage Classroom: A Collection*. Palantine, IL: Skylight Publishing, 1993. 230 pages.

Gaustad, Joan. "Making the Transition From Graded to Nongraded Primary Education." *Oregon School Study Council Bulletin*, 35(8), 1992. 42 pages.

————."Nongraded Education: Mixed-Age, Integrated and Developmentally Appropriate Education for Primary Children." *Oregon School Study Council Bulletin*, 35(7), 1992. 38 pages.

————."Nongraded Education: Overcoming Obstacles to Implementing the Multiage Classroom." 38(3,4) *Oregon School Study Council Bulletin*, 1994. 84 pages.

Gayfer, Margaret, ed. *The Multi-grade Classroom: Myth and Reality*. Toronto: Canadian Education Association, 1991.

Goodlad, John I., and Anderson, Robert H. *The Nongraded Elementary School*. New York: Teachers College Press, 1987. 248 pages.

Grant, Jim, and Johnson, Bob. *A Common Sense Guide to Multiage Practices*. Columbus, OH: Teachers' Publishing Group, 1995. 128 pages.

Grant, Jim; Johnson, Bob; and Richardson, Irv. *Multiage Q&A: 101 Practical Answers to Your Most Pressing Questions*. Peterborough, NH: Crystal Springs Books, 1995.

Gutierrez, Roberto, and Slavin, Robert E. *Achievement Effects of the Nongraded Elementary School: A Retrospective Review*. Baltimore, MD: Center for Research on Effective Schooling for Disadvantaged Students, 1992.

Hunter, Madeline. *How to Change to a Nongraded School*. Alexandria, VA: Association for Supervision and Curriculum Development, 1992. 74 pages.

Kasten, Wendy, and Clarke, Barbara. *The Multi-age Classroom*. Katonah, NY: Richard Owen, 1993. 84 pages.

Katz, Lilian G.; Evangelou, Demetra; and Hartman, Jeanette Allison. *The Case for Mixed-Age Grouping in Early Education*. Washington, DC: National Association for the Education of Young Children, 1990. 60 pages.

Kentucky Department of Education. *Kentucky's Primary School: The Wonder Years*. Frankfort, KY. 155 pages.

Kentucky Education Association and Appalachia Educational Laboratory. *Ungraded Primary Programs: Steps Toward Developmentally Appropriate Instruction*. Frankfort, KY: KEA, 1990. 100 pages.

Maeda, Bev. *The Multi-Age Classroom*. Cypress, CA: Creative Teaching Press, 1994. 128 pages.

Mazzuchi, Diana, and Brooks, Nancy. "The Gift of Time." *Teaching K-8*. (February 1992): 60-62.

Miller, Bruce A. *Children at the Center: Implementing the Multiage Classroom*. Portland, OR: Northwest Regional Educational Laboratory; 1994. 123 pages.

———.*The Multigrade Classroom: A Resource Handbook for Small, Rural Schools*. Portland, OR: Northwest Regional Educational Laboratory, 1989.

———.*Training Guide for the Multigrade Classroom: A Resource for Small, Rural Schools*. Portland, OR: Northwest Regional Laboratory, 1990.

Nebraska Department of Education and Iowa Department of Education. *The Primary Program: Growing and Learning in the Heartland*. 2nd edition. Lincoln, NE, 1994.

Nye, Barbara. *Multiage Programs: An Interview With Barbara Nye*. Nashville, TN: The Center for Research in Basic Skills, Tennessee State University, 1993.

Politano, Colleen, and Davies, Anne. *Building Connection: Multi-Age and More*. Winnipeg, Canada: Peguis Publishers, 1994. 151 pages.

Province of British Columbia Ministry of Education. *Foundation*. Victoria, British Columbia, 1990.

———.*Our Primary Program: Taking the Pulse*. Victoria, British Columbia, 1990.

———.*Primary Program Foundation Document*. Victoria, British Columbia, 1990. This and the accompanying *Resource Document* provide extensive resources that would be of great help in any multiage program, 362 pages.

———.*Primary Program Resource Document*. Victoria, British Columbia, 1990. 392 pages.

Rathbone, Charles; Bingham, Anne; Dorta, Peggy; McClaskey, Molly; and O'Keefe, Justine. *Multiage Portraits: Teaching and Learning in Mixed-age Classrooms*. Peterborough, NH: Crystal Springs Books, 1993.

Society For Developmental Education. *Multiage Classrooms: The Ungrading of America's Schools*. Peterborough, NH, 1993.

Virginia Education Association and Appalachia Educational Laboratory. *Teaching Combined Grade Classes: Real Problems and Promising Practices*. Charleston, WV: Appalachian Educational Laboratory, 1990.

Multiage Education — Audio/Video

Anderson, Robert, and Pavan, Barbara. *The Nongraded School*. Bloomington, IN: Phi Delta Kappa. An interview with the authors of *Nongradedness: Helping It to Happen*. Video, 30 minutes.

Association of Supervision and Curriculum Development. *Tracking: Road to Success or Dead End?* Alexandria, VA: audiocassette.

Cohen, Dorothy. *Status Treatments for the Classroom*. New York: Teachers College Press, 1994. Video.

George, Yvetta, and Keiter, Joel. *Developing Multiage Classrooms in Primary Grades*. Ft. Lauderdale, FL: Positive Connections, 1993. Video, 22 minutes.

Goodman, Gretchen. *Classroom Strategies for "Gray-Area" Children*. Peterborough, NH: Crystal Springs Books, 1995. Video.

Grant, Jim. *Accommodating Developmentally Different Children in the Multiage Classroom*, 1993. Keynote address at the NAESP Annual Convention. Audiocassette available from Chesapeake Audio/Video Communications, Inc. (6330 Howard Lane, Elkridge, MD 21227, product #180).

Katz, Lilian. *Multiage Groupings: A Key to Elementary Reform*. Alexandria, VA: Association for Supervision and Curriculum Development, 1993. Audiocassette.

Lolli, Elizabeth J. *Developing a Framework for Nongraded Multiage Education*. Peterborough, NH: Crystal Springs Books, 1995. Video.

Oakes, Jeannie, and Lipton, Martin. *On Tracking and Ability Grouping*. Bloomington, IN: Phi Delta Kappa.

Thompson, Ellen. *The Nuts and Bolts of Multiage Classrooms*. Peterborough NH: Crystal Springs Books, 1994. Video, 1 hour.

————.*How to Teach in a Multiage Classroom*. Peterborough, NH: Crystal Springs Books, 1994. Video, 25 minutes.

Ulrey, Dave, and Ulrey, Jan. *Teaching in a Multiage Classroom*. Peterborough, NH: Crystal Springs Books, 1994. Video.

Parent Involvement

Baskwill, Jane. *Parents and Teachers: Partners in Learning*. Toronto, Ont.: Scholastic, 1990.

Bettelheim, Bruno. *A Good Enough Parent*. New York: Alfred A. Knopf, 1987.

Bluestein, Jane, and Collins, Lynn. *Parents in a Pressure Cooker*. Rosemont, NJ: Modern Learning Press, 1990.

Butler, Dorothy, and Clay, Marie. *Reading Begins at Home*. Portsmouth, NH: Heinemann, 1982.

Clay, Marie. *Writing Begins at Home*. Portsmouth, NH: Heinemann, 1988.

Dunn, Kathryn B., and Dunn, Allison B. *Trouble with School: A Family Story about Learning Disabilities*. Rockville, MD: Woodbine House, 1993.

Elovson, Allanna. *The Kindergarten Survival Book*. Santa Monica, CA: Parent Ed Resources, 1991.

Frede, Ellen. *Getting Involved: Workshops for Parents*. Ypsilanti, MI: High/Scope Press, 1984. 306 pages.

Grant, Jim. *"I Hate School!" Some Common Sense Answers for Parents Who Wonder Why, Including the Signs and Signals of the Overplaced Child*. Rosemont, NJ: Programs for Education, 1994. 115 pages.

————.*Jim Grant's Book of Parent Pages*. Rosemont, NJ: Programs for Education, 1988.

————.*Worth Repeating: Giving Children a Second Chance at School Success*. Rosemont, NJ: Modern Learning Press, 1989. 194 pages.

————.*Developmental Education in the 1990's*. Rosemont, NJ: Modern Learning Press, 1991. Considers 92 of the critical questions educators and parents are struggling with today, 136 pages.

Grant, Jim, and Azen, Margot. *Every Parent's Owner's Manuals. (Three-, Four-, Five-, Six-, Seven-Year- Old)*. Rosemont, NJ. Programs for Education. 16 pages each manual.

Henderson, Anne T.; Marburger, Carl L.; and Ooms, Theodora. *Beyond the Bake Sale: An Educator's Guide to Working with Parents*. Columbia, MD: National Committee for Citizens in Education, 1990.

Hill, Mary. *Home: Where Reading and Writing Begin*. Portsmouth, NH: 1995.

Karnofsky, Florence, and Weiss, Trudy. *How to Prepare Your Child for Kindergarten*. Carthage, IL: Fearon Teacher Aids, 1993. 79 pages.

Lansky, Vicki. *Divorce Book for Parents*. New York: New American Library, 1989.

Lazear, David. *Seven Pathways of Learning: Teaching Students and Parents About Multiple Intelligences*. Tucson, AZ: Zephyr Press, 1994. 241 pages.

LeShan, Eda. *When Your Child Drives You Crazy*. New York: St. Martin's Press, 1986.

Lipson, Eden. *Parent's Guide to the Best Books for Children*. New York: Times Books, 1988.

Lyons, P.; Robbins, A.; and Smith, A. *Involving Parents: A Handbook for Participation in Schools*. Ypsilanti, MI: High/Scope Press, 1984. 248 pages.

McGregor, G., and Vogelsberg, R.T. *Transition Needs Assessment for Parents*. Philadelphia, PA: Temple University, 1989.

Mooney, Margaret. *Reading to, with, and by Children*. Katonah, NY: Richard C. Owen Publishers, 1990.

Northeastern Local School District. *Every Child is a Promise: Early Childhood At-Home Learning Activities*. Springfield, OH, 1986.

———.*Every Child is a Promise: Positive Parenting.* Springfield, OH, 1986.

Parker, Harvey. *The ADD Hyperactivity Workbook for Parents, Teachers, and Kids.* Plantation, FL: Impact Publication, 1988.

Rich, Dorothy. *Megaskills: In School and Life — The Best Gift You Can Give Your Child.* Boston: Houghton Mifflin, 1992.

Taylor, Denny. *Family Literacy.* Portsmouth, NH: Heinemann, 1983.

Taylor, Denny, and Strickland, Dorothy. *Family Storybook Reading.* Portsmouth, NH: 1986.

Trelease, Jim. *Hey! Listen To This: Stories to Read Aloud.* New York: Penguin Books, 1992.

———.*The New Read-Aloud Handbook.* New York: Penguin Books, 1989.

Vopat, James. *The Parent Project: A Workshop Approach to Parent Involvement.* York, ME: Stenhouse Publishers, 1994. 191 pages.

Wlodkowski, Raymond, and Jaynes, Judith H. *Eager to Learn.* San Francisco: Jossey-Bass, 1990.

Themes

Atwood, Ron, ed. *Elementary Science Themes: Change Over Time: Patterns, Systems and Interactions, Models and Scales.* Lexington, KY: Institute on Education Reform, University of Kentucky, 1993. Set of four pamphlets, 50 pages each.

Bromley, Karen; Irwin-De Vitis, Linda; and Modlo, Marcia. *Graphic Organizers: Visual Strategies for Active Learning.* New York: Scholastic, 1995.

Davies, Anne; Politano, Colleen; and Cameron, Caren. *Making Themes Work.* Winnipeg, Canada: Peguis Publishers, 1993. 88 pages.

Gamberg, Ruth; Kwak, W.; Hutchins, R.; and Altheim, J. *Learning and Loving It: Theme Studies in the Classroom.* Portsmouth, NH: Heinemann, 1988.

Haraway, Fran, and Geldersma, Barbara. *12 Totally Terrific Theme Units.* New York: Scholastic, 1993.

Herr, Judy, and Libby, Yvonne. *Creative Resources for the Early Childhood Classroom.* Albany, NY: Delmar, 1990. 625 pages.

Katz, Lilian G., and Chard, Sylvia C. *Engaging Children's Minds: The Project Approach.* Norwood, NJ: Ablex Press, 1989.

McCarthy, Tara. *150 Thematic Writing Activities.* New York: Scholastic, 1993.

McCracken, Marlene and Robert. *Themes.* (9 book series). Winnipeg, Man.: Peguis, 1984-87.

SchifferDanoff, Valerie. *The Scholastic Integrated Language Arts Resource Book.* New York: Scholastic, 1995.

Schlosser, Kristin. *Thematic Units for Kindergarten.* New York: Scholastic, 1994.

Strube, Penny. *Theme Studies, A Practical Guide: How to Develop Theme Studies to Fit Your Curriculum.* New York: Scholastic, 1993.

Thompson, Gare. *Teaching Through Themes.* New York: Scholastic, 1991. 176 pages.

Tracking

George, Paul. *How to Untrack Your School.* Alexandria, VA.: Association for Supervision and Curriculum Development, 1992. 42 pages.

Kohn, Alfie. *No Contest: The Case Against Competition.* Boston, MA: Houghton Mifflin, 1992.

Kozol, Jonathan. *Savage Inequalities: Children in America's Schools.* New York: Crown, 1991.

Oakes, Jeannie. *Keeping Track: How Schools Structure Equality.* New Haven: Yale University Press, 1985.

Wheelock, Anne. *Crossing the Tracks: How "Untracking" Can Save America's Schools.* New York: New Press, 1992.

INDEX

NOTES

NOTES

NOTES

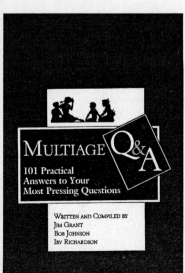

Multiage Videos

Avoid the Pitfalls of Implementing Multiage Classrooms
with Jim Grant

Nationally recognized multiage educator Jim Grant provides you with straight talk about creating multiage classrooms in your school. **He'll tell you about:** The dozen most-often made mistakes when creating a multiage classroom • How multiage grouping accommodates the inclusion of differently-abled children • Grouping/combination practices that work in a mixed-age classroom • The do's and dont's of implementing a multiage continuous progress classroom. Come prepared for an information-packed hard-hitting session which can prepare you to make your move a successful — not stressful — time. (K-6) 60 min. **#4225SC $69.95**

Developing a Framework for Nongraded, Multiage Education
with Libbie Lolli

In this fast-paced information-packed video, you will learn innovative ideas and options to help you develop a plan that will address the needs of your classroom, your school and community. **Key elements addressed:** What a *true* multiage, nongraded school looks like • How to group children heterogeneously and for success • What teaching methodologies are appropriate for multiage classrooms • Practical tips to help with scheduling, team teaching and planning. (K-6) 60 min.   **#4329SC $69.95**

Buy both of Ellen Thompson's videos for only $99 (Save over $20!)

A Day in a Multiage Classroom
by Ellen Thompson

If you've ever wondered what a multiage classroom really looks like, here's your answer. Vermont State Teacher of the Year and acclaimed multiage presenter Ellen Thompson takes you on a bird's eye tour of her multiage primary classroom. This video works well as a training tool either alone, or in conjunction with *The Nuts and Bolts of Multiage Classrooms*. It's also a great way to educate and excite parents and the community about your multiage program. 58 min. **#3743SC $49.95**

Teaching in a Multiage Classroom
with Dave and Jan Ulrey

Why are multiage continuous progress classrooms receiving so much attention? What are the benefits and potential pitfalls of this type of classroom? If you are thinking of starting your own multiage classroom, you've either heard these questions or asked them yourself. This video will address the answers to these important questions to give you a firm foundation for your multiage classroom. **Also included is a 62-page handout booklet.** (K-4) 60 min. **#4265SC $79.95**

The Nuts and Bolts of Multiage Classrooms
by Ellen Thompson

A practical, direct look at multiage classrooms through the eyes of award-winning educator Ellen Thompson. This one-of-a-kind combination of video footage from her acclaimed seminars *and* from her classroom, creates a powerful message for teachers and administrators who are investigating or practicing multiage. If your school is considering multiage grouping, this video is a must! 1 hour. **#3742SC $69.95**

The Complete Lesson Plan Book

This multi-purpose planner was designed with flexibility in mind. The oversized pages can be organized according to days of the week and/or subject areas. Also included are whole language-based ideas integrating math, science, and social studies. Plus assessment suggestions, theme-based book lists, ideas for celebrating special events, and **handy pocket pouch folders.** (K-3) 112 pp.

#3176SC $9.95

Quantity Discount — 25 or more **$8.45**

Childhood Should Be A Journey Not A Race Collection

• **Poster 34" x 21"**
#4327SC $3.95
• **Tote Bag   12"W x 17½"H x 7"gusset**
#3408SC $9.95
• **Button 2¾" x 1½"**
#4500SC $2.00

READ, READ, READ Collection

• **Poster 34" x 21"**
#3093SC $3.95
• **Tote Bag**
   12"W x 17½"H x 7"gusset
#4075SC $9.95
• **Button 2¾" x 1½"**
#3670SC $2.00